PRAISE FOR WHITI

Meeting Company Sergeant Major John Barnes in Trenton on the arrival of bodies from Afghanistan, I was struck by the impact of our war in that distant country. He had the 'thousand yard stare', of men who had been in combat and seen the worst of human behaviour. Even then, his first thoughts, actions and concerns were off his soldiers: those he had lost, those wounded both physically and mentally and their families. Op Medusa is part of our history as a nation, akin to Normandy, Pachino and Hong Kong in terms of courage, service and toughness. I thank him for his leadership, his service and his honesty and frankness in these pages. God bless John Barnes, every soldier he describes and our great country.

- General Rick Hillier, OC, CMM, ONL, MSC, CD

Impossible to put down, CWO John Barnes' delivers a vivid, first-hand account of The Royal Canadian Regiment at war. He delivers a deeply personal account of the courage and sacrifice of Canada's sons and daughters in Afghanistan. The author transports you to the poppy fields and wadis of the Panjwai District as Charles Company, The Royal Canadian Regiment earn their first Battle Honours since Korea. This is a must-read account of this generation's Vimy Ridge.

- Brigadier-General Rob Delaney, OMM, CD, former Canadian Armed Forces Provost Marshal

John Barnes is one of those rare gentlemen who makes you a better person just for having known him. It was an absolute privilege to be with him for some of his adventures and even more of a pleasure to read about the others.

- Lieutenant-Colonel Matthew Sprague, MSM, CD

John Barnes is a legend in the Royal Canadian Regiment. He reveals the experiences which forged him and allowed him to rise, bloody but unbowed after receiving life-changing wounds in battle, to continue leading the soldiers he loved. If you want one book to understand the mettle of Canada's sons and daughters and what they fought through in Afghanistan, this is the one.

Much of the early military experience revealed is from a time when the culture of the Canadian Army was abusive to our own. Through colourful tales told only as John can, we can see the evolution of the Canadian Army. This book will be a great resource to those *looking to understand where we've come from in order to better navigate the way forward as we continue to develop the Canadian Armed Force's culture.*

- Lieutenant-Colonel Trevor Norton, CD

As you read these pages, you will experience a wide variety of reactions—from laughter to sadness and frustration—and a few eye-opening stories. It is wonderful to know that this will help preserve the important lived experiences of those who served and who continue to make a difference in the betterment of our community and our wonderful country.

- Eric Duncan, Member of Parliament (Stormont-Dundas-South Glengarry)

WHITE SCHOOL
BLACK MEMORIES

WHITE SCHOOL BLACK MEMORIES

Chief Warrant Officer (ret'd)
John G. Barnes, MMM, MSM, CD

DOUBLE ‡ DAGGER

Copyright 2022 John G. Barnes

All rights reserved. No part of this publication may be reproduced or transmitted in any form or by any means, electronically or mechanically including photocopying, recording or any information storage or retrieval system, without prior permission in writing from the author.

> Library and Archives Canada Cataloguing in Publication
> Barnes, John G. author
> White School, Black Memories / John G. Barnes

Issued in print and electronic formats.
ISBN: 978-1-990644-27-6 (soft cover)
ISBN: 978-1-990644-28-3 (e-book)

Editors: Samantha Acker and Phil Halton
Cover design: Pablo Javier Herrera
Interior Design: Winston A. Prescott

Cover Photo credit: Russell Knight

Double Dagger Books Ltd
Toronto, Ontario, Canada
www.doubledagger.ca

DEDICATION

I dedicate this story to those who are most important in my life.

To my Dad, John Barnes Sr., who served his country with honour and distinction during World War Two and to my Mother Edna Barnes who supported him throughout his life.

To my wife, Julie, of thirty-two years who, without your love and support, there would be no stories to tell.

To my son, JJ, and daughter, Jana, who are my greatest achievements.

To my grandsons, Noah and Theo, who give me a reason to get up every day.

To my friend, George, who kicked my ass and made me look after myself.

To my fellow soldiers from Charles Company who will forever be my heroes.

To Samantha Acker who did a superb job as an editor.

To The RCR Association for their financial support and input.

To Sandy McQuarrie, who gave me the courage and the ability to share this.

To my friend, mentor and hero, CWO Robert Girouard. You are always whispering in my ear. Rest in Peace!

TABLE OF CONTENTS

Preface..i
Foreword...iii

1. The Battle for Panjwai..1

PART ONE - THE COLD WAR

2. Recruit Centre...7
3. Germany, the First Time..26
4. Army of the West..38
5. A New Command Team..48
6. Cyprus..53
7. Back to Germany..72
8. Marriage..77

PART TWO - PEACEMAKING

9. Gulf War...85
10. UNPROFOR..92
11. Home Again..105
12. Bosnia..118
13. The RCR Battle School..129
14. Back to the Battalion..142

PART THREE - AFGHANISTAN

15. PPCLI Handover to 1 RCR..151
16. Role 3 Hospital...168
17. September 4, Morning...181
18. Ramp Ceremony...185
19. Back to Operations...190
20. Return to Charles Company...194
21. Clearing Objective Rugby...211
22. Ma'sum Ghar..214
23. HESCO Hobbits..219

24. Back to Route Summit..223
25. Mid-Tour Leave...249
26. Escort Duty..258
27. Arrival in Canada..263
28. Home Leave..269
29. Back to Afghanistan..272
30. Sergeants Major Changeover..277
31. Danger Close Fire Mission...284
32. Return of Major Sprague..288
33. Death of the RSM...293
34. Negligent Discharge...296
35. Operation Baaz Tsuka..303
36. Afghan Nomads..314
37. Cold and Damp...322
38. Departure from Afghanistan...328

PART FOUR - POST AFGHANISTAN (2009-2017)

39. Aftermath..345
40. Escorting Families to Afghanistan...349
41. The Rear Party..356
42. Extra-Regimentally Employed...359
43. Promotion to CWO - MSU Chief...363
44. Military Police Group Chief..370
45. Writing as Therapy...389
46. Reflections..392

Lexicon..395

PREFACE

It is 2015, and I find myself sitting in my office in Ottawa, the one place I always swore I would never be. As a soldier, I was immensely proud of the fact that I had spent almost all my thirty-three years on an Army base, but here I was—a staff weenie in Ottawa. I was the group Chief for the Canadian Military Police.

As my time in uniform was getting close to ending, I found myself looking in a mirror and asking the person looking back at me, "Are you okay?"

I was not!

I believe I had started to change after my first tour in Croatia and Bosnia in 1992, and each subsequent tour just added to the emotional baggage I carried around. Following my time in Afghanistan in 2006-2007, my life began to unravel, and the only thing that kept me sane was having a loving family and a career that I cherished.

PTSD was something that happened to others. It still had a stigma attached to it, and that was often a career killer. I found myself having to counsel soldiers that were having issues after returning from Afghanistan. They were abusing drugs, alcohol, and in some cases, their families. Each time one of these soldiers was diagnosed with Post-Traumatic Stress Disorder or an Operational Stress Injury, I found myself defending them and making sure that their comrades and their leadership understood.

As the years went by, the stigma lessened, and the needed resources became more readily available. But I was never ready to admit that I needed help. When the 10th anniversary of Operation MEDUSA arrived, and people wanted me to join them in Petawawa for a celebration and remembrance, I realized I could not be part of it.

I was too angry, too frustrated, too emotional, and I needed to figure this out.

My writing started as a way to talk about my feelings and to keep them secret. So, I wrote them down and would read them back aloud when I was feeling lost. I found comfort in reading them, as if it were okay to feel this way. I started writing about Operation MEDUSA, and the words spilled across the page.

Some days at work, I would spend several hours writing, and someone would have to knock on my office door and say, "Chief, time to go home." I would wake up in the middle of the night, go downstairs to my home office and read what I had written that day. Sometimes I would begin writing again and stop when it was time to go to work.

It was like a weight was being lifted off my shoulders.

The writing continued for a couple of years, and I would be writing, crying and laughing. And it felt right. For the first time in my life, I could be brutally honest because these words were just for me. No one else would ever read them.

I found writing to be a form of therapy. My ability to write things that I had only thought about in the deepest crevices of my brain was a sense of freedom that I had not enjoyed in many years.

Writing the story of Operation MEDUSA led to the rest of my Afghanistan tour. That led me to write about how I got here in the first place. Before I knew what was happening, I had written my story from growing up in Newfoundland, joining the Army, retiring in Ottawa, and all the warts and diamonds in between. The writing led to me finally asking for help in 2016 and receiving a diagnosis of PTSD, anxiety and depression.

I was telling Gilles, a good friend of mine, about my writing, and he said, "I would love to read it." Before I even gave it a second thought, I said, "okay." I was on pins and needles as I waited for him to read it and tell me what he thought. I was feeling a lot of apprehension and concern about how he would see his friend after reading all my secrets, good and bad.

A day or so later, he called to tell me he could not put it down and stayed up all night reading it. I was both surprised and a little excited. He said that he had gained even more respect for me and that my story could benefit others. Only a couple of people have read my complete story, but I am no longer worried about what people will think or say.

I am in a good place.

This is my story, written by someone that had the help of ghosts, demons and heroes of the past. This story is not meant to be 100 percent factual, as years of abuse, injuries, and PTSD have no doubt affected my memories, but it is my story.

To the best of my abilities, my memories are accurate and factual.

I hope that my words will bring some solace to others who find themselves alone in their basements with their darkest thoughts.

FOREWORD

I will start by saying that I am honoured and humbled to write the foreword to Chief Warrant Officer John Barnes' book.

John has had an amazing career in the Canadian Armed Forces and particularly concerning his service in The Royal Canadian Regiment. With great pride, I can say that I served with John as a fellow "Royal Canadian."

While the story of his service to Canada goes from soup to nuts as he relates his career, by his own admission, the focus is on Afghanistan. Arguably, there may not have been a book without that experience in combat in 2006/2007.

During that period and the year leading up to the deployment of the First Battalion, Royal Canadian Regiment Battle Group is when I first met and served with John Barnes. And, though we have only known each other for about sixteen years, as all combat veterans know, the intensity and camaraderie forced upon you by war form a sense of family that only battle-hardened soldiers understand.

As the Commanding Officer of 1 RCR, I was immediately struck by John's professionalism and leadership. He was a soldier's soldier. A bear of a man, gentle and kind by default but also lethal and dangerous when the situation demanded it. In Kandahar in 2006, that was often.

What most impressed me about John was when I was looking for a straight answer; I knew if I approached him, I would get it. Often the response was not necessarily what I was hoping to hear, but I knew there was never any bullshit. To be clear, he was the best Company Sergeant Major in my unit.

I must admit that this book was an emotional read for me on many levels as John recounted the battles that we faced during that tour and the struggles he faced afterwards. It put me back to where I could see, taste and smell the horror of combat. And it is probably by no accident that I write this in my dining room sitting in front of a portrait of John's good friend and mentor and my Regimental Sergeant Major, CWO Bobby Girouard, killed in action on that tour.

To me, this book is about John's courage. His physical courage is unquestionable, as demonstrated by the medals on his chest and the many times I saw it firsthand in combat. If not more important is the moral courage to admit and deal with the aftermath of battles and losing soldiers long after the smoke has cleared from the battlefield. An act of courage that many, if not most of us, fail to summon.

John, I salute you for that, and I know it will be an inspiration to all those who read this book, especially combat veterans.

As the Senior Serving Royal, I will close by saying that it gives me great pride to have served and fought alongside CWO John Barnes. Thank you for your service and Pro Patria.

Omer Lavoie, CMM, MSC, CD
Lieutenant-General

1

THE BATTLE FOR PANJWAI

We crossed the Arghandab River on September 3, 2006, with high hopes and a whole lot of naivety.

Nothing had begun as we had hoped. The Coalition's first deaths during Operation MEDUSA were all fourteen crew of a British Nimrod aircraft killed in a crash. This was the British military's most significant single loss of life since the Falklands War. Before we could begin our own attack, we were dispatched to look for survivors and secure the crash site. It felt like foreshadowing.

When it was our turn to advance, our naivety didn't last long. Before I even had time to realize what a pickle we were in, I was forced to react to our first casualties, including our first soldier killed in action. An 82mm recoilless rifle round struck the vehicle of one of our engineers. Most of those soldiers inside the vehicle were wounded or unconscious, and the vehicle went radio silent. They were out of the fight.

That smell of death is something that remains with you forever; it is not something that can be easily described but, once you smell it, there is no turning back the clock; it is now part of your very fibre. When someone talks about the smell of death, most people immediately think of the detective shows where they find a dead body badly decomposing. But this was different. It was the smell of death itself—a living person who had just been killed.

As the radio buzzed with reports of more casualties and people calling for assistance, bullets whizzed by my ears, none touching me. A strange and surreal feeling of calm comes over you when you realize that you'll probably die in the next few minutes. Once you accept that, you can just go on about your business. It doesn't mean that you're not scared—but you can function.

I realized that I was not going to be much of a benefit standing in the back of the Company Commander's LAV, where I had begun the morning, and so I quickly dismounted. I started running between our armoured vehicles trying to get them moving in the right direction. I could see and hear bullets and grenades hitting the LAVs and ricocheting off into the fields. On the far-right flank, a platoon of Afghan National Army soldiers fought north through the marijuana fields with their American mentors. The marijuana fields were on fire, filling the air with smoke. Through the haze, I could see part of our objective, the white schoolhouse that was where the Taliban were first formed.

I looked around at the chaos unfolding, and all I wanted was to be home in Petawawa with my wife and kids. I did not want to die on a piece of dirt in Afghanistan, and I did not want to be brave. But I was the Company Sergeant Major, and that meant I had no choice.

I tried to figure out where I would set up the Company's Casualty Collection Point. All of our wounded would be brought there until we could evacuate them. I had planned to use the cover of the riverbed for our casualties, but the enemy gets a vote too. There was no way that we could move casualties back to the river with the volume of effective fire the enemy was raining down on us. Buzzing around my head like black flies, more and more bullets were flying around me.

Every few moments, I would catch a glimpse of an enemy fighter as he ducked in and out of wadis or from behind walls. On at least one occasion, my confusion left me too far forward from the Company, and I had to engage the enemy fighters myself. I saw two dirty, hairy guys, and I knew they had seen me because they began firing at me with their AK-47s. I threw myself onto the ground behind a pile of dirt and returned fire. When the two guys ducked behind a rock wall, I immediately jumped up and began running back toward our LAVs. When they reappeared, I fired again, and I saw them both go down. All I felt at that moment was a sense of relief.

When I got back to my LAV, soldiers started yelling and pointing toward the sky. Despite all the fire coming in, some of the soldiers had stopped firing, looking up at the sky in awe. Flying through the air was a black shape that I recognized as a 1000 lb bomb. And rather than flying through the sky to make life bad for the Taliban, it was coming towards us. Soldiers froze, watching it come closer. My thoughts turned to what is most important to me: my family. No one took cover or tried to protect themselves. The bomb represented death, and for what seemed an eternity, we waited for it.

The bomb hit the ground several hundred metres in front of the Company and bounced several times as it came closer and closer. When it finally stopped, it just lay there, close enough that we could read some of the lettering on the side. But it didn't explode.

As quickly as it had appeared, all thoughts of it were gone. The bullets flying around our heads hadn't stopped, and we snapped back to the battle. There was more than one way to die that morning.

I moved forward again, crouching behind the Zettelmeyer, an armoured bulldozer. I wasn't the only one seeking shelter behind it, but it quickly became a magnet for bullets and rocket-propelled grenades. In hindsight, it was probably one of the biggest and most noticeable targets on the battlefield, but when cover from enemy fire is sparse, you take what you can get.

I was trying to coordinate the evacuation of the wounded again when I felt a hot searing wind blow across me, and I recall floating through the air, almost like a dream. I also remember hitting the ground hard, headfirst. It was suddenly quiet, and I was trying to figure out where I was. I thought maybe I was in Petawawa or camping with the kids. Someone touched me, talking to me as well, though I couldn't hear what he was saying. He rolled me over, running his hands under my body armour, and I saw people laying on the ground all around me.

I started to remember where I was. Was I dying? Had I been shot or blown up? I didn't know.

I saw a soldier on the ground only a few feet away, and I knew he was dead. Once you've seen the aftermath of battle, you realize that you know immediately when someone is dead just from looking at them, no need for a doctor. A few feet away I saw a soldier from Charles Company frantically working on another soldier, trying to save his life. The wounded soldier's face was toward me, and he had that look. I knew he was either dead or dying, and nothing that was being done to him was going to change that.

With all this unfolding around me, I was terrified.

Someone gave me the thumbs up, but I didn't know why. I tried to pull off my body armour, afraid it was smothering me, but someone stopped me. I was half-carried, half-dragged onto the back ramp of LAV beside two dead soldiers, falling and crawling over them until I was inside.

I was deaf and confused and no use to anyone. At that moment, looking out the back of the LAV at the chaos, unable to affect it, I hated myself. I was supposed to be the one leading my soldiers, setting the example, caring for the wounded and retrieving the dead. Instead, I was useless. I was a burden. I was not in control.

I had failed my Company.

I had failed my friends, some of whom were now dead.

I had failed their families.

I hated myself.

Years later, I stood in front of the Governor-General of Canada to receive an award. They said that I was a hero for exhibiting leadership under fire. For remaining calm. For wanting nothing more than to get back into the fight with my soldiers.

It was all a lie.

At that moment, I was terrified.

Broken and useless when my Company need me most, I had to wonder:

How the fuck did I get here?

ABOVE: The burned out remains of Callsign 31B, Panjwai. (Charles Company photo)
BELOW: The "White School" and fires set by Charles Company's attack on Objective Rugby, 3 September, 2006. (Russell Knight)

PART ONE
THE COLD WAR

RECRUIT CENTRE

What decisions in my life led me to Afghanistan and a life of service to Canada?

As a kid, I grew up in the shadow of Branch 62 Legion in Riverhead, Saint Mary's Bay, Newfoundland, and from an early age, I learned to have great respect for our veterans. During those early childhood years, we had many WWI and WWII vets around the Bay, and my father was one of those.

My Dad, a young John Barnes, answered the call from England and volunteered to join the historic 166 Artillery. My Dad, like many Newfoundlanders, eagerly accepted the challenge and sailed off to England to train and then off to Italy and Germany to fight our enemies.

He was a quiet man who never spoke of the war and seldom spoke of his exploits. He was a true hero and was an inspiration to me. I remember seeing him dressed in his Legion uniform many times, but I rarely saw him wear his medals, unlike other veterans. I remember asking him the same questions kids have asked me about war: "Were you scared? Did you kill anyone?" He would always find a way to change the subject, and then a bit of sadness would come over his face.

I now understand what he was feeling and wish I had a second chance to talk with him. I would have loved to have known what I know now about soldiers and war back when I was a boy. What a great time I would have had with those veterans walking around our Bay, and now they are gone.

I remember getting the terrible news on September 19, 1996, when my father died and how devastating it was. Even then, some of my first thoughts were, "I never got to talk to him about his experience in WWII." He was remembered as a father and grandfather, husband and brother and friend to many at his funeral. He was also remembered as someone who stepped up and fought for his country when the need arose.

WHITE SCHOOL, BLACK MEMORIES

When the ceremony ended at the church, the president of the Royal Canadian Legion, Branch 62, took his medals off his casket and presented them to me as I stood there proudly in my military uniform. The medals are a constant reminder to me of what a great man and hero my father was.

I remember a few years before his death, I was home in Riverhead for a visit, and I saw my mother looking around for something in the dresser in her bedroom. I went in to speak with her, and I saw something in the bottom drawer that caught my attention. There were my Dad's medals in a plastic bag; they were tarnished and torn and were in overall terrible condition. I told my mom I was taking them to get them fixed and return them as soon as they were done. When I got back to work, I started getting the medals cleaned and the ribbons replaced. After a few months, they were complete.

That Christmas, I gave them to my Dad, and the look on his face made it all worth the time and money I had spent. He could not believe that they had been court mounted and gleaming, but I could tell he was pleased.

Those medals now sit on a shelf in my den, next to mine.

After graduating from high school and making a feeble attempt at the DeVry Institute of Technology in Toronto, I found my way back to the Rock and Saint Mary's Bay, with an uncertain future. At eighteen years of age, I was a typical kid from the Bay with a typical plan - find enough general labour work to get enough stamps to draw unemployment and repeat.

DECIDING TO JOIN THE ARMY

Waking up one morning after a night of drinking, I decided that I wanted something else. I decided that perhaps the military was the way ahead. Now, I just needed to persuade my friend, Don Squires, to enlist with me. Don was a year older, had tried his hand at fishing, as well as the typical labour jobs made available by the government and, much like me, he did not have a plan.

Over a couple of beers the following night, I brought up my plan and, to my surprise, Don did not laugh it off and even seemed a little interested. We discussed it a few times over the next few weeks and finally decided to find a ride for the two hours to Saint John's to the nearest recruiting centre and see what happens.

We arrived in the beautiful city of Saint John's around 1000 hours on a foggy, rainy morning. After walking by the recruiting centre, a couple of times, we decided that we would need a couple of beers to get up our courage. Just across the street was a popular bar called Fiddler's Green, which was frequented by the downtown crowd and the sailors and crew of all the boats and ships that pulled into this fabled harbour. At 1030 hours in the morning, the music was already loud, and the thirty or so patrons were already in a festive mood.

After a couple of beers each and all the while talking ourselves into the next stage, we walked out of the bar, crossed the street and into the unknown.

Inside, the recruiting centre was dark and dreary, and a large man in green asked us if he could help us. When we responded that we were interested in joining, a smile appeared, and we were both sent to separate areas to deal with a recruiter. I remember meeting with a small man, dressed in combats, who said he was a sergeant from The Royal Canadian Regiment.

At the time, it meant nothing to me.

Over the next few weeks, following several trips to the city to write tests, do physicals and interviews, I was told that I had qualified for every trade except three, and I was asked to decide my future. Unlike today, there was no Internet, social media or information sessions; it was a pile of paper that meant little to me. The same sergeant asked me the same questions that have become a part of many jokes, "Do you like the outdoors, hunting, fishing and camping?" I gave the expected answer, "Yes," even though I was not keen on most of that stuff.

My friend, Don, was going through the same process, but somewhere along the track, he got off. I believe it was a medical issue, but he may have just said that and got off on his own. Either way, I was now committed to becoming a soldier. The sergeant told me that he believed the infantry was for me and that it had been the best decision he had ever made. I was sold.

A few weeks later, I was off to Cornwallis, Nova Scotia, and my basic training.

RECRUIT TRAINING

Cornwallis was the beginning of my military journey and the beginning of friendships that would last a lifetime.

I had the opportunity to celebrate my nineteenth birthday in Riverhead with my family and was grateful for the opportunity to have a beer in the Legion with my Dad. He never said he was happy or proud of me for joining the Canadian Forces, but I always knew he was. Perhaps there was a part of him that feared for my safety, the way only a dad who has been to war can.

Nine days after my nineteenth birthday, I officially signed the paperwork on July 23, 1981, and became a Canadian soldier.

Cornwallis was a bit of a shock and an eye-opener for this Newfie. My only military experience was six months in the Army Cadets and playing a politically insensitive game called Cowboys and Indians. I quickly realized that I had a lot to learn about the military, and those friendly smiling faces at the recruiting centre were not the same non-commissioned officers (NCOs) and officers I met in Cornwallis.

After the first few days, you become accustomed to the yelling and screaming, but the personal insults were something that one never got used to.

Looking back after retiring after a thirty-six-year career, I'm happy that the Canadian Forces have come a long way. Even though it took a long time, and we still have a way to go, we have begun to emphasize respect for everyone who wears this country's uniform. I fully agree with the initiative of the former Chief of the Defence Staff, General Jon Vance, who formalized this notion of respect for all into an order called Operation HONOUR.

That said, this problem was a long way from anyone's mind thirty-six years ago when being ridiculed and abused was a regular occurrence, and being a Newfie, I was often on the receiving end. Those early days were all about learning to be part of a team, being able to receive and obey orders without hesitation, and growing from that clumsy son of the Bay to a polished, well-disciplined soldier who looked good in his uniform and was proud of what he was doing.

Not everyone was the right fit for the Canadian Forces (CF) and, during a time when judges still gave young men the option of jail or the army, many arrived with a chip already on their shoulders.

I remember a tall, young man from somewhere out west, who arrived with hair down to his ass, a cigarette hanging out of his mouth and a bad attitude. From the moment we met, he seemed set to become trouble. While everyone else was introducing themselves, he stood alone and snarled. We had to lay all our belongings out on the ground in front of us and anything that the staff believed was not required to be a soldier was taken away. I saw drugs, pills, alcohol, knives, switchblades, porn and a lot of other prohibited stuff get confiscated, never to be seen again.

Then, it was off to the barbershop to get our first military haircut, and, in this case, it was basically a brush cut. When it was the turn of our long-haired friend from Western Canada to get in the chair, he hesitated. The more the staff yelled at him, the more determined he was to keep his locks. My last sight of him was being dragged away, screaming, by two large Military Police officers. We later learned that he was released, due to mental health issues.

I was able to transition to military life easily. Once my body became accustomed to the continuous physical fitness and lack of sleep, I believe I excelled. This was also my first opportunity to see and learn from the different styles of leadership. I did not know it at the time, but some of those young leaders would hugely impact my future ambitions.

The instructors on my Recruit Course 8130 were truly diverse for the day. The names I remember are Warrant Officer (WO) Eisan and Sergeant Cromwell from the Princess Patricia's Canadian Light Infantry, Master Corporal Rivers, a military policeman and my favourite, Sergeant Desmond from The Royal Canadian Regiment. We also had a sailor and an airman whose names I no longer remember.

Sergeant Desmond always had a story to tell to put our training in perspective and to make sure that we were paying attention. When things did not go well, he would always say, "A Royal never passes a fault," a motto that seemed a little bizarre at the time but that I have lived by for the last thirty-six years.

On October 8, 1981, Course 8130 proudly marched onto the parade square and in front of my sister, Joanne, who came all the way from St. John's to be part of this wonderful day; I graduated and became a true member of the Canadian Forces. I was immensely proud to have my sister in Cornwallis for my first graduation parade and even more proud thirty-six years later when Joanne and her husband, Jim, flew to

PART ONE - THE COLD WAR

Ottawa to be part of my retirement celebration.

However, thirty-six years ago, there was only a day or so to enjoy my accomplishment as I packed up and made my way to London, Ontario, the home of The Royal Canadian Regiment and where the First Battalion was located.

It was there that I met up with all the candidates for our basic infantry course.

BASIC INFANTRY COURSE

We landed at Pearson International Airport in Toronto on a Friday evening and were met by Master Corporal Fred Jackson of The RCR. He told us that there was a bus outside for anyone who wanted to go to London, but if we wanted to stay in Toronto for the weekend, he would sign a leave pass, and we would have to ensure we were back in London in our new quarters by 1800 hours on Sunday.

A bunch of us jumped at the opportunity to stay in Toronto, as we had money and energy to burn. I remember hanging with a couple of guys from the area, George Myatte and Rick Farrier. We took cabs to Rick's house, where we changed into our going-out-on-the-town clothes: jeans and a T-shirt. I had lost so much weight in Cornwallis that my jeans were way too big, so Farrier's sister loaned me a pair that fit fine. We had a great time in Toronto, no one was arrested or injured, and we all made it to London in plenty of time.

When we got to London, we moved into quarters, four to a room. The accommodations were simple: four single beds each with white sheets and two itchy grey blankets, a small desk and a wooden locker. And so began my training to become a member of the finest Regular Force Infantry Regiment, The Royal Canadian Regiment.

The RCR Battle School was in Petawawa, Ontario, and was the regular location for all the RCR basic infantry courses. Instead of being there, our course was being conducted in London as part of A Company, also known as The Duke of Edinburgh's Company, or simply 'Dukes'. This allowed more courses to be run and allowed staff to remain close to home instead of having to spend months away in Petawawa.

Those first few days were terrifying to me. I was not prepared for the onslaught of yelling, screaming and abuse. The staff members at Cornwallis were teddy bears compared to the staff from Dukes.

Lieutenant Vincent Buonamici was introduced as our Platoon Commander and course officer. My first impression of him was of a short, stocky man who spoke in a gravelly voice and liked to tell us that he was of Italian heritage, as if that made the rest of us less. As a course, we already thought we had accomplished a lot, graduating from Cornwallis, but we were to learn very quickly that we knew nothing.

We were told to make sure we drank lots of water that first night because Mr. Buonamici was taking us out on day one for a run. We thought we were in good physical shape following our training in Cornwallis. So, after seeing Buonamici, we were not concerned.

That short, stocky man turned out to be a long-distance runner in wolf's clothing.

11

WHITE SCHOOL, BLACK MEMORIES

That first run told us that the next few months were going to be tougher than anything I had ever done. We did a warm-up at about 0550 hours, which lasted about three minutes, and then we were told to get in a double line. Without warning, Lieutenant Buonamici took off at a full sprint. Within seconds, the platoon was spread out over a hundred metres, and several staff were already screaming and insulting anyone who was more than a few inches from the guy in front of him.

The insults varied from person to person, depending on your personal characteristics and your level of fitness and any other information that the staff were able to gain on you, including your hometown, religion and marital status. Words like faggot, asshole, queer, little girl, lady, pussy, fat fuck, homo, Jew boy and every other comment that came to mind could be heard.

After a few weeks of this, you started to dismiss most unless it was specifically meant for you. The one insult that I, and several others, had to endure was "stupid Newfie" or "dumb Newfie". This was one that continued throughout the months of the course and into my first few years of my career. This was one that did bother me because I was, and still am, an immensely proud Newfoundlander.

I took it personally and cringe even today when I hear a "Newfie" joke.

We very quickly learned how to work as a team, and this allowed us to get our living quarters in spic-and-span condition. The floors, including the hallways, bedrooms, laundry rooms and bathrooms had to be stripped of all the wax from the last course. This was a big job that required a buffer with a rough pad, wax remover, steel wool and a lot of muscle.

Each group of four soldiers was responsible for their own room, as well as a portion of the large common areas, which were divided amongst everyone. Every room needed to look exactly like the other and exactly like the layout given to us by the staff. Inspections started immediately and were conducted every morning after breakfast for about eight weeks. After that, they were slowed down to once or twice a week.

We were confined to quarters for the first six weeks and spent all our waking moments cleaning and shining the quarters and our personal kit and learning and practicing a plethora of new skills. During those first couple of months, it sometimes seemed like the staff were more worried about how shiny our floors were instead of how well we could perform our newly learned military skills.

I learned many valuable lessons from those early days in Dukes Company. I remember being rushed out of the quarters one rainy morning, dressed in our fighting equipment, which included an FNC1 rifle, a steel helmet and web gear which held our ammo, magazines, first aid kit, rain gear, camouflage paint, spare socks, a full water bottle and our gas mask. On top of that, we were each carrying a rucksack, packed as per the RCR kit list. In all, our gear weighed about 75 pounds. We did a forced march for about fifteen miles before breakfast. You needed to be ready: your kit needed to be packed properly and everything needed to fit, as something as simple as a wrinkled sock meant blisters and a good "jacking" from the staff.

Following the march, I remember coming around that last corner before our

12

quarters and looking through the downpour of rain and wondering why there were beds and lockers and personal kit all set up on the parade square. I could hardly believe my eyes; everything was soaked but laid out as if ready for morning inspection.

I immediately believed I knew what was going on. The staff had been stressing security since our arrival: weapons needed to be locked in personal lockers and rooms always needed to be locked when no one was present. Anyone who got caught not following these simple rules was in big shit.

Had someone left their room insecure?

My room had an unwritten rule: the last person out of the room was responsible for making sure it had been locked. I thought back to earlier that morning as we were rushed out of our quarters. I believe I was the last out of our room, but I was positive that I had locked the door. I am sure that every other member of the platoon was going through the same mental process as I was.

The staff said nothing.

They formed us up opposite the wet beds, we removed our kit, and we proceeded to do a cool down following the march. Once it was complete, the Platoon's Second-in-Command, WO Doug Bittle, yelled and screamed at us for a few minutes about being lazy, not marching as a team and adding a few personal insults for those of us who had caught his eye. He made no mention of the beds, uniforms, boots, towels and all the other kit that belonged in someone's room sitting outside in the pouring rain.

WO Bittle finished his rant and said that we had fifteen minutes to get upstairs, shower, change into our clean combat uniforms and be back outside to march to breakfast, and then he yelled, "MOVE!" Everyone grabbed their weapons and gear and ran into the quarters, up to our floor and to our rooms.

I was the first one to reach our door, and I was relieved to find the door firmly locked. Good, it was not us, I thought. I inserted my key and, as soon as I opened the door, reality struck me right in the mouth.

Our beds were gone, and the room was a mess.

I heard the groaning from my roommates behind me, and I knew that I had messed up. I was to blame for this. I had been the last person out and because I was being rushed, I must have forgotten to lock the door. We turned around as a group and made our way downstairs to where we knew the staff would be waiting, and they were in a bad mood. I tried several times to explain that it was my fault, but I was not allowed to get a word in. All I could do was stand there with my three roommates and catch the blast from the staff. We had to carry our beds and all the other soaking wet kit up the stairs, throw everything in the room and rush to the showers. We were going to have a busy night. I apologized to my three roommates and told them that I was deeply sorry. They accepted my apology, even though I could tell they were not happy with me.

We all learned a valuable lesson that rainy morning and, even though there would be similar incidents throughout the course, I have never found myself in that position since.

SERGEANT HOLT – SECTION COMMANDER

There was another incident that took place during our basic infantry course that has made me laugh and shake my head a few times since.

It was around the nine-week mark, and we had passed our company commander's inspection; we were no longer confined to barracks and had been enjoying our freedom, especially on weekends. Friday and Saturday nights were a time for everyone to get cleaned up, go to the mess for beers and then downtown to have fun and break loose.

It was a Friday morning and our section commander, Sergeant Holt, decided to walk through our rooms to make sure they were being kept at a high standard. I will categorically state here that our room was fine, and all four bed spaces were immaculate. Sergeant Holt, a scar-faced brute of a man who continually complained about his hemorrhoids and farted more than any human I had ever known, stopped in front of me. Standing only an inch or so from my face, he passed gas and started yelling at me because, in his words, my bed space was exactly what he expected from a stupid Newfie shit.

The smell was disgusting, but like I had been trained, I stood there and allowed the smell to waft around me, took his abuse and even agreed with him about my bed space when asked. Sergeant Holt then went to one of my roommates, Private Rick Button, a fellow Newfoundlander, and proceeded to insult him about being a Newfie and how his bed space was even worse than Barnes, if that was possible. He then told the room to lock everything up and to move outside for training.

The day's training went like many others, and not one word was mentioned about the morning inspection. Rick and I hoped that it was over with, and we could forget about it. At about 1700 hours in the evening, we were formed up for our Friday evening dismissal and the standard fatherly talk: safe sex, don't get in shit, be back in the quarters by 1800 hours on Sunday, followed by a plethora of insults about how crappy we were. It was then time for leave passes to be handed out, which authorized everyone to leave base.

One after the other, names were called out and, when the WO stopped speaking, he asked if there were any final questions. I raised my hand and asked where my leave pass was and, from behind us, I heard Sergeant Holt say, "Barnes and Button, you are confined to barracks [CB]. Come see me after dismissal." My heart dropped. Weekends were the only thing we looked forward to, and now that was gone. The worst part was that our bed spaces were probably better than almost anyone else's on the course.

My thoughts immediately went to Holt hating Newfoundlanders. He would call Rick Button and me his "Newfie Bookends," and that was the nicest thing he said to us.

Sergeant Holt told us to work on our kit all night and to be standing by our beds in combats at 0800 hours Saturday morning, and he walked away. We did work on our kit all night, and everything was even better than before. At 0745 hours the following

PART ONE - THE COLD WAR

morning, we were standing at attention in front of our beds. We heard Sergeant Holt before we saw him as he passed gas several times walking down the hallway toward our room. When he came in, he brought the most disgusting smell with him. Once again, we had to stand there and inhale it.

Surprisingly, he never even looked at our kit. He just said, "Lock your kit up and meet me outside in five minutes," and he walked away. Rick and I looked at each other and wondered what was up? What was in store for us? How was Sergeant Holt going to torture us?

We knew it was not going to be good.

As we exited the quarters, we found Sergeant Holt with a scowl on his face, telling us to get in his car. He yelled, "One in the front and one in the back." Both Rick and I rushed to the back door, neither of us wanted to be in the front. I was slow off the mark and I found myself riding shotgun with a man I believed hated me and, I might add, I was not that fond of him, either. I remember seeing a small smile appear on his face each time he silently passed gas, knowing that we would just sit there and say nothing.

Sergeant Holt never said a word during our fifteen-minute journey, and Rick and I remained quiet, contemplating what was to come. We pulled up in front of an apartment building and were told to get out. It was then that Sergeant Holt decided to tell us what was going on. We were to be his personal workforce; he was moving to a new house, and we were going to be doing the physical labour. We hauled furniture and other crap all day. At lunchtime, we stopped, and Sergeant Holt's wife made us sandwiches. We finished up at about 1800 hours on Saturday night, and Sergeant Holt drove us back to the barracks.

When the car stopped outside the quarters, Sergeant Holt told us that we were no longer confined to barracks and to enjoy the rest of our weekend. Without even a "thanks," he told us to get out, and we could not obey that order any quicker. The rest of the platoon had a great laugh over our misfortune and were glad that they had not been selected.

Monday morning came, and nothing had changed. Rick and I were still two stupid Newfies and Sergeant Holt's Newfie bookends.

The remainder of the course went by very quickly, and relationships were formed through hard work, teamwork and determination. Those friendships have remained as strong thirty-six years later as they were back then. I have photos, certificates, and scars to remind me of my basic infantry course, but the tattoo on my right forearm most signifies what those days meant to me at the time.

It was a Friday night, and after a strenuous exercise and some extensive physical training, we felt invincible. We were the best, and no one could take that away from us. After several drinks and beers, many of us decided that, like all good army guys, we needed tattoos. We stumbled into the first tattoo shop we found with a pocketful of money and some patriotic ideas of what it meant to be a Royal and a Canadian soldier.

We looked through some books the tattoo artist gave us and picked out the tattoo we wanted. This part of the process took about ten minutes, so it was well planned and executed.

I woke up on Saturday morning with a huge hangover, a sore arm and only some bits of memories of the night before. It was like Christmas, as we uncovered our tattoos to see what we had done. I had gotten the tattoo of the day for army folks, DEATH BEFORE DISHONOUR, wrapped around a skull and crossbones. The tattoo was black and red.

It was several days later that someone mentioned to me that my tattoo had a spelling mistake. My tattoo says DEATH BE FOR DISHONOUR. It became a running joke for the rest of the course about why you do not get a tattoo on a whim, especially when drunk. It was worse when Sergeant Holt found out because it just confirmed the stupid Newfie narrative he had been enjoying.

I never got the tattoo covered or corrected, and it remains on my arm, even if a little faded now, as a reminder of those early days.

LIEUTENANT BUONAMICI – COURSE OFFICER

As I mentioned earlier, our Platoon Commander, Lieutenant Buonamici, was a great runner and enjoyed taking the platoon on some long runs until most of the platoon would fall out. Then, he would tell us how weak we were.

Physical fitness was a large part of our basic infantry course and, rightfully so, as has been proven on many operations from Bosnia to Afghanistan and beyond.

The staff would relish seeing us suffer and enjoyed pointing out individuals having difficulty keeping up on runs and marches. I was lucky here as I was a little above average, and there were almost always a bunch of guys that fell out before me and suffered the wrath of the staff. Lieutenant Buonamici enjoyed doing things that would cause us to be miserable and see if someone would break.

One such incident remains clear to me. It happened while we were training in Ipperwash, a military camp and a former Canadian Forces training facility located in Lambton County, near Kettle Point, Ontario. It later became very well known when a land dispute with the First Nations there cost an unarmed protestor, Dudley George, his life.

We were conducting weapons training and each morning we would put on our kit and run and march to the different ranges. They were all between five and seven miles away and Lieutenant Buonamici and his staff would beast us on the way out and then again at the end of the day, returning to quarters.

These forced marches sucked, and even though our bodies were becoming stronger and leaner, our minds could never get used to the abuse, both physical and verbal, that the staff seemed to enjoy immensely.

One specific day in the middle of a rainstorm, we were 'beasted' on the way back to camp, following a full day of live fire section attacks, which are themselves physically gruelling. In particular that day, Lieutenant Buonamici and his staff were not happy with our performance. He told us in no uncertain terms that we were the worst soldiers he had ever seen. We obviously needed to be reminded that we were infantry soldiers and RCR.

The march back was gruelling; we ran most of the six miles at a good clip, carrying our weapons and wearing our helmets and fighting order. We had soldiers spread out over at least a mile, and a few were bent over puking or had just stopped. It made the staff yell louder and get even ruder as they threw more and more personal insults at those who could not keep up.

As we got within sight of the quarters, and an end to this madness seemed near, we suddenly slowed down and went back for those that had fallen behind, and the last guy was at least a kilometre back.

As we made the circle around the last guy, the yelling and screaming increased. The staff were telling us that if we wanted to quit, all we had to do was fall out to the side of the road. A truck would pick us up and drive us back to camp where we could put in a request to quit, and it would be accepted. I am sure it was very tempting for several people, myself included, but I was more scared of the staff than the pain I was in.

It was a great relief as Lieutenant Buonamici slowed down to a jog and allowed everyone to catch up. The quarters and supper were only a few hundred metres to our front, but then the staff once again proved to me that they could be even more abusive than I thought possible.

We passed the quarters and ran over to the Mess Hall. Buonamici had two of the staff hold open the doors, and he ran the whole platoon into the mess hall, around the kitchen and the surprised cooks, who just stood there with their mouths open, and back out through the front doors and back toward the ranges.

I cannot even explain how I felt, but it was like someone had punched me in the gut; I thought I would be sick. We had found the courage and stamina to make it back to camp. When we discovered that the end was not happening and the run continued, it was the most incredible letdown that I have ever experienced.

We ran for about another five hundred metres, and soldiers were falling out at almost every step. Then we slowed down and circled back, picked everyone up who had fallen out, which was about half the platoon, and then stopped in front of the quarters. Lieutenant Buonamici then spoke to us about always remaining ready for everything and expecting the unexpected. He also told us that when we think we can go no further, we must dig deep and find that extra strength to keep going.

I must admit, at the time, all I heard was, "blah, blah, blah," and then we were dismissed to put away our kit and prepare for supper.

As the years have gone by, I realize the critical lesson that I learned that day and how it helped me several times to go the extra distance, even when physically exhausted and under mental stress.

FINAL EXERCISE – CFB PETAWAWA

Near the end of the course, we learned that we would be going to Petawawa, Ontario, to complete our final exercises and the final test to decide whether we passed or failed the course. After what we had endured over the last few months, no one wanted to fail.

On a cold but sunny Sunday morning, we loaded our kit onto trucks and piled onto a bus for the seven-hour trip north to Petawawa.

Our two final exercises were physically strenuous and mentally demanding, but our training had prepared us for the hardship. We were tested as basic infantry soldiers in all phases of war, and sleep was something that we stole when we were on sentry duty and took turns with our fire team partner to watch for staff. They were scarier than any enemy force.

During the final exercise, I also learned a valuable and painful lesson about rushing and doing things so fast that it is not done right. We were going non-stop, conducting platoon attacks during the day, digging defensive positions at night, and patrolling. Sleep was something that we knew was not going to happen. The wind was blowing cold, and everyone was dressed in winter whites, snow pants, long johns and heavy mitts and mukluks. It was hard moving around and even harder doing some basic chores.

We had just finished a platoon attack and had started to replenish ammunition and water when I needed to urinate. The Platoon Commander was yelling for everyone to hurry up, and Sergeant Holt was screaming at our section to get ready to move. I looked at him and said, "Sergeant, I need to piss," he made some half-assed reply like, "Hurry up, pussy."

I got up, moved a few feet ahead of the rest of my section and started the slow process of getting through my long johns, combat pants, snow pants and winter whites, all the time hearing Sergeant Holt yelling at me to hurry up. As I finally freed myself and started to pee, I could hear the section and platoon behind me begin to move off. Sergeant Holt started to scream, "Barnes, get in position now!" I quickly finished, and as I turned around, I am putting myself away and speedily zip up my combat pants.

At first, I felt nothing, and then there was a sharp pain. I looked down, and my zipper was all the way closed and hanging out about halfway down was my foreskin. I do not know why I had a foreskin, and most of my coursemates did not. Maybe it was a Newfoundland thing or a Catholic thing, but at this moment, that was the furthest thing from my mind. I let out a little scream that caught the attention of most of the soldiers that were close by. They just stared as I was grabbing at my crotch. There was a little bit of blood, but mostly it was just skin hanging out of a closed zipper.

I heard some giggles and some comments like, "Shit that must hurt," and "Is that his dick?"

The platoon stopped, and Buonamici, Holt and some other soldiers gathered around. Holt was yelling at me, insulting me about being stupid and to unzip and get going. I was not keen on that plan. I was totally embarrassed as I stood there. Every time I tried to move the zipper, the pain stopped me, and I would say, "I can't." After a few minutes of standing around, Sergeant Holt took off his glove and said, "Let me see." As he reached down, I had a second of dread, but it was too late.

He grabbed the zipper, and with one pull, he yanked it open. I once again let out a little yelp and swore. The Platoon Commander asked me if I was all right and, after a quick look, other than a bit of blood and some zipper teeth marks, I was. We carried on with training.

It was just one more incident that added fuel to the fire of the stupid Newfoundlander narrative.

I tried to remember that lesson throughout my life, and I must say that my foreskin has been safe ever since.

As the last exercise ended, we all breathed a sigh of relief even though the staff continually told us that the course was not over. We still had some stuff to do once we returned to London, including a graduation parade. Any of us could be failed or be sent back to another platoon right up until the moment that we march onto the parade square to graduate. We knew they had the power to do it.

MURDER BALL – ANOTHER LESSON

We did receive some good news at the end of the second exercise when we were told that the following day we would be participating in the Brigade Sports Day taking place in Petawawa. While we had been training and tested on our basic soldier skills, the Brigade had gotten together in Petawawa to train as well. It culminated in a sports day, followed by a barbecue and a couple of beers. The platoon was highly excited to be considered part of the brigade for this.

Because we were part of Dukes Company in London, and 1 RCR was here for the exercise, we just fell in with them. There were several sporting events in which different units competed for first place. I do not know who decided for our platoon to participate in "Murder Ball"—it may have been Dukes Company, but I believe it was probably our platoon staff, especially as they did not participate in the game.

The game consisted of a giant ball that was probably six or seven feet in diameter, and two teams tried to push, drag or drive the ball across the other team's end line. There were rules, but the referees, who were other soldiers, did not enforce them.

We saw the schedule and discovered that we were going to be playing the Canadian Airborne Regiment first. That sucked for us, as their reputation for violence and brutality was well-known. There are many stories from the early '80s about these guys, from gunfights in the quarters to bar brawls that left folks hospitalized to burning cars on the parade square and a lot more.

As we were getting ready to play, our opponents were already harassing us. They would walk by us and lick their lips, make sexual gestures toward us, or simply say, "We are going to hurt you guys." We were young and easily intimidated by these guys, and many of us believed that they would try to hurt us.

No one in our platoon had ever even heard of Murder Ball, let alone played the game, and our staff were not much help. They just told us to work as a team and not to quit.

The game begins at the centre point of the field with both teams on their side of the ball trying to roll it toward the other goal. We were able to hold our own for a while, and then through sheer force, the ball was basically rolled over us, and we were trampled as the Airborne guys continued toward our end zone and scored.

As we started again, we initially had the upper hand, and we were able to get the ball moving toward the opponent's end, but then all hell broke loose. I remember seeing someone coming over the top of the ball and then another and another, and then we had the enemy amongst us. These guys were like animals, and they had propelled their teammates over the ball and onto our unsuspecting team. As soon as they landed, they began kicking and throwing punches. They grabbed our testicles and anything else within reach. I heard screaming and yelling, and then I felt a sharp pain in my left calf. I looked down and saw an Airborne guy with his teeth sunk into my leg. I pulled away as the ball once again rolled through us and across our end line.

Several of our guys had to be replaced because they had been injured. I was one of them, as I had to see a medic to stop the bleeding in my leg. The teeth marks were very evident, but the staff and referees did not seem to care. The game went on and we ended up losing 5 to 0.

Once again, a valuable lesson was learned here: we may all be in the same Canadian Forces, but everyone is highly competitive in sports, and winning is the end game.

I would be involved in many competitions throughout my career, from sporting events to military matches and, to a person, we always wanted to beat the rest. Sometimes the cost was high.

A couple of days later, we jumped back on a bus and made the trip back to London where we had a week of classroom work and a week of parade practice in preparation for our Graduation Parade.

The last two weeks were rather dull compared to the first few months of the course but consisted of morning physical training and hours and hours of drill. I was surprised at how we quickly came together as a platoon and how proud I was when I marched out in front of hundreds of soldiers and families wearing my RCR cap badge. I was a Royal Canadian soldier, and I would remain in Dukes Company with 1 RCR London as my first posting. I was excited and could not wait for what was to come.

ACE MOBILE FORCE (LAND)

My first major event as a full-fledged Infantryman was in Norway, as we deployed with the battalion shortly after graduation on an annual exercise as part of NATO's commitment. Several NATO countries, including Canada, spent several weeks

PART ONE - THE COLD WAR

training in the mountains and towns there.

I was both excited and apprehensive about the upcoming exercise. It would be our first time training with the company and the battalion as qualified infantry soldiers. We anticipated that the more senior soldiers in the unit would probably be watching close by.

The weeks leading up to departure to Norway consisted of some low-level winter training to make sure we were prepared to live and fight in the northern climate. All of our kit, from tents to toboggans, stoves, lanterns and rations were checked and rechecked. We practiced putting up our ten-man tents and tearing them down until we could have the tent up, hot water on and sleeping gear laid out in less than ten minutes.

Once everything was considered ready to go, we had a couple of days to relax with our families. Then we packed our kit, shipped it off and jumped on an aircraft for the long flight to Norway.

Once we were on the ground, we were able to do some low-level training for the first week, including my first attempt at using skis as a form of transportation into battle. We worked with a Norwegian unit and, as they came into our bivouac, I was amazed at their performance. There was a platoon on skis, and they were able to manoeuvre on them with all their fighting gear and full packs as if they were running. It was a sight to see.

One of the things I learned very quickly about our Norwegian brothers in arms was that they use skis like bicycles. They are on skis before they can walk and, while moving through some of the towns and villages in the mountains, it was also evident that they continued to use skis into old age. Everyone was on skis—kids, parents, older men and women—and they were moving around like it was effortless.

For us Canadians, it was not as easy; for starters, unlike the Norwegian soldiers, we did not have good skis. We had something called 'bangy boards,' which were wide, wooden contraptions that were difficult to control and harder to steer. I saw many a Norwegian soldier giggle as many of our platoon guys took a tumble as we tripped over our own feet. Luckily, our platoon did not have to use the skis as part of the actual exercise.

A few events throughout the exercise are still pretty clear to me today, such as one that taught me a lesson about leadership and how we treat our soldiers.

We had a young Master Corporal as our section commander, and he decided that our section was not allowed to use electric razors or battery-powered razors while in the field. During our nightly stove watch inside the tent, the plan was that we would make hot water and shave. For those of us who had electric razors, this was a pain. We did not like being treated like recruits. We were now trained Royal Canadians.

One evening about two weeks into our exercise, Private Dave Gibbs and I walked back to our tent after doing sentry duty. As we approached, we heard someone cursing and mumbling inside the tent. We both looked at each other, wondering what was going on. We reached for the zipper to the tent and pulled it open. The sight inside made us laugh out loud and got us in trouble.

WHITE SCHOOL, BLACK MEMORIES

Standing in the tent was our section commander with a buzzing electric razor attached to his face. Somehow, the razor had gotten stuck to his face, and he was having trouble removing it. He forcefully yanked it off his face, leaving a huge red mark behind. We tried to control our laughter, but that was too much with us lacking sleep and being so tired. The Master Corporal yelled at us to get out of the tent and help the rest of the section build up the defences and keep this to ourselves. We replied, "Yes, Master Corporal," and rushed outside the tent.

Keep it to ourselves—yeah, right! As soon as we got to the rest of the guys, we told them what had happened, and we had a good laugh at our section commander's expense. We had always been told about the principles of leadership, especially "lead by example." As young soldiers, we would giggle and whisper to each other, "Do as I say, not as I do."

As part of the yearly NATO concentration in Norway, there was a competition between nations and between units to show our forces' competitive nature and the esprit de corps that always exists. The competition consisted of a ten-kilometre march, followed by a shooting competition. Canada had several teams and other NATO participants, like Germany, Italy, the United States, the United Kingdom and many more participated.

I believe there had been a ten-minute start between teams, and the time for the march stopped as you crossed the finish line at the shooting range. Your score on the range was then used to either add or subtract from your overall timing.

Our platoon was the Dukes Company representatives, and as we were gathered at the start line, we were inspected to ensure that we had the correct kit and carried the right weight. Lieutenant Buonamici made it clear to us that we were going to win this.

Immediately, we knew we were in for a torturous ten-kilometre march. As the whistle sounded for the start, we immediately started at an amazingly fast walk. As we rounded the first corner and were out of sight of all the spectators, we broke into a run. We would march quickly for about 200 metres, and then we would run for about 200 metres. This routine continued for the first five kilometres.

At about that time, we spotted the Italian team that had started ten minutes before us. It immediately caused Buonamici to become a monster. He started yelling at us that we would catch the Italians, pass them and suck it up. By about the seven-kilometre mark, we had reached the tail end of the Italian platoon. They were spread out over a hundred metres and were giving it their all, but were physically exhausted and hurting.

Buonamici started yelling stuff to them in Italian as we passed them. It was noticeably clear that these proud soldiers were not impressed with this loudmouth Canadian officer. I do not know what he was saying, but there was little doubt from the looks on the faces of the Italian soldiers that he was probably bragging about passing them and maybe insulting them.

As we were almost past the last of the platoon, some of the Italian NCOs started to yell back. Some even made moves toward Buonamici and us soldiers. The yelling got louder, and other soldiers began joining in. The yelling died down as we pulled ahead and left the other team behind.

I learned another valuable lesson here that I have carried with me throughout my career. It's fine to be competitive, and esprit de corps is something that a military unit needs, but you should never treat another unit or country disrespectfully, especially those who are your allies.

We continued at a blistering pace for the next three kilometres and finished with the fastest time out of any unit for the day. We had been competing against everyone but, for me, it was about beating the Canadian Airborne Regiment team. We did so easily, by several minutes.

The shooting competition started as soon as you arrived at the range. Magazines were already loaded for us, and we had to hit targets from 100, 200 and 300 metres. Any misses added penalties to our overall time. We had killed it on the march, but the pace had taken a lot out of us. When I was shooting, I know that I was still shaking and unable to control my breathing. Most of the members of the platoon were the same.

We waited around to hear the final times at the end of the competition and were extremely disappointed to find out that the Canadian Airborne Regiment beat us by less than two minutes. We had obviously not done very well on the shooting part, and they did.

Lesson learned once again. When you are moving on foot to an objective, you need to be fit to fight when you arrive.

The next incident happened during a major part of the exercise. We had been patrolling for several days through the mountains and were supposed to conduct a surprise attack on a well-defended enemy force played by the Canadian Airborne Regiment. Our route took us about twenty hours longer than planned and, by the time we arrived at our attack position at first light on the third day, the enemy had already moved on to another task. We encountered nothing but empty snow and ice defences.

After a quick couple of hours' sleep in our hastily erected ten-man tents, we started back to our company position, back over a mountain and down the other side. After many hours of snowshoeing, pulling toboggans and stumbling around, we finally made it to the other side of the mountain and the rest of the company. As we came around the corner of a trail, my good friend and fellow private, Mike Jordan, spotted someone sitting against a tree.

Our first instinct was that this could be an ambush, and we had walked into a trap.

Because we were the lead section, we dropped the toboggan and moved forward, two of us providing cover while Mike and another soldier approached the man by the tree. It seemed a little strange that he was not moving. There were no tracks on the ground, and it had not snowed for about twelve or more hours. Mike spoke to him, but he did not reply.

It was a young Norwegian soldier dressed for battle with his weapon. As Mike tells it, he crouched down directly in front of this guy while the rest of us covered him with our weapons just in case it was a trick. The guy appeared to have a smile on his face, but his eyes were closed. Then, suddenly his eyes popped open, and he stared straight ahead as if he did not see us. We immediately knew something was wrong. Mike continued to ask him if he was okay and what his name was. His eyes just darted around, he began mumbling, and he started to cry.

We could tell from looking at him that he had been sitting in this cold without shelter or heat for many hours and was near death. We were able to get one of our stoves going and a hot drink down his throat. Then we wrapped him in a poncho liner, put him in a toboggan and got him back to our Company lines in record time.

That night, we put him in our tent, got his wet, cold clothes off and put him in a sleeping bag that Mike graciously gave up. Once he was settled, we had time to look at his kit and noticed that his combat boots were frozen. We had mukluks, and most other soldiers had some sort of arctic boot, but not this guy.

The next morning, Mike's sleeping bag was soaking wet and, when we got our Norwegian soldier up and dressed in dry clothes, we brought him to our HQ to make sure he could get back to his unit.

We heard later that this young Norwegian soldier told someone at the HQ who understood his language that he had fallen through the ice somewhere and gotten wet, and his unit needed to continue with a task. They told him to make it back to his unit lines alone, but he could not walk a step farther on frozen feet, so he stopped to rest. He had probably been sitting there for several hours when we found him.

A week or so later, when the company was leaving, and we were on the tarmac getting ready to take a C130 to Canada, Mike heard someone yelling in terrible English, "Jordan, Mike Jordan!" The same Norwegian soldier came out of the hospital with only a gown and combat boots. His exact words were, "Private Jordan, you and your buddies saved my life. My father made this knife for me. It is all I have to offer. I will never forget all of you. Thank you." He then walked away.

Mike still has the knife as a reminder of that day. Mike Jordan was a hero that day, and his calm and considerate actions saved a life.

The last incident happened near the end of the exercise. After marching for hours and hours, we put in a company attack on a prepared enemy position, played again by the Canadian Airborne Regiment. The attack was a success, but the umpires gave the company several wounded and several killed. This part of the exercise had to be played out as well.

I was designated as a wounded soldier and given a card, which I had to hang around my neck. The card stated what injuries I had. I had a bullet wound to the chest and the upper leg. I had to lay there with several other casualties as the Company immediately did first aid on me and called in medical evacuation. I was excited when two of us were picked up by a helicopter and transported to a NATO airfield for follow-up treatment.

I figured that would be the end of the scenario, but I was wrong. The other casualty and I would be medevacked back to Canada in a Hercules aircraft. We had several medics start doing first aid on us and getting us stable enough for the flight. Then we were strapped into stretchers and loaded on the Hercules. As we were talking, we had medical personnel checking our vitals and hovering all around us. Once we were in the air, we were told to relax, get some sleep, and the medics would check on us now and then.

Sleep came very quickly. I do not know how long I was asleep, but I was awakened by the sound of sirens and horns going off, flashing lights and aircrew running around the aircraft. Someone was yelling about preparing for a water landing, and I started freaking out. I was strapped into a stretcher on a flying fuel bomb that was about to crash in the ocean, and I do not swim. I started to yell for someone to unstrap me and get me a life vest when a young Air Force Sergeant came over and told me to relax because this was just a drill.

I may have been only a young private but, at that moment, if I had not been strapped to a stretcher, I probably would have punched that guy right in the throat. Instead, I asked him if he was a fucking idiot and why they had not told us about the drill as I thought it had been real. I had several people come by to apologize to us, but then they all walked away with a grin on their faces.

The one good thing about being evacuated as a training casualty was that I got home a couple of days before everyone else.

3

GERMANY, THE FIRST TIME

A few months later, it was back to Petawawa for another brigade exercise and then a decision that would change the path my life would take.

We were formed up as a battalion and were told that soldiers from 1 RCR would be posted to 3 RCR in Germany within the next month or so. I immediately volunteered for the posting and, a week or so later, the list came out. I was on it. The list was primarily made up of young, single guys that could move quickly and didn't have to be concerned with families, children and schools.

I was excited about moving to Germany and the opportunity it presented. I had quite a simple move as everything I owned could fit in a couple of boxes. Everything else was in my military-issued kit. I did not have any real connections—no girlfriend, no house, no car—so it was just a quick phone call to my beautiful mother and father in Newfoundland to let them know what was going on. Then, it was Bon Voyage.

I remember my mother being very worried about me going to Germany and all the terrible, dangerous events that it entailed in her mind. I realize now that it may have been a blessing that she had passed before my deployment to Afghanistan in 2006, or she would have had a terrible time coping with it.

We arrived in Germany in the early summer of 1982, and it did not disappoint. I remember that first morning walking across the base, through the gate and into the North Marg. That was part of the airfield that had been turned into the home of 3 RCR, and I was thinking to myself how lucky I was to be here. Everything was green, including rooftops of buildings, and there were bunkers everywhere completely overgrown and camouflaged with grass—all to make it harder to identify if attacked from the air by the Soviet Union. It was the height of the Cold War and all our training, equipment, and everything that we did was in preparation for the Soviets to roll into West Germany from the East.

There were about sixty of us from 1 RCR and as we moved along the Battalion

PART ONE - THE COLD WAR

lines, I felt like an animal in a zoo. All the soldiers from 3 RCR kept coming out of their buildings or vehicles to stop and stare. I quickly learned that 3 RCR was an older battalion, postings in and out were rare, but privates were even rarer. We received catcalls and insults from the corporals and master corporals, as they told us we were 'fresh meat.' I believe they were excited to have some young privates to order around, as back then Corporals held real power over Privates, unlike today when the ranks are viewed as being much closer in seniority.

Those who had just arrived were split up amongst the Rifle Companies, with a few friends and me going to Oscar Company. We met the Sergeant Major immediately. He was a short, stocky man whose reputation did not match his bellowing voice. I thought it was kind of funny that his first question was to ask if any of us were hockey players.

I later learned that our Company Sergeant Major, MWO Sonny McIntyre, was the 3 RCR Hockey Team coach. Hockey was a huge part of being in Germany and could even have priority over such things as work, duties, exercises, etc. I also learned that The RCR and other unit hockey teams recruited soldiers from basic training and trades training for postings to Germany and onto their hockey teams, as well as other sports teams.

A running joke within the battalion went like this, "Private Smith gets the puck, Corporal Smith gets around the defence, Master Corporal Smith shoots, and Sergeant Smith scores." It had to do with what was perceived to be an unfair advantage given to hockey players. I remember hockey players from Oscar Company being let go at 1300 hours to train and, on game days, they would be gone almost all day to go to the Roman baths in Baden-Baden for relaxation and massages. On at least one occasion, a helicopter picked up players from an exercise to take them back to base for hockey, so no wonder there was a perception of unfairness and perhaps some envy.

I had only been in Baden Solingen (the area of Germany where our base was located) for only a couple of days when the four of us decided to rent a car and tour the local area. Cars could be rented from Canex very cheaply and, with the Canadian dollar worth about four deutschmarks, we thought we were rich.

One of my friends who went through our basic infantry training with me and remained in London with 1 RCR had a brother who was a Corporal in 3 RCR. He came to introduce himself to us and offered himself up as a tour guide. He took one look at the bunch of us, young single guys, with money in our pockets and decided to bring us to the seedier side of Germany. Our second night in the country found us in Karlsruhe and the well-known red-light district.

For me, this was a novelty, and I was more interested in looking around than partaking. I was like a kid in a candy store; I was in awe and shock. I was a nineteen-year-old Newfie from a small fishing village, and this was not something I had ever seen or even envisioned. It was like a strip mall.

Everything was out in the open as we walked up and down the street and looked in windows and doors at what was offered. Women would make sure there was nothing left to your imagination and would clearly tell you how much and for what.

There did not seem to be very many limits, and many men were walking around doing the same thing we were doing. Some would disappear inside a door. I was not interested in participating, whether through morals or fear, but others did.

Along the district were bars known as 'pussy bars,' and you could go in these and order a beer or a drink. The rooms were very dark, drinks were expensive, and the walls were covered with small TVs playing every kind of pornography imaginable. The whole time, girls would be coming up to you, partially dressed and making offers to take you upstairs. I never became comfortable in these places but did attend a few times, mostly to fit in and not be made fun of.

I don't know if I was scared, shy or cheap, but it never appealed to me to pay someone for sex. Even though these places were government-controlled, and the women were supposedly checked for diseases, most of them looked a little worse for wear.

Some of the new guys learned some valuable lessons early in 1982 when hanging out in these types of places. If you were in one of these pussy bars and allowed a girl to sit beside you and agreed to buy her a drink, you needed to be prepared to pay. You were not just paying for the drink; you were also paying for her time, even though that was never verbally agreed upon. If you ordered a beer in these places, it could be as much as five marks, but if you decided to buy a drink for a girl, it could cost you a hundred marks.

There was no warning and no forgiveness.

We hung around the Putz Strasa ('pussy street') for a couple of hours that first night and drank a few beers each, as well as a couple of drinks. Once everyone had their fill of the excitement, we decided to leave.

TRAFFIC ACCIDENT – SECOND NIGHT IN COUNTRY

As we were returning to Base Baden from the red-light district, we made a terrible mistake that could have been much worse than it turned out. We had been at the district for about two hours, drinking beer and drinks, as well. We had several before leaving the Base, so none of us should have been driving. We were young, foolish, and perhaps a little overwhelmed by Germany, the excitement of the red-light district, and we made a bad decision. My friend, Mike, was driving, and Dave was in the passenger seat, with myself and another friend, John, in the back. We went onto the Autobahn and headed back to base.

Everything seemed to be going well until we took a side road that led to the turn-off for the base. Because we were still new here and did not know our way around, Mike did not see the turn-off until we were upon it. And, because he was travelling at a higher speed than posted or was safe when he took the turn to go to the Base, the car left the road and started flipping. I remember the car flipping at least five times, perhaps more, and it seemed like it was in slow motion. The car rolled off the road into a ditch and then on a farmer's field, coming to rest in an upside-down position on its

PART ONE - THE COLD WAR

roof.

I just lay there for a moment and thought to myself, "What have we done?" Mike started asking if everyone was okay, and I heard someone say, "Yes," followed by me. I could not get the door to open, so I crawled out a broken side window into the dark and stood by the car. There were already cars stopping along the road, and I heard a mixture of German and English as people came down to help us. As people were approaching, we got together to make sure everyone was okay, and we had our story straight, but Dave was missing. Where was he? We called his name several times and looked in and around the car—nothing.

As people came to us, we told them to look for Dave, and people went for flashlights or moved their cars into position so their headlights could shine toward us, as well as the dark field. We told people that Dave had been in the front passenger seat and was probably not wearing his seatbelt. We also told them that Dave was black and very dark and that he would be hard to see if he were lying in the grass.

At that moment, I heard a voice say, "I am here," and Dave came slowly into the picture. He was okay but had some scratches, as did Mike. The rest of us did not have any marks. We spoke to a couple of folks who had stopped, and we were informed that if no one was hurt and no property was damaged, we did not have to notify the police until the morning. We quickly decided to catch a ride with a Canadian soldier to the Base and worry about the car in the morning, mainly because we were all intoxicated, and maybe we could get away with it.

In the morning, Mike, the driver who had rented the car from Canex, notified the Military Police and then Canex. After morning PT, the rest of us went to see the car and realized that our second night in Germany could very easily have been our last. We had gotten incredibly lucky as the damage to the vehicle was extensive, and we had suffered only minor cuts.

A few hours later, we found ourselves standing at attention outside the Oscar Company's Sergeant Major's office and worried that this might mean we would be sent back to Canada. That was the last thing any of us wanted. As soon as the Military Police were notified, they interviewed Mike, and they then informed our Sergeant Major what had happened the night before.

MWO Sonny McIntyre came out of his office and, even though he was a short, stocky man, he seemed several feet taller as he yelled and screamed at us. He called us idiots and assholes and reminded us that everything we did was a reflection on ourselves, this company, and this battalion.

That was a lesson I never forgot, and I lived by it for the rest of my career.

We were then called into his office one at a time, read the riot act and asked to tell our story. We all told the same story that we had gone to the Putz Strasa and that Mike had been the designated driver and had not been drinking. Because it had been our first time returning to base in a car, we did not know precisely where the turn-off was. When it appeared, Mike took the turn too quickly, and the vehicle flipped.

I know that the CSM did not believe our story because he clearly told us that. He also said that that was our only warning and that if there were another incident, we would be charged and sent back to Canada. We knew that he meant every word.

HALF-COCKED – A SEX STORY

Germany, like much of Europe in the early 1980s, had a highly active sex trade. It was everywhere, and any Major city or town had what was referred to as a Putz Strasa. Like soldiers everywhere, most were men, and many were young, and they were most of the clientele in these red-light districts. German girls looking for a good time or a way out of Germany found a way to become friends with Canadian soldiers, and parties were easy to find and cheap to conduct. Many Canadian soldiers returned to Canada with a German wife. Many more got out of the Army and remained behind in Germany with their new German family.

Like any country and any society, many types of women were hanging around the Canadian base, and soldiers found themselves in some unique situations.

The following account happened in the single quarters in Baden, Germany, around 1982 or 1983. To protect the identity of the individuals involved, fictional names are used.

I lived in the single quarters with many other young soldiers from Oscar Company when I first arrived in Germany, and it was never a surprise or a shock to see some strange events occurring. For example, it would not be a surprise to wake up at 0100 hours to go down the hallway to a public bathroom and find a naked soldier or a naked girl passed out on a couch or the floor in the common area. I got ready for work many mornings and saw women being pushed out the doors of soldiers' quarters as they left.

I remember walking into the common area on the way to my room early on a weeknight and finding two German girls and a soldier having sex on the couch. They just said, "Hi," and invited me to join. I said, "No," and hurried on to my room.

It was in this environment that a more serious event occurred.

It was late in the night or early morning when I heard some yelling going on a few doors down the hallway from my room. I got up and, as I looked out my door, I saw a fellow soldier, a Newfie, naked and holding his crotch as blood ran down his legs. He was yelling for me to get him to the hospital. People kept asking him what had happened, but he just continued to scream for a doctor. By now, others had awakened. Someone called the duty centre for the driver to come to the quarters and take a soldier to the hospital. Minutes later, the duty driver, as well as the base MPs, arrived. The injured soldier was helped to get dressed and then taken to the Canadian hospital while the MPs were seen removing a German woman from the victim's room and taking her away.

Those of us standing around started to clean up the blood on the floor and wondered what had happened.

A few days later, the injured soldier told some of the soldiers in the quarters what had happened. According to his version, he picked up a well-known German girl at

PART ONE - THE COLD WAR

a local bar called Tiffany's, an RCR hang out in the surrounding community. No one knew the girl's name, even though many Canadian soldiers were known to have spent time with her. However, everyone knew her nickname ('Beat Me'). She had a reputation for liking to be roughed up during sex, and many soldiers had told stories of their endeavours with her. I had seen and spoken to this girl on a few occasions, but I had never been interested in having sex with someone that had her reputation.

The injured soldier said they had been drinking all evening at the bar and then returned to his room, where they continued to drink and have sex. His story goes that Beat Me was giving him oral sex, and she continually looked up at him, asking him to slap her. The victim was a quiet individual and did not want to hit her, but she began to insult him, belittle him, and even insulted his manhood.

After a minute or so of getting insulted, the soldier slapped the girl on the shoulder. She called him a pussy, and he punched her in the back of the head, causing her to bite down on his penis. He said he screamed in pain and pushed the girl away to find his penis covered in blood and part of it hanging by a thread. It was around this time that he had run into the hallway.

The poor Canadian soldier had been hospitalized for a few days and had stitches to repair his torn penis, but the damage resulted in the soldier having a penis with a missing piece at the tip.

From that day forward, this young Newfoundland soldier was nicknamed 'half-cocked.' He had to live with this embarrassment for a long time.

FOOLISH GAMES – SERIOUS CONSEQUENCES

I had my own medical incident that resulted from my own immature and foolish actions, but like most young soldiers, I never even really considered the possible consequences.

Alcohol played a significant role in everything we did during those early years in Germany. Most single and married guys drank almost every night and day, and there were very seldom any consequences, or at least serious consequences, for most incidents.

I remember standing in front of a Sergeant Major with four or five other guys, some with black eyes, bruised knuckles and bloody. We were told that getting picked up by the German Police and handed off to the Military Police for fighting in town with local Germans was not a big deal as long as we won. When the Sergeant Major asked what happened, we said, "Yes, we won."

All he said in return was, "Good, the lesson here is to look after each other."

During those early days in Germany, I did not have a car, which was probably a blessing, so much of our drinking took place on the Base, either in a soldier's room or in the Junior Ranks Mess.

Two noteworthy events occurred during those days that I am not proud of today and have difficulty explaining why they happened, other than the effects of alcohol.

WHITE SCHOOL, BLACK MEMORIES

The first was a stupid game that had been going around the mess since London and continued in Germany, called Guts. Like most of my friends and comrades, I was a smoker. The game consisted of putting your forearm tightly against another person's forearm, placing a lit cigarette between the two and seeing who would pull their arm away first. This supposedly showed who had the most "guts."

Yes, it sounds as stupid as it was, but I played several times and have the scars to prove it.

I usually used my left arm because my right arm had my misspelled tattoo on the specific torture area. On one crazy night, I decided for one reason or another to use my right arm. As the cigarette burned down, we could smell singed hair and skin. I just held on and drank my beer and smiled until my opponent finally gave up with a small scream. The following morning, I found that the deep burn scar was right on the outline of my tattoo, and it's a scar that I carry with me to this day.

Many years later, my wife and kids would ask me why a piece of my tattoo was gone. Eventually, I told them the truth, explaining it as a young, gung-ho infantryman trying to prove his toughness to his friends. Still, they knew it was a drunken, stupid, idiotic incident that I am now embarrassed about.

The second event was a bit more dramatic and resulted in much more serious consequences. This one happened outside a beer tent that was on Base Baden but was open to everyone, civilians included. Cheap alcohol was flowing, and I had been drinking all day with several other soldiers and friends, and, as the night progressed, our stupidity also increased.

We had seen many Germans playing a game they called "Smack Mouth," which is exactly how it sounds. Two people square off and punch each other in the face until one quits or is knocked out. This seemed like a great game to me: I wanted to play. I was a big guy and considered myself to be tough. Since joining the military, I had been in several fights, and I had always come out on top, even if I had some scars as a reminder.

I initially watched two of my friends partake and after both had given the other a good smack, they called it a draw and ended the game. It was now my turn to play with my best friend, John. We flipped a coin to see who would go first, and he won. To avoid serious injuries, the rules said that both parties had to sit so that one's entire body weight did not go into the strike. I sat there and realized that the anticipation of the hit was probably much worse than the hit.

John swung hard, but I believe he may have held back a little bit, and as my head went back from the strike, I was relieved to be awake and feeling rather good. I decided to make John suffer a little bit more from the anticipation, so I dragged out my turn as long as possible. I tilted his head a little to the right and then went through a couple of practice swings, all to torture my friend. Finally, I swung a massive strike that knocked John out of his chair and onto the floor, but he slowly got back to his feet with a big smile, saying, "My turn."

Shit, I had hoped he would stop after that one.

John now took enjoyment in making me wait as he prepared and went through some practice swings. The next thing I remember is John and some other friends asking me if I was all right. When I tried to answer, I knew something was wrong. My mouth hurt, and my jaw did not move.

My friends immediately knew it was broken, and the base duty driver was tasked to take me to the base hospital. An X-ray showed that my jaw was broken directly left and right of my chin in two places. The amount of alcohol in my system deadened the pain in the moment, but when I awoke the following morning in my hospital room, it was immediate and excruciating.

I had to face the Battalion Duty Officer and my Sergeant Major, who had been notified. Their immediate concern over my well-being quickly passed when they found out I had been brought in completely drunk with a broken jaw. I made up a story about being jumped by a couple of Germans to protect my friend, even though my chain of command never believed the story.

I was told that I would have to go to the American hospital in Landstuhl to be treated, as the Canadian hospital did not have the proper capacity. I was driven to the U.S. hospital by a civilian driver from the Base. We arrived about fifteen minutes before my appointment. The pain was almost unbearable. It did not help that I was unable to speak or eat and could only drink water through a straw.

Inside the American hospital, I was greeted by a military nurse who had me sit in a wheelchair and pushed me to a waiting room at the far end of the hospital. I waited for about an hour to be seen, and the wait did not ease my already high anxiety.

I saw a large African American staff sergeant go in to see the doctor. His jaw was bloody, swollen and obviously broken. The yells and screams from the inner office made me cringe, knowing that I was next.

I meekly went in when my name was called, hoping that this would not hurt as much as I now thought it would. It only took the doctor a few minutes to look at the X-rays and tell me the plan. My upper and lower jaw would be wired in place for several weeks until it was completely healed. Then I would come back to have the wires removed. The doctor used his fingers to move my lower jaw into the correct position, and he told me that he would put some local anesthetic in my gums to soften the pain. There was a large mirror just above my face, and I could see everything that was happening.

In hindsight, I should have closed my eyes.

Using a long, shiny steel needle, the doctor proceeded to run a wire in and out all the way along my upper gums and then the same to my lower gums. He used more wire to connect the top and bottom in several places. Pliers were used to twist the wire until it was as tight as possible until my teeth were clamped together, and there was zero movement.

When he was done, the doctor talked to me about the importance of avoiding any movement of my jaw for the next six weeks. He showed me a gap between my teeth and told me to use a straw to eat a liquid diet and avoid alcohol and partying.

WHITE SCHOOL, BLACK MEMORIES

He warned me that getting sick could be dangerous, as I could choke on my vomit. He then handed me a small, shiny pair of wire cutters. I was informed that these should always be kept on my person, and if something happened and I was choking, I could use those to cut the wire on the left and right sides of my mouth and force my jaws apart.

I was also informed that I would spend the next three or four days in the hospital back at Base and have to get my meals there for the next six weeks. The next six weeks were a pain in the ass but were also a constant reminder of how stupid and idiotic I had been and that my actions had consequences.

It took only a few weeks for me to forget that lesson.

My first meal at the Baden Base Hospital was a moment in my life that still haunts me. I reported to the hospital about suppertime, and even though I was in pain and discomfort, I was starving. I had not eaten in almost forty-eight hours. Once I was settled into my bed, the duty nurse said she would check on supper for me because she was unsure about what to give someone in my situation. About an hour later, she returned with a large silver cup, like the ones you get a large milkshake in, and it had a straw poking out of it. I could feel my mouth begin to water at the thought of an ice-cold milkshake, but no, that would have been too good to be true.

The cup was warm, and the liquid inside looked like diarrhea and smelled similar. The nurse told me that the plan was that I would be fed the same food as everyone else at the hospital except mine would go through an electric blender to turn it into a liquid. I was so hungry that I did not listen and put the straw in the gap in my teeth and sucked it in. I immediately began to gag, and my first thought was, where are my wire cutters? Fortunately, the gagging only lasted for a few seconds and then I was able to get a grip on my gag reflexes and take a deep breath.

The nurse told me that I was eating pork chop, potatoes and gravy but would get soft ice cream for dessert. The thoughts of that mixture being thrown in a blender and turned into a liquid made me realize that the next six weeks were going to be some trying times. I forced myself to suck a couple of more small bits and pieces and then swallowed, forcing myself to keep it down while the nurse stood by and watched.

I remained in the hospital for three days, and—other than a few melted ice creams, some soft puddings and soup—my meals were all disgusting. I decided that once I was released from the hospital, I would be avoiding the hospital meals as much as possible and eating in my room.

I could not be part of any training or sports for the next six weeks and found myself doing a load of battalion duties, answering phones through clenched teeth, driving and security. I drank a lot of soup, ice cream, puddings and fruit cups and lost about thirty-eight pounds throughout the ordeal.

After the first couple of weeks of being concerned and worried about getting struck or hurting my jaw, I became less concerned and started going back to my old ways of hanging in the Mess and drinking to the extreme. I always made sure that I had my wire cutters in my pocket.

PART ONE - THE COLD WAR

On one weekend night, we had been drinking most of the day and evening in the Mess, mixing beer and Jägermeister shooters until closing time. As we were walking and stumbling back to the quarters, my friend, Mike, noticed an old moped leaning against a building, where it had been for several days. We went over to it, pushed it away from the building, and tried to get it started, but it just turned over and would not start.

Mike thought it might have been a gas problem, so he removed the cap and, after putting his finger inside, he decided to sniff the tank. I understood that the gas had been sitting in the heat for months, and it smelled disgusting. Mike began to gag, and the more he gagged, the harder it was for me to not gag, as well. I remember telling Mike through clenched teeth to stop gagging because I was afraid that I could choke to death if I got sick. I think Mike may have found this a little funny, and he gagged and dry-heaved even more.

It was more than I could take, and without warning, I began throwing up in my mouth. At first, I could swallow it, but that would then make me throw up again. My mouth would quickly fill up and, as some puke would ooze out between my teeth, I would force myself to swallow again. I was gasping for breath and beginning to panic, so I reached into my back pocket for my wire cutters, but they were not there. I had left them in my other pants.

I started to freak out even more. At first, Mike just laughed until he realized that I was in deep trouble and, according to him, I was having difficulty breathing. I was gasping, and my face was turning bright red. I believe that, once Mike stopped gagging and laughing, I was able to get myself under control and, after swallowing the last mouthful of puke, I kept it down. My chest hurt, my throat hurt, and my jaws and teeth were aching. After a few minutes, my heart stopped pounding in my chest. My panic subsided.

We dropped off the moped where we found it and made a beeline for the quarters, where we had a good laugh.

I still had about four more weeks to go with my jaw wired shut, but I did not have another drink of alcohol during that time, as I had learned my lesson. My wire cutters never left my person, just in case.

Four weeks finally passed. I was picked up once again by a civilian driver, and we drove to Landstuhl and the American hospital. I had an X-ray taken, and the same doctor that had wired my jaw shut said he would be removing the wires. I lay back in the same chair and watched in the mirror as he untwisted the ends of the wires and then gave me a look that said, "This will probably hurt a little."

This time, there was no needle to help with the pain. The doctor just grabbed the end of the wire that was sewn in and out of my upper jaw with pliers and, in one steady yank, pulled the wire out of my gums as blood spurted out also. It hurt like hell, and tears came quickly to my eyes. The doctor then focused on the bottom jaw and repeated the same process. Once again, it hurt like hell.

After a good rinse, I was asked to try and open my mouth, but I could only do it about an inch. The doctor explained that it would take a few days to get my jaw moving, avoid chewing anything hard for a week or so and ease my way into eating full meals.

On the way back to Baden, the driver stopped at a local McDonald's for lunch, and initially, I just ordered a milkshake, but then I added fries and a burger, as well. It was probably a funny sight, watching me tear apart small pieces and pushing them into the inch or so gap between my top and bottom teeth. It took about 30 minutes, but eventually, I got through almost all the fries and about half the burger, washed down with a vanilla shake.

About a week later, I was back to eating and drinking as I had several weeks earlier. I have never played Smack Mouth again and avoided as many fights as possible as my jaw might have still been a little bit weak. When I think back to those stupid incidents, I am embarrassed and ashamed that I was ever in a place where that was okay.

That said, I did eventually grow up.

TRAINING – TWO YEARS IN GERMANY

The following two years in Germany were simply incredible. For a young single guy from Saint Mary's Bay, Newfoundland, it was an opportunity to open my mind to the wonders of Germany and Europe.

I had the opportunity to train with soldiers from Germany, France, Britain, the U.S., and most other NATO countries. Exercise REFORGER ("Return of Forces to Germany) was a major training event conducted annually by NATO from 1969 to 1993. It was intended to ensure that NATO could quickly deploy forces to West Germany in the event of a conflict with the Warsaw Pact. Although most troops deployed were from the United States, the operation also involved a substantial number of troops from other NATO countries, including Canada and the United Kingdom.

The training was realistic and challenging and allowed us to rehearse exactly what we would do if the Soviets and their allies came across the East German border. The Cold War was taken very seriously, but there was also lots of time to enjoy living in Germany.

It was a time in my life where alcohol played an important role. It did not help to be living in a country where, in 1981, one Canadian dollar was getting us four German marks, and a large beer only cost around one mark. Alcohol could be found anywhere we gathered, even when we were at work. The battalion had lots of barbecues, sports days, and beer calls, and alcohol was available at every event.

It was not a surprise to any of us to see one of our Sergeant Majors or Company Quartermaster Sergeant, or even some of the soldiers, showing up for morning parade still drunk from the night before or see them come back after lunch half in the bag.

It was never a surprise to hear on a Monday morning of someone getting caught for impaired driving, having a car accident, or a soldier being thrown in jail either on base or downtown for an alcohol incident. I knew one of our Sergeant Majors had three impaired driving charges against him, but was still in his position.

So, it was no surprise to me when we could have a few beers while on Fall Exercise. I was assigned as a driver shortly after arriving in Germany and becoming a member of 7 Platoon, Oscar Company. I did the M113 Driver Course and, once qualified, joined 1 Section, 7 Platoon, which was call sign Three-One Alpha. Then, because I was such a good driver, I was assigned to be the driver for 7 Platoon Headquarters, call sign Three-One.

The M113 Armoured Personnel Carrier was a fully tracked vehicle that offered some protection for the infantry section riding inside. The M113 was only lightly armoured and was prone to mines because of its lightly armoured floor. It featured a hydraulic ramp for allowing infantry soldiers to disembark or quickly get back in, especially under fire.

My time in Germany and 3 RCR was great, and it was with some sadness that we heard rumours in late 1983 that we would be rotated back to Canada and replaced with another battalion.

The rumours were true. As we welcomed in the New Year of 1984, we received official notice that we would return to Canada. 3 RCR was being rotated to Winnipeg, Manitoba, and the Second Battalion, Princess Patricia's Canadian Light Infantry (2PPCLI), would leave Winnipeg and rotate to Baden, Germany.

It would be the first time that an RCR battalion would be part of the army of the west, and most of the soldiers and their families had no connection to Winnipeg. It was not a great time for morale, as the soldiers and their families had come to love their time in Germany, and Winnipeg was not on anyone's short list for a posting. The only saving grace was that we were told that in four years we would rotate back to Germany.

In March, I was moved into Oscar Company Stores and was informed that I would rotate back with the advance party in April 1984.

ARMY OF THE WEST

KAPYONG BARRACKS – WINNIPEG

When we landed in Winnipeg in April, it was a shock to the system. The city had just had a long, cold, snowy winter, and the remnants were still around. Baden might see a flurry or two of snow, but it was gone as soon as daylight arrived.

We arrived at a 64-hectare base sitting on Kenaston Boulevard, surrounded by houses, condos, a park, and the busy streets of Winnipeg. This site was the home of 2 PPCLI and was named after a great battle in the Korean War.

For Canadians, some of the heaviest fighting of the Korean War took place during the battle of Kapyong in 1951. The soldiers of the 2 PPCLI persevered in the face of great adversity to help prevent a potentially costly defeat for the South Korean and United Nations forces. Their heroic efforts did not go unnoticed, with the Americans awarding them the United States Presidential Unit Citation, a rare honour for a Canadian unit.

It was into this highly acclaimed and rightfully named Kapyong Barracks and a city that adored the Princess Patricia's Canadian Light Infantry that a small group of RCR soldiers entered. It was a hectic time as the advance party for the 2 PPCLI was already in Baden, and we were in Winnipeg. Because we were leaving all our equipment, except personal kit, everything had to be accounted for in each of the two locations. All the vehicles had to be signed for, including all the tools, then all the weapons and serialized kit, buildings and general stores. It was an enormous amount of stuff.

As well, everything had to be laid out, counted and inspected for cleanliness and serviceability. If there were issues, the proper paperwork had to be done to have it corrected or replaced. As a young private, I was surprised at the amount of responsibility I was given. I was even more surprised at how much I loved it and even excelled at it.

PART ONE - THE COLD WAR

I was working for a CQMS named WO Donny Smith. He was a guy that liked to give you stuff to do and let you do it. He did not micromanage, but at the same time, he expected that you'd get it right. He was a little surprised at how well I did in this unfamiliar world of stores and accountability, and he placed more and more responsibility on my shoulders, which was almost unheard of in the early 1980s for an inexperienced private.

It was not all work, however, and most nights and weekends were free to enjoy what the city of Winnipeg and the base had to offer.

Even though Kapyong Barracks was 100% owned by the Patricias, and they ran it as they saw fit, it fell under the auspices of Base Winnipeg and the Base Commander from the Air Force Base on the opposite side of the city. Even though the city itself separated the Bases, it was commanded as one. In reality, however, Kapyong Barracks was controlled by the Commanding Officer of the battalion.

One of the first surprises I got was the Junior Ranks Mess. It was extremely popular and always had a party going on. I soon discovered why. In this male-dominated society, the Junior Ranks Mess had strippers. There were typically two strippers every lunch hour, Monday to Friday, and then what was called a 'Striparama' during Happy Hour on Friday evening, with about five or six strippers, from around 1600 hours until 1900 hours or so. Of course, there was also subsidized alcohol to get everyone in the party mood.

It was something that the RCR soldiers on the advance party embraced and was in our report we sent back to the rest of the battalion in Baden, Germany. The junior ranks in 3 RCR were looking forward on arrival in Winnipeg to strippers on the base.

The Patricias had several parades and events to say goodbye to the city of Winnipeg. The Royals were always invited as spectators or to participate and always felt welcome.

The Patricia Battalion set up the drill hall to look like Korea and had bunkers, machine-guns, camouflage nets, sandbags and much more. When you entered, it gave you a realistic picture of the Battle of Kapyong. Mixed in amongst the bunkers and trenches were several bars and displays, and the party went on for several days, twenty-four hours a day. The Royals and Patricias that had to work the next day had to pace themselves, but for the rest, it was one of the best parties I had ever seen. Those guys knew how to say goodbye.

The Patricias were immensely proud of the U.S. Citation that they received and wore on their uniform. They were just as proud of Kapyong Barracks as it was full of their history. Everything they could disassemble and take with them they did, but there was lots of stuff, from paintings to monuments, that would have to stay. At the same time, 3 RCR was going through a similar situation in Baden. We always promised each other that we would not disrespect any of each other's histories, and we did not. Over a few beers amongst ourselves, however, we would talk about how we could not wait to paint over their stuff in RCR colours.

By the time we left Winnipeg four years later, Kapyong Barracks did not resemble the base we had initially taken over. Anything that could be painted RCR colours had been painted, and we made the base our own. However, we never disrespected anything that had historical significance to the PPCLI.

The four years in Winnipeg were a great experience for the Royals and an excellent opportunity to work with the Army of the West, especially the PPCLI. However, I believe anyone from that original group who had moved from Baden in 1984 was secretly counting down the days to return to Germany.

INFANTRY SECTION COMMANDERS COURSE (ISCC) WAINWRIGHT, ALBERTA

While in Winnipeg, I had several personal achievements, including attending the pre-Infantry Section Commanders Course (ISCC) and then the Section Commanders Course in Wainwright, Alberta. Upon successful graduation, this course qualified an infantry soldier to become a Sergeant.

It almost did not happen for me as I initially refused to take the course. I attended the pre-course as a young inexperienced, no-hook private. Most of those attending were corporals, and most of them were very senior, with ten or more years in the army. I was a bit intimidated.

Once the battalion arrived from Germany, I officially became a storeman in Oscar Company stores and did my driver wheel course to allow me to drive the old, standard-steering 2.5-ton stores truck.

A few weeks later, I was told I would be attending the pre-ISCC held in Winnipeg. It was a challenging course, and, in some ways, it was even more demanding than the actual course, but I was told I did very well on it. The pre-course was an opportunity for all the potential candidates to instruct in classes ranging from navigation, Nuclear, Biological and Chemical Warfare, weapons and drill. It also provided a chance to show potential leadership skills in the field, conducting section attacks, preparing defensive positions and patrolling.

Following the pre-course, I carried on with my job as a storeman and did not give it much thought. There had been around sixty candidates on the pre-course, and only about thirty would be selected to take the actual course. I assumed I would not be one of those. I was wrong. A few weeks later, the list came out for about thirty soldiers or so who that winter would be going to the PPCLI Battle School in Wainwright, Alberta to attend the ISCC. My name was on it.

I was having a good time in Winnipeg. I was twenty-two years old, had my first car and a motorcycle. I was partying several days a week, had a good job and was in my glory. This course, if it were anything like the pre-course, would suck. I told my CQ, WO Smith, that I did not think I was ready for the course, that I needed more time and experience to be prepared and would like to be removed. I could tell that he was not impressed with what he saw as whining. He had me write an official memorandum that requested I be removed from the course. Once signed, it was sent up the chain of command for a decision.

The following day, I was summoned to the Company Sergeant Major's office, and it was with great anxiety that I waited outside his office. The Sergeant Major's door was open, and I heard him speaking to WO Smith. Between several cuss words, I heard my name, and it felt like it was spat out. Then I heard, "Barnes, get the fuck in here." I snapped to attention, marched into the office, and came to a halt in front of an old, weathered desk.

My CQMS was standing behind me, and sitting behind the desk was MWO O'Quinn, one of two brothers in our Regiment. Rumour had it that our Sergeant Major was the meaner of the two. His opening remarks told me that this was not going to be a friendly chat. He said, "Barnes, who the fuck do you think you are?" He then continued for about a minute or so. I never really heard what he was saying as I would pick up a scattered word here and there, like asshole, idiot, sack of shit, shit-bird, and many others that didn't even register.

When he finished, he stood up with had my memorandum in his large hands, and with the scariest scowl on his face imaginable, he screamed at me, "So, you don't fucking think you are ready asshole? Well, let me tell you something. That is not your fucking decision. It is my decision, and I say you are fucking ready. Now asshole, are you ready or not?" As I was about to reply, he jumped in and said, "Be careful what you say here, Barnes, because if you say the wrong answer, I will come over this desk and kick your ass." I believed him as he leaned closer and closer to me.

I said, "Yes, sir." He tore up my memo and told me not to fuck this up. He expected me to pass the course and not embarrass him. He then said, "Get the fuck out of my office," and I did so as fast as I could.

That is how I found myself on the ISCC in Wainwright a few months later.

When I look back at that moment, I might disagree with the Sergeant Major's methods, but I am sure glad that he was able to gently "persuade" me to attend the ISCC when I did.

We departed from Winnipeg on a blustery winter day with pretty much all the kit we owned. Sharing several cars, we drove to Wainwright, arriving on a Friday night, knowing that we had to be there by 1800 hours on Sunday night with day one of the three-month course starting on Monday.

We were directed to an old Quonset hut that looked like it was ready to fall down. We were assigned bed spaces and given a paper copy of the kit layout. Several of us young Royal Canadians made our way to what would be our bed space for the next three months, started to unpack our kit and place it where the list directed. Each section had a portion of the hut designated, and all the beds were sitting about four feet from the other with a wooden locker and an old wooden desk. There would be zero privacy for the next few months.

As I was laying out my kit, I thought about how much this experience would suck. I knew that I was here until I passed, failed, or got sent home. We were a little scared and very much nervous over what was to come. We knew it would be the hardest thing we had ever done, and it was on a strange base and in the PPCLI Battle School. We were not looking forward to it.

At about 1900 hours on the day we arrived, the door to our wing of the Quonset hut opened and in walked a young, fit-looking guy in a suit jacket carrying a clipboard. He didn't identify himself but just asked, "Who are you guys?" We told him that we were RCR soldiers from Winnipeg. He replied, "Oh great," in a condescending way before identifying himself as our course officer.

He then started ranting about how messy our bed spaces were and what a shitpit the quarters were and that just because we were Royal Canadians did not mean we could lower the standards at the Patricia Battle School. He then had us do a series of push-ups, sit-ups and jumping jacks for several minutes until we were sweating and panting. Finally, he had us stand at attention while he berated us about being RCR and went through our kit that was all over the beds and floors as we sorted through it. He threw our kit around the room while telling us it was dirty or below standard. About twenty minutes after he arrived, he turned around and walked out. We spent the rest of the weekend cleaning and ironing, as more candidates arrived all the time.

On Sunday evening at 1800 hours, our course of around forty soldiers was sitting in the Base Theatre when a grizzled old WO with a huge handlebar moustache and a face only a mother could love introduced himself as our Course Warrant Officer. He then called out everyone by name and told them what section they would be in. He then had all the staff members come out, and we found out who the Section Commanders and Seconds-in-Command would be.

Then, the course officer arrived. He did not look familiar.

Those of us who had been put through twenty minutes of torture a couple of nights earlier gave each other puzzled looks. Behind us in the last row, we heard some muffled giggling and laughter. I turned around and sitting there was the guy that had made us do all the push-ups. His nametag said "Lloyd." He was a PPCLI Private, and he was grinning from ear to ear. He had gotten us young Royal Canadians good. I could not even be angry with him because it was a prank to be proud of—one I wish I had thought of, to be honest.

I got to know Private Kevin Lloyd over the course. He lived in Wainwright, and we became friends. I have seen him several times over the years and, every time I think of him, I cannot help but smile.

As the course commenced on Monday morning, we immediately found out that this would be a difficult time and that we would have to keep our mouths shut and put up with a pile of crap. We were all confined to barracks the first weekend and spent every waking hour shining floors and boots and ironing clothes, including our underwear and T-shirts. Saturday night was a blustery cold, snowy affair and, when our Section Commander arrived in civvies, we assumed that he was there to help and mentor us on some lessons learned as far as kit and quarters.

He was an RCR sergeant from my battalion who had been tasked to Wainwright as an instructor. I did not know him other than by sight. As soon as he came into our section area, we all knew that he was drunk. His speech was a little slurred, and his walk was chaotic, but he was our Section Commander, and when he yelled at us to stand at attention by our beds, we followed his directions. He proceeded to tear through our kit that we had spent so many hours working on. He never paused until the whole section's kit, half-RCR and half-PPCLI, was totally destroyed.

Our section commander, whom I will call Sergeant Terry, ordered us to change into our dress uniform, including our polished ankle boots. Once everyone was dressed, he told us to grab our snowshoes and to follow him. He led us outdoors into the cold stormy night and onto the snow-covered parade square, where we were then ordered to put on our snowshoes. We all hesitated for a second as we thought of the damage it would do to our boots, but after he screamed and yelled at us to hurry up, we once again followed orders.

Once the whole section was standing with our snowshoes on, Terry began to give us drill commands and, for the next ten or fifteen minutes, we performed drill movements in the snow wearing our full-dress uniforms. Soldiers slipped and fell, and some got tangled up with the soldier next to him and down they would go together. I often wonder how many other NCOs and officers saw what was going on and decided not to interfere. Once Terry thought we had learned whatever lesson he was trying to teach us, he had us return to the quarters and continue working on our kit. He just turned around and left without saying a word.

As we were getting undressed and putting away our uniforms, we started seeing the results of doing drill in snowshoes while wearing dress uniforms and ankle boots. There were tears in the knees of our pants and elbows of our jackets from falling over. For me and several others, it was the damage to our ankle boots that was the biggest issue. The toe areas were smudged and worn. The regions where the snowshoe straps were wrapped tightly left wear marks into the leather. Mine were bad, but some others had boots whose leather had actually been torn.

The following morning, the oncoming Marching NCO arrived in the quarters to give us some work tasks for the remainder of our Sunday, and he spotted some of the damaged uniforms and boots. No one wanted to say what had happened, but the story came out after a few minutes of threats. We did not hear anything else about the incident the rest of the weekend.

Monday morning came too quickly.

As was the morning routine following PT and breakfast, we were all standing at attention in front of our beds, ready for inspection. Our Section Commander, Terry, did not arrive and, instead, it was the Course Warrant Officer. He went through our lockers but never said a word. Once he was done, he called the whole section into the laundry room, closed the doors and told us that Terry had been sent back to Winnipeg where he would be dealt with by 3 RCR.

We were introduced to a new Sergeant who would now be our Section Commander, and anyone that needed a piece of uniform or boots replaced was taken to QM to get it done, no questions asked. I was a little embarrassed that the culprit was an RCR Sergeant, but as a soldier from the PPCLI told me a few hours later, "An asshole is an asshole, and a hat badge doesn't change that." Terry had not been the first poor example of leadership I had encountered, and he would not be the last.

The only other incident of noteworthiness happened one cold, snowy morning about halfway through the course. As was our practice every morning, we awoke at 0500 hours and were formed up outside on the road in front of the Quonset hut to do a warm-up at 0530 hours and then PT. For the most part, this was a run, led by one of the students, but the pace and distance were decided by the staff who continually whispered into your ear, "Speed it up, sprint, speed it up."

As the course progressed, we used to lay in bed until 0515 hours or 0520 hours or maybe even 0525 hours and then throw on our PT kit and run outside ready to go. Every extra minute of sleep helped us get through the day.

This morning, I continued to roll over, get that extra minute of sleep and then jumped up, threw on my regular physical training kit and went outside. The cold struck me like a slap in the face. It was around -35° C with the wind chill and, as we stood around shivering, we saw the staff huddle together to decide whether it was too cold for a run but, as we had become accustomed to, we did a 2-3-minute warm-up and then started off at almost a sprint. We ran up the first hill and turned left toward the Base's front gate, and within the first few minutes, I knew I had messed up.

I had my toque, gloves, T-shirt, heavy sweatshirt, but I had not put on my long johns, something we all wore on PT since that first cold morning. I had been rushing and had forgotten. I initially felt pain in my upper legs and thighs. It was a minor stinging, and then it became worse. I knew I was in trouble when my manhood started to sting and then get worse. I could see the front gate, just a few hundred metres away, and I knew I needed to say something, but fear of abuse and ridicule held me back.

I took my right hand out of my glove, put the glove down inside my pants and cupped my cold, painful penis. Within seconds, my hand was cold, and the glove went back on. By now, I was already falling behind. One of the sergeants saw me with my hand inside my pants and obvious pain on my face. He came up to me and asked me what was going on. I told him that I thought I was getting frostbite on my penis. At first, he thought I was an ass, but the look on my face told him differently. We were just about at the front gate, and I saw the sergeant run up to the Course Officer at the front and say something to him. He came back to me and told me to go into the guard shack and wait there until they returned.

I ran into the tiny guard shack to a commissioner with a surprised look on his face, wondering what I was doing, but he was in for a bigger surprise. I told him what was wrong, and he told me to go over by the electric heater by the wall, which I did. Then I straddled the heater and pulled out my gear and stood there in tears as the heat hit the cold area. I did not have any frostbite that I could see, but I believe it was only minutes away.

About twenty minutes later, I saw the platoon coming back toward the front gate, and I thanked the commissioner. As the course approached the gate, I went outside and joined them. I got several loud comments from the staff, things like, "Barnes, how's your cock?" and, "Did you lose your balls?" And I also got the usual, abusive things like "dumb fuck," but I was so happy to have saved my gear that I didn't care what they said.

After showering and eating breakfast that morning, I was directed to the course officer's office, where I had to sign a red chit, stating that I suffered a self-inflicted injury on training due to poor judgment and lack of preparation. The statement said that because I chose not to dress for the weather, I had to stop training because of frostbite in my private area. I was told that if anything else during the remainder of the course showed poor judgment or lack of preparation, I would be sent home as a failure. I knew that this was not just a threat but was a fact, and I learned a valuable lesson that I continue to carry with me today.

If you fail to plan, then you had better plan to fail!

The remainder of the ISCC was probably the hardest thing I had done up to that point in my life, and there have been only a very few occasions that have come close since. We lost some outstanding candidates and friends removed from the course, some from injuries, others due to failure and a few from a voluntary return to unit or, as the staff called it, quitting. I never looked at any of those guys negatively because, but for the grace of God, it could have been me. I thought about quitting several times, and I came close to failing a reconnaissance patrol because of some navigational errors. It could have been me.

But finally, graduation day arrived, and two courses, with Royal Canadians and Patricias mixed, marched onto the parade square and became the latest graduates of the Infantry Section Commanders Course. I was a young private with about three years in the army, and I was now qualified to the rank of Infantry Sergeant.

RENDEZVOUS 85 – CFB WAINWRIGHT

Not long after returning to Winnipeg from Wainwright in 1985, 3 RCR started preparing for RV 85, a divisional-level exercise. Once again, it would be off to Wainwright.

I had the privilege of driving Oscar Company CQ stores truck, an old and reliable 2.5-ton diesel. I had received my QL4 driver wheel course following my ISCC a few months earlier, and now I was heading to Wainwright on one of the largest exercises to be held in Canada in many years.

RV 85 was a large concentration of troops, with more than ten thousand soldiers, sailors, airmen and women participating, including almost a thousand reservists. More than four thousand vehicles, ninety helicopters, and four thousand tons of supplies and equipment would be moved by rail and air from all over the country to Wainwright.

The exercise focused on all phases of war (advance, attack, defence and withdrawal) up to and including the division level. It was also planned in three phases. Phase 1 was unit-level training, including infantry and armour cooperation. Phase 2 was the attack and defence, and Phase 3 was a road move to Suffield and a twenty-five-kilometre live-fire portion.

Suffield was located about 328 kilometres south of Wainwright and it took several hours to move there as a military convoy. The manoeuvre training area in Suffield covered about 1,588 square kilometres and was ideal for live-fire training. It was also home to the British Army Training Unit Suffield (BATUS) and was their premier live-fire training establishment. It delivered world-class live-fire manoeuvre training.

As part of Oscar Company's CQ staff, we deployed early to Wainwright in the advance party, arriving in late April or early May. We did not make it back to Winnipeg until late June.

I enjoyed my position as a storeman and my role supporting our company soldiers to ensure they had everything they needed to fight. As part of the CQ staff, we were responsible for the resupply of ammunition, rations, water and anything else that the soldiers needed on the battlefield. This was an excellent experience for me and was a crucial part of building my understanding of the logistics that ensure the fighting force can do its job. This understanding allowed me to progress throughout my career, never underestimating the importance of the efforts of the whole team. I was able to practice looking after my troops' needs both in camp and in the field. I had the opportunity to provide hot meals in both tactical and non-tactical scenarios. I learned how to do tactical resupply in the dark of night, without lights, close to enemy lines. I moved as part of a supply convoy during the day and night without lights to guide us.

I made many mistakes, but I had some outstanding mentors and supervisors who allowed me to make those mistakes and then correct them. I learned a considerable amount on RV 85. Many years later, it would help me when I became a Company Quartermaster Sergeant and then when I was a Company Sergeant Major in Afghanistan.

FIRST PROMOTION

I assume that I did a rather good job in the CQ because, before the final exercise in Wainwright, I was promoted to the rank of Master Corporal and moved from being a storeman in Oscar Company to being a section Second-in-Command in Mike Company.

I was both excited and terrified to be going from private to my first position of leadership, jumping over the rank of Corporal. I was lucky to be placed in a section with a very understanding commander, Sergeant Dan Whittaker. I only had a few days to get to know my section and my new platoon, and then it was off on the final exercise in Phase 2 of RV 85.

I made my share of mistakes again, but Sergeant Whittaker was very understanding, and I had some excellent soldiers in the section to lean on as well. I was able to get through the final exercise without any significant issues and without getting Dan Whittaker in any major trouble. Dan was assessed as a casualty during the last twenty-four hours, and I had to step up and command the section.

It was my first real opportunity to be commanding and leading, and I discovered that not only did I like it but also that I was good at it as well. We had a couple of days following Phase 2 to clean and fix our vehicles and equipment, as well as a couple of days to relax, enjoy a beer and get some well-earned rest. Following those couple of days, it was off to Suffield and the live-fire portion of the exercise.

Sergeant Whittaker returned to Winnipeg for either a task or a course, and that left me to step up and be the Section Commander again. I was both scared and excited, and it probably showed, as I had never commanded anything during a live-fire exercise, much less one that included tanks and artillery. Once again, I depended on the more senior soldiers in my section who had already gone through this level of live fire before to advise me and steer me straight.

These early days as a Master Corporal taught me to trust and depend on the soldiers who work for me, and I believe those early lessons were paramount to my success in later years.

5

A NEW COMMAND TEAM

My four years in Winnipeg were very memorable for me. I met my future wife, was promoted master corporal, instructed on an ISCC and a QL3, and survived what was known as the "Jimmy Cox era."

By mid-summer 1984, all of 3 RCR and their families had moved from Germany to Winnipeg, and the battalion was reorganized under new leadership.

On a beautiful sunny summer day in Winnipeg, 3 RCR was introduced to Lieutenant-Colonel Jimmy Cox and Chief Warrant Officer (CWO) Joe Reilly, a Command Team that would be loved and hated for the next couple of years.

The battalion was gathered in Korea Hall, and we were called to attention as Lieutenant-Colonel Cox came strolling out on stage. He was a short, stocky man who walked with a bit of a wobble. As I stood there, the first thing that came to my mind was, "Weebles wobble, but they don't fall down."

You very quickly forgot the appearance of this short, somewhat pudgy man, who was going to be commanding an infantry battalion as soon as he began to speak. Lieutenant-Colonel Cox had a stutter that got worse as he got excited or angry. He would sometimes take several seconds to finish a word, or he would just skip it.

It was difficult for those of us watching not to smile or snicker.

Lieutenant-Colonel Cox took a long time to get his message across to the battalion. In the end, it was evident that we were going to be the toughest and fittest unit in the Canadian Army. Every soldier and officer was expected to meet his high standard and exceed it. If you could not, then he would get rid of us. He sounded incredibly angry and quickly left us with the impression that the next couple of years were going to suck.

When we thought that he had finished speaking, he surprised us again. He brought a dummy onto the stage dressed in RCR hockey gear, and he proceeded to beat the living crap out of it with a hockey stick as he told us that we were going to play hard, train hard and that we would always win. As parts of the dummy flew around the stage, most of the Battalion stood there with our jaws hanging open and concerned about what the future would bring.

We had good reason to be concerned, as we would have many tough hard days ahead of us. Everything we did, from that day forward, was done with the intent to make the Battalion hard, fit and ready to fight.

In that regard, I believe Lieutenant-Colonel Cox was successful.

His Command Team Partner was seasoned soldier CWO Joe Reilly, and they made a good team. They also bore the brunt of many jokes, though obviously behind their backs.

CWO Reilly also had a speech impediment. As told by folks who supposedly knew him, the story was that early in his career, he also stuttered terribly and had difficulty communicating, so he went to a specialist, perhaps in Toronto, to help him overcome his stuttering. After much therapy, CWO Reilly was taught to substitute words like "and" instead of stuttering. With this aide, he was able to communicate much more effectively. It was still amusing to the troops, once again behind his back.

Shortly after returning to Winnipeg from RV 85, I remembered walking by him and had to bite my lip to refrain from giggling. I said, "Good morning, RSM." He stopped and replied, "and a and a and a how are you and a and a Master Corporal and a Barnes." He then asked me how I enjoyed being a Master Corporal and a few other comments in the same manner. I was able to look right at him and answer his questions. As soon as he walked away, I was relieved and chuckled to myself as I rushed away.

ORDERS PARADE – HOLDING MY LAUGHTER

There were some hilarious and comical moments, especially when we were on parade as a Battalion and the Commanding Officer was trying to give words of command.

The Commanding Officer would say things like, "Thirrddddddd Babababattttttalioon Royroyalll Canaancanadian Regggegggiment, attttttennnnnnnnnaaaa" and the Battalion would try not to anticipate the final part. People would be moving as they started to come to attention before the CO was finished. Sometimes, he would just stop and say "fuuuuck," and the RSM would start screaming at us, "andaaaaa don't fucking andaaaaaa move and a and a don't and a and a anticipate the and a and a word of command."

These parade days were always good for a laugh in the Junior Ranks Mess over a beer and a stripper.

Later that same year, I was told a story by someone who was an escort on an Orders Parade, which is when someone was charged under the Queen's Regulations and Orders and would be marched in front of either the Officer Commanding or the Commanding Officer for a trial. The accused would have his beret off, and the escort would have his on. They would be marched in front of the Presiding Officer in double-quick time by the CSM or the RSM, and you had better not fuck it up. I saw many an escort getting in shit for being out of step or for his uniform not being at the highest standard, and they weren't the ones accused of a crime!

There was a story told by the escort for another soldier, who had been charged with drunkenness and fighting for the second time, and so he was going in front of Lieutenant-Colonel Cox. It would have been a regular event, except the accused was also a stutterer. They were formed up outside the Commanding Officer's office, and CWO Reilly inspected them. Then they rehearsed marching everyone in and halting in front of the desk and then marching back out in double-quick time. After several attempts and a lot of screaming, they finally got it right.

The accused and escort were too scared to laugh at the RSM as he used the "and a" every couple of words. The accused had a young officer to assist him and make sure that his rights were not abused. The Assisting Officer rarely spoke during those days, except following the verdict and only talking about the guilty individual's finances and family responsibilities, usually to try to lessen the sentence.

Finally, the trial began. The soldiers were marched in even faster than they practiced and, when halted, they were almost on top of the CO's desk. When they made the right turn, the escort struck the desk with his left knee and received a threat of a size-11 boot up his ass from the RSM.

As the trial proceeded, the Military Police gave their version of events, and then Lieutenant-Colonel Cox asked the accused to give his version. The conversation went something like this:

"Aaaaaaaccused, whhhhaaaat do youuuuuuuu have tooooooooooo say?"

"Siiiiir, IIIIIII waaaaaaaaas not druuuuuuuunk thaaaaat niiiiiight."

He was interrupted by the Commanding Officer. "Arrrrrrrrrrrr youuuuuuu makkkkkkking funnnn of mmmmme?"

"Noooooooooo, siiiiiiiiir!"

Then the RSM started yelling, "Andaaaaaaa, soldier andaaaaaa what the andaaaaaaaa fuck are you andaaaaaa saying?"

It all ended with the Commanding Officer shouting: "RRRRRRRRSM, marrrrch the guillllllllllty basssssstard out."

The escort claimed that he had to do everything in his power not to piss his pants laughing. I don't know how much this story has been exaggerated over the years, but it has been told hundreds of times.

BATTALION PARADE – COMMANDING OFFICER'S INSPECTION

Lieutenant-Colonel Jimmy Cox was a man who was either loved or hated; there was no middle ground. I believe the senior officers and senior NCOs hated him mainly because they were terrified of him. They knew that he would not hesitate to either embarrass them or just fire them on the spot. We were never sure what would happen when dealing with the Commanding Officer, and we were always expecting the worst.

I remember a Battalion Parade on the Parade Square in the middle of a Winnipeg winter held in temperatures well into the minus range. The Battalion had formed up along the length of the Parade Square in Companies, which were then broken into Platoons. Our arctic dress included mukluks, parka, wind pants and toques and heavy gloves, but the bitter wind still somehow got through. Each soldier had their fighting order and travel order with them for inspection, consisting of our rucksack and a kitbag full of gear.

As Lieutenant-Colonel Cox approached each Company, he would give different orders for each Platoon. In my Company, the first Platoon had to open their kitbag and lay all its contents out in front of them to be inspected. The second Platoon had to do the same with their rucksack, and my Platoon had to lay out our fighting order, including weapons and web gear.

I could hear the Commanding Officer jacking soldiers up as he moved along, and the whole time he was yelling at the Officer Commanding and CSM for their soldiers' errors. When he got to my Platoon, he asked the front section to remove their boots, and to our dismay, he inspected the soldier's socks while on their feet. The issued grey socks came with a coloured stripe along the toe and, if they were not the same colour on each sock, or there was a hole, look out. He threatened to relieve people of command for these faults.

I cannot say that I liked Lieutenant-Colonel Jimmy Cox, but I did respect him. I believe that he had one goal in mind: to have the fittest and hardest battalion of fighters possible. I think he succeeded.

However, everything about Winnipeg was not bad—we had one of the best Junior Ranks Messes in Canada. We continued the tradition of having strippers every lunch hour and a 'striparama' at happy hour on Friday evenings, just as the Patricia's had done. Just before we rotated back to Germany, the Base Commander from the Air Force side put a stop to our mess' "entertainment," supposedly because of complaints from the wives of some Air Force folks who would come over to our barracks on Friday evenings instead of going to their own Mess. The Junior Ranks Mess was very profitable and was well attended, not only because of the strippers but because it was our very own RCR Mess on our very own Base. At lunchtime, almost every table was filled, and chairs sat along the floor as two strippers performed before the troops returned to work. On Friday evenings, there was free food and six or eight strippers. The mess was always full.

In 1986, we started hearing rumours that 3 RCR was scheduled to deploy to Cyprus as part of the United Nations Peacekeeping Force for six months. At the same time, I was tasked to go to Petawawa, Ontario, to instruct a Youth Training and Employment Program (YTEP) basic infantry course.

YTEP INSTRUCTOR

Fellow Newfie Master Corporal Jack Gaudet and I left Winnipeg in his brand-new Camaro and drove straight through to Petawawa. Once there, I had the privilege of instructing some of the greatest young men that Canada had to offer. I enjoyed being an instructor and not being on the receiving end of all the abuse for once. I worked as a section second-in-command for Sergeant Ken Saunders, a brute of a man whose hockey skills were known throughout the military.

I quickly became the go-to guy for a lot of the more difficult lessons and most of the drill classes. I thoroughly enjoyed the challenge and, according to my write-up, excelled at it.

Some of those young men that I helped mould into RCR soldiers went on to stellar careers. One, Keith Olstad, not only was my CQ in Afghanistan, but he went on to be a Battalion RSM, Brigade Sergeant Major, Division Sergeant Major and the Task Force Sergeant Major in Iraq.

With only a few weeks remaining on the course in Petawawa, I received word to call my CSM back in Winnipeg, MWO Tom Daigle, a man respected by all as a soldier's soldier. The SM asked me if I was interested in deploying to Cyprus with the battalion? I could not say yes quickly enough. He then asked me if I would be interested in going with the advance party, and my response was the same. He said that the clerks would be working immediately on a plan, and I would be making my way back to Winnipeg as soon as I could clear out of Petawawa.

I was told I would be leaving for Cyprus in less than three weeks, but that was okay with me. I was single, living in quarters and did not even own a car, so I told the Sergeant Major that I could leave tomorrow. I did not even ask what position I was going into and assumed it would be as a Section Second-in-Command. However, he next told me that I would be the driver for the Canadian Contingent Commander.

I did not even know what that meant, but I was game.

During the three or four days it took to get everything sorted in Petawawa and hand over my section duties to the Swing NCO (a spare NCO attached to the platoon for unforeseen circumstances), I took some time to research Cyprus.

CYPRUS

As legend states, Cyprus is the birthplace of the ancient Greek goddess of love, Aphrodite. In contrast, Cyprus' modern history has been dominated by enmity between its Greek and Turkish inhabitants. Cyprus has been divided since 1974 when Turkey invaded the North in response to a military coup on the island that was backed by the Athens government. The island was effectively partitioned, with the northern third inhabited by Turkish Cypriots and the southern two-thirds inhabited by Greek Cypriots.

United Nations troops patrol the 'Green Line' dividing the two parts. Reunification talks have proceeded slowly and have still not resulted in a resolution nearly fifty years later. Cyprus successfully diversified its largely agrarian economy into one based on services, including a large tourism sector and light manufacturing. It has also developed into an important financial hub, especially for investors from Russia and Eastern Europe.

Canada, along with several other countries, played an essential part in the United Nations Force from the very beginning. Now, I would be doing my part as a member of 3 RCR.

A few days after receiving the news, I got back to Winnipeg and was surprised when the taxi driver stopped at the gate to the base and told me that I would have to get out there because his company did not allow him to drive any further. It sounded a little strange to me, as taxis had been going on and off the Base since I had arrived several months earlier, so I got out, took all my kit, and prepared to drag it all to my quarters when I saw the sign attached to the gate. It said that due to training for Cyprus, all vehicles entering the base would have to drive on the opposite side of the road until further notice.

What the heck was going on here? The commissioner at the gate told me that in Cyprus, like in England, cars drove on the opposite side of the road. I had already been a little apprehensive about driving for the Canadian Commander because I had never owned a car and had only driven military vehicles for a few months. Now I found out that I would also be driving on the opposite side of the road. Not having a car, I never did get an opportunity to practice on Base!

ARRIVAL IN CYPRUS

The time flew by as I ran around getting my kit issued, getting vaccinations and filling out paperwork for my upcoming deployment. Before I knew it, I was on a plane and landing in Cyprus. The view of the island as we were landing was amazing. It was gorgeous. The water looked beautiful, the beaches white, and I could not wait to look around. The first thing I noticed as I got off the plane was the heat; it was warm and sunny and would remain that way for most of the six months I was there.

Most of the soldiers from 3 RCR that were part of this advance party jumped on a bus at the airport to go to the beautiful five-star Ledra Palace Hotel, located in the capital city of Nicosia, and, until 1974, was one of the largest and most glamorous hotels on the island. It had been designed by a German-Jewish architect and was built between 1947 and 1949. It originally had ninety-four bedrooms as well as a conference room and several ballrooms. There were also two restaurants, two bars and several cafés. Located within the garden was a swimming pool and tennis courts. In 1968 it had two additional floors added that increased its capacity by more than a hundred rooms.

After the ceasefire, this hotel fell within the boundaries of the UN buffer zone and now served as the Headquarters for Sector 2. It also would continue to play host to many important meetings between the Greek and Turkish Cypriots. This hotel was where most Canadians would be housed and where they would eat, sleep and relax when not out manning positions in the buffer zone.

I was loaded onto a smaller bus with some soldiers from the Administrative Company, and instead of the Ledra Palace we headed for the BBC (Blue Beret Camp). It was where the United Nations Force in Cyprus (UNFICYP) Headquarters was located. The Headquarters of the British contingent was situated within the UN-protected area on the west side of Nicosia, about five kilometres from the Ledra Palace Hotel. This protected area was located on the disused Nicosia International Airport and was primarily open shrubland, dotted with small groups of buildings and structures formerly belonging to the airport. As we drove, I could see the Kyrenia Mountains to the north and the Troodos Mountains to the south.

It would be my home for the next six months.

DEPUTY FORCE COMMANDER'S DRIVER

Typical accommodations at the BBC for Canadians were small rooms, sleeping two or four people, with a communal living area and communal washrooms. However, I was taken to a separate building, where I was given a single room with a bed, dresser, desk, small fridge and a phone.

It was explained to me that the Canadian Contingent Commander was also the deputy commander of the UN Force, and as such, I would always be on call and working some long, irregular hours. A single room was more appropriate so that my schedule wouldn't bother anyone else. I was thrilled with that.

As I was putting my kit in my room, a Master Corporal from the Canadian Airborne Regiment, the unit that 3 RCR was replacing, came to see me. He told me that I was replacing him, and we had less than a week to work together—then he would be gone, and I would be on my own. He said he would be back in an hour; we would go for a drive, and he would brief me on my job.

Within the hour, this young Airborne Master Corporal returned, and we went outside to where my future vehicle was parked. I, of course, was expecting it to be an old Canadian army jeep. To my surprise, I would be driving a shiny, white Mercedes with a licence plate that had a star on it to identify it as the vehicle of the Deputy Commander of the UN Forces.

We had about two hours before the driver had to pick up the commander, so we were going to do a tour of the camp. I went around to the passenger side and jumped in. I heard some giggling, and it became very apparent why. In front of me was the steering wheel. Not only would we be driving on the wrong side of the road, but the driver's seat was also on the wrong side of the car.

I tried to maintain my composure, but, suddenly, I was terrified; this was almost more than I could comprehend. On top of driving on the opposite side of the road and sitting on the wrong side of the car, it had a manual transmission. I'd had my driver wheel course for only about a year, and other than a few hours in the old Canadian Army jeep, I had never driven a standard.

I immediately passed this information on to the Master Corporal who I would be replacing, but he just laughed and said that we would have time to practice. We drove around the BBC, and I was shown where everything was, including the headquarters where all the essential UN folks worked. We parked outside in a designated spot for the Deputy Commander of the UN Forces in Cyprus, and we walked inside.

To say I was intimidated would be an understatement. Folks from several countries were rushing around, all looking like they were involved in important stuff. They ignored us. We walked through the main area and into a more secure one where I had to use the pass I had been given earlier that morning to gain access. Inside was a beautiful waiting area, and sitting behind the desks were two civilian women, who identified themselves as secretaries for both the Commander and Deputy Commander. We walked past them and into another office area where a soldier in a British uniform was sitting. I was introduced as the incoming driver, and the soldier introduced himself as a Warrant Officer and the Personal Assistant (PA) for the Commander.

He told me this was the area where I could hang out when I was not driving or busy. However, a tiny grin came across the Airborne soldier's face as he said, "You won't have much time to hang out."

I was thinking, "How busy can it be? Pick up some guy, drop him off at his office and wait for him to leave." Boy, was I wrong! We stayed around for a few more minutes, then the Master Corporal let the PA know that we would do some more familiarization within the BBC and that we would be back no later than 1630 hours.

This was my first lesson – to make sure that the PA and the secretaries knew where I was at all times. We didn't have cell phones back then, but we did have a radio in the car that allowed us to get in touch with the HQ at any time to receive or pass on messages.

The UN area of BBC was well kept, and everything had UN flags and blue colours on it. We visited the eating and drinking messes for the junior ranks, sergeants, WOs and the officers. We stopped by the Canex and the CQ area, where I drew some more uniforms and kit. I would not be wearing combats but instead the tan dress uniform, including tan shorts. We drove by the British side of the camp but did not go in, as we needed special access to do so.

Then, it was back to the mess for lunch. The food was delicious and plentiful. I knew that I would have to be careful here or I would leave in six months as big as a whale. We then went over to the drinking Mess, where we talked about the daily routine and how I would be spending my days.

I learned that I would be busy when the Commander was away, as the Deputy Commander would be filling in, and he would travel all over the island. I was told that any trips outside of BBC would need to be recce'd beforehand by me. The best route would need to be determined, as well as the exact time it would take, as the boss would expect me to tell him when we needed to leave and when we would arrive. Because we would be travelling in and out of the buffer zone, planning was essential.

Before I knew it, we had to go back to the HQ to pick up the boss. We drove the Mercedes right up to the main door, arriving about fifteen minutes early and while we waited the Master Corporal pulled a cleaning kit out of the trunk and started wiping down the car and shining it—another lesson learned. The car needed to always be sparkling. The next thing to come out was the flag that attached to the vehicle that identified to everyone that the Deputy Commander was in the car and needed to be saluted.

COLONEL DEAN WELLSMAN

The door to the HQ opened and out walked a large Canadian colonel with a briefcase and a smile. The Master Corporal went around, opened the back door, saluted him and then closed the door. We got in the car, and I was introduced as the new driver. Colonel Wellsman said he was glad to meet me and welcomed me to Cyprus. He asked me a few questions about myself and mentioned that his tour was also ending in a couple of weeks.

PART ONE - THE COLD WAR

I was caught off-guard, as I had not been told this. The Deputy Commander said to me that his replacement was Brigadier General MacInnis. He would not only be the Canadian Contingent Commander, but he would also be the Chief of Staff of UN forces in Cyprus. This was a huge deal. This job would usually be given to a more senior Master Corporal, not someone like me who had no experience and only four years in the army.

We drove through the city of Nicosia to the Ledra Palace Hotel, where the Colonel's accommodations were. We pulled in up front, and the Master Corporal and I got out, and we saluted. The Colonel said, "Good night," and told us to be back at the same time tomorrow.

We took the flag down and drove back through the city to BBC. We agreed to go to supper around 1800 and then to the abandoned airfield for me to practice driving the car.

After about an hour on the airfield and some rough starts and stops, I seemed to finally be getting the hang of the Mercedes and its standard transmission, as well as the right-hand driving. I drove around BBC for a short while and then parked the car in my spot right outside my bedroom window. The Master Corporal said to meet him at the car at 0500 in the morning, and we would go through the whole day together.

I did not sleep very well that night. My mind continued to go through all the different ways that I would screw up this important job, and I was scared. Who was this Brigadier General MacInnis? What was it going to be like to drive for him? Was this going to be the longest six months of my life? The next morning, I awoke at 0400 hours, showered, dressed, and was outside waiting by the car at 0445 hours, the same time as when the Master Corporal arrived.

"Well, you are a keener," he said. "Hope that doesn't change because I'm ready to go home." We spent fifteen minutes wiping the car down and shining all the chrome. We even had a small can of spray to make the inside smell nice. The next thing we did was head over to the HQ and picked up any mail or files for the boss that may have come in during the night. We placed them on the backseat so that he could read them on the way to the office. Then, we were off to pick him up.

As we were waiting outside the hotel for Colonel Wellsman to come out, the old driver said to me, "There's no time like the present. You can drive back to BBC." My heart jumped into my throat, and I started to sweat, but there was no time to panic as the Colonel walked out.

I opened the rear door. "Good morning," I said as I saluted.

The Colonel returned the salute and asked, "John, are you driving?"

"Yes, sir."

I was incredibly nervous, and the car jumped a few times when I started. Once I was out on the main road, it was smooth. I was a little too cautious trying to enter the first roundabout, and it was there that I found out that Cypriot drivers were extremely aggressive and did not give the UN or the flagged cars any leeway. I checked my rearview mirror a few times as I searched for the right gear or popped the clutch too early and saw what appeared to be a small smile, or perhaps it could have been pain, on the Colonel's face. The previous driver, relaxing in the passenger seat, made sure I knew the route.

All went well until BBC came within sight.

The main gate to BBC was at the top of a long hill, and there were dozens of cars waiting to show their ID to gain access to the camp. I immediately fell in behind the last car and, as I geared down into first, it stalled. I immediately restarted as the car began to roll backward. I tried to remain calm, but the Colonel was just looking straight ahead when I glanced in the rear-view mirror. The Master Corporal then told me that we did not have to wait in line but to move to the left of the road and go right to the gate.

As I tried to move out and start now up the hill, I stalled again and started to roll backward. I slammed on the brakes, restarted the car, and tried again, but with the same result I was sweating profusely and getting more flustered with each time I stalled the car.

After several failed attempts, the Colonel asked, "John, is this your first time driving a standard?"

I told him that I had a few hours on my driver wheel course but not in a right-hand drive.

As I looked through the rear-view mirror, I saw him smile. "Don't worry about it. You'll get it." His calm demeanour and smile reassured me, and I found the right gear and rolled up to the gate. Two British soldiers snapped to attention, and we just moved on through. I made it to the office without any further problems and, as I stood outside the rear door, Colonel Wellsman once again just smiled, tapped me on the arm and said, "Good job." After he went inside, the former driver and I had a good laugh.

We took the rest of the day to drive around the BBC, Nicosia, and even a few trips outside the area. By 1600 hours, I felt like I had been driving a standard for years. At the end of the day, when I dropped off the Colonel without stalling the car once, he smiled and again said, "John, good job, and have a great night."

I felt much better about my abilities after the second day.

The next day after I dropped off the boss, we spent the entire day driving around the island, both on the Greek and Turkish sides. I was shown all the places that I may have to bring the Colonel. We went to all the other Contingents' Headquarters areas, including Denmark, Sweden, Australia, Finland, British and about a dozen other mostly European countries. I needed to know where they all were located, as my boss would have meetings, parades and visitations to all of them, and I was responsible for getting him to the right place at the right time.

A couple of days later, the former driver packed up his room, turned in his kit and handed everything over to me. A few days after that, John Archie MacInnis took over as the Canadian Contingent Commander and Chief of Staff for UN Forces in Cyprus.

PART ONE - THE COLD WAR

GENERAL JOHN ARCHIBALD MACINNIS

I was now on my own with a new boss and new responsibilities. Although I was a little bit apprehensive, I was looking forward to the challenge.

At that moment, I could never have realized how much driving I would do and how busy I would be for the next seven months. Cyprus is a small Mediterranean island of just a little more than 9,000 square kilometres, making it a little smaller than Cape Breton, but with almost 800,000 people living there. I am sure that I drove every inch of it. Cyprus had a very tumultuous history, including the period around 1960 when it gained independence. Many of the issues centred on ethnic tensions. For thousands of years, Cyprus has mainly been Greek in culture, language, and population, and many of the Greek Cypriots have wanted to join Greece.

However, there is also a sizable minority population of Turkish people who are not as excited about this possibility. It was also the attitude of Turkey's population, which is greatly concerned about Cyprus because it is near to the Turkish coast. During the time of the island's independence, there were frictions between the ethnic groups, which led to violence and unrest. Cyprus asked the UN to establish a peacekeeping force in 1964.

When the UN forces arrived, they were surprised to find that the Turks and Greeks were intermingled across the island, and the UN was expected to maintain the peace with small groups of Turks living among the large Greek populations. Canadian soldiers needed to use their traditional soldiering skills and their ability to manage disagreements and conflicts between civilians and neighbours. It has been said many times by civilian and military scholars that peacekeeping is not a soldier's job but that only a soldier can do it.

With Canadians leading the way, a fragile peace was reached. But that progress was undone in 1974, when Greek Cypriots staged a coup d'état and attempted to make the island Greek. In turn, Turkey invaded the island and took control of the northern part.

United Nations soldiers, including Canadians, found themselves in the middle of a war zone with little chance for peace but lots of violence. After several weeks of fighting, three Canadians were killed and seventeen more were injured. In the end, a cease-fire was negotiated and the UN established the famous Green Line, a cease-fire line and buffer zone stretching across Cyprus. The Green Line separated the island into areas controlled by the Greeks and the Turks. The UN forces patrolled this buffer zone, which in some cases was just a few metres wide. Both sides watched the buffer zone so well that something as simple as moving a sandbag or a post could cause an incident. Canadian soldiers understood that they were between two incredibly angry forces and needed to keep them from killing each other. It was into this volatile situation that I now found myself, and I was both excited and a little apprehensive.

There was a brief ceremony when Brigadier General MacInnis took over from

Colonel Wellsman as the Commander of the Canadian Contingent and, more importantly, the Chief of Staff for the United Nations Cyprus. During the ceremony, I noticed that the General's wife and daughter attended. I thought to myself, "This is a long way to come for an hour-long ceremony." But I soon found out that things were not as they seemed. Brigadier General MacInnis was posted to Cyprus for two years and was entitled to bring his family with him, just like any other posting.

That afternoon I dropped the General, his wife, and their young daughter, who was probably around five or six years old, at the Ledra Palace Hotel. This would be their residence until they found a home. For the next few weeks, that is where I would pick him up and drop him off daily as he took over his new job.

I quickly became accustomed to my job. I found out soon that the Chief of Staff did not spend much time in his office but instead attended meetings all over the island, sometimes two or three times a week. Brigadier General MacInnis was also invited to many social functions—some alone, and others with his wife. Almost all of them were at night. I found myself getting up at around 0430 hours and getting to bed some nights well after midnight.

Brigadier General MacInnis was a very social person who liked to be around people, and people liked having him around. He was considered a typical Cape Bretoner. He enjoyed a drink and loved to play his guitar and sing.

I remember taking him to a high-level meeting somewhere in the Danish sector, and he asked me to come up to his hotel room to bring some stuff down. I was a little surprised to find myself carrying down his guitar and placing it in the car's trunk.

Depending on how long some of his meetings or social functions were expected to last, I may have been told to stay and wait or be back to pick him up at a particular time. At this specific meeting, I was asked to wait. About thirty minutes after the boss had gone inside, he reappeared, grabbed his guitar out of the trunk and told me to be back in a couple of hours. This was the first of many occasions where Brigadier General MacInnis took his guitar to a meeting or social event and stayed well into the night.

There were no days off for us in Cyprus. The normal workweek was from Monday to Friday, but on most Saturdays and Sundays, there were scheduled events. And on any Sunday with no official meetings or functions, I would take the boss and his family to Famagusta Beach in the Turkish Sector.

FAMAGUSTA

Located on the east coast of Cyprus, Famagusta was once one of the most glamorous resorts in the Mediterranean. Its miles of pale sand and the clear turquoise sea made it a destination for thousands of visitors each year. Along with the tourists, the 40,000-strong population enjoyed a life rich in culture, with art, music and theatre that were the best on the island. With the deepest port in Cyprus, Famagusta handled more than 80% of the island's cargo, much of which comprised a vast tonnage of citrus fruit picked from the local orchards.

There were luxury hotels and apartments that were home to primarily Greek Cypriots. Turkish Cypriots inhabited the old, walled-in city that contained historical treasures, including Byzantine churches and a 14th-century cathedral from the Frankish Period. Turkish Forces invaded under the pretense to protect the Turkish Cypriot minority. After a brief cease-fire, the city was bombarded, and then Turkish tanks advanced. The Greek Cypriot population fled in terror, by any means possible—some by car or bus or by foot, taking only what they could carry. They expected help from the outside, but none came. In 1986, while I was there, they still had not been able to return. The Turks had thousands and thousands of soldiers on the north end of the island, and they had drawn a line across the island separating the north from the south.

Even though the Greek Cypriots could not return to Famagusta, we could, and we always went to the same small, very private beach. It was here that I learned how to snorkel, and I enjoyed looking at parts of an ancient city that had sunk below the sea. When we would drive across the buffer zone from the Greek side to the Turkish side, or vice versa, their soldiers would stare in the window, salute and allow us to go through. All the crossing points had photos of all the UN commanders and their drivers. The flag and the star on the plate were also well recognized by both sides, and they dared not hassle us.

I took advantage of this authority once in a way that could have resulted in severe consequences. But I was young, naive and figured I would never be caught. There had been an incident somewhere along the Green Line, and the Turks had decided to close the main crossing point in Nicosia at the old Ledra Palace Hotel until further notice. It would also cause problems for the UN forces trying to cross, and delays were an issue. However, my Mercedes had freedom of movement around the island, and no one messed with that.

A friend of mine, whom I will call Tony, had ordered some gold and jewelry from a shop on the Turkish side of the city of Nicosia. He was getting ready to go on leave and needed it as a gift for his girlfriend. He asked me to help him out. After saying no several times, I finally agreed. After supper on the evening before Tony's leave, we came up with a plan to get across the checkpoint and get his jewelry.

Brigadier General MacInnis had flown to Europe for an emergency meeting regarding the ongoing tensions. So, I put the flag on the car, Tony jumped in the back seat, and we headed for the crossing. The young Turkish soldiers seemed surprised to see the staff car approaching, and they could be seen calling someone on their radio. As we approached, I rolled down my window, nodded my head and smiled. After a quick glance in the car, we were waved through. We managed to get the jewelry, return without incident, avoid an international issue, and thereby preserved my career. Tony was able to go on leave with some jewelry for his girlfriend and owed me big-time.

Looking back, taking that risk was not something that I clearly thought through. In hindsight, this could have been a huge international embarrassment for Canada and a career-ender for both of us. Sometimes, the young and foolish make poor decisions, and in this case, it was a terrible one. If the Turkish soldier had looked closely into the back seat, he would not have seen an older, tall, slim and pasty-white Cape Bretoner but instead a young, well-built black man.

We had a close call that day, and it remained a secret until now.

INTERACTION WITH A TURK DRIVER

The Greek and Turkish soldiers seemed to be worlds apart as far as being professional. It was not surprising to cross a Greek checkpoint and see their soldiers half-dressed, their weapons on the ground, and to maybe even find them sleeping. The Turkish soldiers were all conscripts, and they were terrified of their commanders. They were always on their best behaviour and always seemed to be ready for action. Any time one of them did slack off, they paid for it. I saw Turkish soldiers being beaten, kicked, and on one occasion, struck with a rifle.

I recognized some of the Turkish soldiers because I would pass through the same checkpoint several times a week. If I was by myself, I sometimes stopped and offered them cigarettes or chocolate—stuff they never had.

On one occasion, while driving through a regular Turkish checkpoint, I stopped to hand out cigarettes, but the individual had something else in mind. Through broken English and gestures, I knew he wanted to see if I had any porn magazines. I did not then, but I told him the next time through, I would try to have some.

Porn magazines were easy to get on the Greek side, and the UN was mainly a male-dominated force. Everyone had porn magazines, and the Mess had piles of them available to look at or take. I grabbed a couple and hid them in the trunk of the staff car for the next time I went through that checkpoint on my own.

A few days later, the opportunity arose, and there was the same Turkish soldier on duty. I quickly handed him a bag, which he immediately slipped down the front of his pants and disappeared.

A week or so later, after dropping off the boss, I returned through this same checkpoint, and I saw the same soldier on duty. I slowed down and opened my window. He looked around as if he were scared and then came over. I immediately saw that he had two black eyes and a swollen jaw. He looked at me and said in broken English, "No more fuck fuck books." I knew he had been caught by his Commander and taken a beating.

I felt terrible that I had been the cause of his beating. I continued to give the Turkish soldiers cigarettes and candy bars, but I never again gave them porn magazines.

There was one other Turkish soldier that I met who deserves to be mentioned. I drove the boss to a meeting he was holding in the buffer zone with some senior Turkish and Greek military commanders. All the drivers parked in the same area and waited for the meeting to be concluded. I was tasked to make sure the Greek and Turkish drivers did not try to kill each other. I did this by keeping them separated in different areas.

As I was cleaning my car, the Turkish driver slowly approached me and motioned to me to go around the back of the car to talk. I assumed he wanted cigarettes or porn magazines, but I was totally surprised. In almost perfect English, he told me that he was from Ajax, Ontario, and lived there with his parents and sisters. I asked him why he was in the Turkish military. He explained that he still had his Turkish citizenship. He had gone to Turkey to see his dying grandmother, had been taken into custody at the airport and conscripted into the military for two or three years.

Because he was well educated and spoke English, he was made the senior Turkish commander's driver in Cyprus. For that, he was grateful, as he said he was treated very well, and none of the other senior soldiers dared to touch him. He asked me if I could try to get him some Export A cigarettes and some Canadian beer because he really missed them.

Several weeks later, I learned that the Turkish commander would be secretly brought across the Green Line and through the abandoned airfield at BBC for a meeting at UN HQ. I made sure I had cigarettes and beer, as well as some Canadian treats in the car. Sure enough, the Turkish-Canadian driver arrived. We had about two hours where I looked after the driver, and we had time to talk and relax. I took him to the Mess Hall for lunch but did not consider that all the civilian staff who worked there were Greek. As soon as they saw a Turkish soldier in uniform, they freaked out and started screaming bloody murder. We had to make a quick escape from there before we had another international incident.

My bad, and the boss spoke to me afterward about being more vigilant in what I do.

I gave the young soldier the gifts I had and warned him not to get caught and, if he did, not to mention my name. I wished my Turkish-Canadian friend luck and only saw him once more during my seven months. I hope he did well and is back home in Canada.

YOUNG OFFICER'S LESSON

There were many noteworthy incidents while in Cyprus. The one that brought me the most satisfaction dealt with a young RCR officer who had to learn some valuable lessons the hard way.

When Brigadier General MacInnis took over, he was provided with a Canadian officer as his executive assistant (EA). I believe his name was Holimister. He was responsible for ensuring that the Brigadier General's meeting and the social calendar were free of conflicts and that he knew where the boss needed to be and when even though I was already doing that.

Within weeks of taking over, the boss called the two of us into his office and told us that he was being ordered to UN Headquarters in New York for an emergency meeting about Cyprus. His British PA was booking his flights. He also told us to take the few days he would be away to relax and go to the beach. He reminded me that when he was not using the car, it was mine to use.

Later that day, I was sitting in the outer office when the boss and his British PA discussed his flight the next day. General MacInnis turned to me and said, "My flight leaves Larnaca at 0600." I said, "No problem, sir, I will pick you up at 0430." I already knew the distance and time to get to the location.

Later that night, I was lying in my bed when my phone rang. It was the EA, our young RCR Captain. He told me to pick him up in the morning at his room before picking up the general. He then said, "Pick me up at 0600." I told him that I needed to pick up the boss at 0430 for a 0600 flight, but he told me, no, the pick-up was 0600 for a 0730 flight. I told him I thought he was wrong, but he interrupted me and said, "Shut up, master corporal, I know the timings. It is my job. Your job is to drive, so pick me up at 0600."

I had difficulty sleeping that night because I did not want to mess this up, but I fell asleep thinking that his flight had changed. A part of me also believed that, after putting some doubt in his mind, this young officer would confirm the flight and pickup timings and let me know if there was a change. All night and early morning, my phone remained silent.

At 0600, I picked up the Captain at his room as directed, and we made our way to the General's house. When I pulled into the driveway, his wife was standing on the step in her dressing gown.

We both got out and, and as the captain approached the step, I could hear Mrs. MacInnis say, "He's already gone." I heard nothing else as my heart jumped into my throat. The young Captain came back and slipped into the car, looking like he was about to cry. He said that the General had called the British Duty Centre at 0445 hours, and they had driven him to the airport. I knew better than to say I told you so, or I was right all along.

I remained quiet as we drove back to BBC.

We avoided the subject over the next few days, and I do not think either of us enjoyed our few days off, knowing that the boss would be back soon.

Then it was time for the General to return, and we made sure we had the proper pick-up time for the airport. We arrived at the airport with plenty of time to spare. Neither of us spoke about the incident as if not speaking about it would make it go away. As the plane rolled to a halt, I drove onto the airfield to the bottom of the stairs, got out and put the flag on. At the same time, the Captain got out and was waiting by the back door of the staff car.

General MacInnis walked down the steps, came over to the car and told me to get in. He then stopped by the Captain and spoke a few words that I could not hear, and then the boss got in the car. I waited for the Captain to jump in the front, but I could see him standing there through my mirror. I was about to ask the boss about him, but he spoke first.

"Let's go, John. I just fired the Captain. You don't have to explain what happened. It was the Captain's responsibility."

PART ONE - THE COLD WAR

As I drove off the airfield, I could see the young RCR officer standing there alone. I am sure he assumed his career was over, and I believe he did have a truly short one.

The next day, my old section commander from basic training and Norway, Captain Robert Hay, took over as the EA and did a great job for the next several months.

ONE FUNNY INCIDENT

There was one more funny incident that occurred during BGen MacInnis' stay in the hotel.

It had been a busy day, and I was waiting in the outer office for the boss to finish up for the day. He appeared from his own office with his hand full of folders, a briefcase and a bag. I offered to help, but he declined, and we walked to the car together. Captain Hay had been tasked away for the day. Once he was in the car, he told me to drop by the dry cleaners so that he could pick up his clean uniforms, a task I usually did for him. We went to the CQ area, and he went in, picked up about five or six uniforms, laid them on the passenger seat and away we went.

The uneventful ride ended a few minutes later outside the Ledra Hotel, where he asked me to help him bring stuff up to his room.

I, of course, said, "Yes, sir."

We grabbed all his belongings and entered the lobby of the hotel. The boss went to the front desk, picked up the hotel phone, and I heard him tell his wife that he was coming up with his arms full. We took the elevator to his floor and walked down to his room, the boss leading and me a few feet behind. As he got to his door, his wife opened it, wearing just panties and a look of horror on her face as she saw me standing there, probably as terrified as she was. She ran back into the room, and the General reached back, took the uniforms I was carrying, said, "Thanks, John," and went inside.

As I walked away with a sheepish grin on my face, I could hear a woman yelling and berating her husband, which brought an even bigger grin to my face. It's not every day a young Master Corporal hears a general being yelled at.

The next morning, I was waiting in front of the hotel at 0600 as usual, and the General walked out. After I saluted him, he got in and picked up his mail and started to read as he did every morning. After a few seconds, he said to me, "Master Corporal, I do not want to hear a word about this from anyone else, do you understand?"

"Of course not, sir," I replied. "I don't know what you are talking about."

It has now been more than thirty years, so, hopefully, now I am safe to tell this story.

THE NANNY

As mentioned earlier, BGen MacInnis and his family found a house in Nicosia to rent. It was a large, beautiful home and the UN covered the cost. He was even entitled to a

65

live-in housekeeper and nanny because part of his official duties was to entertain and attend many functions.

His PA set up about six or seven local ladies to be interviewed. I was tasked to go pick them up and bring them to the HQ. I had to pick up these women all over the Greek side of the island. The first four, who spoke only limited English, would probably make a good housekeeper but not a great nanny for a young girl who spoke only English.

As I waited outside a home in Ayia Napa for the fifth person, I was getting a little tired of this whole interview stuff, even though the General would ask me what I thought of each woman. This time was different.

My jaw dropped as a beautiful young blond came strolling out wearing a short skirt and a tight top. She was probably 5 foot, 4 inches, 130 pounds and had the figure and the look of a beauty contestant. I got out to open the back door for her, but instead, she jumped in the front. She told me her name was Adriana, she was nineteen years old and from Sweden. After graduating from high school, she decided to take a few years off, and she had moved to Ayia Napa, Cyprus, to enjoy the beaches and the nightlife. She now needed to make some money, and she had heard about this nanny job from a Canadian friend.

Her English was almost perfect, and her demeanour and style were selling points to me. As we drove back to Nicosia, I tried hard to keep my eyes on the road, but I must admit I took a few glances over at her beautiful legs, short skirt and blue eyes a few times.

When we got back to HQ, I had Adriana wait in the outer office, and I went in to speak with the boss. By now, the General and I had spent many days together, and I was much more comfortable with him. I walked into his office, and I said to him, "Sir, this is the one." He looked up and smiled and said, "Why?" I told him she was young, spoke perfect English, and seemed genuinely friendly and polite. I was told to bring her in, which I did. As I introduced her to the General, I could see just a tiny little grin appearing on his face as he discovered why I thought she was the one.

A couple of hours later, as I was dropping Adriana off in Ayia Napa, I told her I hoped that I would see her again and that I would put in a good word for her.

While driving the General home, we did discuss Adriana again, and he agreed that she was probably the best candidate for the job, but the final decision was up to his wife. That did not seem incredibly positive to me.

I brought Adriana back once more to meet the general's wife and daughter, and they must have hit it off as she was hired. I thought that perhaps I would get to see a lot of her and maybe, just maybe...? I did have an opportunity to have coffee with her one beautiful sunny evening, but other than a casual hello, that was the extent of our relationship.

Adriana lasted only about a month before she moved on and returned to Ayia Napa. She had stayed away several nights, and I would see her being dropped off at the General's home at 0530 or so by her Greek boyfriend. She looked like she had been partying all night and smelled of booze. After being spoken to on several occasions by Mrs. MacInnis, they decided to part ways.

QUEBEC COMPANY SERGEANT MAJOR

During my seven months in Cyprus, there were many occasions to tour the island, sometimes with the General but mostly while doing recces on my own. I came to love every moment of it.

Officially, I belonged to Quebec Company of 3 RCR, which was also housed at BBC. Because I was the General's driver, they learned to leave me alone. During the first couple of weeks, I received messages from Quebec Company saying I needed to report to their HQ for a twenty-four-hour duty. Even though I explained that I would not be able to do it, the Company Sergeant Major insisted. I went to see BGen MacInnis and told him that I would not be available to drive him the next day, as I was on duty at Quebec Company. He just laughed and said, "No, you're not."

That is all I needed to hear, and, a few minutes later, I received a call from the Quebec Company Clerk telling me that I was no longer on duty. I know this pissed off the CSM because he probably thought I was disrespecting him and taking advantage of my position. Every time I would see the CSM, he would say something sarcastic about my job. I would just smile and say, "Yes, sir."

I think that pissed him off even more.

One day, while walking over to the mess, I met the Quebec CSM, and I said, "Good morning, sir." He stopped me and started yelling about my hair. He said that I was an embarrassment to the Battalion, walking around without a proper haircut and that I should remember that I would be returning to the Battalion. For some strange reason, I had just about had enough. I told him that the General and I booked a time for our haircuts together, and I would be getting my haircut the following week with my boss. I could tell he wanted to smash me, but instead, he told me to get a haircut and stay out of his way.

I never did understand why he had it out for me. I had been told to do this job, and I was not trying to rub it in anyone's face. I did, however, have a lot of perks that most soldiers from 3 RCR did not have. When the boss did not need the car or me, I was free to use it and do whatever I wanted as long as I met my timings. If I had a few hours off, I could take the Mercedes and go anywhere I wanted. No permission was required.

I was able to have the kitchen prepare late or early meals for me, and I had my own phone—all things that no one else had. A few months later, I may have gotten back in the CSM's good books when I saw him walking along the road in the BBC in the pouring rain. I turned around, went back and picked him up. He had several things he needed to do that day. I told him that I had a few free hours, and I was his. I also told him that if he needed me for a ride, just to call, and I was his if I could get away.

I believe he really appreciated it, and he was much nicer to me from that day forward.

THE CO'S ACCIDENT

The rest of 3 RCR had a busy time with lots of minor issues along the disputed line, and they dealt with them professionally. Lieutenant-Colonel Cox very quickly lived up to the reputation that those of us from the Battalion already knew. He was a hard-ass, no-nonsense Commander and, if you pissed him off, you would pay the price. That reputation worked well with the Canadian soldiers and maybe even with the two warring sides, but his style and demeanour did not make him a lot of friends with the senior officers of the UN.

Because I worked out of the UN HQ, I heard about Cox and what he did, spoke about throughout the building. Some of the officers would make sure I knew some of Lieutenant-Colonel Cox's antics and would say things like, "Your CO is at it again." The Battalion was always on pins and needles, afraid that they would cross the CO because they knew he would fire them or, at the very least, be subject to his anger. As young soldiers sitting around the drinking mess, we would say that none of our officers or Senior NCOs had the balls to stand up to the Commanding Officer.

Early in the deployment, Jimmy Cox had impressed upon all the soldiers that they were to maintain a top level of physical fitness throughout the tour. Anyone who fell out of a run, dropped out of a march, or came off a chin-up bar early was likely to feel his wrath.

The military obstacle course in Nicosia was a favourite of this small-in-stature but big-in-personality officer, and he had his soldiers install a new death slide to the already gruelling site. Those officers and NCOs who had taken the mountain warfare course knew that this slide needed to have a second fail-safe cable, as was required for all high-level wire slides. Apparently, Lieutenant-Colonel Cox said, "Damn your safety regulations." The death slide almost lived up to its name.

Luckily for the soldiers of 3 RCR or perhaps deliberately (as some rumours have it), it was Lieutenant-Colonel Cox himself who became snagged while traversing the new obstacle. He was seen holding on for dear life at about fifty feet in the air, frantically screaming for help. Very little could be done to help, but a large crowd of mostly 3 RCR soldiers gathered to watch their tough-guy Colonel hanging from a cable.

It is believed that Lieutenant-Colonel Cox waited too long to try and pull himself up the cable. He no longer had the upper body strength even to try. The result was inevitable, and, once his arms gave way, a terrified Lieutenant-Colonel Cox plunged to the ground below, shattering his legs and pelvis. The soldiers admired his courage, they cheered him, and raucous laughter followed.

That night, Lieutenant-Colonel Cox was medically evacuated back to Canada. The parties in the Junior Ranks Mess and the Officers Mess lasted until dawn. As one senior RCR officer said, "There's no denying that the colonel's injuries were serious, but that was the funniest thing I have ever seen." All the troops still talk about it. The word spread like wildfire, and many across the Battalion were delighted to have Jimmy Cox gone. Free beer was laid on in each of the Messes for days. The deputy commanding officer, Major Al Peterson, took over the battalion, and the morale soared.

The next few months flew by, and I continued to put thousands of miles on the car, and then, one day, I overheard some of the British officers saying that Lieutenant-Colonel Cox was returning. I was shocked, but it was an even bigger shock to the battalion who had gotten used to military life without him.

A week or so later, BGen MacInnis let me know that he would be going to Larnaca airport to greet Lieutenant-Colonel Cox on his return. On a beautiful hot sunny day only a couple of months after his crushing injuries, Lieutenant-Colonel Cox returned. I don't remember seeing him get off the plane that day, but others that were there say they watched as the airplane door opened and the easily recognizable Jimmy Cox appeared. He was dressed in his combats, wearing a cowboy hat, and carrying a pickaxe handle painted in RCR colours. There was a noticeable limp, but he looked no worse for wear.

Stories have it that those officers who had been celebrating his unfortunate injuries were now praying that he did not find out. It was believed that he did, and they had to suffer the consequences of their actions.

Nonetheless, my seven months flew by, and finally it was my turn to hand over to a new soldier from the famed Van Doos from Quebec. I was ready to get back to Canada, even though I had a wonderful tour and learned so much.

INSTRUCTOR, INFANTRY SECTION COMMANDERS COURSE (ISCC)

On my return to Winnipeg, I spent some of the money I saved while in Cyprus and bought a new motorcycle, my first. I moved out of quarters and into an apartment with my friend and fellow Royal, Corporal Winston "Smoke" Pinnock.

The joy of this freedom was short-lived when I was tasked to Wainwright to instruct on the Infantry Section Commanders Course a month or so later. I stored my motorcycle, gave my landlord prepaid rent cheques and headed to Alberta.

I learned a lot while teaching on this course, but I also learned a lot about myself. I had been trained by some of the hardest, nastiest NCOs around. That is what I knew, and that is how I was. In retrospect, I was a complete asshole. I am embarrassed by how I behaved and treated some of these fine young men whom their Regiments and units had selected to be future leaders. But I thought I knew best.

The ISCC is not supposed to be easy. It is meant to test the soldiers' ability to lead their fellow soldiers under stressful situations and prepare them to do so again in war. However, I have learned that there is never a time when it is alright to be disrespectful or ignorant to anyone wearing the uniform of their country.

Most of the soldiers on this course were young, with an average age of twenty-four. However, there were a few older corporals, and I decided on day one that this

WHITE SCHOOL, BLACK MEMORIES

one older guy was not going to make it. I made all the soldiers' lives miserable, but I really concentrated on this one RCR corporal. He always had trouble keeping up on the runs and marches, and his breathing would be annoying to me. He had a puffer and had been diagnosed with some type of asthma. He made some weird noises when he was tired. I would get in his face, make fun of him and tell him that he was weak, a waste of sperm and an embarrassment to all Royal Canadians. I would make fun of his manhood and make sexist jokes—all the things I hated having done to me.

It was a vicious cycle; now it was my turn to be on top, and I loved it.

During a morning inspection, I remember I decided to tear this corporal's kit apart, so I threw everything in his locker on the floor. I then told him to get in the locker, close the door and tell himself that he was an asshole until I told him to stop. He complied and, as I was inspecting other soldiers, we continued to hear the muffled voice from the locker.

Today, as I sit here writing this, I wonder how I ever got to that place, because it is not who I am. But, at the time, it was who I believed the Army wanted me to be. I spent the remainder of my career trying to make up for those few years when I was not living up to Canadian values or our Regiment's values.

By the time the course was over and the soldiers marched onto the parade square qualified as infantry sergeants, I had already started to change into the respected NCO I've been ever since. I clearly remember standing in front of the older RCR corporal I had abused on the graduation parade as he stood at attention. I told him how proud I was of his achievement. I apologized for disrespecting him.

He just smiled. "Thank you, and you never disrespected me."

As I walked away, I thought that he was probably like I had been and thought this behaviour was normal and acceptable. It is not.

Today, it makes me angry when I hear a soldier disrespecting another soldier, and I made a point to always step in and correct that action. I hope it has made a difference in some lives. We can be a great fighting force without being physically or mentally disrespectful to our men and women in uniform. I saw many times in my career that senior officers and NCMs said or did something wrong, and I was always surprised by their reaction when I would tell them that it was wrong.

As a CWO, I once approached a CWO and a Lieutenant Colonel who were being very disrespectful and ignorant about the Military Police. After listening to their comments for a few minutes and watching a group of five or six other senior officers and NCMs laugh and say nothing, I decided to step in.

Even though most of the group knew me by name, I introduced myself as CWO John Barnes, the Canadian Forces Military Police Group Chief. I explained that I was both offended and disappointed to hear my peers and superiors being so disrespectful to our fellow soldiers. I then went on to say that I was willing to set up a meeting between themselves and my boss, the Canadian Forces Provost Marshal, Brigadier General Rob Delaney. I explained that this would allow them to voice their concerns more constructively.

They just stared at me, some perhaps waiting for me to laugh and say I was joking, but I believe my facial expression said it all. Then, the Lieutenant Colonel and the CWO tried to explain their ignorance by saying that most MPs were good, but some were not. I interrupted and said, "That is exactly how I feel about CWOs and Lieutenant Colonels. Please let me know when you can find an hour to meet with General Delaney and I." Then, I walked away.

I never heard back from those two guys, so I expect they decided that they did not want the meeting.

Following my time as an instructor on the ISCC in Wainwright, I returned to Winnipeg a more experienced and knowledgeable NCO and a much better person than had left. I believe that my superiors saw my new confidence and ability, and my write-ups told me that I was now on the right path.

JULIE

I still liked to party a little more than I should, and most of my weekends were a drunken stupor with my friends, but that too was about to come to an end.

On a typical Saturday afternoon, my motorcycle was parked at the Junior Ranks Mess. I was drinking to excess and planning for that night's party. My bike would remain where it was until probably Sunday night or Monday morning. While sitting with some casual friends, I was introduced to a beautiful young woman named Julie Sullivan. I just smiled, said, "Hi," and went back to partying. I assumed she was out of my league and I shouldn't waste my time when there was partying to do.

She did, however, get my attention when she said something like, "Hey, is that your pink scooter out there?"

Initially, I was not impressed, as she was talking about my maroon Virago motorcycle, which was my pride and joy at the time. However, I couldn't get mad at her because her smile melted me inside, and so I just replied, "Yes." Over the next few months, we saw each other a lot, mainly because Julie did not give up on me and would show up at bars and other locations where I was partying. I still had not changed my priority.

That January of 1988, I decided to do something I am immensely proud of: I quit smoking. I had been smoking about two packs of Export A Light a day and more when drinking. Even though it was the most challenging thing I had done to date, I succeeded. At the same time, Julie smoked, and it was difficult for me to be around her. After saying that kissing her was like kissing an ashtray and telling her that she had to quit or I was done, she stopped as well.

Neither of us has smoked since, and it has now been more than thirty years.

7

BACK TO GERMANY

At this time, the battalion was getting ready to rotate back to Germany again, and I was both excited and overjoyed. I could tell that Julie was not as excited, and I was not ready or willing to plan to keep us together.

In July, my younger brother flew up from Newfoundland. I gave him my 350, 4-barrel Camaro as a gift, and he drove it back home from Winnipeg. I packed up my few belongings, prepared my motorcycle for shipping and headed off to Germany.

Back to my old stomping ground.

Julie and I wrote and called each other for a few months, and then I planned a trip back to Ottawa, where she had moved. From there, we went to Newfoundland together. We had a great time, but I could tell that something was wrong, but Julie never mentioned anything.

We were in Newfoundland at my sister Karen's home in Riverhead St. Mary's Bay and sleeping on a mattress in her living room when Julie turned to me and said very clearly, "I am not doing this anymore; we either get married, and I move to Germany, or we are done." I hesitated for a moment and then agreed that we needed to get married.

I knew I had to return to Germany in a few more days, so we looked ahead and decided that we would get married on June 3, 1989, in Ottawa. We had a great last few days together in Newfoundland, and then we went back to Ottawa, where we spent a few more days together talking about the wedding and our future.

After a great two weeks back in Canada, I grabbed a flight and made my way back to Germany, knowing that my next few months would be the last of my single life. But I was looking forward to married life.

Once back in Germany, I had a couple of months to get ready to deploy with the rest of the battalion and several thousand other soldiers on another Fall Exercise.

PART ONE - THE COLD WAR

MINOR SURGERY, BIG PROBLEM

Around this time, I had noticed that I had a small lump on the bottom of my right foot and, whenever I did runs or marches, I would be left limping. I went to see the battalion doctor in Baden. She told me I had a plantar wart and that it needed to be removed.

There was only a week or so before we deployed to Hohenfels Training Area. I was concerned about how this minor surgery would affect my ability to soldier on, but I was told, "Don't worry about it. A couple of days after it's removed, you'll be good as ever."

Three or four days before we were scheduled to depart, I went to Lahr, a second Canadian base in Germany, for day surgery. I waited around for an hour or so and then went in for what was about a thirty-minute surgery with some local anesthetics to have my plantar wart removed.

Afterward, the doctor told me that it had gone well but that the roots had been much longer than anticipated, so he had put a couple of stitches in deep and a couple outside. He bandaged my right foot and told me to stay off it until tomorrow. Then I should be able to walk on it. His instructions were simple: keep it clean, the stitches would fall out on their own, and there shouldn't be any problems.

That night, I lay in bed with my foot up, and it felt good. It was aching and throbbing when I woke up the next morning, but I never thought anything about it. That day was spent running around loading vehicles and kit, and I spent several hours on my feet. By the time I got back to my room, I was limping badly and was in pain. After a few Tylenol and a couple of beers, I felt fine. I went to bed early because the next morning would be a busy day, and we had to catch the train and head to Hohenfels for a two-month exercise.

When I awoke the following morning, I had difficulty putting on a combat boot due to my throbbing foot. I squeezed it in, headed for the Battalion lines and then on to the train.

I believe it was about fourteen hours by train to get to the unloading area for our vehicles, and every hour the pain in my foot became worse. I was limping badly and was in a lot of pain as we moved to the camp in Hohenfels and parked our vehicles. I remember the walk from the parking area to our quarters took about five minutes or so, and I was not sure I would make it. I had to stop a couple of times, as the pain was overwhelming.

That night, I had a shower, cleaned my foot, and put on the ointment I had gotten from the doctor. I kept it raised for a couple of hours, and it started to feel better.

It was sore but not intolerable the next morning, and I spent the day running around the camp getting gear ready for the exercise. By suppertime, I was once again hardly able to put any weight on my right foot.

That night was a terrible one, and I was kept awake because of the pain.

WHITE SCHOOL, BLACK MEMORIES

I hobbled over to the newly setup battalion medical centre and saw the military doctor the following day. He did not seem overly concerned even though my foot was very red, inflamed and had pus coming out of it. The doctor cut away the dead flesh and scab so that it would bleed and bandaged it back up. He told me to stay off it the rest of the day.

It did not go over very well with the Company, as this was the first day for deploying into the field for training. I spent the day lying in bed or sitting at the front of the quarters where the CQ had set up to do security. I even had my lunch brought to me.

That night, the pain returned, and by the morning, I had to see the doctor again. He once again cleaned it, cut away dead tissue, bandaged it up and sent me away, telling me I needed to do a better job of keeping it clean, even after I told him I thought there might be a foul smell coming from it.

That night, I was on my feet for a few hours getting ready for the next day, as we would be deploying at noon, and I had planned on going out with the Company.

My foot was very sore the next morning, but I started getting my kit and vehicles ready to go. By 1200 hours, when we were ready to go, I could hardly walk. It is exceedingly difficult to hide a foot injury from others after you throw a 60-pound rucksack on your back and start moving. My CSM saw me limping and told me to remain behind for another day and help the CQ. Hopefully, I would be ready to go the following day. I tried to take it easy the rest of the day, but the CQ had several tasks that needed to be done, so I hobbled around all day on my foot.

The Company got back in from the field around 1800 hours, and I had been tasked to wait at the front of the quarters and sell canteen supplies to the troops, stuff like pop, chips, bars and cigarettes. When the Sergeant Major came through, he asked me how I was feeling. I told him that it was a little better, which was a small, white lie. That night, I hardly slept a wink. My foot throbbed and was painful all night.

The next day, I was sitting in front of the Company stores again. I was wearing running shoes because my boot would not fit on my foot, and the Sergeant Major saw me. He immediately knew that something was wrong. I was sweating profusely and, according to him, I looked like shit. He asked me to remove my running shoe so he could see my foot, and I did. As I pulled off my sock, he could see the stain on the bottom from both blood and pus, and he came closer.

He then stepped back, grimaced. "What is that smell? Is that your foot?"

"Yes, sir," I replied.

He grabbed my foot and held it up so he could clearly examine the bottom and I could see the shock in his face.

"Your foot is rotting," he said. "That's the smell. Didn't you see the red streaks?"

I looked down. Two red lines ran from my foot up past my ankle for about six inches on both sides of my leg. I could tell the Sergeant Major was worried.

"Get a stretcher and get Barnes over to the medics immediately," he said to some soldiers standing nearby. I was carried into the unit medical centre, foot bare and on a stretcher, to the surprise of all the medics and doctors present. Then, when they saw my foot and the red streaks, their demeanour changed. It became an emergency.

I think it was the first time that I had smelled the infection myself. Perhaps it was the clean medical centre, but the smell was disgusting.

The doctor on call got in touch with another more experienced doctor, and they both stood above me, discussing the next step. They were obviously concerned. The first thing they did was put a black mark at the ends of the two red lines running up my leg and noted the time.

I was told that this could become life-threatening and that it looked like I probably had a blood infection. If it continued to spread, they would need to medevac me immediately. One of the staff was sent to contact higher to let them know that there was a possibility of immediate evacuation.

This response got me a little worried, but I just took it in stride.

One of the young medics came in and chatted with me while we waited. I was asked if I wanted to call home. I asked him if it was that serious. He said it could become much more severe, and I could call if I wanted to let someone know. There was no way I was calling my parents, and I did not want to worry Julie, so I just said, "No, thanks."

I was immediately given a couple of needles and some pills to see if it would stop the infection. An hour later, it was apparent that there was still an issue as both red streaks had passed the black mark by about an inch. An hour later, I was on a Canadian helicopter flying to Lahr, where I was quickly brought to the Canadian Military Hospital.

I was immediately admitted. I had doctors working on my foot, cutting away rotten flesh and cleaning the injury. Then, I was hooked up to an intravenous drip and was given a cocktail of drugs to control the infection. One of the doctors was terribly upset that I had been kept in the field for too long and that the doctor in Hohenfels had not medevacked me earlier. I was told that I could have died from this infection very easily, and it should have been dealt with many days earlier.

Twenty-four hours later, I was already feeling much better. The red streaks were fading, and I was much less concerned. I remained in the Lahr Hospital for two more days, and then I was moved to the hospital in Baden, where I stayed another two days. My foot was monitored almost hourly, it was cleaned, and the bandages changed twice a day. I remained on antibiotics the whole time.

The next day, I was released from the hospital, but I was given a room in the quarters and had to report to the hospital twice a day for the next week. I was told to use crutches to ensure I did not use my right foot. I asked the doctor when I would be able to go back to Hohenfels. I was told that he would discuss it with my chain of command and let me know. For now, I was excused from duties and other than reporting to the hospital twice a day, I stayed in quarters.

The 3 RCR rear party had come to see me, and they started to bring me my meals to avoid having me walk to the kitchen. After about a week, I was told that I could move out of quarters and report to the Rear Party, as I would not be returning to the exercise in Hohenfels. I was a little disappointed, but I quickly got into the Rear Party routine of twenty-four-hour duty shifts, day on and day off.

Once I knew I was alright, I called Julie and told her what had happened. I very quickly learned that getting married meant it was no longer all about me. I should have let my wife-to-be know how serious my illness was and that I had been hospitalized for more than a week.

My bad, and one of many lessons I would learn about being a husband over the next couple of years. It obviously worked because on June 3, 1989, I married my best friend. Thirty-plus years later, we are still together, and I am still learning lessons.

MARRIAGE

We decided to have a small family wedding in Ottawa at the church at Canadian Forces Base Uplands, followed by a small reception at Julie's mom's house to save money, as most of my friends and family were in Newfoundland or Germany.

I asked my incredibly good friend and drinking partner, Corporal John Frizzell, to be my best man. He eagerly agreed, even though it had meant having to fly to Ottawa from Germany. John and I had become friends in 1981 on our QL3 Infantry Course in London, and we had been inseparable ever since. John and I were drinking buddies for a few years, and he was known in our circle and within the battalion as someone who could not handle his booze very well. His close friends looked after him, ensuring he did not get in trouble and got home safely.

In early May, the wedding plans that Julie had made in Ottawa were all complete, but I had some bad news for her. My best friend would no longer be my best man, and it was too late to find someone else here in Germany.

I explained that John had gotten arrested by the German police and was awaiting trial, either by the German courts or the Canadian military. In the meantime, the Germans had taken his passport and restricted his movements to base.

As told to me by John, the cause of his legal problems had happened in the small historic German town of Buhl, which is part of the district of Rastatt in southwestern Baden-Wurttemberg. He had gone to the local gasthaus for something to eat and a few beers, a place at which he was a regular customer. As usual, he had drunk too many beers and was highly intoxicated, and the incident occurred around closing time.

He had ordered food an hour earlier and a couple of beers at last call. When the barmaid told him he had to leave because they were closing, he told her he wanted to finish his beer. The barmaid knew John from previous visits, knew that he was very drunk and that he was always harmless in these situations. She gave him another five minutes or so to finish his beer. Then, she told him that he had to leave so that they could lock up.

John said he remembered having a butter knife in his hand from his food. He pointed it toward the barmaid and said he would leave once he finished his beer. At this time, a second barmaid called 112, the emergency number, and reported that a drunken Canadian had threatened a barmaid with a knife and refused to leave the gasthaus.

The German SWAT guys were outside with weapons drawn and declaring a hostage situation within a few minutes. John gave up peacefully and was taken away by the German police. The next day, the local German paper had John's name splashed all over it and told the story of a Canadian soldier taking hostages. John was not only in trouble with the Germans, but he also had to face the Canadian military.

I had to do some scrambling, with only a couple of weeks to go before my wedding, to find a best man. I called a friend of mine from Riverhead, Don Squires, who now lived and worked in Toronto. He was gracious enough to say yes, even though he was my second choice.

When Don showed up from Toronto the night before my wedding, he was a bit of a surprise to Julie and her family. He was a typical Newfie, who spoke with an almost incoherent accent, swore like a fisherman and was missing his front teeth. It was not a great first impression, but you cannot judge a book by its cover. Don became the highlight of the wedding.

Now, after thirty-plus years of marriage, I can look back and have a good laugh at this incident. At the time, I thought that it was not a good start.

After the wedding, we packed up some of Julie's stuff and we headed to Germany as a family. My wife was in for another small surprise. I had failed to mention to her that I was sharing an apartment in Buhl with a friend of mine, and he had the master bedroom, which left Julie and I with a small room. The apartment was really made for a couple of bachelors and was not set up for a husband and wife.

We immediately began looking for another apartment and got lucky when Steve Walker, a friend of mine who I put through QL3 a few years earlier, was moving out of his place. We went there, had a look, and it was perfect.

It was in a small German village called Obersasbach, located at the edge of the Black Forest. Julie soon forgot about me not telling her about the previous apartment and the roommate as we immersed ourselves in the German way of life. We absolutely loved it.

Our apartment was about thirty minutes from the Canadian base, and we loved that we could be part of this little village. The Germans accepted us as their own, and Julie began to learn German. I already could speak some German like "Eine groß bier bitte," and "Dankeschön," but only when I was drinking.

My life as a married man was much easier than I thought. I did not miss the single life of partying and having no real responsibility. We settled into a routine. Julie joined the Air Force Reserves and started working on the base. She made friends very quickly

PART ONE - THE COLD WAR

and began touring Europe either with me or with some of her friends. It was a good time! I was able to come home almost every night, and we started talking about having a family.

Shortly after that, Julie got pregnant, and we started planning for our first child. We were both extremely excited about the future and could not wait for the big day. On July 5, 1990, our son John Jarod (JJ) was born in the Canadian Forces Hospital in Lahr. Our family had grown by one.

A couple of days later, I left for my second Nijmegen March in Holland, and Julie's mom arrived from Ottawa to help with her grandson—which was greatly appreciated. My trip to Holland was a signal of things to come and how much time I would spend away from Julie and our children over the next eighteen years.

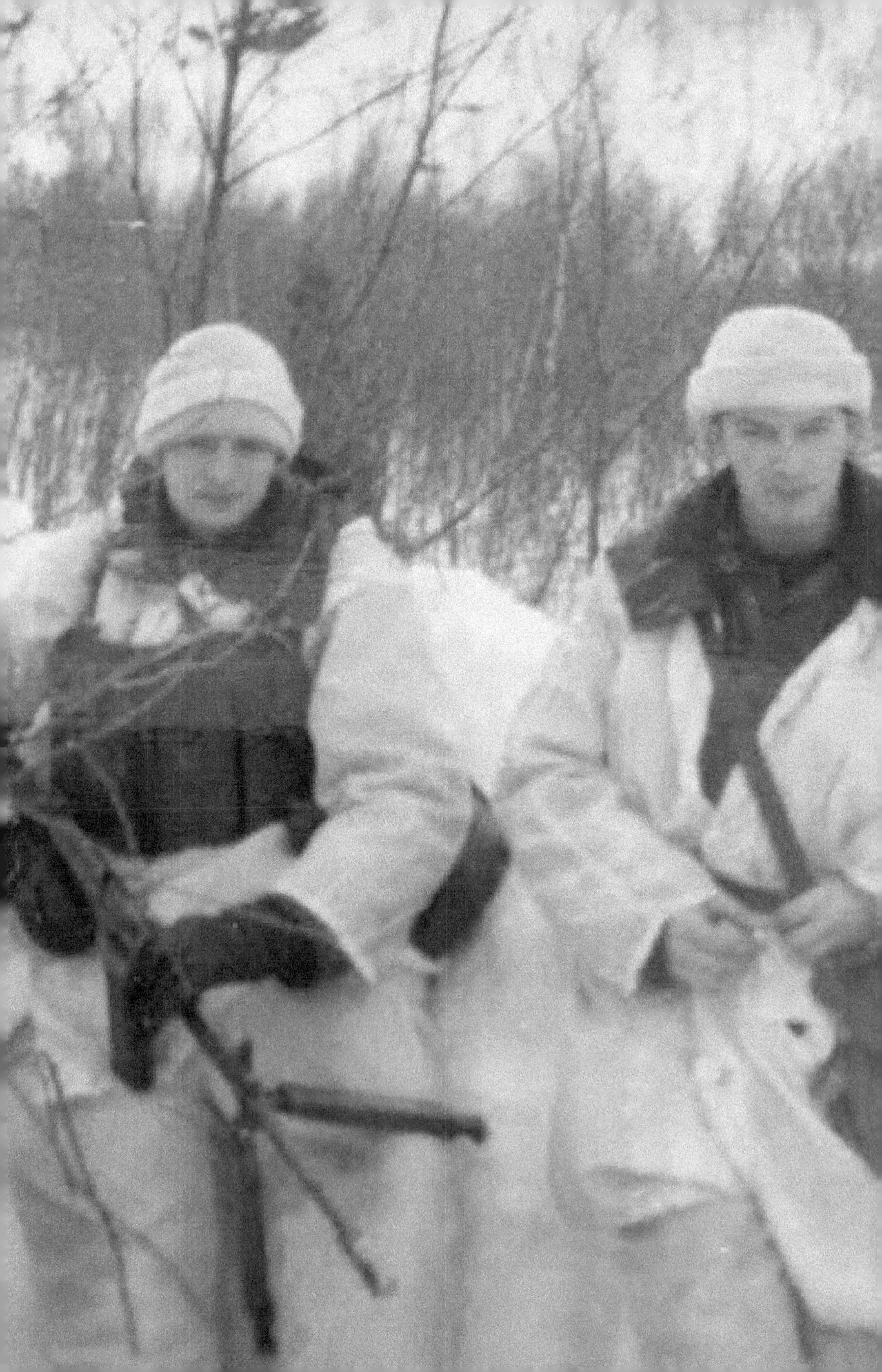

OPPOSITE: Private Barnes, C2 Gunner, QL3 Infantry. (Author's photo)
ABOVE: YTAP Course, 1986. MCpl Barnes seated second from left. (Author's photo)
BELOW: Cyprus, 1986. MCpl Barnes second from right. (Author's photo)
FOLLOWING PAGE: John and Julie's Wedding, 3 June, 1989. (Author's photo)

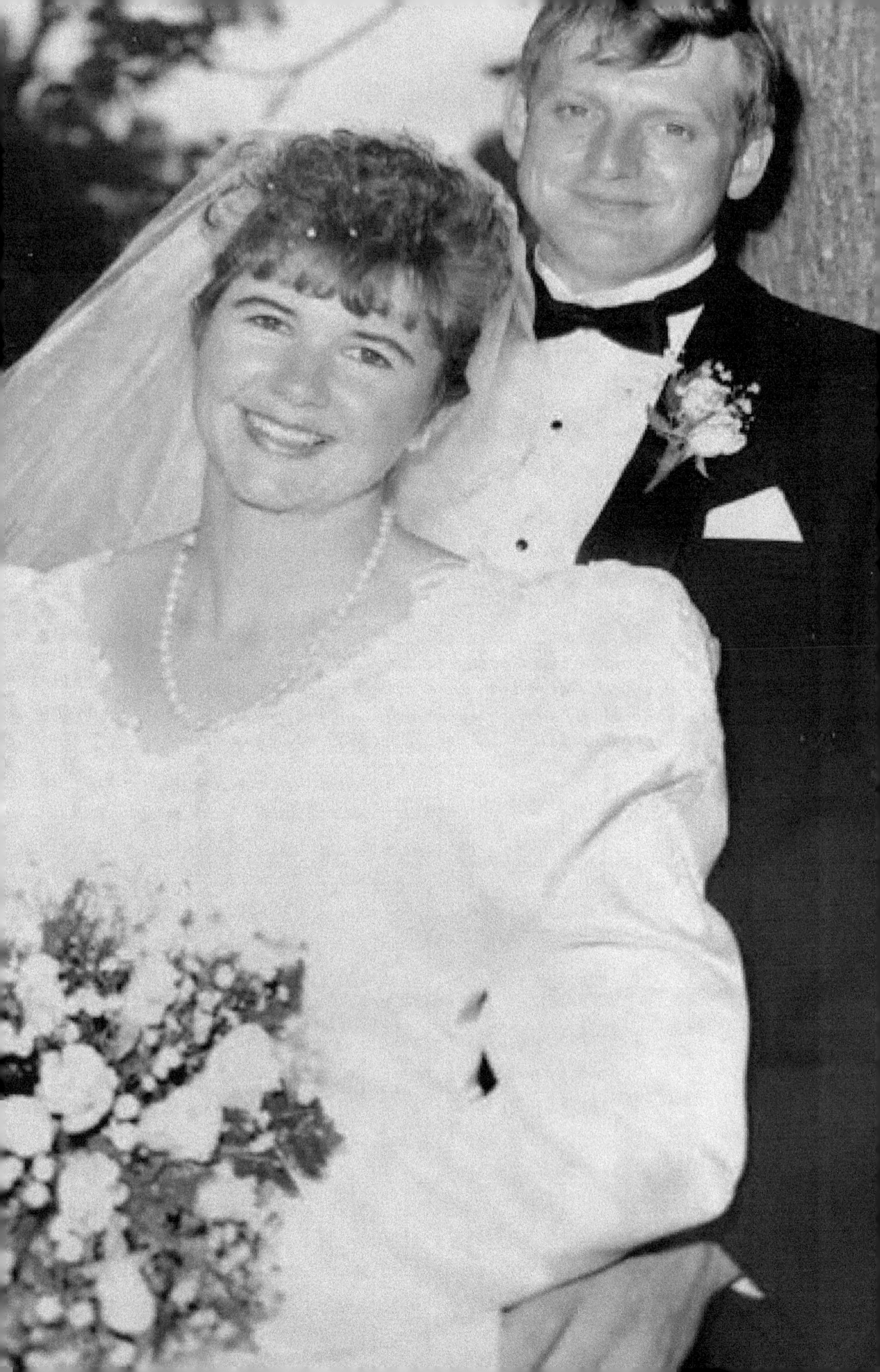

PART TWO
PEACEMAKING

GULF WAR

A week or so after returning to Baden from completing my second Nijmegen March in Holland, things in the world took a turn for the worst. On August 2, 1990, Saddam Hussein sent the Iraqi Army into Kuwait and occupied it. Almost immediately, we started seeing and hearing news reports of condemnation from around the world, including by Canada.

With U.S. leadership, the world started to come together to help Kuwait.

By the end of September, Canada was already planning to send ships and aircraft as part of the coalition effort. Our brigade in Germany was tasked to support. Shortly after that, 3 RCR was tasked to train up a rifle company to provide airfield security for the Canadian task force.

It was an exciting and thrilling moment when Mike Company was told to prepare to deploy to an unknown location in the Middle East to provide security as part of the first Gulf War. We had about ten days to get trained on the Rules of Engagement, the local area, and local issues, coordinate with the Air Force and pack weapons and kit.

The ten days flew by and, before we knew it, we had arrived in Doha, Qatar. The security of Canadian personnel and equipment, primarily our fighter aircraft, was a top priority. It fell to the 118 soldiers of Mike Company, led by Major Mike Blanchette and MWO George Leach. There had been a restriction on how many Canadian personnel Canada would send, and because this was an Air Force operation, we were lucky to get the 118 positions. It had started much higher, but for every new Air Force position required, an infantry position was cut.

The Company size was hardly sufficient to do the job.

Most of us in Mike Company, and perhaps most Canadians in general, had never even heard of Qatar before this deployment. Even today, most could not tell you where it is. I soon learned that it was a tiny state on a peninsula connected to Saudi Arabia, close to Bahrain. Most Qataris lived in Doha, a city of over a million people, which was both the capital and the country's economic hub. A monarchy that had been ruled by one family for over a hundred years, it was one of the poorest and smallest of the Gulf States. Because its population was small, they employed a lot of migrant workers. Most of them had come from India, Nepal and Sri Lanka, and they could not change jobs or even leave the country without a permit.

Even though it accepted the presence of the coalition forces, including Americans and Canadians, Qatar did not boast about it. Even though the tiny state was probably not a military target, like the other Gulf sheikdoms, it was not eager to publicize its role as host to coalition militaries, especially the United States.

It was in this environment that we found ourselves in October 1990.

QATAR AIRPORT

My first impression of our surroundings was not positive.

While doing reconnaissance on the airfield and figuring out how to best secure our aircraft and personnel, I needed to go to the toilet. A local Qatari soldier pointed me in the right direction. Upon entering the modern-looking building on the airfield, I saw several holes in the floor. These were the toilets: no seat, no privacy, and no water for washing your hands afterward. Even more traumatic was the absence of toilet paper.

After a few days of setting up, I started to see the same local soldiers giving me a friendly greeting. Sometimes if I had a vehicle, I would drive them to the gate for their shift, and they were very thankful.

I do not remember the exact temperature during October and November. It was probably around 85 degrees Fahrenheit or higher during the day, but it was winter for the locals. They would have toques and hoods and heavy coats at nights, so a ride instead of walking about a kilometre to their post was a good thing.

I was a little taken aback when, on about day four or five of driving this one soldier a couple of times, he grabbed my hand, leaned in and kissed me on the cheek. Not an everyday event for this Newfie, and afterward, he held my hand for a minute. Through my briefing on the local traditions, I understood that this was quite common between men and showed respect and friendship. I was a little uncomfortable standing around holding this guy's hand as my soldiers looked on.

Upon the arrival of our understrength Company, we had to dig in, build defensive positions, erect fences and observation posts, and place guards all around the perimeter in bunkers constructed by us. We had to control access to the part of the airfield where the Canadian aircraft and personnel were located.

We stacked tens of thousands of sandbags, more than five hundred rolls of concertina wire and more than five hundred pieces of corrugated steel. We had to build dozens of bunkers and individual trenches so that every soldier had a fire position if required. Because our aircraft did not have hardened cover when parked, we also had to conduct constant patrolling at night.

PART TWO - PEACEMAKING

It was a very frustrating tour from an infantry and security point of view, as we were overworked and underappreciated.

It was my first time working under the command of the Air Force, and we discovered early on that their priorities were not the same as ours. There was lots of work to go around between filling sandbags and building our bunkers and trenches (which were a high priority). We began manning those positions immediately, even before they were finished.

I was now a section commander. My section had two main positions, a mortar pit and a .50 calibre machine-gun bunker with a view out over the airfield and into Doha. We had the gun set up and manned within an hour of arriving. We had the position well camouflaged and well laid out with range cards drawn with bearings and distances to possible targets.

The U.S. airfield security folks would drive by in their Hummers, and they would stop and speak to us. They would tell us how grateful they were to have highly trained soldiers with .50 calibre machine-guns and mortars to help them if attacked.

I was embarrassed to tell them the truth, so we kept the secret that we did not have any ammo for the .50 calibre guns. We had been able to get some 5.56 ammo from the Americans for our personnel weapons, but we had no heavy ammo at all. We were told that the .50 calibre ammo had been on the initial manifest from Lahr but that the Air Force had some higher priorities. Someone had decided that the ammo was not something we needed right away.

AIR FORCE PRIORITIES

The NCOs and officers were pissed, as was the whole Company, and our leadership was furious. I know that the Officer Commanding Mike Company and the Sergeant Major immediately went to see the Air Force commander and told him that we needed the .50 calibre ammo now. They were told it would be on the next flight from Lahr in two days.

I was sitting in the .50 calibre bunker with two of my soldiers when the Canadian Hercules came in and landed two days later. I called back to our HQ and told them to send someone to the aircraft and get some .50 calibre ammo immediately for the guns; we could get the rest later.

The Hercules taxied to a stop in front of a hangar the Air Force used for supplies and opened its back end, so my soldiers and I could see inside. It was packed, but that was alright; we would have our ammo.

A few minutes later, my radio buzzed, and it was the Company Command Post telling me that they had seen the plane's manifest, and there was no .50 calibre ammo on it. It had been bumped again for other priorities.

I used my binoculars to watch as the Air Force personnel unloaded the Hercules, and I was shocked by what I saw coming off. There were at least four foosball machines (electronic soccer games, like hockey games), coolers for drinks and ice cream, and at least ten comfy-looking armchairs. I had to stop watching as I was so mad. I was afraid I would do something stupid.

I immediately jumped in the duty vehicle and went to see the Company Sergeant Major to brief him on the contents of the Hercules. He thought I was kidding! When he realized I was serious, he told me to go back to the troops and he would deal with it.

From stories I heard from people in the vicinity, I know that he and Major Mike Blanchette went to talk directly to the senior Air Force Commander. In some very unprofessional terms, he told the Commander that this was messed up and needed to be sorted out immediately, or they would be going outside the Air Force chain of command. The senior Air Force folks were not impressed with this attitude, and there was talk amongst them of replacing both guys. In the end, it did not happen.

Our .50 calibre ammo arrived on the next flight two days later. The embarrassment of being yelled at by infantry guys and the chance that someone would find out how fucked up they were was enough to ensure that the Air Force found room for our ammo. At least now, if something were to happen, we would be able to defend those dumbass Air Force folks who made those terrible decisions.

The little bit of respect I had left for those guys disappeared quickly over the next several weeks.

It was very frustrating having to watch our Air Force friends every day as they strolled around in their ball caps and T-shirts and looked like they were on holiday. I know they had an important job to do; they had to make sure that the aircraft were well looked after and there are rules and regulations about the number of hours one can work or fly without a break. But what was going on in Qatar was pure garbage.

Our infantry soldiers were working between twelve and sixteen hours a day in stifling heat. When we would send guys back to eat or rest, we would find hundreds of Air Force folks sitting around in shorts sunbathing, eating ice cream or playing volleyball.

It pissed us off.

AIR FORCE HELP

As the senior NCOs in theatre, we went to speak with CSM Leach and Major Blanchette to ask them if we could get some assistance from the Air Force to help us get the bunkers and firing positions built so that we could give some of our soldiers a few hours off. We were pretty surprised to hear that the Air Force Commander agreed and thought it was a good idea for his folks to help. It would show that we were all one team.

At this stage, I could not give a damn about team effort; I just wanted some manpower to assist us in getting ready for an attack. I was tasked as the sergeant who would get the Air Force personnel and put them to work. They had agreed to send folks after supper when it was cooler. They would do so every evening until all the work was done and the camp was secure. The infantry soldiers were excited to get help.

PART TWO - PEACEMAKING

At 1800 hours, I was waiting by the sandbags for our help to arrive with about fifty RCR soldiers. They started coming in around ten minutes later, in ones and twos, some in uniform, some in shorts and T-shirts. At that point, I didn't care. Eventually, around a half an hour later, thirty-five people had arrived. I had been told to expect about a hundred. I asked where everyone was, and someone said, "This is it. Everyone else is busy."

I told them I would break them into teams and assign them to my soldiers, who would tell them what needed to be done. I asked who was in charge, and no one spoke up. I asked again, and they just looked around at each other with blank stares. I asked who the senior person was.

One guy said, "I'm a Chief Warrant Officer." Another said, "I'm a Lieutenant Colonel."

I thought to myself that this is not going to work.

I decided to take control myself and, by 1900, we had them assigned to different tasks, mostly filling sandbags or carrying sandbags with my guys placing them. About thirty minutes later, I noticed a few folks starting to walk away. I stopped them and asked where they were going. They told me they had to get dressed for duty, and away they went. A few minutes later, I noticed several more folks gathered around and, when I approached them, they said they were resting and would continue in a minute. I walked away to check on a different group. A few minutes later, I saw the same group heading back toward the main camp.

By 2000 hours, all the Air Force personnel had disappeared, and the infantry guys were back to doing what we had been doing already.

I explained to the Sergeant Major the next morning what had happened the previous night. He just shook his head and said, "Maybe it will be better tonight." A different sergeant was in charge that second night, but I was told only about ten folks arrived. By the third night, no one showed up.

All for one and one for all!

LANDING SCORES

My section was responsible for the .50 calibre bunker at the edge of the airfield where the Canadian jets would take off and land. They would have to taxi in beside the bunker and then roll behind it where they would be parked.

Because we were so short-handed, we had our soldiers doing an average of three to four hour shifts on the gun at a time. It was scorching, and it got very boring after a couple of hours watching for security breaches and staring into the distance. So, the troop came up with something to amuse themselves. They used big pieces of cardboard about two feet by two feet to write large numbers from one to ten in bright colours, and when a Canadian jet landed, they would hold up a card and give them a score on how good the landing was.

This was all in fun, as none of my young soldiers had any experience to gauge a fighter jet landing. If it looked smooth and didn't bounce, they might get a seven or an eight. If it were a rough landing, it could be as low as a two.

We started hearing that the pilots were talking amongst themselves about their scores and were getting upset if they thought it was too low. This made the troops even more enthused to continue with their little game.

A pilot would often stop his jet as it went by the bunker, yell profanity at the soldiers, and belittle them if he disagreed with a score. One pilot from Bagotville took it a little too far after receiving a low score two days in a row. He stopped after the second landing and told the troops to fuck off, as they had no idea what they were doing. The soldiers reportedly told him to get lessons from the other pilots on how to land.

He was not happy.

The following day, as this same pilot was taxiing past the bunker to go on a mission, he decided to teach these ignorant infantry soldiers a lesson. As the jet's tail passed the bunker, the pilot cut the aircraft quickly in front and threw on the afterburners making the cam net catch on fire, forcing the two soldiers to evacuate the bunker and pull off the cam net. The pilot just laughed as he departed for his mission.

Our Command Team got involved and explained how dangerous this was and how my soldiers could have been terribly injured or even killed. I am assuming that the word spread very quickly. The pilot had probably been told by radio to return to base because several minutes later the jet appeared overhead. It circled the airfield and then came in low over an area where the company had set up several sections of modular tents for orders and briefings. He came in so low that the tent was torn off the ground, and chairs and tables went flying. Luckily, no one was inside and no one got hurt.

I can still see the CSM running toward the Air Force Command Post, his arms waving and yelling something that no one could understand. The following day, this pilot was returned to Canada to face the consequences of his actions, and we were asked to stop scoring the landings, which we reluctantly did.

We may have stopped scoring the pilots, but the gap between the Air Force and Mike Company remained. It was made worse when an incident happened in the kitchen tent that caused us to laugh at one of the pilots.

We had several sections of modular tent set up on the airfield as our kitchen area, and inside there were enough tables to seat about a hundred and fifty people at a time. To keep the inside down to a tolerable temperature, the doorways and sides were rolled up to allow a light breeze to blow through. Pilots have a reputation for being spoiled pretty boys. They think they are required to have cool nicknames, let their hair grow a little longer, wear expensive sunglasses and need air-conditioned rooms with real mattresses to sleep well.

This one lunchtime, a young pilot, still wearing his sunglasses, came hopping into the tent telling his pilot friends about some manoeuvre he completed in his jet on the last mission. He misjudged the height of the doorway and slammed his head into the pole that held the modular tent upright. He hit so hard that he knocked himself flat onto the floor, and the swelling and bruising started immediately. The other pilots ran to his prone body showing great concern, while all the infantry guys laughed. The other pilots started yelling and screaming at us to stop laughing and to show some concern, but the more they yelled, the harder we laughed until everyone was almost hysterical. It was safe to say that several weeks of putting up with these pompous asses had finally boiled over, and we just let all our frustrations out.

This incident made it all the way to the Air Force Command Team on the ground, and they were suddenly concerned with the relationship between the Air Force and the infantry. All of us were told to start showing respect for each other.

Perhaps this incident showed the Air Force folks how bad the relationship had gotten. Many of them seemed to try to show some appreciation. Some pilots even said thank you as they taxied by the bunkers, and some of the support staff volunteered to help with security.

We never had an opportunity to see how long this would last because, unlike the Army, the Air Force liked three-month rotations. Since the Air Force guys followed a short replacement schedule, so too did the infantry company. A company from the Van Doos replaced us in December. I arrived back home in Baden on Christmas Eve, just in time for Santa.

Canada did not take any casualties during the Gulf War, but many veterans have come forward complaining of Gulf War Syndrome (GWS). GWS, also known as Gulf War Illnesses (GWI) and chronic multisymptomatic illness, is a chronic disorder affecting returning military veterans and civilian workers of the 1990-1991 Gulf War. Many acute and chronic symptoms have been linked to it, including fatigue, muscle pain, cognitive problems, rashes and diarrhea. Suggested causes have included depleted uranium, sarin gas (a nerve gas), smoke from burning oil wells and vaccinations. I never thought about any of this while I was deployed—those thoughts were far in the future.

For now, I was happy to be home with my beautiful wife and our wonderful little boy. Three months is a long time in a baby's life, and the changes were phenomenal. For starters, JJ didn't remember me. I felt like Julie and JJ had gone on without me, or perhaps they didn't need me as much as I thought. I began to wonder if I was going to remain in the Army after this rotation to Germany or if I would seek another path. I was also considering changing to a trade that would keep me home more. But after being home again for a few months, I started to get that soldiers itch again and was looking for that next adventure.

The remainder of 1991 and the beginning of 1992 were quiet as far as the Canadians in Germany were concerned. We continued to train with our allies and partners, and I even squeezed in a third Nijmegen March.

10

UNPROFOR

However, parts of Europe were starting to unravel following the end of the cold war.

Yugoslavia started to disintegrate in 1991. Both Slovenia and Macedonia declared their independence with little violence. When Croatia declared its independence on June 25, 1991, fighting broke out with the Serbian minority in Croatia, supported by elements of the Yugoslav National Army.

The UN tried to figure out its policy when it was not two nations fighting each other but rather the fighting was between groups inside a country. In response they authorized twelve thousand peacekeepers to deploy into the heart of a civil war.

Canada contributed the largest contingent to the mission, which for us was called Operation HARMONY. It consisted largely of the Van Doos Battle Group, commanded by Lieutenant-Colonel Jones. This Battle Group also included November Company from 3 RCR and the 4th Combat Engineer Regiment.

The Battle Group advance party started to arrive in Croatia in March 1992, with November Company arriving on April 11. Our tasks were to help create and secure one of the three United Nations Protected Areas (UNPAs) where the Serb minorities were located. While the UN deployments into Croatia went well, there were about two hundred ceasefire violations reported per day.

We had departed Germany by train with all the vehicles and equipment required for the operation. The journey to Croatia took several days, as we were an incredibly low priority on the train tracks and had to pull off for hours to allow cattle cars and passenger cars to go ahead. The train was equipped with cars turned into field kitchens manned by Canadian Army cooks, sleeping cars, and passenger cars with bench seats and tables for relaxing—all guarded by Canadian soldiers with loaded weapons.

The long journey was spent sleeping, eating, playing cards and enjoying the spectacular scenery of the Bavarian countryside and the Austrian Alps. I had taken two hundred deutsche marks with me in cash, and I lost it all to a couple of card sharks. As a result, I had to borrow money while I waited for our first pay parade.

As we were switching tracks at the new Slovenian border, a train carrying the Czechoslovakian Contingent to the United Nations Protection Force (UNPROFOR) pulled up alongside us and stopped. For a moment we studied each other with curiosity, but then we started to exchange handshakes, beer, and stories.

Considering that we were on the slow train to Croatia and a low priority, the trip was comfortable and uneventful. Our Battalion cooks, consisting of Master Corporal Merritt and his folks, cooked up some fantastic meals and made the journey that much more enjoyable.

After several days of being bumped from track to track, we crossed into Croatia, and the atmosphere immediately changed. There was destruction everywhere. In some cases, complete villages were destroyed. In other areas, selected houses, those belonging to a specific ethnic group, were gone. Places were marked in red paint for destruction. We saw lots of armed individuals, some in uniforms, many not, and for the most part they just ignored us.

We finally arrived at our destination, the small town of Daruvar, Croatia. November Company, also known as the "Men in Black" for the colour of our company t-shirts, prepared to make this place home for the foreseeable future. We were met at the railhead by our advance party, where we received a brief welcome from Lieutenant-Colonel Jones. Then we began the arduous task of unloading our vehicles and equipment in preparation for our road move to the small Croatian village of Sirač, about ten kilometres southeast of Daruvar.

I took a moment at the railhead to remember how I had gotten here.

TRANSPORT SERGEANT

In late 1991, I was sent to Gagetown, New Brunswick, to attend the Advanced Driver Course, and I was lucky enough to be the top student on that course. Shortly after my return to Baden, the battalion started hearing that 3 RCR would participate in the upcoming UN deployment to Croatia. We did not know who was going, and the plan kept changing.

I was a Sergeant in Mike Company, and we heard that it would not be us because we had recently been deployed to the Gulf War, and it was someone else's turn. That was a real bummer for the Mike Company folks.

Initially, it was going to be Oscar Company and November Company attached to the Van Doos Battle Group. However, a month or so before deployment, it changed to just a beefed-up November Company and a Reconnaissance Platoon.

I was not paying attention, as I knew I was not going, so I just got on with my job. I was walking from our HQ building down to where our soldiers were located when I met a friend walking toward me. Sergeant Steve Jeans, a fellow Newfoundlander, looked upset.

WHITE SCHOOL, BLACK MEMORIES

"How are you doing?" I asked.

"The shits," he said.

He informed me that he had just been told that he had been selected to attend the next 6B Course in Gagetown, which was the course required to be promoted to warrant officer. It was an excellent achievement for Sergeant Jeans, who was still a young soldier. I congratulated him and asked him why he was angry.

He told me that he was the transport sergeant for November Company and was supposed to deploy to Croatia but had just now been told he would not be going and would be attending the course instead. I told him I felt terrible for him, but I was hiding my joy.

As soon as Steve went around the corner, I turned around and made my way back up to the HQ building as fast as I could go without running. I made my way down the hallway to the November Company Sergeant Major's office and took a deep breath before stepping inside. I snapped to attention in front of MWO Rick Clark, who had no idea who I was, and when he looked up, I said with every bit of confidence I could muster, "Sir, I am your new transport sergeant, Sergeant Barnes."

"That was quick," he said. "I just lost Sergeant Jeans a few minutes ago."

"I know that, sir. I just spoke with him." I then told him that I had just completed the Advanced Driver Course, that I had topped it, that I was the best choice to replace Steve, and that I would be a great transport sergeant. He asked me if my Sergeant Major was aware that I was here, and I sheepishly said no.

"Sergeant," said MWO Clark, "You've got some balls. I can't guarantee you the job, but let me speak with your Sergeant Major, and I will let you know."

I think that he appreciated my initiative and my big set of balls for walking into his office the way I did. An hour later, I was told to start clearing out of Mike Company and into November Company.

It was a little bit amusing when folks from the other companies, especially some Sergeants from Oscar Company, found out that Sergeant Barnes from Mike Company was deploying to Croatia as the transport sergeant for November Company. I just kind of shrugged it off and said I was told to clear into November Company. That was all I knew.

I do not know when I told Julie the truth about how I ended up on Rotation Zero for Bosnia when I was not slated to be on it, but I am sure she now understands. She was not as understanding at the time because we had a small baby, and she was pregnant with our second child. Many years later when I told Julie the truth, I found myself having difficulty explaining why I did it. I am still not sure, except to say that I was a soldier and I wanted to be part of something bigger than myself, I wanted to have the excitement of deploying into a war zone. I spent many months and years training to be a good soldier and I wanted to have the opportunity to put those skills to the test.

As the Transport Sergeant, I was responsible for getting all the vehicles offloaded from the train, organized into packets, and moved to Sirač. After a couple of hours of hard work and a bit of yelling and direction, we were able to roll into Sirač as a

Mechanized Rifle Company.

We moved as a company to an area around the local school which had been designated to be our home for the immediate future. WO Terry Riddle showed us where each of the Platoons and Company HQ, including Company Transport, were going to be located.

We immediately went about parking vehicles and setting up bivouacs for everyone.

Later that afternoon, Brigadier General Lew MacKenzie arrived in our area and addressed the newly arrived 'Men in Black' in the Mess Hall, formerly the Sirač Community Centre. He then toured the Company lines, accompanied by Company Commander Major Peter Devlin and the Company Sergeant Major, MWO Rick Clark.

Following the briefing, I took my transport guys and we moved to what would now be the Company Transport Area. The Second-in-Command, Master Corporal Steve Walker, made sure that our area was set up correctly and that we had a place in which to conduct transport business, including the storing of diesel, gas, naphtha, propane and a variety of oils, most of which were on our trucks.

Someone from the Advance Party had dropped off a case of local beer or pivo as a welcome gift for us. After working hard for several hours, I allowed the guys to sit down and enjoy a warm beer. We listened to stories from our two drivers, Corporal Ron Little and Corporal Gerry Carter, two of the finest Royal Canadians with whom I have worked. I considered myself incredibly lucky to inherit these guys. On top of that, I was pleased to have Master Corporal Walker working for me, one of the funniest and most professional junior NCOs in the Battalion.

UNDER BOMBARDMENT

We had just started to relax when we heard what sounded like an explosion somewhere nearby. I must admit that we did not react very well. We just looked at each other and kind of said, "What the fuck?" We had been inside our modular tent, so we went outside as a group with our beers in hand. We heard something whistling over our heads and some branches and dirt falling from the trees above. Then there was another explosion, this time closer.

Even though none of us had ever been under direct or indirect fire before, we knew without a doubt that someone was bombarding us.

We had not completed our firing positions, probably because we had not expected to need them. But were we ever wrong. We hit the dirt and crawled behind cover. I sent the guys to grab our flak jackets and weapons from inside the tent, and I went to get orders. As I ran toward the Company Command Post, more rounds began to land inside our camp. I started hearing yelling and screaming. The orders were clear, "Crash harbour," a manoeuvre we had practiced many times in the past when everyone jumps in their vehicles and makes their way as quickly as possible to the predetermined rendezvous point to escape a bombardment or airstrike. The only issue was that we had not been given a rendezvous point.

Many stories have been written about how our training and professionalism saved lives that evening in Croatia. I saw it a little differently. Canada had been at peace for a long time and, other than a few peacekeeping missions in places like Cyprus, Lebanon and the Congo, the Canadian Army had not been at war since Korea.

It showed!

Our armoured vehicles had been all lined up, one next to the other with drip pans under them in case of oil leaks. The worst part was that the drivers had locked the doors and hatches with padlocks, just like in Germany, and the keys were in their pockets. People ran toward the vehicles in double-quick time only to find their APCs locked with no driver around. It was chaos, and I was trying to get people in any open vehicles and get them moving.

The Company's Second-in-Command told everyone to drive straight out the In Route and across the field to safety. Soldiers were trying to get in vehicles that were already full, and they had to move on to another one. People were running around looking for a set of bolt cutters to cut locks, all while rounds could be heard going overhead and exploding around us. I had the rest of my transport guys keep the vehicles moving to avoid a bottleneck on the narrow road.

Finally, after a lot of cursing and yelling, most of the vehicles were rolling away from the kill zone. I looked up and saw the Company's Command Post vehicle, a version of the M113 called the Queen Mary, come rolling toward me. The Command Post shelter, metal poles that fit over the back of the vehicle and were covered in canvas, was still attached as the vehicle rumbled out the route.

As the Queen Mary departed and it looked like everyone else had found a way out of the kill zone, I yelled at my guys to get in our two trucks. We quickly realized that our vehicles could not follow the tracked M113s across a ditch and into an empty field. So, I turned onto a side road and drove down it for about eight hundred metres. Parked at a bridge were more Canadian trucks, with soldiers outside them, weapons at the ready.

It was only then that I realized that we did not have any ammunition for our rifles.

I believe we were so sure that this would be a quiet tour for us that we had neglected to issue ammo on arrival in Daruvar. In hindsight, it should have been the first thing we did. The CQ staff started throwing ammo at us, and we loaded mags and then loaded our rifles.

It was now quiet, as whoever had been firing at us had stopped.

We were lucky that night as no injuries were sustained other than a few scratches and scrapes from stumbling around, falling, or trying to get in the back of a moving vehicle. Our kit did not fare as well. Lots of tents, uniforms and vehicles had shrapnel holes that were discovered over the next few days.

After the company regrouped, Major Devlin instructed the Company to disperse to Platoon positions around the village and dig in. The Platoons rolled out to their new locations. Company Headquarters spread around our present location and began digging. My Company Transport Section remained where we had initially been placed, and once the trucks were parked, we immediately started digging.

While the trucks were being parked, Steve Walker made a comment that stopped us all in our tracks. He said, "What the fuck were we thinking driving those trucks under artillery fire? They were packed to the roofs with gas, diesel and propane." We just looked at each other and started laughing.

"We wouldn't have felt a thing," I said, and we all laughed harder.

Once we had our bunker completed and overhead protection in place, we unloaded the trucks in an area away from where we slept. It would be more work, but we would load whatever we needed on the trucks when we went to the platoons to resupply them. Better safe than sorry.

At the time, none of us saw any significance to what had happened. It was not until later, when some reporter wrote an article on the "Men in Black," that we learned that we had been the first Canadian infantry unit to come under artillery fire since the Korean War.

MOVE TO SARAJEVO

The next couple of weeks of Operation HARMONY were hectic for everyone, especially for our Company. We were briefed that whoever was responsible for the artillery attack probably wanted to see how Canadian soldiers would react and probably wanted to know if they could intimidate us. That failed miserably as we just got more determined and more prepared for what was to come.

On top of building defences, filling sandbags, building platoon shelters, and stockpiling ammo, rations and fuel, the platoons had to start conducting reconnaissance patrols. Daily patrols were sent out to the cease-fire line between the Croatian Army (CA) and the Yugoslav Federal Army (JNA). This area was to become the area of operations for November Company in the next phase of operations. During these patrols, the platoons looked at sites for future living accommodations, observation posts and vehicle checkpoints. There also had to be patrols done in the neighbouring sector belonging to the Argentinians to confirm patrol routes and safe areas, as this was also November Company's area of responsibility until the Argentinian Battalion arrived, perhaps sometime in May.

Under the guidance of WOs Gord Romard, Wayne Noseworthy, Roger Sheppard, Tim Robinson and Ernie Hall, the platoons continued with the construction of bunkers, bivouacs and command posts. The results were accommodations mostly under canvas, but also some in confiscated buildings. The level of comfort was more than expected.

Back at the Company Headquarters, we also continued to build our defences, and Company Transport started to take shape. We set up an area to look after resupply and another for the company mechanics to work on the vehicles that were taking a beating. They were already old vehicles, and the enormous number of miles being put on them now was causing havoc. The mechanics continued to perform their magic, and the vehicles kept rolling.

Our deployment to Croatia went very well as even though there were on average 200 cease-fire violations a day, things in the rest of the former Yugoslavia were much worse.

In the South, Bosnia Herzegovina was disintegrating, and there were rumours that Bosnia was going to declare itself to be an independent country and receive significant international recognition. The large Serbian minority in Bosnia had boycotted the recent independence referendum, and fighting had started between elements of the Serbian minority and the ill-prepared Bosnian militias on Independence Day, April 6th, 1992.

The UN Security Council ignored the advice of the military leadership from the United Nations Protection Force (UNPROFOR). It directed the UN HQ in theatre to be moved to Sarajevo, more than two hundred kilometres from the mission they were supposed to command in Croatia. The UN wrongly assumed that a few hundred staff officers and support personnel waving a UN flag would somehow ensure peace in Bosnia.

This never had a chance to succeed and, as the fighting got worse in April and May, the population of Sarajevo became angrier with the UNPROFOR folks in the city.

The UN soldiers had been designated as a protection force, and that is what we were doing within the UN-protected areas in Croatia. However, there was no combat capability in Bosnia to protect anything, including the staff officers in Sarajevo. By May, the UN realized they had made a mistake and ordered the HQ to leave Sarajevo and move to Belgrade. The people of Sarajevo were even angrier.

Once in Belgrade, the leadership of the UN Headquarters began to come up with a plan to get a combat force into Sarajevo. Negotiations with Yugoslav President Slobodan Milosevic, the breakaway Bosnian Serb leader Radovan Karadzic, and the president of Bosnia, Alijah Izetbegovic, resulted in an agreement where UNPROFOR would take over the operations and the security of the Sarajevo airport.

Because it would take time for the UN to get a country to provide the force for this new mission, they decided to borrow a unit from the troops operating in Croatia. Other than Canada, none of the other nations were keen on taking on this task. Knowing that the Canadian Battle Group was the most heavily armed and highly trained, a request to borrow the Canadian unit for thirty days went to Canada's Chief of Defence Staff, General John de Chastelain. The government approved it in record time, and Lew Mackenzie was appointed to be the Mission Commander.

SARAJEVO AIRPORT

We got the word before the decision was made that our Battle Group was to prepare to move to Sarajevo by road and fight to take control of the airport in order to secure it for humanitarian operations.

PART TWO - PEACEMAKING

I got the word to go to a nearby camp where the Van Doo HQ was located to receive orders in preparation for the move to Bosnia.

I arrived at the Battalion Headquarters and was directed to Battalion Transport for the road move orders. Sitting in the room were about twenty people who would have an essential role in planning the move. The transport officer asked if anyone did not speak French? I was the only one that raised my hand. "No problem," he said. "Everyone speaks English." And so, orders started.

About five minutes in, someone asked a question in French, and the remainder of the orders were in French. When orders were over, I stayed behind and asked the Transport Officer to repeat the orders in English. I could tell he was a little upset, but he reluctantly gave me the information that November Company needed.

The move from our location in Croatia to Sarajevo was a difficult task. It was hundreds of kilometres away, through mountain passes, winding roads and disputed territory. The M113 tracked vehicles were old and slow, and the troops sitting in the back suffered. We took both our transport trucks and the two CQ trucks, and all of November Company's vehicles made it safely to Sarajevo airport.

We had several hold-ups along the route as we came across illegal checkpoints, some set up by the Croatians, some by the Serbian forces and more by what appeared to be drunk militias or civilians. We had to negotiate our way through. If that did not work, the excessive firepower that we had usually did the job.

The Battle Group arrived in Sarajevo to secure the airport on July 2, the day after Canada Day, which no one had even realized had come and gone. As we rolled onto the airport tarmac, armed soldiers were seen departing, leaving behind destroyed buildings, vehicles, weapons, and bodies. Once the airport was secured and we had a defensive set-up that could protect us, we started planning for the arrival of humanitarian aid, which needed to get delivered to the beleaguered city.

For the next thirty days, the heroic actions of Canadian soldiers and, especially the "Men in Black," were in the headlines of almost every newspaper in the world. While operating in a hazardous environment, Canadian soldiers risked their lives to deliver approximately three hundred tonnes of food and medical supplies a day to a city that had neither. Soldiers risked their lives to help the people of Sarajevo, who were continually being killed or wounded by sniper fire.

Planes from all over the world started landing at the airport. Many of them came in under fire, and many were hit. All the supplies had to be inspected by the UN civil police and humanitarian agencies to ensure it was aid and not weapons or ammunition. Canadian soldiers then delivered the material to distribution centres around the city. Unfortunately, many of the supplies ended up in the black market or the hands of the Bosnian military. Supposedly, this was not unusual, but to the November Company soldiers who were risking their lives and being continually shot at, this was very disappointing.

The delivery of the humanitarian aid did not get off to a good start, but Canadian soldiers were again able to come to the rescue. About twenty large cargo trucks were being used to move the aid around the beleaguered city, and the drivers were locals who were hired and paid by the United Nations High Commissioner for Refugees (UNHCR). Almost immediately, the trucks and their Canadian escorts started to receive fire from the surrounding mountains and buildings around Sarajevo. It came to a head on the second day.

While travelling across a bridge in the heart of the city, the convoy of about a dozen trucks and several armoured personnel carriers came under fire, resulting in some broken windshields and bullet holes in the frames and tarps. The drivers panicked, and most just left their trucks running on the bridge and road and headed for whatever cover they could find. Canadian soldiers could not locate or persuade the drivers to come back. Several trucks were abandoned. That afternoon all the drivers that had remained decided to quit, citing safety concerns. We were left with a bunch of trucks, piles of humanitarian aid and no drivers.

It was decided that Canadian soldiers would become the truck drivers because getting the aid to the suffering people was the most crucial issue. Major Devlin came to see me and asked me if I could train soldiers to drive these big trucks, some of which were large transport trucks. Of course, I said yes, and Master Corporal Steve Walker and I got together and developed a plan.

We planned for about a dozen soldiers to be at the airport around suppertime, and we would run a two- or three-hour condensed training course. Then these guys would be driving the trucks the following morning through Sarajevo.

A simple plan, what could go wrong?

Master Corporal Walker and I went to the airport early to move all the trucks together and ensure we knew how to drive them ourselves before teaching someone else. Of course, nothing was simple in Sarajevo, and we arrived to find that all the trucks were different. Some had two gear shifts, others had a double-clutch and Jake Brakes, and some were just downright scary to drive. After about an hour of playing around with them, we felt comfortable enough to get all the lucky soldiers together and begin.

I started by speaking with the soldiers about the importance of this task and that it would be dangerous. We needed their full attention to give them the best chance of success. Master Corporal Walker started by showing them the different types of trucks and explaining the double-clutch and the use of a Jake Brake. It got everyone's attention. Following that, we designated a driver for each truck and told them to follow the lead vehicle around the airfield. The route would allow them to use the gears and to practice braking.

We drove around the airfield perimeter and had the trucks adjust speed to force the drivers to use the gears and brakes. If not for the seriousness of what we were doing, it would have been the funniest thing I had seen in a long time. Trucks continued to be stalled and would have to be restarted. Some trucks rolled off the paved surface and onto the grass as drivers looked down when they tried to find the right gear. Of course, we had a truck that ran into the back of the one in front of it—all just in the first fifteen minutes.

Eventually, we made it around the perimeter and had just begun the second loop when the first mortar or artillery round landed out in the centre of the airfield. We were already about halfway around the perimeter, so we made a direct beeline to the airport terminal building and, after a few stops and starts and an additional four or five rounds hitting the airfield, all the trucks and soldiers made it to the building and the safety of the bunkers. We watched from relative safety as several more rounds impacted the airfield, and then as suddenly as it had started, it stopped.

By now, darkness had engulfed the airfield, and we decided that the drivers had as much training as they were going to get, and we wished them luck tomorrow with their deliveries.

The following day, the trucks were loaded, and with an armoured escort, Canadian soldiers drove them into the heart of the city and to the aid drop-off points. That evening, when the convoy returned minus one truck, I got an update on the day's task. Most of the aid got to its destination even if it took much longer than anticipated. There had been several accidents on the tight streets, and one truck failed to brake and make a turn at the bottom of a hill and ended up inside a building.

Luckily, while this was going on, the UN had been able to persuade some locals to take on the driving task by paying them more and providing extra security. It was great news for the Canadian soldiers who had found themselves driving transport trucks instead of providing security. The local drivers continued to be an issue every time the convoys came under fire, but thankfully Canadian soldiers did not have to drive the trucks again.

The thirty days in Sarajevo were busy and went by quickly, thanks to the leadership and professionalism of Canadian soldiers and a whole lot of luck. The most serious injury sustained by the Battle Group in the most dangerous city in the world was the loss of a foot to a land mine. Corporal Denis Reid, a fellow Newfoundlander and Royal Canadian, stepped on an anti-personnel mine while working on the security of our camp and gave up his foot for our safety.

BIRTH OF MY DAUGHTER

I had manipulated the system to make sure that I could get on this original tour to the former Yugoslavia, but there was a part of me that felt guilty and concerned. I had left my beautiful wife behind in Germany with a tiny baby and one in the oven.

While in Croatia, I had been able to call Julie at least once a week to make sure she was okay and see if there were any issues I needed to deal with. Julie was very independent and, even if there had been issues, she would never have burdened me with them while I was deployed.

It was a pattern that repeated throughout my career.

Before leaving for UNPROFOR, we had moved out of our apartment in Obersasbach and into military housing in the village of Weitenung. It was closer to base and with hundreds of other Canadians nearby. It would allow Julie to have access to help if she needed it, and it made me feel more at ease. Julie had also decided that, as the time for birth came closer, she would take JJ and go back to Ottawa, stay with her mom, and have our baby in Canada. As August rolled in, I was beginning to feel agitated and concerned. I was stuck in Sarajevo, access to phones was almost impossible, and it was years before Facebook and Twitter.

While driving in a burned-out area of Sarajevo in late August, we stopped our vehicles to try and contact our CP to confirm the location of a distribution centre. I noticed a public phone across the street and, while waiting to move again, I strolled across and picked it up. To my total surprise, there was a dial tone. I pulled my phone card out of my pocket and dialled the operator. Before I even knew what was going on, I could hear the ringing going through. I then heard Julie's mom saying hi, and I was able to speak to Julie for several minutes. She had arrived in Ottawa; she and JJ were doing well and were ready for the new baby to come.

I made sure I was part of any convoys going to that part of Sarajevo, and I was able to speak with Julie on at least two more occasions.

On September 18, I was able to call Ottawa again, and this time Julie's mom answered and said, "You must have heard." I said, "What?" And I was told that I was the father of a healthy baby girl.

Jana Samantha Julie Barnes had arrived.

It was another two weeks before I was able to take leave and return to Ottawa. It was an extremely exciting day when I met my daughter in the Ottawa airport for the first time. The plan was to spend a week in Ottawa and then fly back to Germany with Julie, JJ and Jana. A few days later, I would return to Croatia, where the Battle Group now was.

Ottawa proved to be a bit more complicated than we thought. We spent most of our time together running around government offices downtown to get the proper paperwork and authorizations required to bring Jana into Germany. Finally, the day before our flight, and after dealing with some high-level military and government officials, it all came together, and our family of four went home to Germany.

Another week together with my family in Germany, and I was off to Croatia for the remainder of the tour.

PAKRAC CAMP

While I was away on leave, the French had replaced the Battle Group in Sarajevo, and another long road move had taken place. Master Corporal Steve Walker did a great job getting November Company back to Croatia with all their vehicles in good working order.

Following the Battle Group's return, November Company HQ moved into a new camp in Pakrac, a small town with a population of less than five thousand people before the war. It was well known for a clash called the "Battle of Pakrac," a bloodless

PART TWO - PEACEMAKING

skirmish between Serbs and Croats that took place in March 1991.

It began after rebel Serbs seized the town's police station and municipal buildings and started harassing Croatian government officials. The Croatian government sent Interior Ministry Special Police to re-establish control. Fighting broke out between the two sides. The Yugoslav National Army tried to intervene, but the Croatian government asserted control over the town. After a standoff, there was an agreement to pull out the Special Police and the Yugoslav Army, and the town was restored to what it was before the Serbs tried to seize control.

It left the area of Pakrac in an awkward situation, with both sides stating that the other was committing genocide against them. Serb and Croat papers listed death and murders that had not happened, and the Serb population started to set up barricades around their area of town and adjoining towns to protect themselves.

It was into this quagmire that November Company returned.

We had only a short time in Pakrac before we started our handover with the incoming Battle Group. I can say with some certainty that all of November Company's soldiers were excited about getting home. It would be nice to be back in Germany with my family, and it would be nice to spend some time being a father to my two children. Several months of living in tents, sleeping on a cot, and washing in a basin were about to come to an end.

Simple things, like sitting on an actual toilet and being able to flush, can be sorely missed.

It had been hot in Croatia and keeping bodies and clothes clean is paramount to remaining healthy. We had Porta-Potties in each of the platoon and section locations and at Company HQ, and Battalion Transport had the responsibility to keep them emptied. The Battle Group had two "shitter trucks," fondly referred to as the "Honey Wagons." They were constantly on the go, trying to keep up with all the different locations.

My good friend, Corporal John Frizzell, was one of the drivers. He was continually harassed about his job as he went from one location to the other, but he just took it in stride. Both Honey Wagon drivers had special coveralls and gloves and were always acutely aware of the possibility of disease. The system worked well until one of the trucks was involved in an accident and was out of commission for several weeks. This couldn't have occurred at a worse time, as the heat was almost unbearable, as soon was the smell.

The camps were busy, and the Porta-Potties were distributed to each location with the plan of having them emptied every three or four days. Our Company HQ location had several Porta-Potties around the camp. They were meant for our small group, but HQ always had people coming and going. These toilets would start filling up quickly, even when they were being emptied regularly. The effects of the shitter truck accident were felt almost immediately in my location.

We had a unit sports day and several large meetings to issue and receive orders at our headquarters location, and all the extra folks made use of our limited Porta-

WHITE SCHOOL, BLACK MEMORIES

Potties. On the second or third morning after the accident, I found shit almost level with the seat when I went for my morning routine. Someone had already seen it this way because leaning against the outside was a long stick, obviously meant to push everything around to make room for your contribution. The smell was disgusting, and the temperature inside must have been around 100°F.

After walking around the camp and checking each toilet, I discovered that they were all pretty full. The issue continued for a few weeks, and we were lucky to see the one shitter truck arrive once every seven or eight days instead of every three or four.

The results were disgusting.

I remember seeing John Frizzell, parking the truck next to the Porta-Potty by transport, and then all you heard was swearing and gagging as he tried to put the hose into the overfilled hole. The more we laughed at him, the madder he got until he finally told us to shut up or he would skip this Porta-Potty the next time around. That was enough to keep us quiet, as we had just about enough of full shitters in the 100°F heat.

Thoughts of clean bathrooms and flushing toilets kept me sane during those last days before deploying back to Germany.

11

HOME AGAIN

HEADQUARTERS TRAINING SERGEANT

It was not too long after getting back to Baden and back into a routine of training and work that we started hearing rumours about base closures and major changes to how the Battalion was structured.

3 RCR was designated as a so-called "10/90 Battalion," which was a new and untried concept. The Headquarters was to be based at CFB Borden with companies and platoons spread out amongst the Reserve Units in Ontario. The Battalion would be composed of 10% Regular Force and 90% drawn from the Reserves.

In late 1992 I was asked if I would be interested in a posting to 2 Canadian Mechanized Brigade Group Headquarters and Signals Squadron located in Petawawa, Ontario, as the Training Sergeant. I immediately said yes because I did not want to be part of the 10/90 Battalion fiasco.

So, in February 1993, Julie and I and our two kids packed up everything we owned and said goodbye to Germany. The rumours about base closures proved to be true. The airfield at Baden closed on March 31, 1993. Several of its squadrons were disbanded, and their aircraft returned to Canada for storage. By the summer of 1993, most personnel had vacated Baden, with the Base becoming a detachment of Lahr whose people mainly had left, as well. Baden permanently closed on Dec. 31, 1993.

We landed in Ottawa in the middle of a snowstorm and headed to the Best Western Hotel in Pembroke, several hours north up the Ottawa River Valley. The previous October we had taken a house-hunting trip and purchased a house in the countryside about twenty minutes away from the base. We took possession of the place shortly after we arrived in February. However, we had to remain in the hotel for a month while we waited for our belongings, including our car, to come from Germany.

WHITE SCHOOL, BLACK MEMORIES

During the month in the hotel, I reported for work each day. Julie and the kids would split their time between Pembroke and her mom's house in Ottawa. The time in the hotel gave me an opportunity to paint the whole interior of the house, with the help of Julie's brother, Tim, and his wife, also named Julie. It was a lot of work, but it was easier because the house was empty.

When I reported to CFB Petawawa and then to the Headquarters and Signals Squadron in February, I discovered that Sergeant Dave Patterson, a fellow Royal Canadian, was still in the position I would fill. He was scheduled for posting to 1 RCR that summer, but I had been sent in early because Base Baden was closing.

It was an excellent opportunity for Dave to show me the ropes, as I had no idea what the Training Sergeant's job entailed, and I did not know what the unit was. I worked in a big office area in the Signals Squadron HQ with the Operations Officer and the Operations Warrant Officer, to whom I reported. A training Master Corporal and Corporal worked for me. We were responsible for making sure that the Brigade HQ could move tactically and communicate with all their sub-units while in the field.

While in garrison, we were responsible for training all the Squadron and Brigade HQ's staff. All the folks around me were signals types, and I was the only infantry guy. I quickly realized that all the tactical and field stuff, including security and weapons training, would fall to me. Dave Patterson, who had been with the unit for a couple of years, set a remarkably high standard. They not only depended on him for a lot, but they also adored him.

I knew immediately that I had huge shoes to fill, but I was up for the challenge.

Dave and I got to spend about three months together before he moved to 1 RCR. I took advantage of every minute to learn from this fine soldier and man. He was older, had much more experience, took me under his wing, and taught me a lot.

LOTTERY WIN PRANK

There was one humorous event while we were training in the field on a tactical exercise that is worth telling. We had just finished moving the Brigade HQ into a new location, the Command Post was operational, and communications were good. The staff officers were running the battle when Dave started talking about winning the upcoming lottery draw that night. He was bragging about how he was going to spend his millions.

It was at that moment that I planned to have some fun with him.

We had been running around for about thirty-six hours, and everyone was tired, so Dave took advantage of some downtime to get some sleep. He went into our tent area and, as soon as he was in his sleeping bag, he was asleep. I rummaged through his pockets and found his lottery tickets, wrote the numbers down, stuffed them into my pocket and returned the tickets where I had found them.

Shortly after a delicious supper of Canadian Army Rations, the Operations Officer grabbed Dave and I to play enemy force and attack one of our sub-units.

We did not get back to our HQ until around midnight, and it had been snowing all night. We were wet and cold, so we stripped down to our drawers and tried to dry out. Dave suddenly remembered his lottery tickets, so he grabbed them out of his pocket and asked the signaller on duty in the back of our CP what the winning numbers were. I had anticipated this and given the numbers of Dave's ticket to the signaller earlier in the evening before we left. He started reading the numbers out one by one.

Dave's face began to change, and then he yelled, "Oh fuck! I won!" He stopped and looked at the signaller, then at the Operations Officer, and asked, "Is this a joke?"

"Of course not," we said, "How would we know the numbers? We were with you all night."

Dave still was unsure, so he jumped in the back of the truck, grabbed the phone, and called the Unit Duty Centre on the Base. I had anticipated this as well and had reached the duty centre earlier. As they gave him the numbers, he started to get more and more excited. He once again paused and said, "I am going to call my wife to confirm these numbers." We told him it was 0100 hours in the morning, and his wife would be sleeping, but he did not care. But it was okay! I had anticipated that as well. I heard him saying to his wife, "I am sorry to wake you up, but do you have the lottery numbers?" I could tell she was reading them off. Then, Dave tossed the phone and burst out through the tent's door into the night wearing only his long johns.

It was dark except for the white snow because light was not allowed, and it was noticeably quiet as we were tactical. Dave started yelling his head off.

"Fuck the Army!" he shouted. "Fuck the CF! I'm a millionaire! Fuck! Fuck! Fuck!" I ran after him in my bare feet, wearing only my underwear, trying to get him to stop screaming and explaining that it was a joke. He couldn't hear me or was ignoring me, and just kept shouting.

I started hearing and seeing people come out of their tents and fighting positions to see who was yelling. I was worried that the Brigade Sergeant Major, CWO Steve Douglas, would come out, and we would both be going to jail.

I got closer to Dave, and I yelled at him, "I played a trick on you, Dave. You didn't win." At first, it didn't register on him, but suddenly his face changed. I could see the look of anger, and then it all hit him like a ton of bricks: where he was, what he had been yelling and that it had all been for nothing. He was standing next to one of the fire points set up throughout the HQ area, and he grabbed a pickaxe handle and started for me. I turned and ran for my life, in my bare freezing feet and underwear, sprinting through the snow.

Dave followed me in long johns and boots, yelling, "I will fucking kill you!" In that moment, I believed him.

After a few seconds or so, we both started slowing down. I turned around and told Dave I was sorry. I really was, but I was more scared than sorry. Dave stopped, and so did I. He just looked at me, as the Operations Officer and a couple of other soldiers stood by watching and laughing.

"Fuck, that was a good one," he said. "Let's go inside before Douglas catches us."

WHITE SCHOOL, BLACK MEMORIES

Dave and I have remained friends ever since, and we have worked together several times since.

For my retirement in June 2017, Dave drove up to Ottawa from New Brunswick to attend my Depart With Dignity ceremony and wish me luck. During my speech, I told the story of that day to the hundred and fifty people who attended, including the Brigade Sergeant Major, Steve Douglas. We had a great laugh again.

DETENTION CUSTODIAN COURSE

I spent four years as the Training Sergeant in 2 Brigade HQ and Signals Squadron, thoroughly enjoying it. I learned a lot about working with a higher HQ, and it prepared me for future jobs I would hold.

One of the responsibilities that I looked after was loading personnel from the unit on both career and common courses. I always tried to make sure the folks we sent on courses were as prepared as possible, especially for courses conducted outside the Base. Sometimes that meant placing them on a pre-course.

As I was browsing through the list of courses available to our members, I saw the upcoming Detention Custodian Course in Edmonton, Alberta, which is a nice way of saying a military corrections officer. The Canadian Forces had its detention facility in Edmonton, and anyone sentenced to jail time of thirty days or more would do it there. It was under the command and control of the Military Police; however, other trades could get qualified and were posted there as guards.

I thought this course might be fun. It would get me away from the office for three weeks, and it might open some posting options for me in the future. I loaded my name into the system, not thinking I would be selected.

A few weeks later, the Operations WO, Terry Strickland, told me he had received a message loading me on the Detention Custodian Course. He did not remember authorizing me to put my name forward. I told him that he had not and that I just put in my name, not expecting to be selected. Instead of getting angry with me, I was told there was funding and to enjoy the course.

I arrived in CFB Edmonton with about thirty other candidates, primarily MPs as well as, a cook and a clerk who were being posted to the detention barrack that year.

The course was interesting, and we learned a lot about how the Canadian Forces treated its military prisoners, as well as some Department of Defence civilians and families who were posted to Germany and who found themselves outside the law.

There were only about eight prisoners in the facility during the course, and they had all been there awhile and were very used to the routine. Everything was on a point system, and the more points you earned, the more privileges you got. You either got points or lost points for everything from cell inspections to attitude, personal appearance and discipline. This system was especially difficult on smokers who could take up to a couple of weeks to earn enough points to have a cigarette.

My course ran shortly after the Somalia fiasco, and one of the prisoners was Private

PART TWO - PEACEMAKING

Kyle Brown. Private Brown had been implicated in the death and torture of a Somali teenager, Shidane Arone, along with Master Corporal Clayton Matchee who had taken a leading role. Arone's screams were reported to have been heard throughout the camp as he was being tortured, but no one intervened.

Matchee had attempted to hang himself to avoid trial, but survived and was left with major brain damage and couldn't stand trial. Brown was convicted of manslaughter. He was one of the first inmates I met while on course, and he was an outstanding prisoner. He followed all the rules to a fault and never caused any issues. I was tasked to escort him to the craft area where he liked to draw, mostly with pencil. Some of his drawings were incredibly good.

I was successful on the course and received my qualification and a recommendation to return to the Detention Barracks as a guard. I never got that opportunity, but I did use some of the skills I learned along the way.

BACK TO 1 RCR

In 1996, my career manager advised me that I would be posted back to 1 RCR in Petawawa. I was excited to be going back to a Battalion and back to my infantry roots.

While I was with the HQ and Signals Squadron, I was also selected to attend my Infantry 6B course, the Platoon Second-in-Command course held in Gagetown. This three-month-long course was one of the most demanding courses in the Army, both physically and mentally, but was required if I was to advance in rank.

I had passed the course and, even though I was posted to the Battalion as a Company Transport Sergeant, I knew it would only be a matter of time before I got my promotion to Warrant Officer. My assessment proved to be right, and I spent less than four months as the Duke's Company Transport sergeant before being promoted and moved into 3 Platoon as the Second-in-Command. I inherited a great platoon with some outstanding soldiers.

Duke's Company was known at the time to be the place to avoid because its leaders were two of the hardest men with whom I have ever trained. They were Major Jonathon Vance (later the Chief of the Defence Staff) and MWO Dave Lavery, who had sharpened his teeth with the Special Forces.

During my years with the HQ and Signals Squadron, I had not kept up the same fitness level that I had been used to in the Battalion, and now I would pay for it.

Vance and Lavery took pleasure in leaving our vehicles behind and marching and running to the field for training. After completing hard training all day, we would then run back to Base. By now, I was already having issues with my knees and feet, and all this running in combat boots just made it worse, but quitting was not in my vocabulary. So, I sucked it up and carried on, even if it meant spending most of the weekend on my back trying to recover.

Luckily for me, Major Vance was posted a few months later, and he was replaced by Major Mark Twohey from The RCR Battle School. You could not have a more drastic difference between Major Vance and Major Twohey, the first being a hard-charging, 'git'er-done-at-all-costs' officer and the other being a more intellectual, think-it-through, laid-back-type leader.

After a couple of years with Major Vance, some of the soldiers in Duke's Company were looking forward to a break. One of the issues with this train of thought was that the CSM remained in his job. Dave Lavery continued to push the soldiers whenever he could.

A few weeks after the changeover, the Company was scheduled to do the Annual Battle Fitness Test, a sixteen-kilometre march with a loaded rucksack, fighting order, and weapon. The company had been marching everywhere we went for the past year with Major Vance and MWO Lavery, and we could do the sixteen-kilometre march with our eyes closed in the allotted time of two hours and twenty minutes.

On the morning of the march, the whole Company arrived at about 0530 hours to get our weapons issued, get our gear sorted, and ready to start the test at 0600 hours, as directed the evening prior. Everyone was formed up by Platoon with Company HQ leading, prepared to step off by 0550 hours. The only one missing was Major Twohey. At 0600, I could see MWO Dave Lavery start to get antsy and look at his watch. You could tell that he was not impressed. Where was the Officer Commanding?

A few minutes after 0600, we saw a vehicle driving down the road toward the parking area and pull into the spot designated for the Officer Commanding Duke's Company. Major Twohey jumps out wearing the Regimental PT kit and looks over where his Company is formed up waiting for him. He runs into the CQ area, and about ten minutes later, he came out ready to march. A test that was supposed to kick off at 0600 started at 0625, 25 minutes late. I saw the Command Team exchange a few words, and then Major Twohey gave the order to begin.

After the first kilometre, I knew we were walking too slowly, and the CSM knew it as well, as he marched back and forth alongside the Company, mumbling and swearing to himself. I saw him run forward and speak to the Officer Commanding and then shake his head and come back. I looked at my watch as we passed the one-kilometre marker, timed the next kilometre and was surprised to see it take us about nine minutes and fifteen seconds, which was at least a minute slower than required and probably closer to two minutes slower than we expected.

I saw the CSM go forward again and say something to Major Twohey. Then, he yelled for the rear platoon to run to the front of the Company. As soon as they got there, they started walking again. He then yelled for the next platoon to do the same. It continued for several kilometres, allowing us to get back on schedule and make up some lost time.

A scheduled five-minute halt at the halfway point to get juice and oranges became a walk-through where we grabbed a juice and slice of orange, scoffed it down and threw the garbage on the side of the road for the work party to pick up as we kept marching. We had no choice if we were to make the required timing. As we crossed the finish line, I looked at my watch. It showed that we had taken two hours and twenty-four minutes.

However, the official time for the company was two hours and eighteen minutes, which was just inside the time allowed.

I do not know if my watch was wrong or someone just made the time work to avoid embarrassing the Company and its leadership. Either way, we passed the Battle Fitness Test.

We heard that MWO Dave Lavery was being posted back to Joint Task Force 2 in Ottawa a few weeks later. The rumour was that he had requested it because he was not impressed with the company's direction. The Company Quartermaster, WO Mark Ford, stepped up and became the acting CSM for the next few months.

Around this time, 1 RCR received a warning order about deploying as a part of the NATO Response Force in Bosnia and Herzegovina. The Battalion was being reorganized for the tour, as Duke's Company would not be going.

Almost immediately, the soldiers of Duke's who would be deploying were moved around the Battalion, and I became the Platoon Second-in-Command of 7 Platoon Charles Company. I considered it a great fortune to be a member of Charles Company because the Command Team were two people that I looked up to and admired. The Officer Commanding was Major Howard Coombs, a fellow Newfoundlander and one of the most respected officers in The Royal Canadian Regiment. His Sergeant Major was MWO Derek Ingersoll, someone I had gotten to know and looked up to as a mentor and friend.

For the next couple of months, we did a lot of low-level training. I found it a huge learning experience because I did not have a Platoon Commander, and I was also missing about one-third of my soldiers. This training period was an opportunity for me to find my groove and to discover what kind of leader I was.

ANIMAL ENCOUNTERS

A couple of incidents occurred during this time frame that have always remained in my memory. One was funny, and the other was a bit shocking at the time.

It was late summer or early fall, and we had deployed into the Petawawa training area to conduct some Platoon and Company-level patrolling. My platoon conducted a nighttime raid on an enemy objective, and we got back to our patrol base around 0300 hours. As was usual for patrol bases, there was no light and minimal noise, so everyone except security laid on their air mattresses and quickly fell asleep using their poncho liner as a blanket. I was awakened by one of my Sergeants, John Copeland, and his voice was unmistaken as he whispered, "Warrant, wake up, but do not move."

My eyes pop open, and daylight is starting to peek through the trees, and I can see the soldiers all lying around me. I turn my head toward Copeland's voice, and he is still whispering, "Do not move. There's a skunk on you." I raise my head just a bit so I could look down along my chest and stomach, and there standing on me is a skunk. It didn't not seem to notice me, but my eyes must have been as big as saucers. By now, several other soldiers could be heard moving around, wanting to look at what was going on. Copeland was telling them all to stay quiet and not scare the skunk in case it sprayed.

I thought this is it, a skunk will spray me, and the troops will have a good laugh. I tried to remain perfectly still, but every fibre in my body wanted to fling this animal off me quickly and as far away as possible. As I was trying to decide what to do, the skunk looked me straight in my eyes, casually walked across my chest down onto the ground and slowly walked away as if this was just an everyday occurrence. I would have many more close contacts with animals over the years, but this one was my first, and it was something that the soldiers were able to laugh about for a long time afterwards.

The second incident occurred a few weeks later, during a Company-level exercise. It happened when it had been raining, and Petawawa lived up to its reputation as being infested with mosquitoes and bugs. The troops were given lots of bug spray, but nothing seemed to help. Petawawa, like most of Ontario, has a tick problem. I already knew this because, as pet owners, we were always careful to check our animals and found ticks on several occasions.

The exercise lasted about five days, and then it was back to CFB Petawawa. After accounting for our kit, it was home for a well-deserved rest and some comfortable, sound sleep. I got home late in the evening and, after kissing the kids goodnight, I headed upstairs for a shower and then to spend some quality time with Julie. As I was scrubbing the dirt off my body, I noticed what felt like a zit or pimple on the side of my penis. After several attempts to squish it, I left it and continued with my shower.

When I exited the bathroom wearing only a towel, Julie asked me how I was feeling and if I had injured myself in the field. I told her I was fine, but I did mention the pimple on my penis. She, of course, wanted to see. As she got close enough to get a good look, she let out a laugh and said that it was a tick. I thought she was kidding, but she assured me she was not. After a couple of attempts and a little pain, Julie emerged successfully with a live tick crawling across her hand. It gave me the creeps, but I was glad it was gone.

From that day forward, every time I was in the field, I would be checking myself over from head to toe for hidden creatures. I don't know what it is about me and animals, but the skunk and the tick were only two of several experiences that have left me wondering if I have done something to deserve this treatment from animals. I have always loved animals, and as a kid, I grew up around horses, sheep, cattle and cats and dogs. Other than being stepped on when I fell off our old horse Max, my childhood, as far as animals were concerned, was normal.

RESERVE SOLDIERS

It was probably in late spring or early summer of 1997 that we started hearing that we would be taking a certain percentage of reservists with us to Bosnia. One Monday morning, I saw that about a hundred and fifty of them were formed up in the Drill Hall. As I walked by, I stopped for a look, as did many other soldiers in the Battalion.

PART TWO - PEACEMAKING

Some of our soldiers were concerned because they had heard that the reservists would be given priority to go overseas, even if it meant leaving a Regular Force soldier behind. This rumour did not go over well with the soldiers, and the senior officers and NCOs all tried to ease the tension. They let our soldiers know that this was very unlikely to happen, simply because there were so many positions to fill.

As I looked over the Reservists, I noticed they were a mix of officers, senior NCOs, and lots of soldiers. There were four or five female soldiers as well, which was still an uncommon sight in the infantry.

I don't believe I had any prejudices about having women in my Platoon, but it was certainly not something for which I was asking. I thought the chances of receiving one of the female soldiers was pretty low, given that they would be spread across the Battalion.

The Officer Commanding and CSM told us that the reservists would be reporting into their assigned companies following PT, and we would then know who would be with each Platoon. We were told to be back at 1000 hours.

At 0955 hours, I had my Platoon formed up with the remainder of Charles Company, waiting for the reservists. As they came into our area, the Sergeant Major had them form up in a group on the left flank of the Company. I immediately noticed that there were four female soldiers in the group, and I thought it was strange that four out of the five female soldiers I saw would come to our Company. I expected that I might get one of them in my platoon. I wasn't really concerned.

Once everyone was in place, MWO Derek Ingersoll started calling out names and sending them to their respective Platoons or Company HQ. I was in for a bit of a surprise when I looked at the ten soldiers coming toward 7 Platoon. All four females were with them.

I kind of glanced over toward MWO Derek Ingersoll, and he had a tiny mischievous grin on his face, even though he told me later that day that he had just called the names in order from the top of the list for each platoon. It was just a coincidence.

I do not believe in coincidences, and I knew that this had been intentional.

I remember keeping my Platoon on parade after the Company had been dismissed, as I wanted to set the right tone, starting at that moment. I no longer remember the exact words I used that day, but I clearly remember that the message was to remind everyone that we were now a team. It didn't matter what headdress you wore or what unit you were originally from—we were all Charles Company. I expected everyone to be treated the same.

I also told everyone that we had a lot of strenuous training ahead. Everyone needed to perform at the required standard, or they would not be coming with us to Bosnia. I then told them that none of our positions were confirmed yet, so everyone needed to do their best. I then set up times over the next few hours to personally meet with each of the reservists. It would give each of them a chance to tell me about themselves. More importantly, it was an opportunity for me to introduce myself to them.

One of the soldiers that had arrived was a reserve Sergeant who I'll call "Jones".

He was from a reserve unit in Toronto, and he was wearing a maroon beret as he was a jumper. As I spoke to each of the young soldiers, I told them exactly what I expected from them and that they would be treated like everyone else in the platoon. I also told them that they needed to bring it forward immediately through their chain of command if there were any issues.

When I spoke to Sergeant Jones, my message was a little different. As a Sergeant, my expectations for him were much higher than for the troops. I expected him to act like a senior NCO and to lead his troops. He seemed confident and told me he had been attached to the Canadian Airborne Regiment during the Somalia deployment. He believed he was ready to be an infantry section commander.

Sergeant Jones would turn out to be a big disappointment. Even though we gave him every opportunity to show improvement, he was never able to provide us with the confidence we needed to believe he could take his Section in theatre, lead them and give them every opportunity to come home alive.

I saw him just do silly things at first. On morning PT, when we were running as a Platoon, he would make sure he was right at the front and not where he could be checking on his soldiers. He was more worried about how he looked and making sure he did not fall back.

On exercise in Petawawa, the weather was in the minus teens and very damp. I noticed that Sergeant Jones always seemed to be overly tired or looking for an excuse to be in the vehicle with the heater on. On about the third night, I walked around at about 0100 hours, checking on security and talking with the soldiers on sentry, when I noticed a small light in one of the section vehicles. The policy was clear; no one slept in the vehicles. So, when I looked inside and saw Jones curled up, sleeping in the corner with his parka wrapped around him, I was a little surprised.

I banged on the vehicle to get his attention. When he saw me, he started whining about not feeling well, so he crawled in the vehicle to be away from the troops and try to rest. I took him at his word and told him to see the Company Medic in the morning if he was still feeling ill. In the meantime, he should remain in the vehicle and try to stay warm.

A few minutes later, when I was speaking with a couple of soldiers manning an observation post, I mentioned in passing that their Sergeant was sick.

"I'm not surprised," one of the soldiers said, "seeing as he didn't bring his winter sleeping kit."

I asked the young soldier to explain, and he said that Sergeant Jones had not brought his sleeping bag, liner or poncho. I went back to see him and asked about his kit. He said he did not think he would need it because it was not supposed to be very cold. I asked him what he would have done if one of his soldiers had requested to leave their sleeping kit behind? He said that would be their choice.

I was not happy with him and reminded him that it was his job to make sure his soldiers were prepared to live tactically in the field and that, in this case, he could not even look after himself. The following day, I placed Sergeant Jones on verbal warning. I

PART TWO - PEACEMAKING

had him sign the document and warned him that he needed to start acting like a Senior Non-Commissioned Member and look after his soldiers and himself, or I would not be taking him with us to Bosnia. He looked shocked to be signing something negative, but I hoped it would sort him out.

The next day, Major Coombs came to see me and said that he had some good news and bad news for me. Which did I want first?

"Give me the good news," I said.

He told me that I was getting a Platoon Commander that day.

"That's good news?" I enjoyed being the Platoon Commander, but my role was really the Second-in-Command, and I did not want to do both jobs. I then asked for the bad news, and he said that my Platoon Commander was a reservist. I did not necessarily consider it bad news, as I was fine with whoever came, as long as they could do the job.

That afternoon, I was introduced to Captain Fred Moore, a reservist from Toronto. He had little experience and no operational tours. I shook hands with him, and then we went inside the Platoon Headquarters vehicle to talk alone. I told him I would be very frank with him, and I wanted him to listen to what I had to say carefully.

I don't remember my exact words, but I told him that 7 Platoon was mine, that I would still be here long after he had moved on and that I was not going to let him fuck us around. I told him that I had lots of experience. Major Coombs had been fine with me taking the Platoon to Bosnia as their commander, as he had lots of faith in me. If he wanted to get through this intact, he needed to listen to what I say and talk to me before making decisions. I then told him that if he followed those simple rules, I would look after him and we would get through this together.

I told him not to mistake my little chat as taking control, as there was no doubt in my mind about him being the commander and me being his Second-in-Command, but this needed to be a team effort for it to work. He looked like he was unsure how to react but said he was good with that plan. I then briefed him on the Platoon and some of its interesting characters and then took him around the position and introduced him to the soldiers.

Captain Moore did listen to me most of the time. When he decided to go it on his own, more often than not, he received the wrath of the Company Commander for messing something up. At the same time as Captain Moore was getting chewed out, the CSM would pull me aside and, with that sly grin he always seemed to have on his face, tell me to get a grip on my commander.

I was happy with the performance of most of our soldiers and NCOs during training so far, but Sergeant Jones continued to be a pain in my ass.

RELIEF OF A SECTION COMMANDER

As part of that winter exercise, Charles Company was tasked to seize a significant bridge between the warring sides. It had been taken over by a belligerent force that had wired it with explosives. Our task was to take control of the bridge and make sure it was not destroyed, as we needed it for future operations.

The plan was developed over several hours and was rehearsed until we were happy that we could get the task done.

We moved by foot all night, with our armoured vehicles taking a different route and remaining a couple of miles away from the objective. Before first light, we had all our folks in position, including a covering force of machine-guns and mortars. The Company advanced toward the bridge along the river with two platoons up front and one in depth. 7 Platoon was on the right side of the river, and we had Sergeant Jones and his Section closest to the water. We had divers in the river, whose job was to get to the bridge unseen and cut the wires to the explosives before we attacked, as it was paramount that the bridge is saved.

It was still dark, and the bridge was just coming into view when we stopped the advance to allow the divers to move silently down the river to the bridge and complete their task. There was complete silence and, from my position directly behind 7 Platoon, I could see the divers pass by and then, suddenly, I heard splashing and grunting and some muffled yells.

What the heck was going on? Had the divers been spotted and, if so, why had we not been fired upon?

Captain Moore kept the rest of the platoon still, and I moved as quietly as possible to the river's edge, where I saw a scuffle going on in the river.

"What's going on?" I asked.

The nearest soldier said that Sergeant Jones had jumped into the river and attacked the diver. I waded into the edge of the river and yelled for Jones to get back onshore. He looked at me standing there in the cold icy water in the dark and walked back to land. I asked the diver if he was alright and got an affirmative.

"That guy is freaking nuts," said the diver, "and he's lucky to be alive."

The divers continued with their task, and I knelt directly in front of this young, soaking wet and shivering Sergeant and asked him what he was doing. His response was confusing.

"I spotted an enemy diver in the water, so I jumped on him."

I just shook my head and said, "They're friendly, you dumb ass."

It was in the orders, and we had rehearsed it. But he just shook his head as if he did not understand.

The attack was about to start, so there was little to be done at this time. I told him that we would get him dry and warm once we had seized the bridge. The attack was successful despite Sergeant Jones effort to the contrary.

Once we were in control, I had the Jones vehicle come forward and had him get in the back. I had them crank up the heat to dry him off and avoid hypothermia or worse. He was so cold he could hardly walk or talk when he got in the vehicle.

Captain Moore and I located the diver from 2 Canadian Engineer Regiment to get his side of the story. He said when they received word to get in the river and move

PART TWO - PEACEMAKING

to the bridge, they did so. Because of the depth of the water, they were using snorkels. As they passed the lead Platoon, he heard a splash and then someone jumped on his back. He said that they rolled around in the water several times. He was panicking and was about to reach for his diver's knife when the individual got off him.

I realized how serious the situation had been when he said, "If he hadn't gotten off me when he did, I was prepared to stick my knife in whoever this crazy fuck was."

I huddled together with Captain Moore, and we discussed what should happen to Jones. I was pleased when the Captain recommended that Jones sign another warning, and that he would request he was returned to his Reserve Unit. It was exactly what I was thinking. I told him I supported his decision and suggested he discuss this with Major Coombs while I went to speak with the CSM.

An hour later, while still holding the bridge, we had Sergeant Jones pack up whatever personal kit he had brought with him, pass on all the section kit to his Second-in-Command, and he was relieved of command.

The remainder of our time in training went by quickly and, before we knew it, we were finalizing our company and platoon-manning list. Besides one reserve Sergeant and a Master Corporal who were moved to Bravo Company, the remainder of the team stayed together, including the four females, which sometimes got us called Charlie's Angels or Johnny's Angels.

One of the young Reserve women whom we will call Private Sacks was the most difficult one to get ready for deployment. She was small in stature, very girly and did not like to get dirty or work excessively hard to the point of sweating. I had many one-way conversations with her, and the one positive that I always walked away with was that she never quit. I could tell sometimes she got angry with me or even at herself, but she always kept her cool and walked away.

I remember one incident where she was not on parade on a Monday morning following a weekend on leave at home in Toronto. Finally, around 1000 hours after we had checked with hospitals, jails and her friends, she came strolling in. She was brought straight to my office. I had her stand at attention and read her rights before questioning her. When I asked her to tell me what happened, she reached into her pocket and handed me a handwritten note from her mother. The letter said that the mother had arranged a ride back to Petawawa from Toronto for her daughter. The individual had let them down, that they were unable to get her a different ride last night, so she could not leave until early this morning. It ended by saying that the mother was sorry and to forgive her daughter.

After I finished laughing, I started yelling at Private Sacks about taking personal responsibility for her life and that she was not a child. I told her that if she couldn't be on time here, she should perhaps stay behind. Private Sacks was charged and marched in front of Major Coombs by the Sergeant Major. She was found guilty of being Absent Without Leave and was given a fine.

I had hoped that this would be the turning point for Sacks, but it was not.

12

BOSNIA

Following Christmas leave with our families, I departed Canada on December 29, 1997, as part of the Company Advance Party and arrived the next day as part of SFOR, or the " Stabilization Force in Bosnia and Herzegovina."

I was driven to the town of Drvar and then onto the main camp, commonly referred to by those of us living there as Pigeon Palace. The camp was centered around an abandoned flour factory that had several floors. The top floor had been home to hundreds of pigeons for a long time, hence our nickname, Pigeon Palace. The other floors were used as living quarters for the Company Headquarters and the Platoons. Drvar is a town in Western Bosnia and Herzegovina in a valley in Southwestern Krajina. This was a very hilly and mountainous area covering over a thousand kilometers. Drvar itself is about 120 kilometers from Croatia.

On August 3, 1995, the Croatian Army and Bosnian Croats started shelling Drvar from the mountains, killing two citizens. This started an evacuation of civilians. Almost immediately, the Croatian Government Armed Forces began Operation Storm, a military operation. The shelling on the outlying areas of Drvar by Croatian forces continued for many days. In late 1995, after the Dayton Peace Accord was signed, Drvar became part of the Federation of Bosnia and Herzegovina. Croatian politicians persuaded up to six thousand Bosnian Croats, mainly displaced from central Bosnia, to move to Drvar, promising them jobs and vacant homes, mostly belonging to Serbs who had been forced to leave. A large contingent of Croatian troops and their families were stationed there, occupying the homes of displaced Bosnian Serb citizens. This action drastically changed the population from mostly Serb before the war to almost all Croatian now. It was in this situation that I found myself on New Year's Eve of 1997. I was welcomed to my new home for the next six months with thousands of rounds of tracers being fired from machine guns, mostly celebrating the New Year, but

PART TWO - PEACEMAKING

I am sure some were neighbors against neighbors.

CHARLES COMPANY

The rest of Charles Company and the remainder of 7 Platoon arrived in early January 1998. Drvar and the area around it was beginning to have significant issues between the Croats living and running the town now and the minority Serbs who either remained in place or were trying to return to their occupied homes.

On January 10, Charles Company started aggressive patrolling with a 24/7 routine. The patrols had staggered timings so that there was no way to figure out when a patrol was going to be out and in what area. During the handover with the former occupants, we were told that things had quieted down recently and there was lots of free time. We quickly discovered that there was no free time, and we did not have the time or the troops to carry out the mission the way we would have liked.

Very soon after the complete Company was situated in Drvar, we had our first significant snowfall. Many of the mountain passes, as well as some of the local routes, were closed. It affected our ability to patrol all our areas of responsibility. It also made it impossible for the rest of the Battle Group on the other side of the mountain to visit us.

That was a good thing! Not having to put up with VIPs and other dignitaries allowed us to relax just a little bit, especially while hanging out at the camp.

The remainder of January was a steady rhythm of patrolling and trying to meet with some of the locals and get their feelings and opinions on how things were going. Depending on whom you spoke to would define the information you received. A small number of Serbs had refused to leave their homes during the war and remained through all the harassment and intimidation, including widespread looting and having their houses burned down.

In February, the snow was gone, and there was unseasonably warm weather. It increased the numbers of displaced persons, primarily Bosnian Serbs, who were trying to return to their homes in Drvar. Most of their houses were now occupied by Bosnian Croats who themselves had been displaced from Serb areas and were persuaded to come to Drvar with the promise of homes and jobs. The Bosnian Croat opposition to the returning Serbs was extreme and culminated in riots and murders. Buildings and houses were torched. Two elderly Serbs who had recently returned to Drvar were murdered.

During this time of very intense feelings between the two ethnic groups, we started Operation NERO. There were more fires in Drvar during this time than there had been during the L.A. riots. Charles Company did not have the workforce to patrol all the volatile areas and try to stop the fires. The Battle Group responded, and the population of Camp Drvar grew by 30%. Operation NERO involved increased patrolling and resulted in many long hours and days for all the platoons.

This operation was noteworthy for a couple of reasons. The first was the number of resources that were made available to Drvar. Once the Division Commander decided that this operation would be his priority, assets started showing up immediately. Among the many items that we received were several helicopters, one equipped with a Night Sun, the number one searchlight for law enforcement and the best in the world. There was also P-3 Orion reconnaissance aircraft constantly monitoring the town of Drvar.

The second reason that the operation was noteworthy was the unprecedented number of high-ranking visitors interested in Drvar and what was going on here. Among our guests was the Supreme Allied Commander Europe. The most enjoyable thing about his visit was watching all his security guys running around trying to look cool, not being happy with the layout of our camp and the helicopter-landing zone.

They tried to get a little pushy with some of my guys, but as I told the one security guy, "You are now in my camp. Don't expect my guys to get out of your way or stay out of the kitchen area while you secure it. It's already secure."

As the same guy was rushing down the steps before the Commander departed, he dropped his rifle and, when he bent down to get it, his $200 sunglasses fell off. Of course, some of my folks laughed. He was not impressed, but I just shrugged at him and smiled.

Despite all of our efforts, Drvar still looked like a town that had been bombed and burned for months. Sadly, most of the damage to the town hadn't happened during the war, but in the ethnic violence afterwards. Unemployment was sky high, but people came back to the town because it was the only home they knew.

To demonstrate NATO's resolve to provide a peaceful environment despite this chaos, Charles Company was tasked in early April to participate in Exercise Dynamic Response. It was a test and training exercise for NATO's Strategic Reserve to deploy quick-reaction units into Bosnia.

Once again, we had a massive influx of personnel to our little camp in Drvar. We got about two hundred Marines from a U.S. Naval Task Force and a platoon of Polish airborne soldiers. This group of soldiers and Marines augmented Charles Company for about five days, allowing us to increase patrolling of our area substantially. While 9 Platoon worked exclusively with the Poles, 7 and 8 Platoons worked with the Americans.

We deployed outside the camp and into a Patrol Base to conduct combined Canadian and American patrols. Even though the Americans were very professional, other than their NCOs and officers, most were young and inexperienced. I believe we learned from each other, and they were very keen to be involved in operations after floating around on a ship for several weeks. It was the first time for many of my soldiers to work with Marines. The experience was great for both sides.

A LESSON FOR AN OFFICER

I had the opportunity during these combined operations to influence Captain Moore

PART TWO - PEACEMAKING

about what I deemed to be a bad decision, and to remind him of our initial conversation many months earlier in Petawawa. And at the same time, I learned a valuable lesson about my own leadership style and what an ass I could be. We were deployed outside Camp Drvar for a couple of days and even with a platoon of American Marines we were still having difficulty monitoring our whole area of operation. With soldiers away on leave, the multitude of internal tasks in Drvar and the platoon being only at 30% strength, we were being stretched to the breaking point. We set up our Platoon HQ next to a burned-out home and all our headquarters personnel took shifts manning the radios in order to monitor the sections while they were on patrol. About thirty-six hours later we received a message from our higher headquarters directing Captain Moore to return to Camp Drvar for new orders. He took the platoon jeep and headed back to camp while the remainder of the platoon under my command continued with the mission. I sent our combined Canadian and American patrols out into the most volatile areas to show a strong presence to the locals as well as to any bad guys.

A couple of hours later Captain Moore returned, and I gathered the American and Canadian leaders together to receive new orders. He explained that the operation would end at first light the following day, but we were to increase our patrolling until then. We were also directed to start thinning out our non-essential kit and return it to Camp Drvar before dark. He also gave us some information on specific individuals we were to keep an eye out for while patrolling, as well as some mundane stuff on our redeployment to camp. On completion of orders, I directed the section seconds-in-command to have all the kit that needed to be returned early ready to go within the hour. I would be along to pick it up with a truck.

As I was about to leave, Captain Moore pulled me aside to pass on one more piece of information. He said that the Battle Group was looking for a section of soldiers to assist in security at the main camp and that our platoon had been tasked to provide them. I let him know immediately that I was not happy about this and reminded him that of the three platoons in the company, we had the least number of soldiers available. I also told him that we had completed the last company task and that it should have been someone else's turn. Captain Moore said that he had explained that to Major Coombs, but it had not changed his mind. I once again let Captain Moore know that I was angry by letting out a flurry of curses as I walked towards the platoon truck. At least Captain Moore had stood up for the soldiers and tried to get the task changed.

A couple of hours later the driver and I pulled into Camp Drvar with our excess heaters, rations, and water. As we pulled up to the unloading area I saw the Company Sergeant Major, Master Warrant Officer Derek Ingersoll, standing by the HQ. I waved to him as we pulled in and parked. I directed the driver to start unloading the truck and I wandered over to speak with the Sergeant Major about the section task as I was still fuming. As I approached him, he smiled.

"I figured you'd be pissed," he said. "I told Major Coombs that you wouldn't be very happy that Captain Moore had volunteered one of your sections for the Battle Group task."

WHITE SCHOOL, BLACK MEMORIES

I just stared at him, and he could tell that I wasn't aware of that part of the story.

"I guess he forgot to tell you that," said Derek with a grin. He then pulled a small piece of paper out of his pocket and handed it to me. Written on the note was "Barnes will be pissed". As Captain Moore was volunteering our section, he handed this note to the Company Quartermaster who was sitting next to him, and they both nodded and smiled. He was right, I was not happy.

I yelled over to the driver to finish unloading and five minutes later we were rolling back towards our platoon headquarters. I don't think I spoke one word the whole way back and when we pulled into our area, I jumped out and immediately looked for Captain Moore. Everyone in the area knew something was up.

"Let's talk," I said to Captain Moore when I found him. He followed me around the side of the house, and I immediately got in his face. I told him that I knew he'd lied to me and carried on from there. I ranted and raved for another minute or so and finished by telling him that he needed to go back to camp and speak to Major Coombs to get the task changed.

Captain Moore didn't say anything, he just nodded and headed to the jeep. After he'd left, I had a moment of reflection and immediately knew that I hadn't handled it very well. Captain Moore may have come into the platoon with little experience, but he'd come a long way. He didn't deserve to be disrespected as I'd just done. After telling several soldiers and Marines that were standing around listening to our interaction to get back to work, I took a moment to collect myself.

I know that Major Coombs and Captain Moore had a long and thoughtful conversation, and the task was rescinded. For that, I was happy. When Captain Moore returned, he pulled me aside and apologized for his actions and I also apologized to him for how I'd handled the situation. We shook hands and got back to running a platoon on operations.

I believe that we both learned some valuable lessons from this incident and in the end we were better soldiers, and better men as well.

As is the practice for Canadians on operations, we inserted a leave plan within the operational timeline. Many soldiers planned their leave in a location other than Canada and had their families meet them in Germany, Thailand or wherever. I decided to return to Petawawa and spend time with my family there, as well as taking a short trip to the Dominican Republic with Julie and the kids. My holidays were very relaxing, and it was an excellent opportunity to spend time with loved ones and to have no contact with the unit. Unlike leave periods of the future where I would spend almost all my time watching the news or calling the unit to see how things were going, that holiday was all about family time. Like all good things, my leave period ended too soon. Before I knew it, I was saying goodbye to Julie, JJ, and Jana again and heading back to the terrible situation in Bosnia.

Things had not changed very much during my absence. There was still the ongoing conflict between the Croats who had made Drvar their own and the Serbs who wanted to return to homes that their adversaries now occupied. While I was away, Sergeant

PART TWO - PEACEMAKING

Coughlin, one of my Section Commanders, had been tasked to replace me as the acting Platoon Second-in-Command and was very eager to turn things back over to me. He briefed me on a few incidents that I needed to be aware of and gave me an updated brief on the tactical situation in Drvar. At the end of his brief, he said there was one other thing he needed to tell me.

Sometimes it seemed like there was always one more thing.

AN INCIDENT OVER A HELMET

Sergeant Coughlin asked me if I had noticed anything missing out of my bed space, located in a separate area from the remainder of the platoon. I said that I had only thrown my bag in there and had not really looked around. He then told me that Captain Moore had gone in there a week earlier, even though he had told him not to. He had taken my helmet and had been wearing it even as late as an hour ago. I thought this was a little strange, as he had his own helmet. Sergeant Coughlin told me that Captain Moore had somehow lost his helmet on patrol and said he needed to borrow mine. I went into my bedroom, and sure enough, my helmet was missing. I went across the hall and into Captain Moore's bedroom, which was also the platoon office. There he was, all smiles, welcoming me back.

Straight away, I asked him where my helmet was. His face went white and he just looked at me. I assume he was terrified that I was going to yell at him again, especially after our incident a few weeks earlier. He pointed to the corner of the room where I saw my helmet sitting on his kit. I went and put it on my head, and it went all the way down over my ears. He not only took my helmet without permission, but he had adjusted it to fit his head.

After three weeks with my family, I was relaxed and in a good mood. I also was remembering the lesson I learned a few weeks earlier when I had been very unprofessional towards Captain Moore, and so I didn't yell or scream. I just asked Sergeant Coughlin, who was standing inside the door enjoying this uncomfortable moment, to leave. As the door closed, leaving Captain Moore and me alone, he once again started to look uncomfortable and started to apologize. I just stopped him and asked him what was going on. He told me that he had been on patrol in the vehicle and that they had dismounted to speak with the locals. After getting back in the vehicle, he had placed his helmet on the back hatch to put on his soft cap so he could use the headset for the radio. He thought he must have left it there, and when they got back to camp, it was gone.

They had gone back along the route but could not find the helmet, which was probably now on the head of a local kid. I told him that he had been careless but that it was not the end of the world. Once he had reported it lost, he should have gotten a replacement, even if it meant paying for the old one, which was less than $150. What he told me next caused me to have to hold my anger. He hadn't reported the helmet missing, even though it was an essential piece of personal kit required for safety. He then went on to say that he was avoiding telling the CQ because WO Grant Gervais was going to be angry with him. I knew that the CQ could be very tough to deal with, but he still needed to sort this out. He needed to go immediately and report the helmet missing.

WO Grant Gervais was a massive man with arms and legs the size of tree trunks who worked out like there was no tomorrow. He was intimidating to a lot of people, not just Captain Moore. Grant could be very intense, but he was a genuinely nice guy who, like myself, could be a little rough around the edges at times. Captain Moore timidly approached the CQ area, and I stood back, watching the show. Other than a few colorful comments towards Captain Moore about being a dumbass, it went very well. After the paperwork was done, a new helmet appeared. Once again, Captain Moore learned a valuable lesson. Afterwards during a light moment, I told Captain Moore that I would break his fingers if he touched any of my kit again.

Captain Fred Moore arrived in Petawawa as a young inexperienced Reserve Officer. He took command of a regular force Infantry Platoon with a strong-willed Platoon Second-in-Command. He took this responsibility very seriously and, after some bumps in the road, was very successful. Even though the Charles Company Command Team expected me to make sure he was prepared and ready to lead us, I learned as much from him as he did from me. I saw Captain Moore several times over the next couple of decades and it was always nice to shake his hand and tell some stories. He went on to have a very successful military career, eventually commanding his Reserve unit. Every time I saw him over the years, his smile never failed to brighten up a room.

OPERATION HAMLYN

Almost as soon as the Quick Reaction Force departed, we started Operation HAMLYN.

We knew for weeks that the international community had been talking about bringing in many displaced Serbs back to Drvar, their home before the war. Finally, after exhaustive talks lasting for months, it was going to happen. We knew that this was not going to be easy. The Croats now living in the former homes of the Serbs were not going to give them up without a fight. We were going to be in the middle.

The Company started planning for the return of approximately one hundred and eighty Serbs to the downtown area of Drvar. We started increasing our presence downtown while the international community started preparing the present population for what was to come. Two apartment buildings were cleared and readied for the returning Serbs. Once again, other elements of the Battle Group arrived in our camp to assist and increase our presence.

Things seemed to be going very well for the next few weeks as preparations continued for the Serb's arrival. Then the lid was blown off, and the tensions exploded into the open. We started hearing rumours about massive protests being planned for

PART TWO - PEACEMAKING

arrival day, and we started seeing an increase in incidents between the locals and SFOR.

On April 28, a mob protesting injustices being committed to the Bosnian Croats stormed the municipal building in downtown Drvar. As our soldiers arrived to intervene, the mob grew from seventy people to several hundred in minutes, showing that it was a pre-planned event. The mob destroyed the offices of the NGOs working there. They then moved to the building that had housed the HVO, the Bosnian Croat military, but would now be the new home of the Serb returnees.

The Battle Group had left our mortar platoon in that location, and they had the initial task of holding back the angry mob until reinforcements from Charles Company could arrive. We immediately sent about fifty soldiers to assist, and the Company soldiers held their ground. At the same time, the rest of Camp Drvar—including our cooks, clerks, medics, and any other available support troops—were mobilized to act as reinforcements, if needed, to extract the returnees. Every soldier on the ground that day placed themselves between the mob and the Serb returnees and undoubtedly saved many lives.

While the mob was being held back, Company HQ and 8 Platoon were organizing the extraction of all foreign personnel, as their safety could no longer be guaranteed. Everyone had to work together, and they were dispatched to several areas where there was the potential for things to become deadly. In all cases, the foreign folks were happy to see friendly Canadian soldiers help them.

After that terrifying day, the population of Camp Drvar was never the same. The camp population more than doubled to four hundred people overnight, and it was no longer exclusively Charles Company living there. The larger force was needed to help provide a stable environment for everyone in the area, whether they agreed to it or not.

Visits to the camp became quite common. The relaxed and comfortable camp that Drvar had become had turned into a patrol base for the entire international community. Our platoon continued to soldier on and did our part to ensure the area was peaceful. Once the area was safe enough to get back to a routine, we gave the returning Serbs an opportunity to decide if they wanted to stay or leave. Those who chose to leave were taken back to the Banja Luka area and the Republic of Serbia.

I believe that most of us went into this deployment expecting a quiet tour and lots of free time; however, it quickly became one of the busiest tours I have ever been on.

In many ways, that was a good thing.

RSM BOBBY HODGSON

There were a few more memorable moments from the tour that I believe need to be told. One was the loss of our beloved RSM, CWO Robert (Bobby) Hodgson. He was a warrior who stood only 5 feet, 7 inches tall. He was an iconic figure, immensely powerful both in strength and character. He was respected by all the soldiers and officers alike. He was a very calm man who was equally relaxed when speaking with either a private or a general, yet he could also be very stern. He never demanded respect because it was given to him naturally. He was a genuine outdoorsman who loved to show his skills with a rifle or an axe and was a leader who never expected a soldier to do anything that he would not do himself.

I know that the people closest to him knew that he was having some medical issues during the early days of our deployment. Finally, he could no longer ignore it, and he had to return to Ottawa to be seen by a doctor. The news was the worst, and CWO Bobby Hodgson would not be able to return to join his beloved Battle Group. The Drill Sergeant Major would be promoted to Chief and replace Bobby Hodgson in theatre. Mr. Hodgson was diagnosed with cancer. Even though he would walk into our drill hall a few months later and speak with the Battalion, he could never reclaim his position as our Regimental Sergeant Major. A few months later, in November 1999, CWO Bobby Hodgson would leave us for good after fighting a great fight. He may be gone, but he will always be remembered. Rest in Peace, brother!

CORPORAL RONNIE ANDERSON

As mentioned earlier, 7 Platoon was lucky to have a genuinely diverse group of people. It made us the best Platoon in the Battle Group and allowed us to be successful.

One of those soldiers was a young man named Ron Anderson, born in 1974 in Lahr, Germany, while his father had been serving there. Ronnie would continue to serve the Canadian Forces and Canada for twenty-one years before retiring. In 2014, Ron Anderson would take his own life and join the list of many Canadian soldiers who have committed suicide after being diagnosed with Post Traumatic Stress Disorder. Ronnie had completed seven tours overseas, including two in Afghanistan.

That, however, was all in the future.

In 1998, Corporal Ronnie Anderson was in my Platoon. He was a character that always brought a smile to my face, even when, at times, he made me mad. I remember in September 1997, while holding a platoon parade in 1 RCR area, I told my soldiers that, because tomorrow was the first day of the new school year, those with young children could come into work late the next morning if they wanted to go to school with their kids. I asked all those coming in late to raise their hands to make a note of it for the next morning's parade. Only a few soldiers raised their hands, and then I noticed Corporal Anderson's hand up. I knew he had no kids, so I asked him why he had raised his hand, and without missing a beat, he said, "I would like to walk your kids to school, Warrant."

I wanted to be angry with him, but when I saw the sly grin on his face, I just said, "Fuck off, Anderson." Everyone laughed.

During one of our exercises after the Reservists had arrived, there was another incident with Ronnie. Once again, I was unable to be angry about it. It was around dusk, and we were on a narrow trail in our Grizzly armoured vehicles in the middle of a field when Anderson tried to get my attention. He was in the commander's hatch of the vehicle because the Platoon Commander was preparing to dismount. I was

PART TWO - PEACEMAKING

standing in the back in the air sentry hatch.

I was facing the rear when Anderson said something like, "Warrant, Nortel wants you." Master Corporal Nortel was another of the female reservists attached to my platoon, and she was in the vehicle in front of us. After Anderson yelled at me that Nortel wanted me, I turned around, and he was pointing to the front of our vehicle. I leaned out and looked forward. Nortel was squatting beside the trail with her drawers around her ankles peeing, and I was looking directly at her. She looked up and saw me, quickly jumped up, fixed her clothes, and got in her vehicle.

Corporal Anderson and a couple of other soldiers, including our driver, were all bursting out laughing and once again, I was probably mad, but it was so funny that I just laughed and said, "Good one, Anderson."

I could only imagine what Master Corporal Nortel was thinking. Something like: "The creepy Platoon WO was spying on me while I was peeing." Even worse, I had just recently talked with the whole platoon about respecting everyone's privacy. Because we were all together, men and women, it was even more critical.

I jumped out of my vehicle and walked forward to Nortel' vehicle and pulled her aside. I apologized for what had happened and told her that I had not been intentionally watching her. I never mentioned to her that Anderson had tricked me into looking, as that did not seem appropriate at the time.

I did get Anderson back several months later in Pigeon Palace. The platoon started playing tricks on each other in their sleeping area, things like putting boots in the bottom of someone's sleeping bag or gun taping the opening to the bag with an entire roll of tape.

The Section Commanders came to see me about sending a message to stay out of other people's sleeping areas because they were concerned that this would get out of hand since we were living in such close proximity to each other. I spoke to the platoon and told them this was to stop immediately. If it did not, I would start putting someone on duty in the quarters at night.

While I was returning to camp from a patrol the next day, we stopped to do a navigation check. On the side of the road was a huge cow's skull that had been weathered by the sun from several years of lying around. I threw a small tarp over it and put it in the vehicle without anyone seeing me. When we got to Drvar, I took it to my room, which was separated from the troops.

That evening, during supper, when most people were eating, and Corporal Anderson was on shift at the Company Command Post, I took the head, laid it directly on Corporal Anderson's pillow with a small note that read, "Enjoy. This is the only head you will ever get."

The head was disgusting, and I made sure no one knew that I had anything to do with this. I also knew that there was no chance in hell that anyone would ever think that the Platoon Warrant was responsible for this, especially after I had just threatened the platoon for pulling pranks on each other.

That evening, following his shift, Corporal Anderson came back to his bed to find a cow's skull and note on his pillow. He was furious, and he immediately blamed another prankster in the platoon, Corporal Johnny O'Neill. Both of those guys were friends, but they had been part of the prank patrol for the last week, so he was the first culprit that Anderson thought of. O'Neill obviously denied it, and Anderson started blaming other folks in the platoon, all of whom were innocent.

The pranking got worse after that. I held another platoon meeting and jacked everyone up for the havoc they were causing, especially the dirty bastard who put a disgusting disease-ridden cow's skull on someone's pillow. Anderson often brought up the skull incident and said he would find out who it was and that there would be hell to pay. I never did tell anyone what I had done to Corporal Anderson, and every time Ronnie would bring it up, he would get angry, and I would walk away with a smile on my face.

In 2007, I was on Kandahar Airfield (KAF) in Afghanistan many years later, and I ran into Sergeant Ronnie Anderson. I had not seen him in many years, and we immediately connected again. We went for coffee on the boardwalk, and we talked for a couple of hours. He knew that I had been injured earlier in the tour and had lost some good friends and soldiers. He was genuinely concerned about me.

As we were getting ready to leave, I remember standing in front of him, and I said to him, "Listen, buddy, there is something I want to tell you because I could be dead tomorrow." I then asked him if he remembered the cow's skull in Bosnia many years earlier.

"Of course," he said. "I'm still trying to find out who did it."

I told him that I knew who it was, but I did not tell him back then because I enjoyed the interactions between him and the others.

He smiled. "It was Johnny O'Neill, right?"

"No, it was me."

He just stood there, looked at me and then started to laugh uncontrollably. Then I started laughing, as well. We hugged each other like long-lost brothers, and we wished each other the best. I remember his final words to me as he walked away: "Shit, you got me good."

That was the last time I saw Ronnie Anderson. Rest in peace, brother.

The remainder of the tour in Bosnia was much more of the same, and we spent the last couple of months trying to find a way to protect all those who were being victimized, but we were not always successful as hate will always find a way to persist. In July of 1998, we started our handover, and mid-July found us back home with our families.

There was a month of leave followed by another reorganization of the Battalion, and then it was back to training and preparing for the next operation. The next four or five months were an opportunity for the Battalion to reorganize and get its young soldiers some well-needed courses and training in basic and advanced winter operations.

Then December came around, and it was off to the Christmas holidays.

THE RCR BATTLE SCHOOL

I returned to work in 1 RCR in early January 1999 and was called into the RSM's office for a meeting.

I was asked if I would be interested in a posting to The RCR Battle School in Meaford. I said that training new young infantry soldiers was something I always wanted to do, but I needed to speak to my wife first. I was asked if I could call her right away, as this was a fastball. A Warrant Officer in Meaford had put in his thirty-day release, and they needed a replacement immediately, as a new course would be starting in late February.

I kind of stopped. "So, I would be posted immediately?"

The reply was yes.

I called Julie from work and told her about my discussions with the RSM, and she asked me where Meaford was. I did not know but told her someone had told me it was about a five- or six-hour drive from Petawawa. She said, "If you want to go, so do I, but the kids and I will not be moving until after the school year finishes."

I went back and told the RSM. He told me to come back after he made a phone call, and after only an hour, he told me that I was posted to Meaford and to see the clerks about a posting message.

I was posted a month later and moved into quarters on Imposed Restriction, which meant that quarters and food were free while my family remained in Petawawa. I would have time to do some house-hunting, and my family would move later that summer.

Julie and I started looking for a new home in Meaford and the surrounding area. We did not see anything that was in our price range or to our liking. We finally decided to purchase a piece of land in Meaford and have a home built. We spent a couple of weeks working on a plan and dealing with our real estate agent and the building contractor to ensure we got the house we wanted. We were lucky to find a nice lot on the edge of Meaford in a small subdivision next to the water and a just short walk to Memorial Park.

I was excited about the move, and within a few weeks, I was the Platoon Second-in-Command for a new infantry course. I had always been a good instructor, and I was extremely comfortable speaking in front of people. I thoroughly enjoyed it, so I was able to fit into my new role very quickly.

GETTING INVOLVED

Even before the course started, I decided that I would be involved in all aspects of it. I would put all my time and effort into training these young soldiers, and I would expect the same from my staff. I did, however, have to remind myself several times that I was on IR and, therefore, I was able to spend a lot more time at work because my family was still in Petawawa. However, most of my staff had families and a life in Meaford. They needed to have a routine which saw them at home at a reasonable time each day.

The course staff consisted of a captain as the platoon commander, on loan from a battalion; me, the platoon second-in-command; three sergeants as section commanders; three master corporals as section second-in-commands, a master corporal as the swing NCO and a corporal as a storeman and driver.

I first sat down with the Platoon Commander, and we agreed that this was probably the most important thing we would do in our career. We spoke about our vision for the course, and once we decided, I called in the rest of the staff. I introduced the Platoon Commander and myself, and we gave our backgrounds and experience. Then I spoke for about thirty minutes on how I saw the course being conducted.

I watched their faces as I spoke. I saw a few strange looks from some people, and I noticed a small smile from a few others. Some of these staff had been here doing the job for two, three or even four years, and they believed they were the experts. I was the new guy trying to tell them how to do things. So, I also said to them that I was the new guy and that I would be leaning on them to make sure that I was heading in the right direction, but I would be holding them to a high standard.

The Royal Canadian Regiment did not always post the best people to the Battle School during this time frame. As a result, we sometimes did not get the finest trained soldiers sent to the battalions. I remember hearing many a Sergeant Major and Warrant Officer complaining about how shitty some young soldiers were when they arrived from Meaford. I'm sure I had the same complaint.

Posting staff to the battle school was one of those jobs that RSMs never really paid much attention to until they needed to get rid of someone. Many young sergeants and warrant officers who got on the wrong side of the RSM found themselves posted to the school or elsewhere. Also, some of the staff that ended up at the Battle School fought to stay there longer than they should.

I believed that staff should remain at the school for only three years but a maximum

PART TWO - PEACEMAKING

of four. Then, they needed to be posted back to a battalion. I noticed some of the staff that had been at the School for five or even six years had become very bitter about the process and the recruits. They no longer had credibility with some of the newer staff because they had been away from a battalion too long, and so much had changed.

I had one of those sergeants on my first course, and I had several issues with him. He was very disrespectful to the students, was always in a bad mood and did not seem to enjoy what he was doing. I also noticed that the students never approached him or asked him questions. I always impressed upon my staff that any soldier should feel comfortable enough to come and ask them any question. If they noticed that the students were not approaching them, they needed to have a look in the mirror.

I remember reading somewhere, perhaps in General Colin Powell's book on leadership, that the day that soldiers stop bringing you their problems is the day you stopped leading them. They have either lost confidence that you can help them or concluded that you do not care. Either case is a failure of leadership.

During the first several weeks of training, the students were confined to barracks and had to meet a certain standard within the quarters and their personal kit to gain their freedom. We had a marching NCO, a section commander or second-in-command in the quarters 24/7 during this time. Their job was to supervise the students and make sure they were prepared for all the upcoming inspections.

Early on, I believed that the course was not aligned correctly and that too much emphasis was placed on kit and quarters. I thought that three weeks was long enough to be confined to barracks and more than enough time for gear and quarters. I started having the marching NCO redo some training at night to emphasize the important stuff from that day and make sure the troops understood it. I would rather have the soldiers practicing gas mask drills for an hour than waxing floors for that same hour.

This minor change caused some animosity with the staff, especially those that had been there too long. They looked at their time in the quarters as marching NCOs as a chance to watch movies or sleep. When I left a few years later, the policy had changed, and the troops were confined to barracks for only a few weeks.

The other significant change was that The RCR decided that only the best folks would be sent to the School to ensure the best candidates were graduating. So, they gave extra points on the promotion boards to those who were posted to the school. This change made the RSMs really look at whom they were sending. If they sent their shit birds to the School and the individual did okay, plus got the extra points on the boards, the RSM would not only get the individual back but at a higher rank.

It was in everyone's interest to make sure only the best people were posted to the Schools.

During my four years in Meaford, I did various jobs from the course second-in-command to standards NCO and Company Sergeant Major for a three hundred person company during summer reserve training. My last year was as the Sergeant Major for the newly formed Soldier Qualification Company.

All these jobs brought me a sense of accomplishment. Watching these young men and women go from what we characterized as "flat-face civvies" to become proud, disciplined and professional infantry soldiers and watch them march out on their graduation parade as Royal Canadians was one of the highlights of my career. I learned early on that these young soldiers would look at everything we as instructors said, did or did not do and start emulating it, so we always needed to be professional.

I remember one of the courses that I was running had a Royal Canadian named Sergeant Jack Murphy as one of the section commanders. Jack was one of a kind. He was the epitome of what an infantry soldier should be. He kept his hair shaved short, he was well-muscled, and he was as fit as any soldier I had met. He was a hard charger, and he acted and behaved like a tough son of a bitch.

He did have one habit that I was not happy with; however, some flaws can be overlooked. Jack chewed tobacco, and it was a disgusting habit that sometimes caused us to be at odds. He would chew all the time, and anytime you spoke to him, you could see the wad of chew bulging out from his bottom lip. He would have a can or bottle with him that he would spit in. Many times, I would find the can left on a desk. Sergeant Murphy's section looked up to him, had massive respect for him, and he genuinely cared about his soldiers. He could be seen spending many long hours after others were done still teaching and mentoring.

I had often wished that all my instructors were like Jack Murphy.

We were out on the ranges at about month two of the course, and, after shooting all morning, we stopped for a hay box lunch. It was a beautiful day, and all the staff and students were sitting together in a relaxed and joking mood. I noticed that several soldiers were chewing tobacco, and I knew that none of them had chewed a few weeks earlier. I realized that most of the soldiers chewing were from Sergeant Murphy's section, so I asked Jack to grab all his soldiers to let me speak with them. Jack had no idea why, but he got his guys together. I asked them to raise their hands if they chewed tobacco and, out of his twelve-man section, I believe nine or ten students now chewed.

It was the moment when I realized how much influence we had over these young men and women. From that day and every day since, I always made sure that I, and my NCOs, acted professionally in front of the soldiers. I passionately believed that young impressionable soldiers would follow the good examples, but also the bad ones.

CSM, SOLDIER QUALIFICATION COMPANY

In 2002, I was called into the School Sergeant Major Ben Dufresne's office. He wanted to talk to me about taking over as the Company Sergeant Major for a new Company. I was told that both he and the CO had discussed this in detail. Instead of having a Master Warrant Officer posted to the School out of season, they wanted me to fill that position as a Warrant Officer. I was surprised but excited and said that I would absolutely love the challenge. MWO Stew Hartnell would remain as the CSM for Soldier Skills Company, and I would become the CSM for Soldier Qualification Company.

PART TWO - PEACEMAKING

The following week saw the Company start to come together. We were able to have Base Meaford move some folks around to give us a complete building to house the Company HQ, staff and administration. I asked for and was able to get my old friend WO Dave Patterson moved over from Soldier Skills to be my CQ, and as well we got a couple of permanent drivers. I was also introduced to the Company's Officer Commanding, a Captain Cushman, an artillery officer with lots of experience.

Captain Cushman and I had a couple of weeks to get everything set up before our first staff would arrive, followed by the first students. It was a lot of work, but we were prepared by the time the first course was ready to kick off.

The first course had some typical growing pains with both the content and a couple of the instructors who thought that having a WO as the CSM instead of an MWO meant that they could cut some corners on training and get away with it. They were in for the surprise of their life as they realized that I did the job of the CSM just like I did as the course second-in-command, hands-on and involved.

I showed up unexpectedly at 0200 hours during the defensive exercise to find all the staff sleeping inside one of the buildings used for training and all the students outside in the trenches. It was about -18° C, and I was pissed. I had all the staff get up and gather around. I reminded them that they were not only staff but also filling the roles of section commanders and seconds-in-command. Every section would always have either the commander or second-in-command with them, otherwise who was mentoring and training the students?

I could not tell if they were angrier with me for showing up unexpectedly or the fact that I was telling them the way I wanted it done.

The Platoon WO for the course had been in Meaford for four years and had run several courses already. He started to say, "But this is the way we have always done it."

I stopped him. I said, "Just because you have been doing it wrong for four years does not mean we will continue to do it wrong. I have told you how we are going to do business in this company, and that is the end of discussions."

I could tell he was not happy, and I saw him roll his eyes and kind of shake his head as if to say, "Yea, whatever. Once you are gone, I will decide."

Unluckily for him, I saw the eye roll and called him outside, away from the remainder of the staff. I looked him in the eyes and said, "You have two options: get on board with my decision or go get your kit, get in the truck and you can come back to base with me. I will have one of the Sergeants take over the course." I asked him where the Course Officer was and was totally caught off guard when he said he had gone into base for the night. He explained that he or his officer went in each night, as well as one of the section commanders and one second-in-command, and they would switch day on and day off. I was furious. I told him so and asked him what his decision was.

He replied, "I'm with you."

That Platoon Commander was quite surprised to have me banging on his door at 0430. I told him that he had one hour to be back out with his troops, or I would be going to the CO to have him fired.

From that night onward, the performance of the course staff was excellent. Both the students and I told them so at the end of the training.

I always spoke with the young soldiers about discipline and how it was the cornerstone of forming a good team and unit and how a lack of discipline would quickly erode unit cohesion. Every opportunity I had to demonstrate the importance of what I was saying, I would make sure that the young soldiers knew it. The RCR Motto, 'Never Pass A Fault,' was something that I always tried to live by, and it was something that we tried to impress upon the young soldiers and the staff.

If someone messed up, even if it was minor, I ensured that we dealt with it. It didn't mean that we hammered the young guys every time they screwed up, but we did highlight the error to make sure it didn't happen again. All the soldiers needed to be aware of the mistake so that they all learned from it.

I had investigated two soldiers for minor offences that had occurred, and after speaking with legal counsel, I formally laid charges against both. One was for being Absent Without Leave (AWOL), and the other was for drunkenness. These young soldiers needed to know that they would be held accountable for their actions and needed to take that knowledge with them throughout their careers.

I believe there have been several very public incidents in the military where soldiers were not held accountable for their actions—whether in Somalia, in the Canadian Airborne Regiment or later in Afghanistan—and I wanted to try to change that.

SUMMARY TRIAL

I decided to hold the summary trial for these two individuals in front of the whole course and staff to make sure that they not only saw the procedure and the fairness of it but to hopefully deter them from behaving similarly themselves in the future.

This was during a period of training when the course was in the field from Monday to Friday for several weeks in a row, and I believed that a timely trial was required while the incidents were still fresh in everyone's mind. I spoke to the Course Commander and Second-in-Command and picked a time when the whole platoon would be together in a patrol base. I told them that Captain Cushman would be conducting the trial there. At first, I got a couple of strange looks, but they were on board once they realized I was serious.

On the day of the trial, it was raining, and a little chilly, but nothing was going to stop justice from being carried out. I had the CQ staff bring out a six-foot table and a couple of chairs, and a tarp to protect the paperwork and Bible from getting wet.

At 1300 hours on a Friday, the course was seated in a semi-circle around a clearing with the table and chairs in the middle. All the troops were in camouflage, dirty and had all their weapons and fighting gear with them. I conducted the trial as if it were in the headquarters building minus the shiny uniforms. I rehearsed the march in and out of the clearing while waiting for Captain Cushman, the Presiding Officer, to arrive. He was watching from a distance until I gave him the thumbs-up.

PART TWO - PEACEMAKING

This rehearsal was all part of my lesson to the troops. I yelled and screamed at the accused and escort, also known as the Orders Parade, to make them as miserable as possible. After ten minutes of marching them back and forth, they were sweating. The accused looked like he was going to cry. I then had the Orders Parade stand at attention away from the centre of the circle while the Presiding Officer and the Assisting Officer for the accused moved position.

Once everything was ready, I marched in the Orders Parade, and the trial began. We did this for both accused. The Presiding Officer announced the guilty verdict at the end of each trial and then pronounced the sentence. In both cases, the guilty soldiers were confined to barracks for three days, which meant they lost their freedom for the upcoming weekend. The weekend was particularly important to them following a week in the field.

Once the trial area was cleared away, I spoke to the soldiers about the importance of what had just occurred. I reminded them that they would always be accountable for their actions during the remainder of this course and throughout the remainder of their careers.

I believe that this had been a positive experience for everyone present that day. I had several of the staff come up to me and thank me for setting this example. I hope that all involved that day continue to be an example to everyone else to be accountable for their actions.

A DISGUSTING EVENT

One other incident had me shaking my head and wondering where we found some of our recruits. I had instigated a policy, which stated that students were not allowed to take photos or videos during training unless specifically authorized by the staff. This mainly was part of operational security and because we did not want students to have bits and pieces of stuff on tape that they could use when they were being counselled or re-coursed for something.

It was a Saturday late in the course, and all the students were off for the weekend. I was at home enjoying some family time when my phone rang. It was the Base Meaford Duty MP, and she wanted to know if I could come into the Base because she needed to talk to me about a serious incident involving one of my courses. I jumped in the car, drove to base, and parked in front of the Military Police Headquarters. Once inside, the Duty MP proceeded to tell me what was going on.

One of the students had called the MPs to complain about a couple of other students. According to the individual, he had been in his room working on his kit when one of his roommates came in and told him that he might want to go to the TV room because several of his coursemates were watching a video that he was in. He said that he had gone down to the TV room and, as he approached, he heard uncontrollable laughter coming from about a dozen or so students. According to the MP, the student was told by some of the guys gathered there that a couple of other students had played

WHITE SCHOOL, BLACK MEMORIES

a disgusting joke on him while they were in the field and that they had recorded it. The guys gathered there said they had watched it but had not known about it when it happened. The young female MP said that instead of telling me what happened, she wanted to play the video.

The video disgusted me, and I immediately decided on the spot that the two guys involved were going to pay a hefty price. It happened during the offensive exercise that took place in the winter months. The sections were living in ten-man arctic tents, and this incident occurred while half the platoon had gone out on a patrol and the other half remained behind to provide security and keep the tents warm for the returning patrollers.

The video showed a young student standing inside the tent holding a bag of long red licorice, and he can be heard saying to the guy videotaping, "Are we really doing this?"

"Yeah," replied someone off-camera. They both laughed.

The guy then pulled down his combat pants, his long johns, and finally his underwear and bent over for the camera. He removed one of the pieces of long red licorice, inserted one end into his anus and then pushed it in and out for a few seconds. All the while, both individuals were laughing hysterically. The licorice was then removed from his anus and placed in the bag with the others, but it was left out a couple of inches further than the rest to identify it more quickly as the right one.

The camera then shut off, and the next time it came on, the same soldier was standing outside the tent holding the bag of licorice, and the video showed the patrol returning from their task. They could be seen heading toward their tents and, as the victim got close, the soldier with the licorice said, "Hey, welcome back. How was the patrol? Have a piece of licorice."

The victim reached out and grabbed the licorice that was sticking out of the bag, and he started eating it. The video continued until he had eaten and swallowed the whole piece, and then it went black. After watching the video, I did not know if I wanted to throw up or head to the quarters and throw punches at these two pigs.

I looked at the MP and told her that I didn't want to do this investigation. I wanted the Military Police to contact the National Investigation Service (NIS), who investigate serious crimes, so they could handle this. She agreed, and I told her that I would brief the Company Commander immediately, I would have him call the Commanding Officer and that I would call the RSM. I made the second call to the base doctor, a civilian who lived about twenty minutes from the Base. I told him what had happened and asked if there was a concern for the soldier's health. When I told him that the incident had occurred about a month earlier, he did not seem to have any immediate concerns for the soldier but said to have him see him first thing Monday morning.

On Monday morning, the Company Commander and I got together with the RSM and Commanding Officer to discuss the situation. I wanted to remove both soldiers from the course immediately. The Commanding Officer was more hesitant

PART TWO - PEACEMAKING

and wanted to get some legal advice first. I was angry that we had to continue training with the victim and the two accused together. I did remove the two accused from the victim's section and moved them to a different one so, at least, they did not need to sit next to each other or sleep next to each other. I spoke to the victim, and I apologized for the disgusting behaviour of the two accused and told him that they would be dealt with accordingly and that the NIS would be coming to do interviews.

I then pulled in the two accused and had them at attention in front of me for about ten minutes as I told them what I thought of them and that I hoped they would be kicked out of the military. I then spoke to the Platoon as a group because, by now, everyone was aware of what had happened. I told them that there was going to be an investigation and that everyone was to cooperate fully and, other than with the MPs, I did not want to hear anyone speaking about this. I gave them my normal speech about teamwork and looking out for each other and how this Platoon had failed one of their own. I left every soldier and staff that was present that day with the same message: "This was totally unacceptable, and we did not want people in the regiment who would disrespect another soldier in this manner."

I had investigated many offences by this time in my career, and after a week or so, I decided to see the MPs for an update. I found out from the base MPs that they had not seen anyone from NIS yet, and they had not even asked for the videotape. I went and spoke to the RSM, who called the Military Police Chief in Ottawa to find out what was going on and remind them that unless they got the investigation done in the next couple of weeks, it was going to be exceedingly difficult. The course would graduate in about eighteen days and then they would be posted to different battalions in different provinces.

The RSM came back later that day to speak with me, and I was not happy with the news. The NIS had reviewed the incident and did not believe it would be in the best interest of justice for them to carry on with the investigation. They thought that the unit should conduct the investigation and the charges could be heard by a Summary Trial rather than at a Court Martial. I told the RSM that I would do the investigation immediately and have my recommendations to the lawyers within a few days.

It was a simple investigation. There was the video, the victim and the two soldiers who made the video and caused the incident to happen, and, finally, there was the Military Police report.

I made sure that I followed all the rules for an investigation and that both the accused were read their rights each time I spoke to them. When they agreed to write me a statement regarding the incident, I had them begin by saying they understood their rights and knew they did not have to give or write a statement. I had the investigation report and draft charges ready for the lawyers to see just two days later.

I recommended that each of the two accused was charged with conduct to the prejudice of good order and discipline and disgraceful behaviour. The latter was a serious charge, and I was not surprised when the lawyers returned with their recommendations. They recommended that both be charged only with Article 129,

"Conduct to the prejudice of good order and discipline," which is a minor offence.

I thought this was a mistake because the trial would be in front of Captain Cushman and his powers of punishment were minimal, at best. I was not happy with the recommendations, and I told the lawyers such. Then I went to see the RSM. I reluctantly followed the lawyers' advice, and I laid a single charge under Article 129 against each accused. We prepared for a Summary Trial in front of Captain Cushman.

The Summary Trial, although not what I had wanted, was a serious procedure. Even though the Presiding Officers' powers of punishment were a lot less than that of a Superior Commander or a Court Martial, we had to make the best of a bad situation and make sure justice was done. I had given Captain Cushman a copy of the Charge Report, as well as a list of the witnesses and evidence but did not discuss anything else I had gathered or learned during my investigation. Even though Captain Cushman knew about the incident in general terms as the Officer Commanding Soldier Qualification Company, he did not know the details, allowing him impartiality and fairness as the Presiding Officer.

On the day of the trial, I had the accused and their escorts show up early. I rehearsed marching them in and out of the trial room and inspecting them, all done with a sense of anger and disappointment to teach a lesson. As Captain Cushman took his place behind his desk and the accused Assisting Officer was in place, I marched the accused in, and the trial began.

Just as we had done in the field, the trial was a formal affair and followed the sequence laid out in the Queen's Regulations and Orders to ensure that the accused and the victim's rights were maintained. The accused pleaded not guilty, and the first witness was called, the Military Police Officer who was initially called to the victim's quarters. She was placed under oath and told the Presiding Officer about the night she was called and that she had confiscated a video as evidence. Captain Cushman had not seen the video, but I had set up a TV and video player so that it could be played for him. Captain Cushman observed as the video begins, and then I could see the disgust and anger come over his face as the licorice was inserted in the accused's anus. The video continued to when the victim was offered the soiled licorice and took it; Captain Cushman's face started to change colour.

As the victim placed the licorice in his mouth, I heard Captain Cushman say, in a quivering voice, "Sergeant Major, march them out now."

I called them to attention, marched everyone out, and returned to the room where Captain Cushman was visibly shaken. I grabbed a garbage can for him in case he had to throw up, but it wasn't required. I got him some water and asked if he was okay to continue. After taking a few more minutes to compose himself, I had everyone move back inside, and I marched the accused back in. The Presiding Officer apologized to everyone for having to pause the trial and explained that he had a fragile stomach and certain things would very quickly make him gag. He assured everyone present that he was okay to continue and that nothing had changed as far as the trial was concerned.

After the video was finished, the Presiding Officer called the victim into the trial.

PART TWO - PEACEMAKING

He gave a heartfelt story about how he felt that day after seeing the video and hearing all the laughter. He spoke about the disgust he felt afterward and that the video was probably out there somewhere even though the Military Police had confiscated all the copies from the course. He said he was angry with the two guys accused of doing this, but he was angrier with all his coursemates, who watched and laughed along with everyone else but never thought they should come forward and tell him what was going on.

After the victim left, it was time for the first accused to call his witnesses or make a statement on his behalf. However, he did neither. He said that he would like to change his plea to guilty. The second accused also wanted to change his plea. The Presiding Officer wanted to ensure that the accused understood what they were doing and asked a few more questions to confirm. In the end, he was satisfied and changed their pleas to guilty and then promptly found them guilty. Because they both had changed their plea to guilty, seemed sorry for their actions and apologized to the victim, the Presiding Officer took that into account. Both soldiers received a fine and a reprimand. I would have liked to have seen them get a much harsher punishment, but Captain Cushman believed they were sorry and gave them a punishment that he thought was justice.

I ran into all three of the soldiers involved a few years later in 1 RCR, and they had all moved on with their careers. The victim had accepted the apology, and all three were now good friends and good soldiers.

I guess everyone deserves a second chance.

ADVENTURE TRAINING

During my posting to Meaford, the Company bid for some adventure training and was successful in getting it approved. My friend and mentor, MWO Paul Benoit, planned to take about eighteen of the staff from Meaford to British Columbia for a week of adventure training. We would become part of the crew on the HMCS Oriole, a training vessel of the Royal Canadian Navy, based at CFB Esquimalt in Victoria. She is a sailing ketch and has room aboard for one officer and five enlisted crew, as well as eighteen trainees. Sailing on the Oriole was the best adventure training I had ever been involved in and, other than an incident with a local animal, all went well.

We had been out practicing our sailing skills all day and, by early evening, we had arrived back at the main dock in downtown Victoria. The Captain had us trainees remain on board and sleep in the bunks, but we had to have a security detail always awake as we were in the city and not on a Base. My duty shift was between 0200 and 0300, and I enjoyed sitting on the deck of the Oriole in Victoria Harbour, listening to the city going about its business around us.

Suddenly, I heard a strange noise coming from the pier a few metres from the ship. As any good infantryman would do, I went to investigate. I had nothing but my flashlight and my wits as I climbed over the side and down onto the cement. I begin walking forward of the ship toward the strange noise. Shining the light ahead of me,

I moved forward slowly and quietly. As I got closer, I heard what sounded like the crunching or cracking of something. My light then found the reason for the noise as I shone it directly into the face of a sea otter eating a seagull.

I was unable to stop looking as it continued to chew and crunch through bone and flesh. As I continued to watch, the sea otter looked up and saw me. It stopped eating, let out a terrible growl and started coming toward me at a full sprint. I turned and was running as fast as I could, straight toward the Oriole with the ferocious sea otter only feet behind me. As I came in line with the ship, I jumped, grabbed the rail, and pulled myself up and over onto the deck. I looked over the side, and the sea otter was looking up at me with a facial expression as if it were saying, "You're lucky this time." Then, it turned around and slowly went back the way it had come. A few moments later, I could once again hear the sound of crunching bone.

YET ANOTHER ANIMAL ENCOUNTER

The next animal event occurred while I was still in Meaford. It was a beautiful summer weekend day, and I decided to take my bicycle out of the garage and ride up to the local cemetery. This place was beautiful and peaceful with an artificial lake, birds and benches. It was a great place just to sit and think. This lake was also home to a pair of nesting swans familiar to most of the residents.

I parked my bike at the top of the hill by the monument and headstones and strolled down the fifty metres of a grassy hill to the lakeside. As soon as I was by the water, I saw the first swan go into the water across the lake and head toward me.

"Shit," I thought to myself, "I forgot to bring some bread." I was very relaxed as I stood there on the water's edge by myself, watching the beautiful swan gracefully approach.

As soon as the swan was within a few feet, it suddenly became aggressive. While uttering loud noises from its throat, it half-flew, half-ran out of the water right at me. I turned and ran at a full sprint up the hill toward my bike, but the swan was only feet behind me. I knew if I stopped to get on my bike, I would be caught and attacked, so I continued past it and into the rows of headstones. The swan stopped by my bike and just glared at me. I walked away and tried not to look back at the swan. After a few minutes, it turned and headed toward the lake.

I waited a few minutes more and then headed for my bike. I was about to throw my leg over the bike when a swan came out from behind a small structure and immediately attacked me. I dropped the bike and ran into the cemetery again, using my arms and hands to protect my face. The swan continued to hiss at me and act aggressively while it once again stayed close to my bike as I cowered amongst the headstones. I tried the same procedure a couple more times, and each time the swan beat me to my bike, and I had to retreat.

Luckily, there was not anyone around to watch me being humbled by a swan.

After my last attempt, I rested amongst the headstones and came up with a more deliberate attack plan. I walked away from the bike area, and when I was out of sight of the swan, I quickly ran down to the water and began splashing and making noise. As I expected, the swan had come down its original path to the water and, after getting in, made its way toward me farther down the lake. I planned to wait until it was well in the water coming toward me, and then I would break for my bike and leave. The swan swam toward me and, when it was several metres from me with its full attention on my present location, I turned and ran up the hill toward my bike, letting out a little yell to proclaim my victory over this dumb bird. I rounded the corner only feet from my bike and ran headfirst into a swan that came at my face with a flurry of wings and squeals. I once again retreated into the cemetery, quite frightened by the unexpected second swan.

A few minutes later, both swans could be seen walking around my bike, seeming to enjoy their victory over this dumb human. I watched as they suddenly turned together and strolled toward the water without even a backward glance. I waited a few more moments for them to vanish from sight and then moved stealthily toward my bike, expecting another attack at any moment. When I was a couple of feet from the bicycle, I quickly covered the last distance, jumped on it, and pedalled as fast as I could toward the exit to the cemetery. I did not relax until I was several hundred metres away.

But enough about my animal encounters.

14

BACK TO THE BATTALION

I was involved in several courses and a reserve summer concentration during my four years in Meaford. It was an excellent opportunity for me to influence young minds and prepare them for a future as soldiers. I am immensely proud of that. It was also a great time for our family, as Meaford allowed us to spend a lot of time together. I had a schedule, so I always knew what I was going to be doing and when. Other than a few weeks in the field as a Platoon Second-in-Command or visiting as a Sergeant Major, I got to sleep in my bed almost every night.

SECOND-LANGUAGE TRAINING

In early 2003, I got a call from the Regimental Chief Warrant Officer (RCWO or Regimental Chief) who wanted to speak directly to me about their plans for me going forward. I had done very well in Meaford. My last personal evaluation report wrote me up as a Company Sergeant Major, which moved me up the promotion list very quickly. I was told that I probably would not get promoted that summer, but I could get promoted around Christmas or as late as the following summer. I was told that I would be posted back to Petawawa that summer so that I was on location to take over a Company as the CSM whenever the promotion happened.

He then asked me if I would be interested in attending the yearlong French Course in Petawawa while I waited for my Company. I immediately said, "Yes."

Bilingualism had become a point of contention within the Canadian Forces and other Government of Canada agencies. Those who were proficient in French or English as their second language got extra points on the Merit Boards and were promoted ahead of their peers. There was a belief in some corners that French Canadians had an advantage as more of them spoke English than the reverse. I knew it would be more and more difficult in the future for anyone to be promoted to Chief Warrant Officer, as they would almost certainly need second-language ability. It was a no-brainer for me to say yes to the training.

It was not something that I was eager to do. My knowledge of French was almost nil, and being older than forty years of age, it just seemed like a road too far. But, I was willing to give it a shot.

One night a week, I started attending some French training at the Family Resource Centre on Base in Meaford. It was what was considered the "sandbox" level, which was exactly where I needed to be. Even the basics did not come easy to me, and I would spend hours looking online for stuff or asking my wife Julie to assist.

I was finally in a place where I was looking forward to the course in a couple of months when the old Regimental Mafia stepped in. I got a call from the career manager telling me that I was no longer going on a French Course but would be posted back to 1 RCR as a Company Quartermaster Sergeant.

COMPANY QUARTERMASTER SERGEANT

Now, I had never been posted into a Company Quartermaster position in the Battalion before. Still, I had done the job in Charles Company for seven months when the Company Sergeant Major put in a request for a thirty-day release as the current CQ had to fill in as the Company Sergeant Major. I also did my CQ stuff in Meaford and did a full year as a CSM, so it was a bit disingenuous when I was told that I had to go back as a CQ. It was a stepping-stone to becoming a CSM, and I had not officially filled the spot already.

I explained that I had already filled the position of CQ, that I had even been appointed to the next higher position as a Company Sergeant Major here in Meaford, and a French Course would be much more beneficial to me than a CQ job.

It was like speaking to a rock: no one would listen. I was continually told that specific jobs needed to be done before going to the next. No matter how much I tried to explain my side, it always came back to, "That is the way it is."

The Regimental Chief called me personally, again to explain the Regiment's position. He told me that I would be going back as the Administration Company CQ, the most senior WO in the battalion. It would serve me well and that the French course would come later. I never actually believed a word he said to me, but I accepted the facts as they were.

We packed up our home and family again and moved to Petawawa.

While I was in Petawawa on my house-hunting trip, I stopped by the 1 RCR and went in to see the RSM. I told him that I was house hunting but wanted to drop by and say hi. As well, I was going to drop by Admin Company to see the outgoing CQ, as I was his replacement. Once again, I was introduced to the Regimental Mafia. The RSM asked me to sit down, and then he told me that he had decided to change my position from Admin Company to Combat Support Company, the second most senior Warrant Officer's position.

I was taken aback and told him my story about why I was coming here and the loss of the French Course. He said he understood, but because I was already able to be promoted, I didn't need the extra points that the senior job would bring me. Another Warrant Officer in the battalion would benefit from that job, so the change was happening. Now, the other individual in question happened to be a particularly good friend of mine, and I held no animosity toward him. I do not even know if he knew about the switch.

After moving my family and all our belongings to Petawawa, I reported for work and went to see the Quebec Company (also known as Combat Support Company) CQMS.

When I walked into the company area, the first thing I noticed was the fact that there was no one around. No soldiers telling stories or cleaning weapons or vehicles. It was just empty. I went into the stores area where a Master Corporal and a Corporal were sitting around with their feet on a desk, each reading a book. I asked them where the CQ was, and the Master Corporal piped up and said, "That's me." He explained that as most of the Company had been deployed to Afghanistan, he had been tasked to sign for the stores and look after it for the Rear Party.

I was not happy. I not only lost my French Course and my position in Admin Company, but now I would be a CQ for a Company that was Rear Party. I asked the Master Corporal how many people were in Quebec Company, and he said, other than the Signals Platoon, which had its own stores for everything and needed little support, there were about thirty soldiers. Great, I would be a CQ for thirty people, which would then prepare me to be a Company Sergeant Major for a mechanized rifle company.

I just shook my head and said, "Well, boys, I am your new CQ."

I can't say I learned very much over the next several months about becoming a CSM or even how to be a good CQ, but thankfully, I believed I had already mastered those jobs. I think I proved that over the coming years.

I rolled into my job as CQ of Quebec Company just when the Battalion was extremely busy trying to support those few soldiers still in Petawawa and more importantly those who were overseas on deployment. Even though it was not where I had seen myself after Meaford, like all positions that I have filled throughout my career, I decided that I would be the best CQ that Quebec Company had ever had.

It was also another great opportunity to spend more time with my family and have a schedule that did not change very much. I also took the time to complete an online military course on military law, which I aced. I was also lucky enough to get qualified on all-terrain vehicles (ATVs), which were beginning to be used more and more in the Battalion and were also a lot of fun.

Following my qualification, the Battalion was able to get funding to run four one-week ATV courses. I volunteered to be one of the instructors. WO Mike Graham, a friend of mine who was the Battalion Transport Warrant, would run the courses. We

PART TWO - PEACEMAKING

went to a local dealer and rented ten brand new ATVs, all of them were different to give the students more variety. Mike and I were able to grab the two we wanted as the instructors and use them for the course duration.

It was an amazing four weeks. There were a few hours of theoretical classes, but the remainder was driving. We would begin driving around 0800 and finish around 1530 each day, except for the days we did night driving, and then we could go until 2300 or so. What a great way to spend a month; it was probably the most fun I'd had in many years. There were no significant incidents, however, some damage was done to some of the ATVs, which I considered all part of the training.

The summer and fall of 2003 went by very quickly, and it was a great time as far as family and relaxation went. I certainly was not overworked, and I took advantage of this time to become part of my family's daily routine.

At Christmastime, I again got a call from The RCR Career Manager, informing me that my promotion message would come early in 2004. I would be remaining in 1 RCR and taking over as the CSM of one of the Rifle Companies. It was great news for me, as I had little faith in the Regimental plan for my career.

The next year rolled in much like 2003 had rolled out. 1 RCR continued to look after those in Petawawa, as well as those who were deployed. Most of our troops returned early in the year. In early May, I received word from a friend in Ottawa that my promotion message had been sent, and it was now in the hands of the Battalion. A couple of weeks later, I was promoted to Master Warrant Officer with little fanfare at morning PT. I remained in Quebec Company for the next several weeks. In early June, I became the CSM of Charles Company.

It set me up to deploy to Afghanistan as the Sergeant Major in 2006.

WELCOME TO
LITTLE TORONTO

OPPOSITE: .50 calibre machine gun bunker, Doha, Qatar, 1990. (Author's photo)
ABOVE: Sergeant Barnes, Qatar, 1990. (Author's photo)
BELOW: Sarajevo Airport, 1992. (Author's photo)

ABOVE: Sirac, Croatia, 1992, Company Transport, MCpl Steve Walker, Sgt John Barnes, Cpl Gerry Carter, Cpl Ron Little. (Author's photo)
BELOW: Road move from Sarajevo to Croatia, 1992. (Author's photo)

PART THREE
AFGHANISTAN

15

PPCLI HANDOVER TO 1 RCR

In early August, Charles Company Headquarters and one of our platoons landed at the Kandahar Airfield, universally known as "KAF." They started our handover with the headquarters and one of the platoons from the PPCLI Battle Group, known as Task Force Orion, commanded by Lieutenant-Colonel Ian Hope. The standard procedure for the rotation of units into a theatre of operations is that it is done in phases. This ensures there is no loss of firepower in the companies and that the enemy doesn't get an advantage over us during the change.

We did a couple of days of briefings, received orders to deploy to the Panjwai area to patrol some of the local villages and to speak with the locals to see what information we could gather about the Taliban in their area. This would be an opportunity for the outgoing soldiers to show us new guys the ropes and talk about lessons learned.

When we departed KAF, we had a mixture of RCR and PPCLI soldiers within the headquarters and the platoon, which was still under the command of the PPCLI Company commander, Major Bill Fletcher, with Sergeant Major Shawn Stevens. Major Fletcher would be awarded the Star of Military Valour for his extraordinary bravery while leading his company. We needed to suck as much information from him as possible in a truly short period of time to ensure we were ready to lead this new force. From my perspective, MWO Shawn Stevens had an immense amount of experience to pass on to me within a few days and I intended to take it all in. He was later awarded the Meritorious Service Medal for his courage and calm under fire,

There was a huge distinction between our Charles Company soldiers and the PPCLI soldiers who had been in combat for several months. They had the look of someone who had the weight of the world on their shoulders, and although they knew they were only a few days away from going home, they were prepared for anything. The way they carried themselves had that look of confidence, as well as that look of "Do not fuck with us." On top of that, most only had a few days left, and no one wants to die just a few days before going home.

I could tell that my soldiers were nervous and full of energy, but I had every faith that they were ready and prepared for whatever we were going to face. One of the first things we did was allow our soldiers to adjust their kit and equipment to make sure it was functional for them. The Patricias had learned some valuable lessons about how to wear their combat gear and things like the number of magazines of ammo you carried needed to be changed. The six or seven that we trained with did not do the job in some of the extended firefights in Afghanistan, and so we doubled that number and carried several hundred more rounds on us.

We left KAF, and every soldier ensured that their weapons were loaded and ready, which means a round in the chamber and the weapon on safe. When, and not if, we needed to use our weapons, we needed to have the ability to engage immediately. The LAV cannon and machine-guns were readied and the radios were checked, and then (and only then) were we ready to exit the relative safety of KAF. As we left the inner perimeter, we rolled into an area that was still within the confines of the airfield but didn't have access to the inner base and the Coalition soldiers working and living there.

In that area lived hundreds of interpreters, or as we called them "terps.". Major Fletcher stopped the convoy as we rolled by, and MWO Stevens, the Platoon Warrant and I got out and went inside the building that acted as their living area to pick up our terps. Our Ops folks had arranged this a few days in advance, so they were ready when we arrived. We learned from Major Fletcher that if you get a good terp, that you needed to try and hold onto him and get him each time, as some of them were useless.

We picked up a terp for the Company and one for the platoon, and I learned that neither of these guys had been with the Company before. These guys were screened and tested by an American civilian company that had a contract with the coalition to provide interpreters for all the Coalition partners. I learned that the company was paid thousands of dollars a month for each individual, but the terps only received about $60 a month.

MWO Stevens told me they had been lucky and had a few good ones, but most could hardly speak English and couldn't be trusted. He also informed me that they were not allowed to have cell phones or communicate with anyone on their own, as it was believed that some of them had given away the Battle Group's locations and plans to the Taliban. I learned that most of the terps were from Afghanistan and Pakistan. However, the few from Canada or other Coalition nations were designated for use by other Canadian Government Agencies, senior Task Force personnel or the Special Forces. The leftovers were for the Battle Group.

We had some excellent interpreters over the next several months who became part of our team. In some cases, they became our friends, but we also had some that were useless. These guys had to live with us and sometimes fight for their lives, just like we did. They also had to continually worry about their families because if their identities were ever discovered the Taliban made it very clear that they would kill all of them. There were stories of this happening several times throughout my tour. On one occasion we allowed one of our interpreters to go home to Kabul after his family had received a letter threatening their lives.

FIRST TIME OUT

We exited the outer perimeter of KAF and found ourselves on the highway used by everyone travelling in this part of the province. We took Highway 1 toward Forward Operating Base (FOB) Wilson, and I stood in the back hatch with MWO Stevens. I was a little bit excited, as well as a little bit scared. I observed children running around barefoot, in tattered clothes, women wearing burkas peering at us from around corners, and bearded men just glaring as we passed by. My first impression of the people of Afghanistan was that they were poor, very conservative and not very friendly. For the most part, that would not change.

As we approached Kandahar City, Major Fletcher came over the intercom and told us to be on high alert, as there have been several car bombs and attacks on this route over the last couple of weeks. Our vehicle was behind three LAVs from the platoon. Behind us was the artillery LAV, the engineer LAV, and the Company LAV Captain, with the fourth platoon LAV bringing up the rear. We had a lot of firepower, but our biggest concern was IEDs and suicide bombers and not necessarily a concentrated attack.

As we entered the outskirts of Kandahar City, the first thing I noticed was the smell and then the noise. The scent was a mixture of spices, exhaust fumes and shit. It permeated everything and got in the back of your throat. The hundred-degree weather was compounded by the hot exhaust blowing back on me from the LAV engine, and it made it hard to breathe. The streets were very narrow and bustling, and people seemed to ignore our convoy. Horns blew continuously, but people were just going about their business.

The lead LAV continuously radioed warnings about suspicious vehicles or people to our front as they cleared a pathway for the convoy to move through. Then, suddenly a warning came over the radio from the rear LAV that a white car was closing on the convoy at high speed. The commander of the rear LAV informed us that the gunner in the back hatch was waving his arms and his weapon to tell the vehicle to stay back as per the warning on a large sign on the back of the LAV. The large red signs attached to the back of our LAVs had a message in Pashtun saying to stay back a hundred metres or risk being shot. As well, most of the locals in Kandahar had already either experienced the results of not listening or knew of someone who had, as escalations happened daily, sometimes resulting in fatalities. Even with all the warnings and threats, civilians continued to take the risks.

Then, I heard a burst of machine-gun fire, followed immediately by a second burst. The radio crackled again, and the rear LAV let us know that there had been an escalation of force. The C-9 machine-gunner in the rear had fired a burst into the road in front of the car, and it had continued to close on them. A second burst had been fired into the car's windshield, and it had crashed into a parked car. The convoy did not stop, and we continued with our mission. Major Fletcher got on the radio and passed the information about the escalation of force on to his Command Post and told them to notify higher. We continued through Kandahar City without further incident. This was my first taste of having to drive through the city, and it never became any easier. We then continued down Highway 1 to FOB Wilson and pulled in there for about an hour. We had an MRE for lunch and got a tour by the on-scene security folks.

FOB Wilson, during this timeframe, was not big, and other than a couple of buildings on site, there was truly little else. The district police chief and his cronies occupied one of the buildings. Everyone there was walking around at the ready. This was not a secure area where folks could take off their gear and relax—it was an obscure staging area in the middle of the Taliban heartland.

We spent the hour at FOB Wilson talking to our counterparts about how they did business. They told us about the area we were going into and how they had been attacked every time they came through here.

Silently I was wondering to myself why we would be going into an area like that although I obviously knew it was our job.

SPEAKING WITH THE VILLAGE ELDERS

Around mid-afternoon, we departed FOB Wilson and headed northeast into the desert to visit the locals in a couple of villages that the PPCLI had not yet been able to speak with. We left the LAVs sitting outside the village to provide security and firepower if needed. About thirty soldiers, a mixture of PPCLI and RCR, dismounted and walked the last few hundred metres into the village. The plan was to have a shura, an Arabic loanword for a meeting or consultation, with the village religious and tribal leaders to see how things were, if they needed any help and whether they were having difficulty with the Taliban.

Major Fletcher had his soldiers spread out around the centre of the village in areas that allowed them to observe anyone approaching the village as well as the villagers who were now gathering around the inside. They always kept their weapons pointed down and avoided eye contact with any women who appeared. A tall man with a long, flowing grey beard approached and identified himself through one of the terps as the village elder and invited Major Fletcher and the Charles Company commander, Major Matthew Sprague, to sit down. Once they were seated on the ground, several other men appeared and sat down as well, about ten of them forming a circle. MWO Stevens and I sat down beside our commanders, and the meeting began.

The village men seemed to be paying attention as Major Fletcher introduced himself and Major Sprague to everyone. They asked the elder about the village and if they had any trouble with the Taliban. The village elder told us that there were no Taliban in their area and that the village did not need our help. He went on to say that our soldiers were scaring the women and children by driving around in our big vehicles and shooting at anyone that moved. He also complained about how our convoys forced drivers off the roads and even shot up civilian vehicles.

Several men now started speaking amongst themselves, and when Major Fletcher asked the terp what they were saying, the terp replied that he was not sure because they were talking really fast and the dialect was different. Around this same time, I noticed the second terp, who was standing behind us with one of our soldiers, began putting his scarf around his face so that only his eyes could be seen. Then the terp who had been translating for us did the same. I found this to be a bit strange, but lots of men wore their scarves like this, so maybe it was nothing. I then noticed four men sitting on a low wall about fifteen metres or so from us, and they appeared to be different. They were younger, had long, black beards and dressed in black robes and turbans.

MWO Stevens leaned over to me and whispered, "Taliban." I gave him a confused look, and he just shook his head as if to say, "I'll tell you more later."

My first thought was that if those guys were Taliban, why weren't we taking them into custody? I would find out that our ROEs were known not only by us but also by the Taliban. If they did not have weapons or present a threat, we had to treat them as locals.

Some of the PPCLI soldiers had already noticed these guys, as a couple of them had already moved their positions to keep a close eye on the four perceived enemies. I did not see any weapons or any hostile intent—they just sat there and stared. As quickly as the shura had begun, it ended, and the village leader shook our hands, gave us a blessing, and walked away.

We stayed spread out and slowly made our way back to the LAVs, where we did a quick debriefing. Our counterparts informed us that this was not out of the ordinary and that most of the shuras they had attended in this area had what they believed to be Taliban or their supporters in attendance. Major Fletcher went on to say that a lot of these villages either supported the Taliban or provided their sons as fighters. He asked us if we had noticed that there were no fighting-age males in the village except for those four suspicious guys? He went on to say that it was probably because they were either hiding or had already gone off as fighters and perhaps had been killed. The villages in that area that did not support the Taliban were under constant threat and had Taliban visitors many nights to terrorize them until they gave in and offered their support and loyalty.

NIGHT LEAGUER

By the time we had finished our debriefing, it was late in the evening, and Major Fletcher decided to set up a Company leaguer for the night in a relatively secure area. He gave quick orders to the Platoon Commander and pointed to a spot on the map northeast of FOB Wilson where the convoy would adopt an all-around defence. They had obviously done this many times. We took this lesson to heart as we did these leaguers many times ourselves over the following months.

As we were moving to our new location, Major Fletcher explained to us over the intercom that it was much safer for a large force like ours to set up in the desert than in a confined FOB. The Platoon Commander picked a location in the middle of nowhere that did not have any villages, people or structures within a kilometre of our vehicles for 360 degrees. The LAVs were spread out in a circle, each about twenty metres apart, with our headquarters in the middle. With the weapons systems and sights on our LAVs, nothing could approach us without being seen, and we had the firepower to reach out thousands of metres away.

The soldiers were all ordered to start digging individual firing positions, and, once they were completed, the outer LAVs would always have gunners and commanders mounted and awake, while the rest of the soldiers could get some well-deserved rest.

Major Sprague and I spoke well into the night with the Patricias about lessons they had learned and why they did things the way they did. This information would assist us throughout our tour. We finally laid our air mattresses on the ground at about midnight, and I was surprised that I was asleep within seconds. An hour later, though, MWO Stevens woke me up by kicking me because a pickup truck was approaching us from the south. I jumped up, grabbed my gear and went with him to an area where we could see the headlights coming toward us. The truck was still about eight hundred metres away, but it was way too suspicious to ignore.

Major Fletcher had the two LAVs facing south turn on their headlights and flash them, hoping to get the truck to turn around. It continued to advance. When it was about six hundred metres from us, one of the LAVs fired a burst from its machine-gun into the dirt in front of the truck, and it stopped. The LAVs' night vision capability allowed our soldiers to see two men jump out and start setting up what appeared to be a mortar tube. One of the LAVs then engaged the enemy with machine-gun fire as the first mortar round was fired. The mortar round landed well east of our position, and no one was hurt, but I cannot say the same for the enemy.

Both men were hit, and a second LAV opened fire on the truck with the 25mm cannon, setting it ablaze. The two fighters didn't move, and Major Fletcher sent a dismounted section to confirm that the enemy was dead. While this was taking place, I heard a commotion at the platoon headquarters LAV. I saw two soldiers moving someone along who had their hands tied behind their back and a pair of black-painted goggles over their eyes, and a set of ear defenders over their ears. I immediately thought that somehow, even with the night vision and infrared sights we had, someone had been able to sneak in, but I was wrong.

Being pushed into the middle of our position was the interpreter that had been with the platoon and who we had picked up only a few hours earlier in KAF. We learned that a few minutes before the mortar attack, one of the Patricia soldiers spotted this terp behind the LAV speaking on a cell phone. Not long after, the headlights were spotted coming our way. The interpreters are not allowed to have cell phones, and they understand this very well.

Because there are no coincidences in Afghanistan, we believed that this terp had called his Taliban friends and gave them our location. This unfortunate Afghan, either because he was Taliban himself or he was being forced to betray us because the Taliban had his family or something else, spent the remainder of the night tied up, deaf and blind in the bottom of a hole in the ground, under Canadian guard.

AFTERMATH

At first light, we moved as a convoy back out to the closest road, past the burned-out truck and two dead Taliban, and waited for the Afghan Police that our CP had requested. Two trucks approached us with Afghan flags flying, carrying many young men, none in uniform but all armed to the teeth. We were on high alert even after they identified themselves as police.

This problem would continue to be an issue for several more months until we could get them proper uniforms, standardized weapons and vehicles and training so that they could be easily identified. Even then, we had to be careful, as many were Taliban sympathizers and paid off to betray their country and us.

Once we confirmed that these guys were police, we handed off the traitorous interpreter to them. They violently threw him in the back of one of the trucks, then grabbed the two dead guys and threw them in as well, before heading back to FOB Wilson. I don't know what happened to that terp, but I don't believe anyone saw him again.

We also headed back to FOB Wilson, where we would leave the LAVs and do a dismounted patrol out into the village of Pashmul. We got to FOB Wilson around mid-afternoon and then spent several hours walking around Pashmul carrying about forty pounds of gear in hundred-degree heat. It was an uneventful patrol, but once again it allowed us to see how the Patricias were doing things after several months in theatre and some hard lessons learned.

We had an MRE for supper while sitting around the PPCLI Command Post and discussing the remainder of our handover. The plan was to move back through Kandahar City that night, using the cover of darkness, when hopefully there would be less local activity. After that, we'd head back south into an area where at first light we would approach a small village that had been friendly to the coalition on the last visit.

It was around 2200, and other than the moon, darkness enveloped everything. Even though there were about eighty people at FOB Wilson that night, there were no lights. Everything remained black to avoid making ourselves a target.

Major Wright, who was commanding A Company PPCLI and was part of our Battle Group, was also preparing to depart FOB Wilson and we decided to attach ourselves to his convoy for more security. We received a quick set of orders from him and then we departed.

Little traffic used Highway 1 at night other than Coalition forces because it was way too dangerous, so as we turned left toward the mosque, we turned off our headlights and running lights. It felt a little strange to be driving on a highway at night without lights. I don't think this was an official SOP for the PPCLI, but it was only common sense to these guys who had learned their lessons the hard way.

As we passed the mosque, I noticed several men hanging around outside. They weren't armed and didn't pose a threat. It seemed odd that these guys were outside at 2200 hours in the middle of a war zone, and most were talking on cell phones. We had already been briefed that the people at the mosque were keeping an eye on FOB Wilson, and we believed that they informed the Taliban every time anyone came or left and told them which direction we were going.

ROLLING FIREFIGHT

Only about a minute had passed since we saw the men at the mosque when I heard the first explosions and rifle fire. I saw flashes off to the right of the highway, but it took a few seconds for me to realize what was happening. Over the radio, the lead LAVs called in a contact, and Major Wright was sending his initial contact report to higher. These initial reports were critical because, as soon as a TIC (troops in contact) happened, it took priority on the radio. The QRF, helicopters for medevac and all other resources were put on standby to support us.

I have spoken to a few soldiers from both the PPCLI and the RCR who were present for this engagement in mid-August, and they all remember the time and distance a little differently than I do, but the main elements of the incident itself are clear.

I saw many flashes around us, some coming from areas only a few metres off the road and others from areas that were a couple of hundred metres away. The Taliban seemed to be lined up as far as I could see in a straight line along the highway and were throwing everything they had at us. I could hear rounds hitting the LAVs and saw sparks fly off the LAV in front of us. I heard a grenade explode and saw flashes all over the place. I listened to the crack and buzz of bullets and shrapnel flying by our heads.

Major Wright came over the radio and told everyone to slow down, stay spread out, and engage any targets of opportunity. I was thinking to myself that slowing down was crazy and that we should get the fuck out of there, but the PPCLI didn't panic and wanted to kill as many of the enemy as possible.

The convoy rolled slowly along Highway 1, and all our LAVs were engaging enemy fighters. I saw a figure stand up about ten metres from my vehicle and fire a burst, and I heard rounds go over my head. I instinctively pointed my rifle and fired three to five rounds at him and watched as he twitched and went down. Next, I heard Major Wright tell everyone standing in the back hatches to get down inside, except for those in the rear LAV, and for the LAVs to continue firing. I did not have to be told twice as I sat inside the LAV, and the hatches were closed.

I thought this would bring some comfort, but it did not. Being trapped inside a square box and not having any control over what was happening was not a good feeling. All the while you're in there, you're waiting and expecting that sooner or later something is going to penetrate the LAV and kill. It's terrifying. I could hear the gunner and the commander picking out targets over the intercom and the excitement in their voices after neutralizing them. I could hear both 25mm and the machine-guns firing and saw our headquarters signaller passing up more ammo for both.

The Taliban were getting their asses handed to them, and I was surprised to see how calm the PPCLI soldiers were from top to bottom. We would become like them in short order. I could hear bullets hitting the LAV and explosions as rocket-propelled grenade (RPG) rounds exploded around us and above us, but the LAV remained intact. It seemed to go on for several minutes and at least a few kilometres while our LAVs slowly rolled on. Eventually, silence returned. I listened on the radio as Major Wright sent his situation report to higher and informed them that we had one Canadian injured. We were heading for Camp Nathan Smith and would require a medevac.

Camp Nathan Smith was in the heart of Kandahar City and had been an abandoned fruit factory reconstructed in 2003 by the U.S. Army and then turned over to the Canadian Army in 2005. It had been named after Private Nathan Smith of the 3rd Battalion, Princess Patricia's Canadian Light Infantry, killed in the friendly fire incident at Tarnak Farms.

The rest of the trip along Highway 1 and into Kandahar City was uneventful, and we made it to Camp Nathan Smith and safety about an hour later. I found out that one of the Patricia medics had received a severe head wound that was threatening to cost him an eye. Within thirty minutes, two helicopters arrived and our casualty was taken away to the Role 3 Hospital at KAF. The rest of us got ourselves refocused, and we carried on south to our village objective.

A few days later, when we were speaking with some of the senior leadership of the incoming and outgoing Battle Group, we were told about the assessment of what happened that night. From intelligence reports, through phone and radio chatter between the insurgents and from local Afghan police and local leaders, as well as from one of the Special Forces communities, we were able to put a picture together.

It was believed that hundreds of Taliban fighters had been moving into Kandahar from all over Afghanistan and Pakistan, and they could not resist the opportunity to attack our convoy when we drove by. The numbers of dead fighters varied and was never agreed upon, but I have seen and heard reports as high as eighty and as low as thirty. We also received reports that at least that many again had been wounded.

This incident reminded me of what some of the Patricias had told us about the Taliban. Other than the hard-core fighters and some foreigners, especially the Chechens, many of these fighters were young, inexperienced guys who always seemed to fire high and always exposed themselves when shooting, and that seemed to be the case here. As one Patricia gunner said to me, with a big shit-eating grin, "Sir, it was like shooting targets on a range, maybe even easier. It was great! I think I probably killed twenty myself."

After only about twenty-four hours in the field, I had been bloodied and involved in a serious firefight. I'm sure that I had killed the one guy that popped up so close to our LAV, but it never really crossed my mind again. Keeping a count of how many people you've killed was never one of those things that I did. Others like to talk about personal exploits, but it's not my style. That's okay—I was always bragging about the exploits of my Company instead.

What I brought away from my initial battle was how careless the Taliban were with their lives. The Taliban commanders and their followers would soon learn that gathering together in large numbers to take on Canadians and our Coalition partners was a huge mistake. It would eventually result in them going back to their run-and-gun approach, using small groups instead.

That night they were willing to stand up in a field and fire their rifles and RPGs at about ten armoured LAVs and about fifty Canadian soldiers. It resulted in an exceptionally good night for our side, and a terrible one for them.

Major Sprague and I were now in command of the remainder of the PPCLI soldiers and our Charles Company soldiers. I believe we were both excited and perhaps a little apprehensive, but we also had no idea what was to come. Over the summer, the PPCLI had been engaged in running battles with the Taliban in Panjwai, trying to eject them from what had become a stronghold. By August, the Taliban were still able to mount operations from Panjwai that threatened Kandahar City. Our first major task as a Battle Group was to clear them out, codenamed Operation MEDUSA.

The plan was for Charles Company to be in the south, acting as the hammer. Major Geoff Abthorpe and MWO Ken Lockyer would have Bravo Company in the north, serving as the anvil. To the east and west were other coalition forces, primarily the Dutch, Americans and Danes, acting as a blocking force and destroying any Taliban that squirted out. In addition to our battalion were contingents from 2 Canadian Engineer Regiment, the Royal Canadian Dragoons, the Royal Canadian Artillery, a company from the Princess Patricia's Canadian Light Infantry, and the 2nd Military Police Platoon, as well as a small group of Afghan soldiers. In the shadows were Canadian and Allied Special Forces soldiers operating in support.

The first soldier of the Battle Group killed in action was an engineer, Sergeant Shane Stachnik.

He was standing in his armoured vehicle's hatch trying to find the best routes for us and providing freedom of movement for Charles Company when an 82-millimetre recoilless rifle round blew him apart. Most of those inside the vehicle were wounded or unconscious, and the vehicle went radio silent. His team, call sign Echo Three-Two, was out of the fight.

Master Corporal Jean-Paul Somerset, our Company Medic, immediately jumped out of our LAV and started treating casualties with assistance from Corporal Derrick Lewis. We were fortunate to have Master Corporal Somerset as our Company Medic, and I fought a few personal battles with the Battle Group Medical Officer to make sure that he remained with us. He was a unique individual in that he was a great medic and a great soldier and was able to find a way to do both without blurring the lines of ethics.

His sense of humour was a treat, and his smile always seemed to make bad situations a little better. He continues to serve Canada proudly today.

Things got real extremely fast that morning. I remember the overwhelming grief and anguish I felt having to touch someone who, only a few minutes earlier, had been alive and excited to be part of this great battle and who had dreams and aspirations, who wanted to go home to his family. Now I was involved in putting him in a body bag and moving him off to the side so that we could continue with the fight.

It is strange how today, something as simple as taking a garbage bag from the garage and putting it on the side of the road will bring back this memory. I am not comparing the body of one of our Canadian heroes to garbage, but I believe it is the process of putting something aside in black plastic that causes the memory to return with extreme clarity. That memory comes back often, the blood, the terrible wounds, the smell of death and knowing that, at any moment, I could be next.

WARRANT OFFICER RICK NOLAN – 7 PLATOON, SECOND-IN-COMMAND

One of our next casualties was 7 Platoon's Second-in-Command, Warrant Officer Rick Nolan. He was a friend and fellow Newfoundlander, and he too was killed on 3 September.

Rick was his platoon's heart and soul. He was sitting in the passenger seat of a lightly armoured G-Wagon when a rocket-propelled grenade came crashing through the windshield. How is it possible that Rick Nolan, someone I knew well and respected as a soldier and friend, was gone?

And why was Rick Nolan in a lightly armoured jeep in the middle of an intense battle in Afghanistan in 2006? That is a question that would be asked by many, including myself, many times over the following days, months and years.

Soldiers voiced concerns in the early days of Afghanistan as the G-Wagons (or Gelaende-Wagon from the German word for "cross-country vehicle") began arriving. However, it was better than the Iltis it was replacing, and the troops appreciated the air conditioning. Its small size allowed it to go into areas of Kandahar City other vehicles could not fit.

But there were complaints. Soldiers complained about the cracks that would appear on the floor, and as we had done years earlier in unsafe vehicles in Bosnia, they put Kevlar blankets on the floors and seats for some added protection, hoping for the best.

The G-Wagon arrived in Afghanistan to fulfill the purpose of a patrol vehicle, but, as Major General Leslie said at the time, "The ideal patrol vehicle doesn't exist. The type we are getting is essentially a slightly bigger Iltis," Major General Leslie continued. "Quite frankly, it's not much different than that which we have now. Is that a suitable vehicle for the light infantry battalions to do their business? I've got my doubts."

I still question how, a few years later, we allowed soldiers to roll into a deliberate attack on a dug-in enemy in a vehicle that was not even acceptable as a light battalion recce vehicle?

Our enemies in Afghanistan very quickly identified the G-Wagon as the weak link in Canadian convoys and would target them accordingly. I remember reading media reports describing G-Wagons as heavily armoured and thinking that this was false. Armoured vehicles are built with heavy structures to hold armoured plating, while the G-Wagon is an SUV, a cross-country vehicle with some armoured panels attached to a light steel body.

Rightly so, as the G-Wagons began to arrive, they were hailed as a significant advance over the unarmoured Iltis. It had armoured glass windows that could stop some attacks but, in Kandahar, it was a much more hostile environment than Kabul. Praise for the vehicle quickly changed as casualties mounted.

However, it was not until four soldiers were killed in April 2006 in a G-Wagon that the government, DND and the Canadian media addressed the unsuitability of the lightly armoured jeep. The response from Defence Minister Gordon O'Connor was swift. By the end of May, he announced that "most" G-Wagons were to be restricted to camp in Afghanistan. It sounded like a reasonable precaution, even if not realistic.

Canada had bought around 1,200 G-Wagons. Those in Southern Afghanistan were to be replaced with fully armoured vehicles, such as the Bison, LAVs and the newly acquired Nyala Armoured Patrol Vehicle. However, the problem with small, poorly financed armies is that there are not enough of these armoured vehicles, so the G-Wagon continued to be used in Southern Afghanistan, one of the most dangerous places in the world.

The DND said that G-Wagons would be used only where deemed appropriate, based on the threat assessment on the ground. As an opposition MP in 2005, O'Connor criticized the G-Wagon, saying that it was not suited for Afghanistan and that the government of the day had sent our soldiers to Afghanistan without the proper equipment. Opposition MP O'Connor was proven right, so it makes me wonder why he was so slow off the mark to fix the problem when he became the Minister of Defence.

General Rick Hillier had already identified the solution. More armoured patrol vehicles were required and pull the G-Wagon off the roads. Instead, there was some silly statement about placing restrictions on the use of G-Wagons and leaving the decision to commanders' threat assessments on the ground.

Why was the safety of our soldiers not at the top of the Minister's priority list?

So, on September 3, 2006, just a few months later, Rick Nolan found himself in the front seat of a G-Wagon in the middle of one of the biggest battles Canada had fought since the Korean War.

WO Richard Nolan grew up in Mount Pearl, Newfoundland, just an hour from Saint Mary's Bay, where I grew up and was a soldier's soldier. Now he had made the ultimate sacrifice.

He was an immensely proud Newfoundlander, and we would often have conversations about how much we missed home and how great the people were. He would often be heard talking to the troops with that beautiful accent and using phrases that would stop people in their tracks to get an explanation. The phrase I remember the most was, "G'day, get in, get wet, get out," which summed up his view of the world.

He was an exceptional leader who had a great future in The Royal Canadian Regiment and the Canadian Forces. There was no limit to what he could achieve as a soldier. He was born to be a soldier, and he loved the very idea of serving his country. He was a proud Newfoundlander, but he was also a proud and loyal Canadian.

He joined the Canadian Forces at 19 years old and had big dreams and ambitions. He was a great family man and adored his children. He has been described as a committed soldier with a genuine soul who took the most pleasure in spending hours playing outside with his three sons and his stepdaughter. All who knew him knew his love for his spouse and fellow soldier Kelly, and he never wasted an opportunity to tell us how lucky he was to have someone like her in his life. I can say with complete confidence that Rick died as he lived, a true warrior and a true hero. He did more in his thirty-nine years on this earth than most will do in an entire lifetime. He has left a lasting impression on his children and friends and a whole generation of young Canadian soldiers. Rick, you are a great Canadian hero.

Later, I would have the great pleasure and honour to have my photo taken in front of a street sign, reading Richard Nolan Drive, in Mount Pearl, Newfoundland, and it was on the day that would have been Rick's 50th birthday.

CORPORAL SEAN TEAL – STAR OF MILITARY VALOUR

Sitting in the back seat of Rick's G-Wagon when it was destroyed was his platoon medic, Corporal Richard Furoy (Doc), who had his shoulder torn apart by shrapnel and an Afghan interpreter, who was also gravely wounded. Corporal Sean Teal, the driver, dazed but mostly unhurt, jumped into a hail of bullets and went to find help.

Enemy rounds were tearing up the ground and whipping past and into the burning vehicle. The G-Wagon would never roll again. It sat and burned as soldiers fought bravely all around it. Though wounded himself, Corporal Teal made sure that Doc was looked after.

According to Corporal Furoy (Doc), he had pretty much given up and assumed he was finished. The only Canadian soldier he could see was Corporal Teal, and he was frantically fighting off the Taliban in the immediate vicinity. Corporal Teal brought him back to his senses with the butt of his rifle. Teal then placed the C8 rifle, belonging to WO Nolan, in Furoy's hands and told him, "Enemy fifty metres to the front, defend yourself." So, Furoy did what he could.

While under direct enemy fire, Corporal Teal went back to the G-Wagon twice to help the wounded. Sean Teal received the Star of Military Valour, Canada's second-highest award, just below the Victoria Cross.

Hearing the news of Rick's death had a profound effect on me, as this was not only a Charles Company soldier, but he was also a friend and someone for whom I had tremendous respect.

That loss is still something that I continue to deal with today, and I often wondered what we could have done differently to change the outcome of this terrible incident, but still worse was yet to come.

WOUNDED IN ACTION – CSM DOWN

Crouching behind the Zettelmeyer did not bring the safety and comfort that I had been looking for, and this became apparent very quickly as rocket-propelled grenades and bullets exploded above and against the enforced steel.

Just before I was wounded, I remember another one of my fine Warrant Officers, Frank Mellish, and another soldier came running toward me, yelling about how we needed to send someone forward to get Rick Nolan's body. What was Frank doing here? He was part of the reserve platoon in the rear, but I was sure that he started moving forward as soon as he heard that Rick had been killed.

Frank and Rick were not only Platoon Seconds-in-Command from Charles Company, but they were also friends. The news had been devastating to Mellish.

I remember telling Frank that we would get Rick's body but that we had other more important things to worry about at this very moment, such as the living. He needed to get back to his soldiers as we were probably going to need them. I hope that my tone was not too harsh, and I hope that my words did not make him think that I was dismissing Rick. Those were the last words I would ever speak to my friend, WO Frank Mellish.

The same explosion that wounded me killed Frank almost instantly.

WO FRANK MELLISH – 8 PLATOON, SECOND-IN-COMMAND

Frank and Rick were good friends, and there is a part of me that believes that Frank needed to be with Rick. Sounds crazy, but who really knows? Frank was someone who had been the backbone of Charles Company, and he was the key to the leadership of 8 Platoon. His soldiers respected and adored him, and the Company leadership and I depended on him, maybe too much.

As I sat there in pain, my mind flashed back and forth between what was happening and how we got to this moment. I felt the tears flowing, and I sobbed for Frank, just thirty-eight years old, and Kendra and their two boys. Childhood sweethearts who met at age thirteen in the Air Cadets on Prince Edward Island, they later became a military service couple and had been together since.

Now he was lying dead in a shithole called Kandahar. Was this my fault? Could I have changed this event if I had done something different, made another decision, listened a little better? I think so.

Several months earlier, I'd arrived at my office in 1 RCR early in the morning, as was my routine. I liked to read the news and relax before doing Company PT. I was usually the first in, and this morning, as I walked by the platoon cubicles on the way to my office, I heard the clicking of computer keys—someone was in 8 Platoon. I stuck my head around the corner, and there was WO Frank Mellish working away. I said, "Good morning, Frank," and he replied, as he always did, "Good morning, Sergeant Major." We were friends, but Frank was a true professional and would never call me John at work, even when we were alone. We chatted for a while, and I asked him why he was in so early. He just said he had a lot to think about and couldn't sleep. I asked him if he was okay and if there was anything we could do. He said no, he was good. I told him that he could talk to me anytime if he had concerns.

Over the next few weeks, WO Mellish was a true professional and, if anything, his performance was better than ever. I don't know what Frank was concerned about, but it didn't seem to have affected him.

The timelines and the sequence of the following events are blurred by time and a brain injury, but I remember getting an email or a phone call from Frank's wife Kendra, and eventually I had a one-on-one talk with her. She was concerned that Frank was not himself, and that he needed to step away from this deployment to Afghanistan. Many thoughts went through my head as I heard this, and my initial reaction was that WO Mellish was a true professional and I hadn't seen any noticeable effect on him or his platoon. He was doing the job we expected from him every day, and his performance was second to none. His platoon was ready to deploy and they had their shit wired tight, but there was a tiny voice in my head that said: "be sure."

I spoke with the Company Commander and the Second-in Command and explained what Kendra had told me. We didn't really see any concerns and Kendra never really told me why she felt this way or what the problem was. She did say that she and Frank had discussed a move to Gagetown and she wanted him to sit this tour out. I thought back to that early morning after seeing Frank at work when he'd said he couldn't sleep because he had some "concerns." The way I saw it, we all had concerns about deploying to a war zone.

A day or so later, there was another message from Kendra once again voicing her concerns. She said that it was very apparent to her, being the person who knew and loved Frank the most, that he was not ready to deploy to Afghanistan. If he went, he would not come back alive. That statement hit me hard. I never told Frank that I was in contact with Kendra, and to this day I don't know if he knew.

I had dealt with spouses for many years. Some were incredibly supportive, and others were not. Kendra had always been supportive of Frank and there were many times that Frank would remind us how lucky he was. She was a devoted and exceptional woman who was looking out for her husband and her family. I know that she was genuinely concerned and that her love for Frank was at the heart of her comments, but she was also just worried, and I had to consider that too.

We have a saying in the Army that may be used too freely, "We have done our due diligence." Saying it is like giving ourselves a pass, because we can always claim that we did everything we could. At the time, I believed that we had done our due diligence, and I deployed with Charles Company thinking that WO Frank Mellish was at the top of his game. Similarly, the Company leadership had no concerns. I spoke to Kendra once more before we deployed. I don't remember exactly where or how, but she never mentioned anything about Frank not going and I took that as a good thing.

I had initially heard her words loud and clear, but I also knew that she wanted her husband to remain home. She was disappointed with his decision—or ours or both—to deploy him. I have questioned my decision to deploy Frank a thousand times since, and I have torn myself apart over whether I could have changed the terrible outcome.

Did Kendra really know? Did she have a vivid premonition? Frank described his recurring dreams of combat to her in detail, months prior to the battle in September that led to so many deaths, including his own.

Kendra later wrote to me to explain how she felt after Frank's death:

> As a family, with a new home not yet fully settled into and new schools for all, we were forced to face a new and strange existence, but now, without the strongest link in our chain. The most difficult duty I have ever endured as a wife was to say good-bye, let him do and be all he wanted to be. That final goodbye was the most trying and painful I had ever endured in our marriage.
> It was as though someone took a sword and pierced my heart.
> The question I've continually asked myself since is: must it always be soldier first, tradesman second? Could or would a chain of command dare to put a spouse first? Here too, there appears to be a fine line drawn in the sand.

Had I missed the signs? Did I ignore them? Was I preoccupied with the big picture? To this day, I do not have a satisfactory answer. I live with these feelings daily, and I have been angry and sad and guilty about it ever since. Those feelings will remain with me for the rest of my life.

Wounded and in the back of that LAV, I sat beside Frank's lifeless body. Next to him was another great soldier from 7 Platoon, Private William Cushley. Originally from Port Lambton, Ontario, he was just twenty-one years old when he was killed.

EXTRACTION AND BREAKING CONTACT

The sounds and the pounding of incoming rounds on the LAV's metal hull brought me back to my senses. I knew that these brave young soldiers of the Charles Company Combat Team were fighting for their very lives. I don't know if I blacked out or if I just went somewhere else in my mind, but I don't remember the ride to the riverbed or the arrival of the lifesaving helicopter.

My next memory is landing at Kandahar Airfield. What a relief, not for myself but for the injured that were with me, as now they were in the best hands that God ever made, and their chance of survival went through the roof.

As I flew from the battlefield to the Role 3 hospital on Kandahar Airfield, Charles

PART THREE - AFGHANISTAN

Company had to continue fighting. No longer for ownership of the white school or the dirt fields or marijuana, they were now fighting for each other, the soldier on the left and the right, and that is the greatest reason of all.

From start to finish, the initial attack and subsequent firefight lasted about three and a half hours. A section dismounted to retrieve the dead and injured from the G-Wagon, while their LAV gunners fired into the marijuana fields and surrounding buildings, burning through more than a thousand rounds of 25mm and 7.62mm. Three-One Charlie burned through three uploads of ammunition before pulling back and was the last vehicle to leave the battlefield.

Three-One Bravo's LAV had technical issues with its gun and, with the back filled with casualties, they reversed through the marijuana at high speed and crashed into a four-metre ditch, or wadi. It was immediately stuck, with its hydraulic system jammed, and the rear ramp would not go down. They took two direct hits from a rocket-propelled grenade launcher before the soldiers inside could break through the emergency hatch and get outside. Three-One Bravo would never leave the ditch.

Many of these soldiers made their way to Three-One Charlie and squeezed themselves into the back, in a compartment made for a maximum number of eight. They stacked themselves like firewood, with the wounded laying on the laps of others. There was no room for everyone, and some soldiers had to use fire and movement and sprinting to get back to the main Charles Company area instead.

During this whole time, Major Sprague was standing in his hatch, controlling everything that he could. He had every available vehicle lay down a barrage of fire as WO Nolan's body was retrieved and returned to the casualty area. He kept the company fighting despite the chaos all around him. Major Matthew Sprague is my friend, but he is also a hero.

16

ROLE 3 HOSPITAL

While these great Canadian heroes fought for their lives, I was already back at Kandahar Airfield. Once again, I only remember bits and pieces of the next few hours, and I am no longer sure my memories are real. I remember being in a screened-in area, and all my bloody clothes had been removed. I felt naked and vulnerable. Most of my injuries turned out to be internal, and I have often wondered whose blood I was covered in.

I saw someone get wheeled by who was obviously close to death, but he was not a Canadian soldier; he was either a bad guy or an interpreter. Everyone got treated here at the Role 3, and everyone got the same great level of medical care.

I thought to myself, "Could I do that?" If I had to treat someone responsible for the death of my friends and soldiers, I could not guarantee them a good result. That is probably why I am an infantryman and not a medic or a Padre.

Before this tour in Afghanistan, I have always practiced and preached that we treat our enemies with respect and dignity, especially once they are under our control. At that moment, I am not sure that I would follow those rules.

It was tough dealing with some of the locals as they would smile and give you their hand and share their food with you, and the whole time you knew that they were Taliban or, at the very least, supporters of the Taliban. In my book, that makes them all the same. There were often locals wearing black turbans with long, black beards who sat on the sidelines of our discussions and just glared at us as we spoke with the village elders. I am sure that my soldiers felt the same as I did; we wanted to walk over to them and smash the smug look off their faces. The fact that we did not says more about our professionalism than it does about our feelings. While I controlled my actions, I knew that as the locals were taking our money and our gifts, they would also sell us out.

I remember lying on a hospital bed with people scurrying around and seeing that look on people's faces as they go about their business of saving lives. My hearing had

PART THREE - AFGHANISTAN

not returned yet, but I was able to start recognizing loud noises, indistinguishable voices, yells and even some screams.

For the first time, I was terrified. I had no real idea what was wrong with me. I had some sort of mask on my face to assist me in breathing and an IV in my hand, which would cause numbness in my fingers, even today. I remember a young lady trying to put the IV in my arm and, after several attempts, she looked frustrated. A male doctor kind of brushed her aside with what appeared to be contempt and tried to put it in himself.

For some reason, he also failed, and then he seemed to explain to the young lady (who turned out to be an American nurse) that the hand was best when the arm failed. He then put the IV needle in just above my left thumb. I remember it really hurting, and I yelled, but everyone ignored me. My left hand continued to hurt for several days, and the numbness in my thumb and finger remains today.

I believe the doctor who was treating me was German. I think I recall seeing a German flag on his scrubs. He was a big man, and I remember he had huge hands, which continue to haunt me every time I see a doctor.

I remember being told a story by one of the nurses about the next few minutes. I sort of recall it was happening, but I did not hear specific words or comments. I certainly did not expect it to become a story that would be remembered for years. While this German doctor was checking my whole body for any other injuries, Corporal Lewis, a great soldier and a great Canadian hero, was lying on a hospital bed across from me after receiving terrible injuries in the same attack. He would receive the Meritorious Service Medal for his actions, which "brought credit to himself, the military and Canada."

He had been part of our Charles Company HQ (Three-Niner) and had been on the ground with me as the day's events unfolded and had distinguished himself as a great and brave warrior. Even though he had profoundly serious injuries, I was told that he was more concerned about me, his Company Sergeant Major, more than himself, and he reacted every time I yelled or screamed.

The first time was when the German doctor put the needle in my hand and obviously hit something he was not supposed to, and I yelled.

That was the first time that Corporal Lewis, who himself was undergoing initial assessment, yelled out in a very loud and worried voice, "Sergeant Major, are you all right?" When he did not get an immediate response, I am told that he continued to yell and even tried to get up. He continued these actions until he was told that I was okay.

Now, at about this time, and for medical and personal reasons that I cannot understand, this German doctor with huge hands and even larger fingers violated me without any warning. My mind flashed to the jokes and stories about seeing a doctor about a cough or an earache and being asked to bend over. To this day, I don't know what injuries this guy was assessing inside my ass. The running joke has been about a spinal adjustment, but the real reason is still lost on me. Maybe it was a huge temperature gauge.

I don't know if it was pain, shock, or a combination of both, but I began yelling and screaming. I am told that, because I was completely deaf at this moment, I did not realize how loud I was yelling, and people all over the hospital came running. Corporal Lewis also heard this and knew the scream had come from me, and his concern intensified. Once again, I'm told he was yelling, "Sergeant Major, are you alright? Are they hurting you?" He was yelling almost as loud as I was screaming. It went on for several seconds, and apparently it became a little hilarious in an otherwise serious atmosphere.

When the story was relayed to me later, I almost pissed myself laughing.

A few hours later, after coming out of emergency surgery and waiting to be medevacked to Germany, Corporal Lewis insisted that he be allowed to come to see his Sergeant Major immediately. He had just awoken from surgery and, after several minutes of arguing with doctors and nurses, they allowed him to come to see me.

A nurse brought him in a wheelchair. He looked like shit covered in bandages and blood, and I was concerned about him, but he rolled himself over to me and grabbed my hand. I could tell that he was speaking to me, and I knew he was telling me that he would be all right, and so would I.

A huge wave of emotion swept over me as I looked into his eyes. I had been lying there feeling angry, guilty and ashamed that, as part of the leadership of this great Company, we had failed, soldiers had died, and many were struggling for their lives. Here was one of those great soldiers, and he was concerned about me.

I had truly little time to dwell on this, as Corporal Lewis opened his mouth, and the effects of battle, his terrible injuries and the anesthetic from surgery resulted in a gush of vomit heading for my bed. The nurse tried to get a bedpan between him and my bed, but most of the contents of his stomach hit the bed and me.

Now, yes, my breathing was still sluggish, my hearing was gone, I still had a terrible headache, I was on a plethora of medications, but, for some reason, God had a sense of humour, and my nose worked fine. The smell was overbearing, and the stress of the day's events, along with the pungent smell, was more than I could handle. I reciprocated in kind and started vomiting, as well.

I do not know if I ever told Corporal Lewis how those two stories helped me get through the next few days as things got rough, but those tales would make me smile, usually in private.

After many more surgeries and time to heal back in Germany and then Canada, Corporal Lewis, once again, insisted that he be able to return to battle in Afghanistan. Because he did not allow others to say no to him, he returned and continued the fight that was interrupted only by his extensive injuries.

I now settled in for what I thought would be several days of rest and recovery from injuries that were minor in retrospect compared to the injuries that my Company had inflicted on the Taliban. My hearing would return to a level that would allow me to continue and my balance would come back, even if not quickly enough for my liking, and my partially deflated lung was reinflated. Other than a bit of soreness while breathing, I was ready to re-join the Company and the fight.

The headaches would remain, and, as I write this now, over a decade later, the headaches are there every day, and I have accepted the fact that I will have to live with chronic pain for the remainder of my life. I wear hearing aids in both ears to enjoy day-to-day conversations and allow my wife and I to enjoy our time together.

Unless you or your partner has extensive hearing loss, you will never understand its impact on the other. Basic conversations always seem difficult, someone is always asking "What?", having to repeat oneself a thousand times a day over the years becomes an issue in your relationship. When I was enjoying a hockey game or a football game on TV, everyone else in the house was forced to enjoy it as well, no matter where they were, because the volume was cranked. The headaches continued to affect my quality of life and would have a part to play in everything that I did or refused to do from then to this day.

Over the years, I have had many people ask me to describe my headaches, and I have now started to answer by saying, "Imagine the worst hangover you've ever had and multiply that by ten, and picture waking up with that every day of your life."

But all that was in the future.

For now, I was lying in a bed that had just been changed to get rid of the smell of vomit, a nurse had cleaned me, and the smell was finally gone. I was now left to my thoughts and, before they could even get a foothold, I had to go pee.

There is something about people like Corporal Lewis, Major Sprague, WO Frank Mellish, WO Rick Nolan and the other soldiers of Charles Company and even me. Some folks will call it stubbornness, and others will call it a little bit of craziness. Some others will just say we are infantry guys, as if that explains everything.

No matter what it is, I was not using a bedpan or a tube or whatever the nurse offered me. I wanted to stand up and pee like a man, and that was the end of it. I could tell the nurse was getting a little pissed at me (no pun intended), but I did not realize that, because of my hearing loss, I was once again yelling very loudly at her. She may have taken that as a sign of anger or disrespect. It certainly was not meant that way. I have huge respect for everyone who worked at the Role 3 Hospital, but I wanted to go pee like a normal person.

While thinking that my bladder was going to burst and trying to get up, another nurse arrived. She would have a considerable effect on me for the rest of my days. I did not know her, but she approached me with a huge smile, hugged me, and it was like a sense of relief flooded over me.

At a time I really needed it, I felt comfort and kindness.

CALLING HOME

She knew who I was, and she knew my family. She was CWO Rose St. Croix from Saint Mary's Bay, Newfoundland, the same place that I called home. She had a pen and paper and, between the few words I could hear or lip-read and with her using pen and paper, she told me who she was and that I needed to call home and let my wife and children know I was all right.

A good friend of mine, MWO Mark Brander, who was part of the 1 RCR Rear Party, had already notified my family that I had been injured. Before leaving for Afghanistan, I approached Mark and asked him for a huge favour, which he immediately accepted. If anything happened to me, I wanted only him to tell Julie and not some stranger who did not know either of us. I had known Mark for twenty-five years, and I knew he was a good choice to perform this thankless task.

I had only been able to call Julie on a few occasions when satellite phones were made available to us and, during those times, I did not tell her what we were doing both for security reasons and because I did not want her to worry. Julie, like most Canadians, knew from the news that something big was up, and the upcoming attack in Kandahar was no secret, not even to the Taliban, as we dropped leaflets to give them a chance to leave.

Like during many other weekends, Julie had packed up our camper and, along with her brother, Tim, had taken JJ and Jana to a local campground where they did not have cellphone service. I later learned from Mark that he had made several attempts to reach her and that he had gone by our house many times, to no avail. Finally, as Julie was getting home from the camping trip and trying to back our trailer into our long driveway, Mark pulled up in uniform.

Julie was already stressed by my deployment, having to look after two young kids by herself, and trying to back the trailer down our driveway, and the sight of Mark pulling up in uniform was the last straw.

She reminds me today that this event has affected her in ways that I will never understand. Julie stopped the car where it was, jumped out and yelled at the kids to get into the house, as she honestly believed that I was dead. I can never fully understand how she felt that day as she watched JJ and Jana go inside. With the kids peering out the window, Mark immediately told Julie that I wasn't dead but that I had been injured and that they didn't have a lot of information yet.

It was 2006, and I will never understand how we failed to get full and timely information back to the families in Canada, but Julie was told that I had been injured and had trouble breathing. She once said to me that because of the little bit of information she got, she believed I could have had a heart attack, and no one corrected her for hours.

She started calling the rear party personnel immediately, and it was several hours later before she got the correct information about what had happened. Those several hours must have been a nightmare for Julie and the kids. I often think about how our families must deal with the results of our decisions.

As I lay in my hospital bed waiting to get through to Julie and having no luck with the unreliable phone service (even satellite phones have limits), I began to think about what a crappy thing I had talked Mark Brander into doing for me.

PART THREE - AFGHANISTAN

MWO MARK BRANDER – A FELLOW PRANKSTER

At the time, I could not even imagine telling families this type of terrible news, but a few years later, that is precisely what I would be doing. I had known Mark for many years, and I had a lot of respect and admiration for him as a friend, soldier and Royal Canadian.

Several people stayed behind in Petawawa that Julie and I liked and were friends with, but none that we had more trust in than Mark. Mark was a great soldier, and I had learned a lot from him over the years. We had been on several courses together, and he had always proved himself to be reliable. He was an advanced mortarman, a course that only a few were selected for and even fewer passed. Mark was also one of only a tiny handful of infantrymen qualified as observer controllers and posted to a helicopter squadron to perform that task.

Mark and I liked to pull pranks and laugh at each other, all in a friendly way. I remember one such incident that took place on our Platoon Second-in-Command course in Gagetown in 1996. We had arrived from all over the country on the weekend before the course began. I was glad to find Mark on the course because he was a friendly face and someone I could look to for help and assistance.

All the English and French students were gathered in the Base Theatre that Sunday evening. We were introduced to the staff, got a brief on the conduct of the course and what we should expect from the staff and what they expected from us.

At the end of the briefing, the course Second-in-Command WO Gary Cook informed everyone about how we were to behave while on course and what he expected from us regarding discipline and dress. He informed us that we would be responsible for running a formal mess dinner that many dignitaries and Royal Canadians from Gagetown were invited to attend during the last week of the course. He said he wanted two volunteers, one to be the president of the mess committee (PMC) and another to be the vice president of the mess committee (VPMC). These two individuals would be responsible to WO Cook and the RSM of the school for the conduct of the mess dinner.

I assumed no one would be interested in these positions, as it would entail a lot of work outside of all the course activities that already needed to be done. I was wrong, as a fellow Royal Canadian shot up his hand and said he would like to be the PMC, so Sergeant Leo Saccery was selected. WO Cook then asked for a volunteer to be the VPMC, and no one moved.

"You have thirty seconds," he said, "and then I pick a name from the nominal roll." I was immediately concerned because my name was either at the top of the alphabetical list or awfully close, and so it could be me he picked. I reacted without thinking and put my hand up.

WO Cook didn't know me, and so he pointed at me and asked, "What's your name?"

I replied without missing a beat, "Sergeant Mark Brander."

Before Mark had a chance to interject, WO Cook said, "Thanks, Brander," and walked out.

I think everyone except for Mark had a great laugh, and I just told Mark that I would wait for payback. I am sure that Mark was always looking for an opportunity to get one over on me, but I never gave him the chance. Mark never took life too seriously and was always up for a good laugh even at his own expense. He never got angry when I pulled these pranks and as I lay in that hospital bed, I knew I had picked the right guy to deal with my family and he would be there to support them.

ZAP NUMBERS

Laying in hospital all I could think about was what my family was going through. They would be scared and worried, and here I was, lying in a bed arguing with a nurse about having to pee. At the same time as this was happening, I got a visit from the Commanding Officer and Sergeant Major of the National Support Element at Kandahar Airfield, two fellow Royal Canadians. The Sergeant Major was a friend of mine, MWO Ken Miles, a larger-than-life figure within the Canadian Forces, Army, Airborne Regiment and The RCR. He looked worried but pleased to see me, and it would not be until later that I found out why.

Before leaving for Afghanistan, every Canadian soldier was given a four digit "ZAP" number which would be used to identify a soldier instead of using names, especially over the radio, for security and privacy reasons. We knew that ZAP numbers allowed us to identify soldiers who had been declared VSA (vital signs absent) or injured to ensure that families were notified before the names got out.

In some cases, as in Charles Company, we had soldiers who had spouses in another Company who might hear this information over the radio, so it was vital to use ZAPs. My understanding of what happened when I was injured was that somehow my ZAP, or some other identifier, was given over the radio as VSA, which, of course, was incorrect.

Somehow this information got passed through the Company to the Battle Group, so people like MWO Ken Miles and Major Sprague, who was standing in the turret trying to control the battle, initially thought I had been killed. It was a relief when they discovered the mistake, and I was happy that it was only a mistake as well!

I was thrilled to see Ken, and he was a great asset to me during my phone call home. I don't remember if I gave them my home phone number or if they just had it from my documents, but Ken made the call and told Julie I was okay and that he would give me the phone but that I had temporary hearing loss. Through writing, hand signals, lip-reading and using Ken as my ears, I was able to have a conversation with Julie and let her know not to worry. I was good and would be back on my feet in a few days.

PART THREE - AFGHANISTAN

MAJOR ERIN SAVAGE AND CWO ROSE ST. CROIX

That timeline was one that I had decided on and I would use that stubbornness to talk doctors into following. After speaking with Julie and saying goodbye to the CO and Sergeant Major, the urge to pee came back like a tornado.

Once again, I said to the nurse, "I'm going to pee. Where's the toilet?"

As the young nurse again reached for a pan, my newfound angel, Rose St. Croix, said something and put out her hand.

It was my first time standing since the explosion, and only my will to go pee standing up pushed me on. Rose and the other nurse had to help me stand up. With my IV bag on a portable pole with wheels, oxygen in my nose and Rose holding me up, we headed down the hallway. It was a long journey that should have taken about a minute. But I felt like I was drunk…one step forward and a stumble and one back, but Rose did not even blink an eye. She just held me up, and away we went.

Now, this was Afghanistan, so we had to go outside to a Porta-Potty, like the ones you see at major events and outdoor concerts. The hospital was air-conditioned, and when I eventually stepped outside, it was like hitting a wall. I do not remember it ever being so hot, I don't know if it was the stress, the medication, or the injuries, but I was gasping for air, even with the oxygen. It was September 3, it was early evening, and the temperature was around 50° Celsius.

I had to stop and rest for a minute, and then, with Rose's assistance, we made it across some gravel to the portable toilet. After several attempts, and with Rose's help, I was able to get inside. My mobile IV and oxygen pole remained outside with Rose, who stood by the door because it would not close with wires and hoses running through it. I could hardly release myself from my gown before I started to pee, and it continued for an extended period.

What a trooper Rose was to stand outside with her hand inside, holding me up in case she needed to stop me from falling and having to listen as I relieved myself and put up with that disgusting smell that all portable toilets give off in the 50°C heat. The long trip back was just as painful and awkward

It was a relief to be back in bed where I had some control.

The next few hours were filled with a steady stream of doctors, nurses and visitors, who all wanted to show their support and concern. My favourite visitor was the Battle Group Medical Officer, Major Erin Savage, who was as much a part of the 1 RCR Battle Group as any soldier and perhaps more than most. She was an amazing doctor, soldier and person, and she would be my lifeline over the next couple of weeks. Unfortunately, this wonderful lady and friend lost her fight with cancer a couple of years ago and is missed every day. She had so much more to offer.

That evening, she sat on my bed, grabbed my hand and smiled, telling me that I was going to be all right. Using words, hand signals, and writing on the paper that Rose had left, Major Savage said they would decide soon whether I should go to Germany to analyze my head and brain further. They knew I had a bad concussion, but they weren't sure if there was further brain damage.

Without a specific plan, I immediately started to tell her that I was already feeling better, some hearing had returned, and the headaches were subsiding. I said to her that Charles Company needed me now more than ever, and I needed to go back out. Truthfully, though, while some of my hearing was returning, the headaches were worse.

Even still, I needed to get back out with my Company. They needed me for what I knew was coming, a hard-fought battle to remove the hundreds of Taliban dug in and prepared to defend Panjwai, the pathway to Kandahar City and the homeland of the religious movement and their leader Mullah Mohammed Omar. It is a well-known fact that any invader that has wanted to take Kandahar City, from Alexander the Great on, has had to take Panjwai first. The Taliban had been able to do this, but as has been evident throughout history, no outsider has ever been able to conquer it.

From the look on Major Savage's face, I could tell that she did not buy one word that I was saying, and I was worried that she would send me to Germany.

Shortly after that and, as I was just starting to fall asleep, I had more visitors, the CO and RSM of 1 RCR Battle Group. Lieutenant-Colonel Omer Lavoie and CWO Bobby Girouard were not only the Senior Command Team for the Battle Group, but they were also two of the most respected men I have ever known. They had both been on Ma'sum Ghar when we had crossed that morning, and I knew that Omer Lavoie had not been 100% behind us going early. Bobby Girouard was also my friend and confidant and someone I had known for almost twenty-five years.

I could see the stress on the faces of these two fine men, the pressure of leadership, of having to send men and women into battle knowing that some would die and others would have terrible injuries that would affect the rest of their lives. They visited with me for several minutes, and then I must have fallen asleep because the next time I woke up, it was about an hour later. It was dark outside, and my Company Quartermaster Sergeant was standing by my bed.

WO KEITH OLSTAD

WO Keith Olstad was someone I had known since he first joined The Regiment as a private and was now my senior Warrant Officer in the Company and, by far, one of the best soldiers with whom I have had the privilege of serving. Keith would continue over the next several years serving this country, and later became a Command Sergeant Major deployed in Iraq.

Keith had a black duffel bag in his hand with The RCR emblem on it. Inside he had all the items that an injured soldier would need in the hospital. There was underwear, socks, RCR sweatpants and shirt, an RCR jacket, sandals, a toothbrush, and several other great articles. The CQ had a black bag just like that one for every wounded Charles Company soldier.

It was then that I realized that I had made my long journey to the toilet and back in one of those stupid paper gowns that are made for boys and girls, not men, and, when I decided to put on the pants, I realized little was covered in the gown. Oh well, I was so messed up during the toilet trip, I did not care. Some of the folks here at Role 3 may have enjoyed the show.

Keith gave me a breakdown of which soldiers had been killed and injured and how they were doing. His professionalism and calm demeanour kept me relaxed as he showed me the names. I remember tears starting to flow, and Keith did not react. He just reached out his hand, placed it on my shoulder and continued. At the end of his report, he told me he was getting his gear ready and heading out to replace me as Company Sergeant Major because we would be recommencing the attack in the morning.

I was immediately scared for him and the rest of my soldiers, but I forced myself not to react. I asked him to have one of his CQ folks try to find my gear that had been removed from me somewhere along the evacuation route, as I wanted personal items in my tactical vest. He said that most of my equipment had been bagged up because it had been contaminated with blood and would be burned. I told him to have someone put on gloves and remove my mini binoculars, my GPS, and, most importantly, to look for my Saint Christopher medal that I got many years ago from my Great-Aunt Margaret Lee (known by all as Aunt Mag).

Aunt Mag was a beautiful and wonderful woman who was adored by everyone who knew her. When I was sitting in her tiny kitchen a few weeks before joining the military, she gave me the Saint Christopher medal and said it had been in her family for many years, and it would protect me on my travels. It was later that I came to understand that Saint Christopher is the patron saint of travel. I was never able to locate that Saint Christopher medal, and it was something that gave me pause many times over the next few months as we headed into battle.

I wished Keith good luck, and he left to catch a ride out to Ma'sum Ghar.

I slept little that night between the headaches, my IV and the thoughts of Charles Company going back across the Arghandab River without me. My one positive thought was that Major Sprague and WO Olstad were the right guys to lead, and the Company would get revenge for those lives lost. I finally fell asleep with thoughts of dead and dying Taliban as Charles Company rolled over them.

I woke up the next morning just as it was getting light outside. I knew something bad had happened. The hospital was a flurry of activity, with doctors and nurses running around and lots more flowing in. Some were in civilian attire and were hastily changing into uniform. They weren't all Canadian either—I saw the uniforms of a lot of different countries.

What was going on?

A-10 STRIKE

I then thought of the Charles Company attack, which should have just been getting started around then. Could things have gone wrong so fast, or had something bad happened to someone else? Many coalition forces were doing the same things that the Canadians were doing, and many other Canadians were involved in Operation MEDUSA. And, of course, there were the Afghan army and police who were taking the brunt of the action and receiving huge numbers of casualties every day.

I was sure it was someone else, and my thoughts went to the smell of food. I was hungry. I had not eaten in more than twenty-four hours . I had only eaten MREs for the last couple of weeks, and I smelled real food. I looked up and saw Major Erin Savage walking toward my bed, and my heart stopped. Her face told the story. I could see the stress, the concern and the sadness, and I knew, at that moment, that Charles Company had been hit.

Had the attack faltered? Did someone hit an improvised explosive device (IED)? Had we had more injuries? I waited for Major Savage to get closer. She sat on my bed and took my hand in her hand, and she asked me if my hearing had returned. I told her that I could hear her, at least with my left ear, but to speak up.

She then spoke the words I had been dreading.

"I have some bad news about your Company. They've been hit, and there are multiple casualties."

She then said that there was at least one dead, and they were expecting more, as well as many wounded. I was in shock. Once again, I could not control the tears, and when I looked at Major Savage, she was crying as well.

I had never cried in public, and I always thought it was a sign of weakness, but I never thought that way again after that day.

I asked her what had happened, expecting to hear of an attack gone badly, an IED, or hand-to-hand combat, but her answer both surprised me and angered me. She said it had been a friendly fire incident, and she did not have any other details other than that it happened at Ma'sum Ghar before the attack started and that the attack had been cancelled.

I hated it when someone used the term 'friendly fire' even though I understood why it is used that way, but the facts are obvious for anyone who has been under effective fire. There is no friendly fire. I much rather use the term "blue on blue." My thoughts went to the thousand-pound bomb of yesterday and wondered, "Was this another one that had gone off track?"

I got out of bed and started walking around with my portable pole. After stumbling several times and getting in the way of the medical folks getting ready for what they called a mass-casualty event, I was ushered back to bed by my angel, Rose. I told her I needed to know what was going on and that I needed to see my soldiers when they started coming in. Rose kept me informed the best she could over the next couple of hours and even allowed me to see some of the more severely injured.

The next couple of hours were some of the worst of my life…seeing soldiers being rushed around on gurneys but not being able to identify them. Seeing doctors and nurses scurrying around and knowing that they were trying to save one of my soldiers was more than I could handle, and I threw up what little was left in my stomach.

PART THREE - AFGHANISTAN

I cannot explain how useless I felt and how years of being responsible for soldiers had left me feeling like a failure once again at this critical moment.

After about another hour, Major Erin Savage again came to my bedside. She had a piece of paper, which had the names of the Charles Company soldiers that were either killed or injured. She first told me that they were still receiving information and that the names and numbers could change.

She said that an American A-10 Thunderbolt, an aircraft affectionately known by infantrymen as the "Warthog" or "Tank Buster," had mistakenly strafed Charles Company as it was preparing to assault across the Arghandab River.

I knew what an A-10 could do. I had seen it in action several times, and the results were unforgettable. It is an old American plane that is probably known throughout the world as the best killing machine ever invented. Its autocannon fires 30mm depleted-uranium armour piercing ammunition that will punch straight through a tank at a rate of about seventy rounds per second.

To describe the impact to someone that has never seen it is impossible. These rounds come so fast all you hear is a BRRRRP, and then the shit hits the fan. I had seen the results on a small enemy convoy that had been hit. Vehicles were torn apart, and I will leave what it did to the Taliban inside to your imagination. It would have been like putting together a puzzle, and not even their mothers would have been able to identify them.

Major Savage now handed me the list that she had been able to compile, and she told me that there had been only one VSA, but they believe somewhere between twenty and fifty soldiers were wounded, some very badly. She also explained that not all the injured were coming to Kandahar because of the huge numbers. Some were being diverted to other Coalition hospitals. I slowly looked at the list, and I am sure that my jaw fell because I was floored. All thoughts of headaches and a sore neck and poor equilibrium were gone—my beloved Charles Company had been devastated.

Major Sprague, WO Keith Olstad, all my Platoon WOs, almost all my Sergeants and Master Corporals and many of my soldiers were on that list. I was in shock. Practically all the company's leaders had been hit, and the heart and soul of the Company had been taken in less than twenty-four hours. Major Savage gently touched my arm and left me to my thoughts.

In the next few minutes, the thoughts that went through my head made me realize just how human I was. The guilt, the shame, the anger rushed back, and it was all almost more than I could handle again.

Why had I survived?
Why didn't I die?
How would I keep going?
Did I want to?
What would I tell all those families?
How many more were going to die?
Why did I do this to my family?

I should have been there that morning. I hated all Americans. I hated Afghanistan. They didn't deserve our help. I hated Muslims.

This was bullshit.

I again tried to get up and get some answers. I needed to know who was hurt badly, who was dying, and I needed to see them. Once again, Rose came to my side. She sat by my bed with a list of most of the injuries to my guys, and just knowing that helped me. I wanted to know if their families had been notified, and I wanted to know right away when I could visit them. Some of the guys were being stabilized, and as soon as they were ready to travel, they were being evacuated to Germany to the American hospital at Landstuhl. Some were going on to Canada for treatment.

Rose told me that the bullets and the ricochet from rocks and pebbles had caused massive injuries. She said to me that both Major Sprague and WO Olstad each had shrapnel in their heads, and she did not know how they were doing or even if they were here at Kandahar yet.

Over the next few hours, and with the great help of Major Savage, CWO St. Croix and MWO Miles, I was able to get a clearer picture of what had happened, as well as the conditions of the wounded. I also spoke to some of the walking wounded, who had massive pieces of flesh torn off arms and legs and backs and every other body part, but they were the lucky ones—they were alive and walking.

From these walking wounded soldiers, I was able to get the story of the morning of September 4, 2016.

SEPTEMBER 4, MORNING

The soldiers of Charles Company had received their orders the evening of September 3. With apprehension and perhaps a little hope for revenge after the first unsuccessful assault and the loss of their comrades, they found a place to sleep on the rocky enclave of Ma'sum Ghar. The soldiers gathered their thoughts, knowing that they would be attacking back across the river in the morning. They took shelter behind walls and rocks or their armoured LAVs, knowing that, at first light, they would once again cross the Arghandab River and try to kill the hundreds of Taliban who were dug in and waiting for them.

The company was reorganized, with fine young men stepping up and replacing those great leaders lost just a few hours earlier. Men like Olstad, Benedict, Fawcett, Pickering and others never hesitated and made sure that the soldiers were prepared and ready for battle the next day.

After what had happened a few hours earlier, soldiers were probably now thinking about their mortality, and some looked at photos, wrote letters and prayed. There was some solace in the fact that throughout the entire evening and night before their second attack, artillery, "fast air," helicopter gunships and A-10 Thunderbolts were pounding the Taliban positions. It would have been the perfect way to fall asleep, knowing that those who had killed and injured your friends and comrades were now themselves being torn apart by artillery shells and 1,000-pound bombs.

I believe I would have enjoyed that night had I been there because revenge can be sweet. That may not be politically correct, but until you stand in the shoes of a soldier who has seen his friend torn apart, do not judge. Let the bombs kill them all; God can sort the pieces out.

For those that could, they got a few hours of sleep. But, for most, it was a night of lying awake to the sounds of explosions across the river and counting the hours and minutes before you had to advance into the mouth of the lion once again.

A couple of hours before first light, soldiers began moving around. It was an opportunity for the Company Commander to gather his leadership for one last review of the plan. Soldiers ate MREs, drank crappy coffee and did their last bathroom thing.

That morning, a fire had been lit to burn all the garbage accumulated from rations and ammo boxes. While Private Mark Graham, a great soldier and Canadian Olympian, completed his last-minute preparations for the upcoming battle, he was engulfed in a massive eruption of metal and rocks as an A-10 mistakenly strafed the Charles Company assembly area. The ground erupted in flames and sparks. Soldiers scrambled for cover in LAVs, behind rocks, wherever they could, but an A-10 strike is unforgiving.

Only seconds passed as the A-10 fired, but it was described to me by my soldiers who were on the ground as being an eternity—in slow motion—as they scrambled for their lives. Then, after the BRRRP and the flames and the sparks were over, there was screaming and yelling and death and destruction. Soldiers who were injured tried to save the lives of other soldiers. Soldiers who were not in the immediate location came to help. Medics arrived, first aid kits were located, and soldiers started helping their friends.

Forward Air Controllers could still be heard screaming into the radios about friendlies, and evacuation was requested. By some small miracle, Private Mark Graham was the only soldier killed by the strike. Born in Gordon Town, Jamaica, he had grown up in Hamilton and attended university in the United States on track and field scholarships. He was a world-class runner who competed for Canada in the 1992 Olympic Games. He was only thirty-three years old when he made the ultimate sacrifice for his country and comrades.

Many other soldiers needed help to survive, and the Company and others in the vicinity stayed calm and provided first aid, which resulted in many lives being saved. The evacuation took a long time. The numbers were astounding: one dead and about forty injured, but at the end of the next several hours and through the courage of American helicopter pilots and Coalition doctors and nurses, no other lives were lost.

That is the one positive from a terribly damaging twenty-four hours. I will forever be thankful to all those who assisted from the battlefield, evacuated wounded to the Coalition hospitals, or provided the great care in Germany and in Canada that continues today for many.

The one funny story that came from that terrible event involved an American evacuation helicopter. For some reason, the pilot got confused about the location of the casualty-collection point and accidentally landed on the wrong side of the Arghandab River. I can picture the look on the faces of the Taliban, who were probably looking across the river with joy at the carnage when that helicopter landed among them. Their shock and surprise probably saved the day as the pilot realized where he had landed and was able to lift off without even receiving any enemy fire and finally land safely to collect the casualties. I doubt there was much laughter that day, but now, it causes a few

PART THREE - AFGHANISTAN

laughs and comments.

While the soldiers of Charles Company were thinking about families and writing letters or praying the evening before the attack, the Forward Observers from the Battle Group were controlling the artillery, fighter jets, drones and helicopters that were bringing death and destruction to the Taliban across the river in hopes that this assault would go better than the first. The plan was to destroy as many Taliban and their positions as possible before sending over the infantry.

We will never know how that assault would have gone, but I believe in my heart that Charles Company would have swept through that objective and killed every Taliban in the area.

The night had been dark, and the A-10 pilots had been wearing their night-vision goggles, which would have allowed them to see their targets in infrared and would have given them a considerable advantage. The attacks went on all night. The Forward Observation Officers had to coordinate all the air assets and artillery to ensure that there were no mid-air collisions and that as much firepower as possible was brought to bear on the enemy.

Just before dawn on the morning of September 4, the A-10s had reported that they had enough fuel to do only one more run, and then they would have to depart. They were thanked for their support and given one last target. They were to hit the area of the previous attack and use the fire from an earlier bombing to align themselves.

The night had been long and dark. As the A-10s came around behind Ma'sum Ghar to prepare for their last attack of the day, the sun started to come up and there was a haze over the ground. The lead pilot directed his wingman to remove his night-vision goggles, and he did the same. After many hours of stress and flying and destroying enemy positions, the pilot in the lead aircraft saw a fire and knew that his new target was the area of that fire. He was now committed to his new target. His aircraft alarms told him he was off target, that he was on the wrong side of a huge river (about a kilometre wide), but his brain was not allowing him to see the mistake. His finger was on the trigger, and he squeezed.

I know the forward observer on the radio that morning, and I know he blamed himself for what happened for many years. But I know that his quick reaction and his screaming into the radio not only stopped the U.S. pilot but also stopped his wingman who was just about to fire. A terrible situation could have been a lot worse but for the quick action of that forward observer.

The investigation that followed found that the pilot was responsible for the death and injuries of the Canadian soldiers. The report that was released said that the pilot had lost his situational awareness. He was tasked with strafing a target that, moments earlier, had been hit by a guided bomb dropped by another American aircraft. He was supposed to use the fire and smoke generated by the bomb to identify where he was to shoot. But the report determined that he had mistaken a garbage fire at the Company's location for his target without verifying it through his targeting pod and heads-up display. The report concluded that the incident was preventable, had he only verified the target. He was disoriented as night transitioned into day, and by the fact that he had removed his night-vision goggles and hadn't had time for his eyes to adjust.

I do not personally blame the U.S. pilot for what happened that day. I believe that having to live with the results of his decision is a terrible burden. I have so much gratitude for the support provided by all the American and Coalition pilots. They saved the lives of soldiers in Charles Company on many other occasions and were always there when we needed them. We did not have Canadian air power to support us in Afghanistan and, although there were Coalition aircraft in theatre, we primarily depended on the Americans.

If we were speaking directly to the pilot of an American aircraft and needed support, all we needed to do was give them the target, and they destroyed it and saved our asses every time. Blue on blue incidents are terrible, but they have always been a part of war and will likely continue to be, no matter how hard we try to mitigate and prevent them.

Lying in my hospital bed in Kandahar, I waited for news about all the injured soldiers of Charles Company who were being medically evacuated to Germany and Canada, as well as those who were to remain here to heal. It was a painful few hours, but the picture became much clearer. The soldiers who had initially been sent to other Coalition hospitals, including Major Matt Sprague, were eventually brought to Kandahar Hospital to reunite with the remainder of the Company.

I had the opportunity to see Major Sprague, who was being sent to Germany and then back to Canada, and his only concern was for Charles Company. He was obviously shocked and angry about what had happened, but he was much more worried about what was next for his soldiers. I assured him that I would be back on my feet quickly and that Charles Company would be okay.

As I left his side that day, I did not expect him to ever return to command Charles Company, but he would prove me wrong. I also went to see WO Keith Olstad. His head was bandaged, and he was covered in blood, but when he saw me, he smiled.

"I don't ever want to replace you again," he said.

"I don't ever want you to have to," I replied.

18

RAMP CEREMONY

With so much going on and so many soldiers injured, it caught me by surprise when MWO Ken Miles came to see me about the Ramp Ceremony for those who had been killed. We had all agreed that we needed to do a proper send-off for Sergeant Stachnik, WO Nolan, WO Mellish, Private Cushley and Private Graham, but I was not ready to talk about the Ramp Ceremony. I was unprepared, and it showed.

While my friend Ken was by my bed, I was not even sure I could handle the Ramp Ceremony and, deep down, I did not know if I wanted to attend. That negative thought quickly disappeared, as I knew that I had to attend. I needed to put on a brave face.

It would not be my first Ramp Ceremony, and it would not be my last.

Every time a member of the Coalition is killed in Afghanistan and is being sent home, everyone who is available, from every country, gathers to send them off. The flag-covered coffins are paraded in front of them and up the ramp into the back of whichever aircraft is designated to take them home. This time, it was Canadian soldiers, and they would be loaded on a Canadian Hercules.

By the third day in hospital, I was starting to feel much better. The IV and oxygen were now gone, and I could walk short distances by myself, albeit with a cane to assist in keeping my balance. I had to be careful of any sudden movements as dizziness was always just around the corner.

Around this time, I started working on my plan to get back to what was left of Charles Company. They had arrived in Kandahar Airfield the previous night by LAV and would attend the upcoming Ramp Ceremony.

The Company was now considered combat ineffective, a term used to describe a unit that has lost so many of its soldiers and leaders that, without reinforcements, they are not ready for battle. No one in the Company was pleased with this designation, and we all immediately started the process of getting ready to get back to the fight.

Even though the headaches had persisted, and the balance and hearing were not returning as quickly as I wanted, I knew that I was going back out with the Company. It was only a matter of time. Captain Steve Brown was the Company Second-in-Command, and he was now looking after what was left of the Company until a decision was made for someone to take official command from Major Sprague. I let Captain Brown know immediately upon seeing him that I would be ready to go in a couple of days, and I always made sure to keep my balance and my better ear toward him.

I also started to speak to Major Savage every time I saw her, which would sometimes be four or five times a day. I would say, "Hey, ma'am, I am feeling good, and I think I will be ready in two days."

She would always smile and say, "Sergeant Major, I will let you know when you are ready. We are still considering sending you to Germany for another head scan." I would just smile and walk away as sharply as I could.

I did not want to deal with the upcoming Ramp Ceremony, but, once again, it was not a choice. It was going to be hard for everyone, and in my muddled thinking at the time, I unfortunately made it worse for one of my soldiers.

I went to see Corporal Ryan Pagnacco from the Royal Highland Fusiliers of Canada, a young Reservist who was as much a part of Charles Company as any other soldier. He had received terrible wounds to his legs, arms, hands and back, with huge pieces of flesh missing, but when he saw me, he smiled. I put my hand on his shoulder, and I asked him if he could play the bagpipes the following day for the Ramp Ceremony.

What was I thinking? I should never have asked him that. He held up his right hand to show me a terrible mess. It looked like it had been in a shredder, and that was when I saw tears running down his cheeks. I told him it was okay, that he has already done more than anyone could ask. He was devastated. Not only could he not play for his Platoon Warrant Officer, Frank Mellish, and his other comrades, he also wouldn't even be able to attend the ceremony because his wounds were too severe for him to be taken out to the airfield.

I spoke to him once after returning to Canada following the tour and found out that missing the Ramp Ceremony was something that bothered him for a long time.

CORPORAL RYAN PAGNACCO

Corporal Pagnacco, like many other Reservists, became part of Charles Company in Petawawa many months before we deployed so that they would be able to complete all the same training as the Regular Force soldiers. I committed to all the Reservists that they would be treated exactly like every other soldier in Charles Company. I told all the soldiers that our goal was to make the Company seamless, and that from Day One we would not look at individuals as being from the Regular Force or Reserve. By the time we deployed, Charles Company would be one team and we wouldn't even know the difference between the two.

PART THREE - AFGHANISTAN

It worked out better than I could have imagined. A few weeks following those terrible days of Operation MEDUSA, I was asked to draw up a list of all of those who had been injured and whether they were Regular Force or Reservists. To my surprise, not only did I not know for certain which was which, but the new Platoon Warrants had to check as well. What a great team we had become.

I remember back in Petawawa that as soon as WO Frank Mellish found out that Corporal Pagnacco not only played the bagpipes but also had his own, he became his platoon piper. As soon as I found out, he became the Company Piper. Like me, Frank loved the sounds of the bagpipes.

My many years of serving with 3 RCR and marching to their pipes and drums had made me a big fan. Whenever the opportunity presented itself, we brought the pipes out. We especially loved to have Corporal Pagnacco play when the rest of the Battle Group was around, just to show off Charles Company and perhaps to piss everyone else off. We had Corporal Pagnacco play on long marches, on the ranges, during an attack and, even though many others from the Battle Group would yell and scream about Charles Company sounding like a bunch of screaming cats, we had Pagnacco keep playing.

One of the Battle Group exercises we did before we deployed was to go through the process of moving onto an abandoned airfield north of Petawawa and using it as if we were moving to the Kandahar Airfield. Charles Company was the last to arrive, and we ended up furthest from the main HQ area and the field kitchen, which had prepared a fresh supper for all. As soon as we arrived, we started receiving runners from the Battle Group HQ to hurry and get the whole Company up because they were waiting for us before serving supper. It was a good feeling to have hundreds of hungry mouths waiting for us.

WO Mellish came over to see me and asked if we could have Pagnacco pipe us up to supper as a Company? At first, I was hesitant as I knew the CO and RSM were waiting for us before allowing anyone else to eat and that this was a semi-tactical exercise and the bagpipes may not go over well. But, after receiving a second runner in a few minutes to rush us, I agreed.

We formed up, dug out our unofficial Charles Company flag, which had a bear on it, and marched sharply to the kitchen area. It was a great feeling as we passed every other soldier of the Battle Group with Corporal Pagnacco playing the pipes the whole way. CWO Bobby Girouard just shook his head as we went by but then gave me a wink, and I knew he was a big supporter.

Charles Company was by far the best company in the Battle Group, and we liked to put on a show, even if it did piss off everyone else.

RAMP CEREMONY

The Ramp Ceremony in Kandahar was a very sombre event and all but the most critically injured soldiers attended. Some were in wheelchairs, others were on crutches, and several were on gurneys hooked up to lifesaving machines with doctors and nurses at their sides. That stubbornness that I mentioned earlier was not going to stop anyone but the most critically injured from attending, and even then, only because the doctors said absolutely no.

Hundreds of Coalition soldiers and civilians were on the airfield as each casket, draped in a Canadian flag, was driven to the aircraft on the ramp of a LAV. There, it was carried by our soldiers inside for its final trip back to Canada.

As a Company, we had the opportunity to salute these heroes one last time, as we would not attend their funerals in Canada. Once the ceremony was concluded, the soldiers of Charles Company had one last chance to go inside the aircraft and say their final goodbyes. Lieutenant-Colonel Omer Lavoie stood among the caskets and had some exceedingly kind and comforting words for Charles Company. Then we filed by the caskets to say our final goodbyes.

That was very tough, and as I placed my hand on each casket, I silently said a few personal words and moved along. Saying goodbye to Frank was the most difficult for me, as the guilt for his death was a huge burden. I remember placing my hand on the Canadian flag covering his casket. With tears in my eyes, I whispered, "I am sorry."

We continued to mingle outside the aircraft, almost afraid to leave because it would mean a total goodbye. Infantrymen and women are considered the toughest of the tough, and we portray that characteristic even when it is to our detriment. However, what I saw that morning was an excellent infantry Company dropping the façade. People hugged and cried and told each other that things would be okay, that we would get our revenge, and that they had not given their lives in vain. Following the Ramp Ceremony, I took the time to see the rest of the Company wounded that I had missed or had not been able to see because of their critical injuries.

I saw Private Mike Spence, a man of small stature with a big heart. I could see him for only a moment, as he was still struggling for his life, and he would eventually be placed in an induced coma. After many head surgeries, he would recover. I would see him a few times over the next few years after he changed trades and moved to the Air Force, where he continues to serve Canada.

I also saw Corporal Bruce Moncur. He had terrible injuries, and after many surgeries, he would recover and become an advocate for veterans. I got to see Macdonald, Cousineau, Mitchell and many others, some who would return to the Company and others who would have to go back to Canada to receive the treatment they needed, but to a man, they all wanted to return to the fight to finish what they had started.

I remember reading an article from the CBC News, posted on September 6, 2006. They interviewed with Major Nick Withers, a senior medical officer with the Canadian Forces in Landstuhl, Germany, who talked about the Canuck Ward, where several of the Charles Company wounded were being treated. He stated, "They're telling war stories, their moods are good, and several of them are saying, 'Get me back to theatre, I want to get back with my buddies.' " I believe they are Canadian heroes, one and all.

PART THREE - AFGHANISTAN

The plane departed, and the dead were on their way home. The seriously and critically wounded were on their way to Germany and eventually on to Canada. The twenty or so wounded left in Kandahar Airfield tried to get on with their new daily routine of changing bandages, physiotherapy and rest. The brief period of mourning was over, because now we needed to remain focused on the mission. I thought there would be time to mourn them fully when we were safely back in Canada.

It sounded good in theory, but a few were unable to get their focus back on the fight. On at least a couple of occasions, those individuals needed to be replaced and sent home to get the help they needed. For most, it was a daily visit to the hospital to have wounds cleaned and dressed. The dirt and the filth of Afghanistan caused terrible infections. The concern they would lose limbs or die of infections caused some of those walking wounded to be sent back to Canada to heal. Most went kicking and screaming, but every one of them would eventually return.

The remainder of Charles Company needed to be reorganized into a fighting force while we waited for reinforcements from Canada. The Battle Group was supposed to have a 10% reinforcement pool remain behind in Canada to backfill anyone sent home. Many of these reinforcements had already been used before we deployed due to last-minute illnesses, drug testing failures, and other reasons that caused folks not to be deployed.

There was no expectation that they would have to provide trained infantry to replace twenty or twenty-five positions in one crack, and it was becoming difficult to get that many folks ready to deploy quickly.

It meant for Charles Company that we would have to reorganize from within while we waited for new soldiers. My immediate plan was to request privates and corporals as reinforcements from Canada, and I would promote soldiers who were already part of Charles Company into the more senior positions that needed to be filled. I wanted these combat-proven, highly trained soldiers to lead their fellow Charles Company comrades, not a replacement from Canada.

When I finalized my plan, I passed it by the Battle Group's RSM, and CWO Bobby Girouard agreed to every promotion recommendation, even a few controversial ones. Over the next few days, we promoted several soldiers to Warrant Officer, Sergeant and Master Corporal, and those soldiers became the new leadership of Charles Company.

The Company remained in Kandahar Airfield for a few days as we transitioned. Soldiers were able to heal physically and mentally while sleeping in air-conditioned rooms and eating fresh meals. However, to a man, we were all asking when we would be able to return to the fight.

Each day, I would visit Major Savage in her office to let her know how well I was doing and that what was left of the Company would be moving out shortly and I was ready to go. She would smile, and some days when she was not overly busy, I would sit, and we would chat. One day, as I was standing at her door speaking to her, I lost my balance and fell up against her wall. She just looked at me and smiled.

19

BACK TO OPERATIONS

A couple of days later, Charles Company got orders to send one of its understrength platoons to relieve an armoured troop that was in Spin Boldak, a town on the border of Pakistan and the second-largest port of entry between the two countries. The remainder of the Company was to deploy to Ma'sum Ghar under the command of Major Andy Lussier, commander of the ISTAR (Intelligence, Surveillance, Target Acquisition, Reconnaissance) Squadron. All those physically able to go would deploy the next day.

When I heard, I moved as quickly as I could over to Major Savage's office.

By the time I got there, I was out of breath and feeling weak and dizzy but, putting on my best face, I knocked on her door and walked in. She took one look at me and said no even before I had spoken. She already knew what was going on with the Company, as she attended the Battle Group orders. She was already expecting me, but there was no way she would allow me to deploy with my soldiers. She did give me some hope when she said, "Come back in a few days, and I will look at you again."

Of course, as I mentioned earlier, math is not my greatest asset, and to me a few days meant tomorrow.

I did what I could with Captain Brown to get the soldiers ready. It would be the first time that they would be going outside the wire since Operation MEDUSA, and I could tell that some of them were a little apprehensive.

As we were preparing, Captain Brown pulled me aside to tell me that the acting Task Force Sergeant Major (the actual Sergeant Major was in Canada on holidays) had visited our soldiers in their quarters. After speaking to several of them, he had told the Task Force Commander that he was concerned that the soldiers of Charles Company did not trust the chain of command and should not be deployed outside the wire. I was furious. How dare the acting Task Force Sergeant Major visit my troops without me knowing and being present? There were unwritten rules, and he should have contacted me first.

I went to see him. He was an infantry soldier from the PPCLI, and I had met him several times over the years. Even though he was senior to me, I had no problem confronting him, as this was about my soldiers.

He immediately went on the defensive, telling me that he didn't need my permission to talk to any troops in the Task Force. He had found my soldiers to be very unprofessional. He said that he had asked them how they were feeling, and they began whining about how the chain of command had changed the plan and sent them into battle early before the enemy had been softened up with airpower and artillery and, as a result, we had lost soldiers.

'That's true," I snapped back at him. "They did send us in early. And if you didn't want to hear their opinion, you shouldn't have asked them."

I then told him if he wanted to see my soldiers again, he needed to contact me first and otherwise to stay the fuck out of my quarters. He then spoke to me in a way that someone who has never had a round fired at them would talk. He told me, as he had told my soldiers, that they needed to get on with the job and that the reason we have infantry soldiers was to fight and die. That was our role and to suck it up.

I just looked at him in amazement. "That's easy for you to say, living here behind the wire drinking Tim Horton's coffee. Stay the fuck away from my soldiers."

He never had a chance to respond as I turned around and left.

The whole way back to the Company lines, I kept thinking that this was it: I would be fired and sent back to Canada. But I also knew that I'd say it all again, in exactly the same way, if I had to. I never heard another word about the incident and, when I saw the individual again a few weeks later at Ma'sum Ghar, he acted as if it had never occurred. That was fine with me.

When I got back to Captain Brown, I could tell he was upset about something. He told me that the Battle Group Command Post had called him in. They told him that the Task Force Commander had ordered every Charles Company soldier to see the Coalition psychologist before they would be allowed to deploy outside the wire. It was obviously the result of the Task Force Sergeant Major's comments to the Commander about our soldiers' lack of trust in the senior leadership.

I was just as angry and upset, but fortunately, Lieutenant-Colonel Lavoie had flown into the airfield for orders, and as I was walking toward the HQ, I ran into him. I could freely express my disgust to him about what was happening to our soldiers, and he was not happy about this decision either. He took it up with the Task Force Commander, and the order was rescinded.

I informed Lieutenant-Colonel Lavoie that Captain Brown and I would speak to every soldier and decide if any should remain behind for additional rest and treatment. We wound up deciding that other than the soldiers that still needed time for their physical wounds to heal, only two soldiers should remain behind. They just needed some more time to get their head on straight, and we set them up to get some help from the professionals. However, after making that decision, I understood the predicament I was putting Major Savage in regarding my injuries.

Understanding it is one thing, but I was still not giving up.

I remember that feeling of dread as I watched the Company depart for the badlands and knowing that, once again I was safe and sound, I was dreading their next contact with the enemy. I stayed up to date on what was going on with the Company over the next several hours by dropping into the Battle Group Command Post and getting up-to-date situation reports.

I spent the next couple of days eating well, showering daily, and sleeping in my air-conditioned room, all the time wishing I were with my soldiers. From Major Savage's attitude and comments, I knew that she was close to allowing me to deploy, and I was getting excited.

In the meantime, I tried to enjoy the advantages of Kandahar Airfield and the nightly Tim Hortons meetings with MWO Rob MacRae and Terry Beers. Rob worked in Ops and kept me up to date on all the operational stuff, while Terry Beers was our Chief Clerk, and he had all the skinny on administration, allowances, and reinforcements from Canada for which we were still waiting.

BREAKING THE RULES

I went to a kitchen on the airfield for breakfast with Terry Beers and Rob MacRae one morning. Even though I was feeling much better, my hearing had not improved as much as I thought it had. As a result, I put Terry and myself in a very awkward position. I will keep this story vague to protect the innocent and the guilty.

While sitting in the mess hall at a table across from each other, Terry told me about a married Canadian soldier who worked here on the airfield behind the wire. He had found new love with another married Canadian soldier also here at the airfield. After only a few weeks, he called home to tell his wife in Petawawa that they were finished and that he had found true love.

I cannot imagine how his wife must have felt as she looked at their two young children, terrified about daddy being in Afghanistan. I remember thinking the man was a coward—calling home from this shithole to tell his wife that they were done and to be out of the PMQ when he got home. It was bad enough that these two were fraternizing, which is against the rules when Canadian soldiers are deployed. That kind of behaviour has resulted in people being charged, sent home, and even meant an end to their careers for a few. But, on top of that, these two were both married with kids.

After my experiences of the previous few weeks, I found absolutely no compassion or empathy for these two cowards. When the individual in question walked in through the door with his new love in tow, those were my thoughts. Now, I know this is not politically correct, but I said exactly what I was thinking to Terry and Rob.

"Are you telling me that he left his wife and kids for that hog?" The thirty or so people sitting around us stopped, looked at me and then looked at the two people coming through the door. Terry Beers lowered himself in his chair.

"Have you forgotten that you're fucking deaf? Everyone just heard you."

What I had thought was a low voice to Terry and Rob was really a loud, boisterous voice heard by all. Maybe even by our two lovebirds. However, they did not react, so perhaps they just wondered why everyone was looking around and why it went quiet when they walked in. To be honest, I didn't care if they had heard.

Terry looked like he was in shock. It was made worse when Rob began laughing, and I did too. What's done is done. I don't know how it turned out for these two lovebirds, but what I do know is that on return to their home base, his wife and two kids and her husband and two kids were at the assembly area to welcome them home. I wouldn't have wanted to be them, and I hope those cowards haven't found happiness.

Early the following morning, I went to see Major Savage and asked her once again to sign off on my medical limitations to allow me to re-join the Company on the battlefield. She said that from what she had seen and heard from the medics at the hospital from my daily check-ups, I needed more time to allow the concussion symptoms to go away. I argued that the Company needed me more and that they would soon start sweeping through the same area of Pashmul that we had previously attacked. That was more important than a few lingering health issues.

I explained how the leadership of the Company was gone and that it was vital that they see their Sergeant Major back at the front with them as they begin sweeping through the area that had taken so much from them. I told her what she needed to hear—I had no balance issues, the headaches were gone, and my hearing had returned—which were all lies, of course.

She finally looked up at me and said, "Sergeant Major, if you're so eager to go get yourself killed, go ahead."

I said thank you, and she stood up, hugged me, and I left.

A part of me felt terrible for lying to her, but I think she knew and just gave in. As I said previously, she was a great officer, a great Royal Canadian, a great doctor, and a great Canadian.

She is sorely missed.

20
RETURN TO CHARLES COMPANY

It took me only a few minutes to head over to Ops and ask my friend, Rob MacRae, to find me the next transport out to Ma'sum Ghar to link up with Charles Company. He informed me that my Company had just moved across the Arghandab River and into the killing fields we fought on a few weeks earlier. They had encountered little resistance, as most of the Taliban had either been killed or captured, and the remnants had slipped away, with only a few hard-core holdouts left to slow down the Coalition. My soldiers had been sweeping toward the white school and would probably be there in a couple of days.

Rob was able to get me booked on a helicopter for the following morning and, after almost two weeks of waiting, I was finally going to be re-joining my Company in the field. That night was spent getting ready and making sure my replacement kit was all working and was comfortable and accessible. I called home and spoke to Julie, JJ and Jana and told them not to worry, I was fine, and it was quiet here now.

I went and had a fresh meal and spent a few minutes with Terry and Rob over at Tim Hortons. I had a coffee and doughnut too, knowing it would be a while before I had that opportunity again. Then I went back to my room and checked and rechecked my ammo, checked my weapons to make sure they were good to go, and strapped on my knives, which I always carried with me and had been lucky to get back from my burned kit. Then, I tried to sleep.

Sleep did not come easy. I had nightmares and woke up sweating and gasping for breath, worried about the next day.

Was I ready to go back out?

I knew I had some issues I would have to deal with physically, but mentally, could I carry the burden?

Would the Company welcome me back, or had they moved on without me?

PART THREE - AFGHANISTAN

Finally, I fell asleep and two hours later my alarm woke me up and I jumped out of bed, ready for a great reunion. I found out that jumping out of bed quickly with a concussion is stupid. I found myself on the floor and struggled to get up and keep my balance. I knew that there were still lingering issues, and this scared me. Was I ready to go? After sitting on the bed for a few minutes, my equilibrium returned.

I got dressed and headed for breakfast.

An hour later, Sergeant Chris Pickering, the acting Company Quartermaster, dropped me off at the airfield. A few minutes later, I was on an American Blackhawk helicopter on the way to Ma'sum Ghar, one of our largest Forward Operating Bases (FOBs) in Afghanistan.

I soon found out that concussions and combat flying in a Blackhawk do not go well together either. I had a massive headache, and I had to do everything in my power not to throw up or scream. Those American pilots knew how to fly in enemy territory. I would have enjoyed it during normal circumstances, but rolling and diving at high speed with the doors open can be a nightmare for someone who has recently been concussed.

After what felt like a lifetime but was actually less than an hour, we landed at Ma'sum Ghar. As I got out of the aircraft I was met by an armoured soldier and led to the ISTAR Squadron Command Post. They, of course, had not been expecting me, so I told them I needed to get across the river and rejoin my Company as soon as possible. The Command Post notified Captain Brown and the ISTAR commander, Major Lussier, that I was here and that I would be brought across in about an hour. I was excited and relieved to be here finally and hoped the Company felt the same way.

I spent the next thirty minutes or so drinking water, checking my weapons and ammunition and trying to recover from the helicopter ride. I took the time to go to the exact location in Ma'sum Ghar where the A-10 aircraft had hit Charles Company, and where so many of my soldiers and friends were killed and wounded. I sat in silence and reflected. I cried over those lost and those who would live with invisible wounds for the rest of their lives.

A few minutes later, the Squadron Second-in-Command came to tell me that his vehicle would take me across the river and to grab my kit. I had all my fighting gear and rucksack, and when I got to his vehicle, I realized it was a Coyote. It is the recce version of the LAV and is much smaller, as it is not built to carry a section of soldiers. I threw my kit into the back and crawled through the narrow door, where I found myself squeezed into a tiny space that did not have a seat. I lay across a pile of kit and ammo boxes and waited for the Coyote to leave.

The Second-in-Command yelled down from the turret that they were having trouble with the air conditioning, so it would not be comfortable. That was the understatement of the day. The ride was a nightmare. To begin with, I am a big man, and once all my fighting gear is on, I do not fit well into small spaces. The vehicle bounced and bumped its way across the base of the mountain, then into the Arghandab River and out the other side into the burned-out fields of Panjwai.

As a passenger, you cannot see anything from the back of a Coyote and you're at the mercy of the driver as he takes every bump and pothole at his pleasure. Some drivers take pleasure in making the drive a total nightmare, especially when their passenger is an infantry Sergeant Major. I probably would.

I had initially removed my helmet because my headache was back, but about thirty seconds into the drive, I put it back on. I could not afford another head injury. I made the right decision as my head hit the roof hard on several occasions.

After about thirty minutes which felt much longer, the vehicle came to a stop. I did not feel well. I had been bounced around, hit my head several times, and it was probably about 130° Fahrenheit inside that cramped space.

The commander yelled down from the turret, "Sergeant Major, you're here."

I felt like I had to throw up, but I did everything I could to keep it down. In hindsight, perhaps I should have left a little surprise for the driver who seemed to take pleasure in making sure I had the roughest ride possible.

I had no idea what to expect or where I was, but I needed to get out of that vehicle. I threw open the back door, and the light burst in and hurt my eyes. I squinted, but I could not see anything, just shapes moving around. I hauled myself over the kit to the door, swung my legs out and then my body. I landed on my feet on the very ground that had taken so much from Charles Company and me personally.

My vision cleared, and I saw Captain Brown about five metres in front of me, and I took a step toward him. I am sure he must have thought I was drunk. I remember swaying left, then right, and then I did a face-plant in the dirt and the dust. I tried to get up, but I could not. Then hands grabbed me and pulled me onto my feet. Two HQ soldiers had come to my rescue. Now, directly in front of me, was Captain Brown with his hand stuck out and a huge welcoming smile on his face. I know he was concerned about me, but I quickly regained my composure, and I made a joke about the hot, sweaty, cramped ride that was the cause of my stumble.

It was like a homecoming. Every soldier that came by welcomed me back. I made my way over to my LAV, put my rucksack inside and took a moment to see exactly where we were. I also allowed myself to think of Shane Stachnik, Rick Nolan, Frank Mellish, Will Cushley, and Mark Graham for just a moment. I then turned to Captain Brown and asked him for the latest orders.

OPERATION MEDUSA – PHASE 2, TASK FORCE GRIZZLY

I had arrived back at the Company when the next phase of Operation MEDUSA was in full swing. Major Andrew Lussier's ISTAR Squadron, an element from the Royal Canadian Dragoons that was the equivalent of a company, took the remainder of Charles Company under command. Lussier's squadron was assigned to Task Force Grizzly, commanded by an American Special Forces Colonel named Steve Williams, known on the radio by the call sign "Grizzly 6." He was now in charge of holding the southern battle line in Panjwai and disrupting the enemy forces in the south.

PART THREE - AFGHANISTAN

His initial orders were simple. We were to take ISTAR Squadron and the remnants of Charles Company, with attached snipers and forward observers, and make ourselves look like a thousand-man organization. We had to make the Taliban believe that we were still 1 RCR Battle Group, so other elements could manoeuvre around and attack them where they didn't expect it.

They carried out this mission for several days from Ma'sum Ghar by hammering the Taliban positions with fire from the LAVs, artillery, fast air and helicopter gunships, all the while giving the impression of a much larger force.

As this was going on, the Battle Group had regrouped and executed a methodical, phased attack from the north, led by Major Geoff Abthorpe and MWO Ken Lockyer, the Command Team for Bravo Company. Bolstering these forces in the north was Alpha Company of the 2nd Battalion PPCLI, led by Major Charles Wright and MWO Shawn Stevens.

In addition, there was Task Force 31, which was composed mainly of U.S. Special Forces, and Task Force Mohawk, a company of American soldiers from the 10th Mountain Division, who were also involved in the fighting. Backing up the whole operation were the big 155mm guns of a battery of 2 Royal Canadian Horse Artillery, commanded by Major Greg Ivey and MWO Bob Montague.

Task Force Grizzly carried out their mission with precision for several days, ensuring a continual bombardment of direct and indirect fire on the enemy positions across the Arghandab River. The Taliban were being squeezed from three different directions. Task Force Grizzly continued their mission until they received word to move across the river in force and onto Objective Rugby, centred on the white school. This was the area that had proven so deadly on the third day of September, and where Charles Company now needed to go again.

After getting briefed by Captain Brown, we headed off to meet Colonel Williams. I immediately saw a man who looked at war and the art of war a little differently than most Canadians. He was an American soldier who had cut his teeth in the world of Special Forces. He had a uniquely aggressive approach to war fighting, described by those who served with him as 'ballsy' and that he was a "cowboy." Williams was always out front, leading the advance, but both Captain Brown and Major Lussier were not convinced about this run-and-gun approach to war fighting. Both Canadian officers would confront Colonel Williams over the next few days.

I have great respect for both of these fine Canadian officers. It was not easy to confront a Colonel when you are a Major and even more challenging as a Captain, and Williams was a hero in the U.S. Special Forces community. They both had the welfare of their Canadian soldiers at heart, and I believe they both knew that Charles Company was not only understrength, but we were still vulnerable.

That evening and night, I got a firsthand look at how Colonel Williams handled the battlefield and his view on this next phase of the operation, which was to sweep through to Objective Rugby, destroy any last Taliban, and find and secure any IEDs and explosives.

He would give us a distance. For example, "Clear the next thousand metres," and off we would go, sometimes with him up front and leading and sometimes in the way.

We had cleared less than one kilometre of compounds, wadis, trenches, and fields during my first day back, the Company was tired and hungry, and the night was coming quickly. We now went about getting our LAVs and soldiers into position for night security and working on the plan for the next day's advance. Individual firing positions were prepared, LAVs and machine-guns were placed, and soldiers settled down for the night.

I took the opportunity to walk around the position to check on security and speak to all the Charles Company soldiers that I had not already seen throughout the day.

It is the best that I had felt in weeks.

They had many questions about how all the wounded soldiers were doing, and I updated them on what I knew. I asked them how they were doing, and they were all happy to be out of Kandahar Airfield and back out in the dirt and the filth of Panjwai.

Colonel Williams had three or four Humvees with him that was part of his HQ, and they were at his beck and call. As I made my way back to the HQ location that night, there was Colonel Williams, gazing out over tomorrow's area of advance, smoking a cigar, and looking like General Patton. Even though his attitude toward war and the life of his soldiers seemed a little too casual for some, I had great respect for him. The thought of taking the fight to the enemy brought a smile to my face. I stood next to him and asked him if he thought tomorrow would be a tough fight as we got closer to the area that was so heavily defended a few weeks ago.

He replied in a very casual manner with his American drawl, "Well, Sergeant Major, if there are any fucking Taliban or fucking terrorists or anybody fucking else that wants a fight tomorrow, you Canadians will kill them all and enjoy every minute of it."

I smiled up at him and said, "HOOAH, sir."

And I believed it.

One of the Humvees that was part of Colonel Williams' headquarters carried his Psychological Operations Team (Psy Ops), composed of two American staff sergeants who had one purpose in life: to mess with the enemy's heads. As we were standing there together, Colonel Williams turned to one of the sergeants and told him to get on with the show. I had no idea what he meant, and I was in for a total surprise.

I made sure that I did not stand too close to Colonel Williams because as he stood there smoking his cigar, he was in plain sight of any enemy to our front, and I did not want to be a prize for some Taliban sniper. However, Colonel Williams was fearless, perhaps a little too much so.

As I was standing there in the dark, the PsyOps team set up these massive speakers and ran wires to their vehicle. They then handed a microphone to call sign Grizzly.

In that same U.S. drawl that he had spoken to me in earlier, he started talking in English to any remnants of Taliban or their terrorist supporters that were in the vicinity. The fact that most of these maggots did not speak English seemed lost on him.

PART THREE - AFGHANISTAN

The speakers boomed as Colonel Williams told anyone listening: "Tomorrow, we are coming to kill you. We are not going to ask you to surrender. We want to kill you. If you do not want to die tomorrow, put your weapons on the ground and leave now. Anyone still in the area tomorrow will be considered the enemy and will be killed."

He went on for another minute or so, explaining how good it would feel to kill them and that, please, they should remain behind so he would not be disappointed. I was gobsmacked. It was a first for me, and I must say, I enjoyed the show.

When he was finished speaking, he had one of the staff sergeants repeat his message in Pashtun, and then the PsyOps team began blaring music over the speakers. I am not a connoisseur of music; all I know is that it was the loudest head-banging heavy metal tunes I had ever heard. I was not exactly sure how much damage the explosion of September 3 had done to my hearing, but after this, it was worse.

A couple of hours later, as I lay there on the ground, covered by a poncho liner, I was thinking that anyone who was out there waiting for us had probably packed up and gotten out of town. If I had been out there, I would not want to face these freaks. I remember smiling as I fell asleep to AC/DC's Back in Black.

The next morning, an hour before first light, the soldiers were up, ate an MRE for breakfast, used the public hole that was hand dug for their toilet needs, and made sure that their kit was sorted and ready to go for the upcoming advance.

Colonel Williams called this a clearance operation, but as Captain Wessan (one of the platoon commanders) correctly said, what we were doing in Canadian military terms was called an Advance to Contact, and he was right. We would move toward the next objective until someone tried to stop us, and then we would kill them and continue.

The LAVs were unable to always move with us, as the terrain was just not suitable. Large wadis, which are ditches that mountain water has run through for thousands of years, crisscrossed the land. There were large compounds with two-foot-thick mud walls and grape-drying huts that looked like castles from a time long ago. On top of all of that was the constant threat of IEDs and unexploded ordnance. And so, the LAVs usually remained at a distance and provided overwatch and security as we advanced on foot.

We moved forward with one platoon up front, our HQ behind that and a small reserve in the rear for emergencies. We wanted to be slow and methodical, but Colonel Williams wanted to go quickly and bypass areas not deemed a threat. It caused some heated conversations on the radio between Brown, Lussier and call sign Grizzly.

In the end, Captain Wessan, the lead Platoon Commander, did it the way he was trained to do so and the way he had promised his soldiers—slowly and carefully. He had already sent home too many soldiers in body bags, and there was no rush to clear the areas, so he wanted to do it right. The Afghans have a saying, "The Coalition may own the watches, but we have the time." It meant that eventually, we would go home, and they could just wait for us to leave.

In this case, we believed we had the time and to rush to failure made no sense. As

WHITE SCHOOL, BLACK MEMORIES

I walked by Captain Wessan, I touched his arm and said, "Slow is smooth, and smooth is fast." I wanted this young Canadian infantry officer to know that I had his back and trusted his instinct and experience.

By 0600 it was already stinking hot. The ground was rough and rugged. The constant threat of enemy engagement or stepping on an IED caused us to be even more slow and meticulous, which continued to irritate Colonel Williams. I would often see him move ahead of the advancing Platoon with a handful of his headquarters staff. The Canadians would ignore him, and eventually, he would return.

We had to secure every compound, every ditch, and as we got closer to Objective Ruby, we started to see more and more battle damage from days of artillery and bombing. There were large holes, destroyed compounds and both bodies and body parts. Many of the dead had been removed and buried by both the Taliban and some of the locals to follow the Islamic tradition of doing so within twenty-four hours of death, but their own safety prevented them from getting them all.

We did not touch them as we advanced other than to ensure that they were dead. In most cases, that was obvious. Someone else would have to worry about cleaning up. Sometimes bodies were booby-trapped, and we did not have time to deal with that as we were still looking for a fight.

As the hours went by, it got hotter and hotter, and the troops had used up most of the water they were able to carry on their person. It was now around 1200 hours. We had advanced less than one kilometre and had not had any contact with the enemy.

Perhaps the fatherly advice from Colonel Williams the night before had persuaded all the bad guys to leave, or maybe they were waiting just ahead. However, we found several IEDs and had to mark them for the engineers to come and blow. As each IED was blown, we would take cover and thank God that no one had stepped on it or driven over it.

Around this time, we could get some of our vehicles to join us, using a route that we had cleared. They were able to bring us some much-needed water.

Here, once again, is an event that I will always remember with fondness. I have always been a big fan of cola, and my drink of choice was Diet Coke. As I walked through the field with about sixty pounds of spare ammo, medical supplies, water and rations on my back, in about 120°F heat with a massive headache, waiting for some asshole to shoot me, I was summoned by one of my soldiers. Sergeant Craig Dinsmore was sitting in the passenger seat of a lightly armoured vehicle with his driver as he watched this disabled old Sergeant Major stumbling around under the weight of a heavy pack. As I got closer, he yelled over to me with a grin on his face, "Sergeant Major, I bet you would love an ice-cold Diet Coke."

I looked him right in the eye and told him to fuck off. When I was hot, tired, and under stress, the last thing I needed was one of my senior guys messing with my head. Maintaining that shit-eating grin, he says, "Sergeant Major, do you want an ice-cold Diet Coke?"

Something about the way he said it the second time made me stop. I walked over to

PART THREE - AFGHANISTAN

his vehicle and said, "I would love one." He got out, opened some container I couldn't see and handed me a can of Diet Coke with a layer of ice on it. After rubbing it on my face a few times, I opened it and swallowed it in two or three gulps. I had a sharp pain behind my eyes and my chest hurt like hell, but all I could do was smile. That was the best Diet Coke I have ever drunk and likely ever will. I thanked Sergeant Dinsmore and moved along to catch up with Captain Brown.

I meant to ask Sergeant Dinsmore how he was able to accomplish that, but I never did. Maybe the next time I see him, I will ask, as he is still serving his country. I have never underestimated the abilities of Canadian soldiers to find a way to bring a little comfort to their lives. In this case, one of them made my day, month and year.

Once again, I could tell that Colonel Williams was not happy that we were having the LAV vehicles come up and that we had just told the soldiers to put out security while the remainder grabbed some water and food. Even though our progress was slow, the stress and heat of the advance and lack of water can cause exhaustion, and heat exhaustion can be extremely dangerous. The break was much needed.

We had stopped in an open field that had been used to grow pomegranates and melons, and to our luck, it was picking season. After warning the soldiers not to overeat, as we had a lot more work to do, we enjoyed the fruits of our labour. The melons and pomegranates were delicious and juicy, and I enjoyed a couple while talking with some of the troops.

While sitting there, I had the opportunity to think about my last twenty-four hours. I realized that I was so busy, focused on the task at hand and ensuring the soldiers were performing well that I never even thought about myself. I never stumbled once, my hearing was not a concern, and I had not even thought about the headaches.

But they were there, and for the first time, I realized that my head was pounding. Luckily, my medical contacts within the battalion had given me enough meds to get me through the rough patches. I had put about thirty pills loose in my pocket, and as I had been advancing, I had been eating them like candy. I put my hand in my pocket to realize that I had taken about twelve of these enormously powerful painkillers in six hours—no wonder I felt okay. My medical friend had suggested I take two every eight hours; I was never particularly good at math. I would continue taking large amounts of painkillers over the next six months in Afghanistan and after returning to Canada for several years.

After our much-needed break. a delicious MRE lunch, and freshly filled water bottles, we were ready to advance again. I could see the white school just a short distance to our front. That was Objective Rugby and had been the objective for Charles Company on September 3 during the opening hours of Operation MEDUSA.

It was now today's objective.

We continued to advance, and the ground began to look like pictures I had seen from the First and Second World Wars—everything was utterly destroyed. Truly very little remained standing. Every compound and structure had been hit and, in most cases, eliminated. We started seeing lots of sandals, torn and burned clothing, weapons, ammunition, combat vests, magazines and what appeared to be body parts and bloodstains. I felt a sense of relief seeing it, knowing that this was the remains of my enemy, and that many of them had been killed, maimed and torn apart by the Coalition forces.

There was no doubt that they had bloodied us, and they had also earned my respect for standing their ground under relentless bombardment and overwhelming force, but in the end, I was standing here on their most sacred ground, and most of them were dead. The insurgents' gamble of massing their forces and taking on the Canadians had failed miserably.

As we cleared the remains of compounds, we started finding IED components and piles of dried poppies, opium, and marijuana—sometimes by the ton. Once again, we marked it, called in its location, and left it for the engineers and the exploitation teams to look after.

Sensitive exploitation teams would sift through everything, gathering intelligence to add to the big picture of what was happening in the area. Explosive Ordnance Disposal Teams were constantly destroying unexploded shells and bombs as we found them, some dating back to the Soviet invasion.

We would also use our engineers to blow holes in compound walls so that soldiers could go in and clear them without having to use obvious entrance points that could be booby-trapped. Similarly, bulldozers would clear routes or make new ones for our LAVs to use for resupply.

In one compound we found a pile of books, notes, maps, unmarked DVDs, and a huge amount of money, both Afghani and U.S. I do not know how much it was, but it was more than I had ever seen in my life and was certainly in the thousands. There were also pictures of Mullah Omar and Osama Bin Laden. Those did not always survive our visits. We left everything else as we found it for the experts who would be following behind us. The engineers and the exploitation teams took anything that could be used for intelligence purposes. Everything else was destroyed in place.

There was no doubt in my mind that the Taliban, despite what they preached, had no problems using the poppy trade to fund their war. I also learned later that many Afghans, including soldiers, police officers and yes, even the Taliban, used drugs daily. Hypocrites, one and all.

We continued to advance and, other than a few donkeys and some goats and sheep, we did not encounter any life, either locals or Taliban.

So, we continued to push forward, getting extraordinarily little information from Colonel Williams, other than basic directions like, "Two hundred more metres."

At one point, I noticed that Captain Wessan and his platoon seemed to be standing around, distracted. I rushed forward to tell them to get into firing positions and keep their heads in the game. Standing around without being behind cover will get people killed, and did on several occasions.

But as I was speaking to Captain Wessan, I realized where we were. We were back on the same ground where WO Mellish and Private Cushley had been killed and where

PART THREE - AFGHANISTAN

I had been injured. I was not sure how to feel, but things started to become familiar as I looked around. Not even the relentless bombing that this area had endured over the last two weeks could hide the events that had unfolded here. It was getting dark, and our vehicles had been able to move forward to our location. As I was trying to situate everyone for the long night ahead, I could see the remains of our vehicles that had been left behind nearly two weeks ago.

We had abandoned an armoured Zettelmeyer, a LAV and a G-Wagon. Coalition airstrikes had destroyed them to make sure the enemy did not have the benefit of their use or the propaganda of photos.

As I had envisioned it many times, we were the first soldiers on this position since September 3. It was very appropriate that it was soldiers from Charles Company—we may not have taken this ground on September 3, but we had it now.

That night was spent in all-around defence, securing the ground where so much Canadian blood had been spilled. Except for the explosions and firefights to the north and east, the night was quiet. The soldiers of Charles Company had time to think about those who had sacrificed so much here in this very dirt. I believe that there was a sense of redemption for many soldiers who now found themselves occupying the same piece of dirt they had failed to take on September 3. I don't think I slept a wink that night, and it wasn't just because of the head-banging music coming from the PsyOps guys. My mind continually replayed the actions of September 3.

What could we have done differently?
Was there a better way?
Did we make the right decisions?
I then spent hours playing the blame game.
Why did we go early?
Was General Fraser getting pressure from his higher headquarters?
Had he decided, himself, to change the plan?
Did the Commanding Officer fight back hard enough?
Did Major Sprague and myself push back hard enough?

Eventually, I was able to put those thoughts aside and force myself to worry about the now. I got up and patrolled around our defensive position to ensure that we were in the correct posture for the night's security. As always, we were. Charles Company soldiers were manning the LAVs, using our night vision capability to watch for any Taliban that would try to sneak in, machine-guns were manned, and soldiers were alert. In contrast, their comrades who weren't on alert tried to get some well-deserved rest. However, I don't know if anyone got to sleep that night.

As I once again lay on the dirt under my poncho liner, my mind could only focus on those who we had lost here, and I silently cried to myself, knowing full well that others were doing the same.

The next morning, we were ordered to head north into the maze of compounds and the very tight and vulnerable terrain around the white school. Again, I do not remember any real plan from Colonel Williams, just a direction and a distance.

WHITE SCHOOL, BLACK MEMORIES

I remember Captain Wessan kind of losing control a little bit and yelling about how this was not how we do things and that we were going to lose people. I saw Captain Brown quietly speaking with him and touching his arm.

I went by him, and I remember saying to him, "Sir, just carry on the way you have been doing it. Slow and steady wins the race."

He smiled at me, but I could see the stress on his face. I knew he did not want to cause any more soldiers to go home in body bags.

FLASHBACK – SEPTEMBER 3

My thoughts went back to a few weeks earlier when we had crossed this river the first time.

In the middle of all that carnage and, while trying to gather the wounded and get them undercover, I had seen Captain Wessan running by with his pistol in his hand, and no rifle, yelling about something. My first thought had been, "Where's his rifle?" He had just lost his Platoon Warrant and friend, Rick Nolan, and I believe he had snapped just for a second, but he recovered and carried on with the fight. I had every faith in him that he would continue.

Just a few minutes after both Platoon Warrants had been killed and everyone was gathering up for the withdrawal, Captain Hiltz, commander of 8 Platoon, discovered that one of his sections was still out on the left flank. Coming from that direction were the sounds of a tremendous firefight. One way or another, the Section Commander had ended up back at the LAV without his troops, and they were pinned down. After a quick glance from Hiltz to Captain Wessan, who just appeared beside him without his rifle, they headed in the direction of the section. Wessan hit the berm first with Hiltz sprinting behind him, carrying the heavy radio in his backpack, and it was obviously slowing him down.

They both stood on the forward edge of the berm with enemy bullets cracking past. They could hear the trapped soldiers yelling for help. Hiltz immediately started to fire his C8 rifle toward the enemy, with Wessan firing his pistol. They were hoping that the covering fire, such as it was, would be enough for the trapped section to find the courage to start moving back.

It worked and the trapped section, using a manoeuvre called the Aussie Peel Back, used fire and manoeuvre to cover for each other. Even though they endured a tremendous amount of enemy fire, they all survived and made it back to the LAV, thanks in part to the courageous actions of those two fine young officers.

TASK FORCE GRIZZLY – DAY 2

The following morning, it was clear that the Taliban had been torn apart. Except for a few minor contacts with some hard-core remnants willing to sacrifice themselves for

PART THREE - AFGHANISTAN

the cause, there was no major fighting. Objective Rugby fell to us.

There was one incident that occurred that at the time gave me pause, but today causes me to laugh. We were on foot, moving through a small open area adjacent to a compound that had just been cleared. I approached Colonel Williams and a small group of his staff as they stood around what appeared to be a tunnel entrance but could have been an abandoned well. Colonel Williams did not want to send anyone down into it to clear it as he wanted to continue the advance. But he also wanted to make sure no one would pop up as we left and shoot us in the back.

As we are standing there and, without discussion or fanfare, he took a grenade off his belt, pulled the pin, and dropped it in the hole. I threw myself back away from the spot and lay on my belly as close to the ground as I could get. Others did the same, except the Colonel and an American staff sergeant who just stood there as the grenade exploded, causing dirt and dust to fly everywhere.

My concern was that we didn't know what was in that hole, which could have been an ammo store that would have blown us all to kingdom come. But I am sure those thoughts didn't cross the Colonel's mind. As I was about to get up, I saw the staff sergeant pull the pin from another grenade and toss it in. Fuck, were they nuts or what? I planned to make a comment to the Colonel but, instead, I just shook my head and carried on with the advance.

Now that we were here on Objective Rugby, it was a little disappointing—all this blood and treasure spent for what? The white school, which was part of so many conversations, stories, and future songs and was the cause of so much grief, was now a pile of rubble and did not deserve the importance it was given.

We established a line of defence just north of the remnants of the building and started seeing all the damage that was done. There were dozens of IEDs visible from our positions, and people were told to stay where they were and not move around. The Taliban may have been gone, but it would take days, and perhaps weeks, to make this area safe, and even then, things would be missed.

While preparing our fighting positions in case of attack, we started seeing LAV antennas coming from the north. I couldn't believe it; Rugby was secure, and the link-up with the forces from the north was complete.

With this part of the operations finished, I took a moment to look over at Colonel Williams. He was smiling and happy, mission accomplished.

"Sergeant Major," he said, "I'm so proud of you Canadians. You are true warriors."

Grizzly Six was a man heralded by one and all as a great and brave combat leader, most often seen driving or walking in the direction of enemy fire. Not everyone agreed with his methods, and some believed his willingness to risk his soldiers' lives was a mistake, but no one doubted his courage.

As he was about to leave us, he pulled Captain Brown and I aside and told us how proud he was to have served with Canadians, and that there was not a better partner in the world. He told us that we should be immensely proud of our soldiers and that he had fought worldwide from Iraq to Afghanistan to South America and places that will never be talked about. He said that he would fight with Canadians anytime. He then shook our hand and presented us with the Task Force Grizzly coin. It is a part of my collection today.

From my perspective, it was a privilege to work with such a courageous leader. I believe that Major Sprague would have liked him as they both thought outside the box and were unconventional leaders.

BATTLEFIELD INTELLIGENCE – A KEY TO ALL BATTLES

I believe that Canadian soldiers and Canadian leadership have learned many valuable lessons from Operation MEDUSA, and those lessons would be used in many battles to come. Unfortunately, they would quickly be forgotten in others.

One of the constant themes in Afghanistan was the struggle to find the right balance between aggressive operations and reckless operations. A common denominator to both should be battlefield intelligence. Without sound intelligence, any advance will have to endure significant risk and possible calamity.

Charles Company learned this the hard way on September 3, 2006.

I believe we went into battle during the opening days of Operation MEDUSA without the intelligence picture we needed. The information we needed was out there and in the hands of both Canadian and Coalition partners. For some reason, it did not get passed to us.

A few days after this event, I saw a Canadian intelligence officer briefing an American Special Forces Colonel. He was using a detailed drawing of Objective Ruby, including fighting positions and routes he had access to before commencement of Operation MEDUSA.

It made me incredibly angry, and I had to walk away before I said or did something that I would regret. I believe that there was tremendous pressure to conduct that operation from both our military and political masters, and the result was that we rushed into initial failure. I don't know if it was pressure to get a good news story for Canadians or about making military and political careers. Still, a good plan agreed upon and understood by all was replaced by a frontal assault against a superior number of enemies dug in behind a prepared defensive position. The result should have been foreseen.

By the end of Operation MEDUSA, Charles Company of The Royal Canadian Regiment was the most decorated and bloodied company in the Canadian Army. Men such as Funnel, O'Rourke, Teal, Niefer, and Fawcett would receive medals for their bravery and valour, while many others would receive other awards.

The rest of the fighting men and women of Charles Company may not have received formal recognition, but their heroics over that first twenty-four-hour period have made every Canadian proud. Whatever the historians decide about this battle is a thing for the future, but I know what I know.

With the combat phase of Operation MEDUSA theoretically finished, the reconstruction phase could begin.

LEAVE

By mid-September, the Canadian Battle Group were operating well into what was considered enemy territory. Lieutenant-Colonel Lavoie noted that the ground that had once given the insurgents an advantage was now being turned against them. It was the perfect defensive ground, and it was now ours, and we were going to hold it.

We had enjoyed the full support of NATO for this operation and even had air support from the USS Abraham Lincoln in the Indian Ocean. The sound of artillery and bombs had become normal background noise, and the troops hardly noticed. Even the distinctive sound of the A-10 cannon, described by a fellow Newfoundlander as "the sound a whale makes when it hits a ship," had become second nature.

At the same time as all this was taking place, a persistent rumour started that a squadron of Leopard C2 tanks from Canada would be arriving shortly and joining the fight. Although they would come too late to affect this battle, they would become an essential piece of future operations.

I guess some rumours do come true.

Shortly after Task Force Grizzly departed, Charles Company was reunited with our Platoon returning to the fold from Spin Boldak. We still had not received our reinforcements, but I had received word that we would be getting the first group within a few days. That was great news as not only were we missing about thirty soldiers from death and injuries, but we had also started to commence the mandatory leave period.

Every soldier in the Battle Group would receive about three weeks leave, which ended up being closer to three and a half by the time travel was accounted for, including in and out of Kandahar Airfield (KAF) and home and back.

Leave has always been a big issue for all deployments, and most of the leadership agrees that it should not happen and should be given at the end of the tour. You can only imagine the difficulty in planning individual periods of leave for every person in the whole Company, trying to prioritize the needs of the individual with the needs of the unit.

We always needed to have enough leaders, drivers, gunners, and other qualified folks on the ground. Of course, leave periods often overlapped by a few days at a time, which meant that you were missing double the people for that period.

The company leave plot was planned in Petawawa. My CQ, WO Keith Olstad, and I took on the task, and with assistance from the Platoon Warrants, we came up with a workable solution. This task took weeks and literally hundreds of hours of work. Soldiers wanted their leave during kids' birthdays, anniversaries and, of course, everyone wanted Christmas. We looked at whether soldiers were married or single, if they had kids, what date they preferred, and, of course, most importantly, we always had to keep a fighting force together.

It was probably one of the most challenging and time-consuming things we had ever planned. We finally completed it, and WO Olstad came up with a beautiful chart, which showed all hundred and fifty soldiers and their leave periods, all colour-coded with dates and overlap times. Then we presented it to Major Sprague and Captain Brown. They liked the plan and were impressed with the beautiful chart. There were a couple of changes that they wanted to make as part of the bigger picture, things that we had not considered, and of course, with such a finely tuned plan, a couple of changes affected the whole thing.

It crumbled like a house of cards.

After another couple of days of hard work, we had the final solution. It was presented to the Company about a month before deploying to allow the soldiers to brief their families and make plans for their holidays.

But once we were in Afghanistan and leave had begun, there were new concerns. The Taliban continued to try and kill us, and there were now fewer of us as well. Trying to do combat operations was much harder, and we were always looking for people. We had to shut down complete sections while people were on leave, including their LAVs, so firepower was missing. We knew during the planning phase for leave that it would make things difficult, but we never realized how difficult it would really be.

Many soldiers approach me over the next couple of months, volunteering to give up their leave and remain behind. The response given was the same each time: leave is mandatory, and you will take it. If you do not want to go home, go sit in a hotel in Dubai, but you will not be here.

I found myself in the same position the day before I was to go on leave. We had been in constant contact with the enemy for several weeks, and I believed I was needed in theatre. I got the same answer from the Company Commander that I had given to the soldiers and again from Lieutenant-Colonel Lavoie the morning I was leaving.

"No, you cannot stay. Go home."

REPLACEMENTS

The only bright spot during this time was the arrival of our first replacements. It had taken a little longer than we anticipated, but they were finally here. The ramps dropped on the vehicles in FOB Wilson, and out came the first dozen or so bright-eyed and confused-looking soldiers. Some I immediately recognized, while others had never trained with us but were trained by other companies. I think everyone was excited to get the new troops, especially with all the vacancies we had and the absence of those on leave.

There was, however, a little bit of concern. These guys had not been in combat yet, and none of them had been bloodied in battle. Charles Company had learned many valuable lessons over the past couple of months. There was concern from some of the junior leadership that these guys may not be up to the task.

I spoke to the leadership of Charles Company, and I told them that they would have to try to ease these guys into operations and make sure that, over the next few days, all those valuable lessons we had learned were passed on. I reminded them that these young men were Royal Canadians and that, just like those of us who had been here for a while, they would also step up and make us all proud.

I do not know if my little chat helped, but I never heard anything negative after that, and all those replacements were forced into battle within days.

We spent the next week securing the area around the white school and searching the compounds and grape huts around Route Summit and beyond. It was a very sombre moment when we could get to the area of the destroyed Canadian vehicles, as this was hallowed ground and was soaked in Canadian blood. We would find a Canadian flak jacket and tactical vest and some Canadian clothing that we buried in location with a small, hastily built cross. We even found a notebook that had not been destroyed, and a variety of personal kit with soldiers' names on it. Many of the individual items and damaged military kit that we found were also buried in location.

It was a very personal moment for many of us as we stood at the exact spot where our friends had been killed and were able to take a moment to remember them. As I stood by the remains of Three-One Bravo and the G-Wagon, I took a moment to remember my friend, WO Rick Nolan, and the story relayed to me by a Coalition sniper who was in a perfect location to observe what went down that day. He reiterated the heroic tale that was discussed earlier about the initial withdrawal of Three-One Bravo with the wounded and WO Nolan's body and how he watched as it ended up on its side in the ditch.

Even though not all our soldiers may have been aware, this sniper and his partner provided covering fire as the soldiers got out of the LAV and made their way to Three-One Charlie or the rear. The snipers watched as Taliban insurgents swarmed the LAV and tried to get inside where Rick's body had been left and how our snipers were quickly able to kill several of them before the rest of them gave up and finally withdrew. They then watched as the Company laid down an enormous amount of fire as a section LAV returned and rescued Rick Nolan's body.

The sniper told me that once again the insurgents returned to the LAV in force. His team and other unnamed snipers killed many more, and how they yelled in unison as a thousand-pound bomb destroyed the LAV and the twenty or so Taliban who were still trying to get inside.

The immediate area around the LAV and G-Wagon was littered with enemy sandals, clothing, destroyed weapons and ammunition, body parts and the rancid smell of death. The remains of the LAV and G-wagon would be eventually taken back to KAF, while the Zettelmeyer would be buried in place and become the reason for the name FOB Zettelmeyer.

Initially, we did not have a lot of contact with the enemy. Still, there were scattered firefights that typically ended with us forcing one or two bad guys into a building or compound, keeping them busy with direct fire until we could use aircraft or artillery to destroy them. We would then send in a section or a Platoon to sweep through and confirm that the threat had been neutralized. Sometimes there would not be any sign of the Taliban, but often we would find bodies or body parts and some weapons or explosives.

We did, on a couple of occasions, take prisoners. How we treated them and the process for moving them on would become an issue in Canadian politics and Canadian society in the future. But, for now, they were just the enemy. There would be many people swept up in operations over the coming months. Many were legitimate enemy fighters, while a small portion were either local farmers or, at the worst, Taliban sympathizers.

In the early days of 2006, all prisoners taken were handed off to the Afghan National Police as soon as practical, and they were processed through the Afghan system. However, as 2006 was coming to an end, we heard that the Afghans were perhaps mistreating these prisoners, and we now had to process all prisoners back to KAF through the Canadian system. It was a little bit more time-consuming but also allowed our intelligence folks to gain valuable information.

I understand that the Canadian military police and our intelligence folks did an amazing job with the huge numbers of prisoners they had to deal with. A lot of these bad guys were the worst of the worst, and dealing with them must have been difficult.

21

CLEARING OBJECTIVE RUBY

During this timeframe, A Company, PPCLI, worked at setting up a Forward Operating Base at Ma'sum Ghar to our south. It had a great view of the whole area and would be beneficial as a staging area for many future operations.

We were a little surprised as we went about securing Objective Rugby to find out how sophisticated the Taliban position really was. We had the opportunity to look at it from the enemy's point of view, looking at where we had crossed and attacked on September 3.

I have had many years of experience looking at how to defend positions and how to attack them. I believe that the Taliban had set up the perfect kill zone. Once Charles Company had entered that area, we were incredibly lucky to have escaped with the minimum number of casualties that we took. If not for the great fighting spirit of the Company, the leadership of Major Sprague and the fire and air support that was quickly provided, it could have been disastrous.

There were interconnected irrigation ditches that served as a deep, wide trench system. Connected to those ditches were real trench systems that ran into fortified compounds. Leading into and out of these compounds and to the trenches were tunnels. These tunnels allowed hundreds of Taliban to move freely around Objective Ruby without being seen from Ma'sum Ghar or our air assets. The enemy had to appear only when they needed to engage us with direct fire and then could disappear again. Miles of the typical two-foot-high Afghan grape walls that were about two feet thick ran throughout the area, and trenches were dug behind them with firing ports dug through the mud walls to allow weapons to be fired without the shooter ever revealing themselves. Some of the tunnels had elaborate rooms that consisted of eating and sleeping areas and an area for the wounded.

Mixed in amongst this elaborate defensive position was a maze of endless bisecting tree lines and dense fields of marijuana growing so high you could see only the antennas of the Canadian LAVs as they moved around the battlefield. Placed all around the defensive position were dozens and dozens of IEDs, mines and booby traps. I believe that the battle for the white school and objective Rugby was to Charles Company what the fight for Vimy Ridge was to Canadians a hundred years earlier—a defining moment.

We spent days doing nothing except locating IEDs and explosives and waiting for the engineers to come out with the exploitation teams to study them before blowing them up. I saw one IED that sent shivers up my spine as I realized how devastating it could have been for one of our sections or platoons. A ten-foot walled compound lined one of the main routes through the extensive ditches and fields and would eventually have been used if we had continued the attack on September 3. The wall was about two feet thick made with baked mud and rock, and from the outside, it looked like any other wall in Afghanistan.

Once inside the compound, however, we saw the mother of all improvised explosive devices. It was embedded in the wall about three and a half feet high and twenty inches deep, with about a half-inch of dirt to cover it from the outside. It appeared to me to be at least three 120mm shells and another ten or so 81mm mortar shells and piles of sharp metal and nails, all pointing out from the wall toward the road, set up to be manually fired from inside the compound with a wire leading to one of the adjacent rooms. It was obviously set up to fire at one of the Coalition's armoured vehicles, specifically a Canadian LAV. After he saw it, a Canadian engineer captain told me that if it had been fired as a section or platoon was going by, it would have destroyed everything within a hundred metres.

From our interpreters listening in on the Taliban chatter, we had heard that getting a Canadian LAV and later a Canadian tank was a huge prize. Every fighter wanted that opportunity. They had come remarkably close.

The Taliban had a nickname for our LAV. I no longer remember the Pashtun word, but loosely translated, it meant big green monster that shits out little red men. Our terps would always tell us this because they knew it would make us laugh, and they liked to explain from where it came.

The Taliban and their supporters were always watching us, and they were terrified of the LAV's cannon and coaxial machine-gun, as it had killed many of their fighters from hundreds of metres away. They knew we could destroy one of their trucks from a mile away as it sped across the desert and, if one of their fighters was hit by the 25mm cannon round, it left little to recognize. And so they rightly feared it and us. On top of the firepower of the LAV, the rear ramp would drop, and a bunch of Canadian soldiers would come pouring out with a lot more firepower. The red men part was hilarious because most of us were lily-white Canadians and would burn badly under the relentless Afghan sun. So, big green monster that shit out little red men made perfect sense to me.

Lying in the compound with the massive IED were three enemy fighters who had been decomposing for several days, and it looked like they could have been killed by sniper fire as all of them had suffered head and upper torso wounds. There was no doubt in my mind that, while the battle was going on, we had Battle Group snipers, as well as men with no names from Canada and other Coalition Special Forces, who were moving in and out of the shadows taking out targets of opportunity. Someone had taken these guys out without ever knowing that they probably saved a considerable number of Coalition troops. These dirtbags would never again have a chance to kill.

After securing and removing the bodies and handing them off to the Afghan police, we cleared out of the area and allowed the engineers to come in and exploit the compound. Once they were done, the decision was made to destroy this IED in place, as it was not safe to try to disarm it. We moved all the soldiers back to Ma'sum Ghar and watched the show from a couple of kilometres away. The explosion not only destroyed the wall but the compound and the adjoining compound, and it shook the ground at Ma'sum Ghar.

It was one of the biggest explosions I had ever seen, and I have seen many. All that was missing were the hot dogs and marshmallows—what a show.

Yes, this might have been some innocent farmer's home or the home of the Taliban or a supporter. However, I never lost a minute of sleep over its destruction. We knew, before deploying, that Kandahar was the birthplace of the Taliban and that Panjwai was the gateway to Kandahar City. So, they were going to defend it. They had obviously been working on this system for a long time, perhaps months, if not years, knowing that they would have to defend it one day. They had decided to change the hit-and-run insurgency tactics that were working so well and gather their forces in the hopes of dealing the Coalition a decisive blow. Instead, they were defeated after some fierce fighting, and hundreds of their fighters were killed and maimed.

Days turned into weeks, and we spent our time clearing compounds, patrolling the area for bad guys, and pushing out into new areas to contact the locals. We lived on MREs and jerry cans of water from the weekly resupply. I had brought a few containers of wet baby wipes, and they became my daily bath, as water was too scarce to use for anything other than drinking.

MA'SUM GHAR

We were able to roll into FOB Ma'sum Ghar a few times a week and get resupplied as the Patricia company and their engineer support were doing an amazing job of getting it up and running. Some sea containers held extra ammo, water, rations, and generators to provide electricity to the Command Post. They had set up immersion heaters, which are large self-contained drums with a diesel system for heating water. I allowed the soldiers to skip a few days of shaving when we were out in the desert, but each time they rolled through Ma'sum Ghar, they were to take advantage of the water and shave. Most followed the rules, but a few needed the old Sergeant Major to kick them in the ass.

Eventually, FOB Ma'sum Ghar would become a sizeable self-contained camp with electricity, showers, and a temporary kitchen that could provide at least one fresh meal a day, but that was still a few months in the future for Charles Company.

For now, our new orders were to provide security for a project to build a road from Highway 1 to the farming district of Panjwai, a total of fewer than five kilometres. The road was to be known as Route Summit. This road would run from Pashmul at the base of Ma'sum Ghar, across the Arghandab river in the same location that Charles Company had crossed on that fateful day, through the fields of Panjwai and Objective Rugby and then north to Highway 1 where B Company was located at the start of Operation MEDUSA. In between these two points were five kilometres of wadis, grape huts, grape fields, miles of walls, compounds, farmers' homes and Taliban with the mission of not allowing the road to be completed.

This project was not just a road to us—it was a promise. Completing it would mean that farmers could bring their produce to bigger markets in Kabul to the north, Herat to the west, and from there to Iran. Travel times in all directions would be cut dramatically. It would mean that the Panjwai farmers could finally begin to prosper.

PART THREE - AFGHANISTAN

We were trying to win the hearts and minds of the locals, and the Taliban were trying to stop us.

The initial path had been cleared as a combat corridor for the Coalition Forces to advance from the south and the north during Operation MEDUSA. It was now used to allow the same forces to move freely throughout Panjwai. However, almost daily, Coalition forces would hit or find an IED and were continually ambushed by insurgents with rocket-propelled grenades or small arms.

It was now up to the Canadian combat engineers to survey and shape this path into a road. I was amazed at the ability of these fine soldiers and their local contractors to complete the first mile. We provided security, but it was a big area, and it took only one or two Taliban to sneak in to cause disruption. They did it on an almost daily basis. The insurgents could also sneak in at night and plant hastily buried IEDs, which the engineers would hope to find on their daily sweep. We brought in truckload after truckload of gravel and rock, and slowly the road took shape. Then, to finish it off, the engineers had it paved to make it more difficult for the Taliban to plant IEDs. The engineers also dug ditches and installed culverts to prevent flooding. That mile of road took a lot of blood, sweat and tears and was finally completed under the most trying conditions.

A soldier from Bravo Company was killed when he stepped on a mine along Route Summit before construction even started. Then, a few days later, a security detail from the ISTAR Squadron was hit by mortar fire, and two more soldiers lost their lives. Regretfully, they would not be the last deaths along Route Summit.

REPLACING THE OC

Sometime during these first few days, following the combat phase of Operation MEDUSA, we had a visit from the Battle Group Commander and RSM while at FOB Ma'sum Ghar. Lieutenant-Colonel Lavoie pulled me aside so we could speak in private. He asked me how it was going and how the soldiers of the Company were doing. His concern for my soldiers was authentic, as he was not just a leader doing what he thought was right. I told him that we were shorthanded and needed more soldiers, but that we were getting the job done and morale was high. He said that he was in the final phase of deciding on the leadership of Charles Company, and he wanted my input.

He said that the discussions with his senior leadership had narrowed it down to the Battle Group Operations Officer, a Major working out of KAF, and Captain Brown, our Company Second-in-Command, who had been acting as the OC for the last week or so. Lieutenant-Colonel Lavoie told me that whatever I thought was best for the Company, he would agree with. Lieutenant-Colonel Lavoie earned my respect forever by allowing me to be part of such a huge decision.

The next Officer Commanding Charles Company would be taking this reorganized force into battle and making difficult life and death decisions. I knew the

Operations Officer back at KAF and had watched him perform admirably under some incredibly stressful and trying conditions, but this decision was an easy one for me.

Charles Company was a team. The Company Commander prepares the Company Second-in-Command to step up if required, and we had trained for this very scenario. We weren't expecting it to happen, but we still had almost six months to go, and we needed an OC who the company would trust.

I told Lieutenant-Colonel Lavoie that the Company had every faith that Captain Brown was ready to command, and an outsider would not be the best decision at this trying time. A few hours later, while in the middle of Objective Rugby, Lieutenant-Colonel Lavoie came back with his tactical headquarters, gathered the soldiers of Charles Company that were in the immediate vicinity and, without fanfare, promoted Captain Brown to Major. Lieutenant-Colonel Lavoie told the new Major that he had confidence in his ability to command and then told the Company that we were still his go-to combat unit. He would continue to rely on us to complete the mission.

After some quick congratulations to Major Brown, we quickly dispersed so as not to be a big target for the Taliban. I know that Major Brown was ready for this day, but I also know that he did not envision becoming a Company Commander this way. I already had a great working relationship with Major Brown. Over the next few weeks, it would come in handy as we continued to receive replacements and being attacked almost daily by the Taliban.

ERADICATING POPPY FIELDS

During this time, we started hearing bits and pieces about a NATO plan to start eradicating the drug harvest and try and persuade the farmers in our area to start to grow other crops. We knew immediately that this would be a dismal failure, as it did not make sense economically. Farmers were able to grow poppies with the protection of the Taliban and, in most cases, the federal and provincial governments. They made more than those growing traditional crops, like corn or potatoes. It is a bit ironic that it was the presence of NATO forces that restored the opium harvest instead of eradicating it. From 2000 to 2001, during the Taliban's rule, a drug-eradication program led to a 94% decline in opium cultivation. According to UN figures, in 2001, opium production had fallen to record lows to 185 tons, and immediately following the U.S.-led invasion, production increased dramatically to historical levels. In 2006, there were 165,000 hectares cultivated, compared to 7,606 hectares in 2001. There was a 59% increase in opium in 2006. When the Taliban were part of the government, they were adamant that growing, selling or using drugs was against the teachings of Islam, and anyone involved would be punished. However, by 2006, they were using the taxes and subsidies they received from this trade to buy weapons, vehicles, explosives and pay soldiers. Many of them were full-time drug users.

Canada did not get involved in the counter-narcotic operations, and we destroyed drugs only when they were located during operations. The supposed anti-narcotic

PART THREE - AFGHANISTAN

operations only made things worse for the soldiers on the ground, as we started to encounter more hostile farmers, corrupt district Chiefs and well-armed local militias intent on protecting poppy fields. I often heard our soldiers say that the worst possible way to win the locals' hearts and minds was to destroy their livelihood.

I remember seeing an old farmer and what looked like his whole family out in the fields harvesting the poppies, and when we stopped our convoy, he agreed to speak to us. He told us that he had the permission of the provincial governor and the district Chief to grow poppies. He could not afford to grow anything else because the price was too low, and he would not be able to afford to feed his family. Abdullah said that his family grows enough poppies to harvest about two hundred pounds and that he makes about $10,000 U.S. a year. He also said that he tried to grow cotton and corn one year, but the prices were so low, he had to destroy most of it, and he made only about $800. He said that he understands that opium is bad, but it is difficult to see his neighbor provide for his family while he cannot do the same. He made the decision for his family.

That kind of says it all, and I think about being in his place and having to decide on how to best support your family and how most would probably do the same.

During one of the U.S. eradication patrols, they came across a compound that had truckloads of drying marijuana, poppies and opium, along with a pile of weapons and explosives. The decision was made to take all the drugs, move them out into the desert, and burn them, making sense at face value. At around this same time, our HQ LAV, 39er TAC, was moving along the combat road, known as Route Summit, to FOB Wilson when we started to get the initial smell of marijuana. It was not a big deal because, as I said, drugs were everywhere, and lots of the locals were users. However, as we approached Highway 1, we could see the smoke rolling over FOB Wilson.

At first, we thought the FOB was under attack, but then we heard the radio crackle and a message telling all non-essential personnel to get under cover and protect their faces from the smoke. The call went on to say that the U.S. had just dumped several tons of drugs about two kilometres north of the FOB in the middle of the desert and had ignited it, and the wind was blowing the smoke toward Highway 1.

What a stupid thing to do; one of those decisions that were not thought through. The smoke continued to blow over FOB Wilson for another day or so until the wind changed direction. As we rolled into FOB Wilson, the smoke was choking us, so we decided to depart. We waved to the gate guards wearing their gas masks and headed back south away from the smoke.

As I had said, during the event where Charles Company was camouflaging their vehicles with marijuana leaves, we would have all been sent home if any of us had been piss tested for drugs. It is difficult to persuade the government, the districts, or the farmers to give up this lucrative trade of drugs for corn when it provides about 92% of the world's opium and is a multi-billion-dollar trade. Over the next several weeks, the eradication teams became less involved, and from an Afghanistan perspective, things became normal.

WHITE SCHOOL, BLACK MEMORIES

Luckily for a few of us, about this time our Company Headquarters and one of our Platoons were able to go into KAF for a thirty-six-hour respite. Even though the road move through Kandahar City was a nightmare, it was something to which we were looking forward.

23

HESCO HOBBITS

Conditions at the Strong Points were very primitive, but we did not want to be living on Kandahar Airfield (KAF) with the "Hesco1 Hobbits," as the troops liked to call those who lived in air-conditioned rooms and ate fresh meals every day in relative safety. I tried to disparage them from using that term and a few others that did not do justice to those at the airfield. However, it wasn't easy to enforce, and sometimes those Hobbits did not do themselves any favors.

Every soldier who spent any amount of time outside the wire has a story or two about why dealing with those in KAF was frustrating.

I have several!

On one occasion, after a couple of months of living in the dirt in the Strong Points on Route Summit, we were able to rotate about a platoon of soldiers into KAF for forty-eight hours to rest and relax. For most of these soldiers, other than coming through KAF on arriving in Afghanistan and perhaps attending the ramp ceremony for their comrades, they had not been there. These soldiers had not eaten a fresh meal nor had a shower or clean laundry in months, and now they would have forty-eight hours to refresh themselves before returning to the fight.

I used the satellite phone to contact my CQ back at KAF and had him get ready for the arrival of the troops. He would now prepare for things like laundry, kit exchanges, barbers, and personnel available to check and repair weapons and vehicles.

The platoon used the dark of night to travel the dangerous roads of Kandahar, and, after the two-hour trip and several scary moments, they arrived at KAF at about 0500. I am told that the soldiers were given air-conditioned rooms. They all showered, put on clean clothes from barrack boxes they had not seen since Canada and had a fresh, hot meal for breakfast.

Shortly after that, I received a call on the satellite phone from the CQ. He is not happy as it happens to be a Saturday and, as was the routine for KAF, they had an Afghan market. NATO had arranged for twenty or thirty local vendors to bring their products to KAF, and hundreds, if not thousands, of Coalition soldiers, would purchase the items. You could buy things from pirated DVDs to rugs, gold and other stones and everything in between. The problem was that the Coalition had to provide security, and armed soldiers had to be watching the vendors even though all outsiders would have been searched and vetted.

My CQ tells me that the Task Force has said to him that now that Charles Company had soldiers in KAF, we would have to provide the security. I told the CQ to tell whoever was asking for this that our soldiers would not be doing security as they had just arrived after months of living in the dirt, and they were leaving the following day to come back to the dirt. The CQ told me he had already explained that and was told it did not matter. Everyone had to do their part while in KAF.

I try not to get mad over little things, but this made me angry, not because it was a huge deal if we provided a few guys for a few hours, but because of the stupidity of the decision. There are tens of thousands of coalition soldiers and civilians on KAF, including hundreds of Canadians. I don't envy the fact that they can enjoy a Tim Horton's coffee or a smoothie, as well as burgers and pizza and even movie nights and salsa dancing. And let's not forget the boardwalk massages. My soldiers are happier out in the desert; however, don't ask my soldiers to secure your market so you can stroll down and buy a souvenir.

I told the CQ to go back to the Command Post and tell whoever was asking that you had spoken to me, and I said, "No." If they have an issue with that, tell them I said, "Get off your ass and come out and see me." I know that I was putting WO Keith Olstad in a bad situation.

He knew how I thought after being wounded while replacing me and being with me for a few years now. I knew he was up to the challenge.

Off he went, and that was the end of it. The soldiers were left alone, but these stupid decisions gave the fighting troops a bad impression of the Hesco Hobbits.

Later, my HQ and a different Platoon, after about three months of no showers, fresh food or a private toilet, were able to rotate into KAF for forty-eight hours. I must say that, even though we were happy to be out in the dirt, I was looking forward to a shower and a fresh meal.

The good thing about being out in the desert with the Company is that we were all dirty and smelled terrible, but we never even noticed. Baby wipes were a lifesaver.

About forty of us arrived in KAF around 1800 hours, and after securing our kit, clearing our weapons, and making sure the vehicles were good to go, the OC allowed the soldiers to head to the quarters. They were told to be back at the CQ's compound at 2100 to do kit exchanges and turn in dirty laundry. The OC and I stayed in the compound a little longer to discuss some issues with the CQ. While we were waiting, MWO Rob MacRae, who worked in Operations, came by. He told me that some staff from the Task Force Headquarters had just jacked up a bunch of our soldiers for wearing their field hats instead of berets.

This sounded crazy, but the CQ said that it had been passed on a few weeks earlier that field hats could only be worn outside the wire, and berets needed to be worn in KAF. Once again, I was amazed by the stupidity of this. They were trying to treat KAF like a base back in Canada, and the cushy life these Hobbits were living did not help dispel the idea.

The OC was a man of very few words, and he hated stupidity more than anything else. Even though our berets were stuffed somewhere in our LAV, we put on our field hats and started walking toward the main camp. We had gone only a few hundred metres when we saw a Canadian Sergeant Major from the National Command Element coming toward us. He had clean combats, clean boots, a nice haircut and, of course, was wearing his beret. I could see it in his eyes that he was about to tell us that we couldn't wear our field hats, but something changed when he was directly in front of us.

I don't know if it was the smell of three months of disgusting filth, the fact that we needed haircuts and had a few days' facial hair growth, or perhaps it was the major and sergeant major ranks. It may even have been the blank stare that soldiers who have seen too much combat have, but all he said was, "Welcome back, boys."

The OC, of course, couldn't let it go.

"I thought you were going to tell us we couldn't wear our field hats here," he said. "I was going to tell you to fuck off and to let your folks know that my soldiers are only here for about thirty-six more hours, so leave them the fuck alone. Most of the guys have no idea where their fucking berets are, anyway. Over the next day or so, they'll get haircuts and shave and get clean uniforms. Until then, do not fuck with them. Have a good day, Sergeant Major."

We walked away, and I could see the most mischievous smile on the corner of his mouth. He looked at me and said, "That felt good."

An hour later, I got another complaint because a handful of soldiers decided that getting a fresh meal was more of a priority than a shower. They had gone over to one of the several kitchens on the airfield, and they walked in as a group smelling like three months of body odour and whatever else someone that has not showered in three months smells like. Upon entry, someone complained that they were too dirty and smelly to be in a kitchen, and it was not sanitary, so they were asked to leave. The soldiers put up a bit of a fight, and after some poorly thought comments about Hobbits and crappy food, they left.

The Task Force decided to make a big deal out of it instead of just laughing it off. I had to pretend I was angry and ashamed of their conduct and said, "I would sort it out." I just passed on the word that from now on, make sure everyone showers before going to the kitchen, problem solved. However, this just added to the idea of Hobbits, at least in the mind of those soldiers.

Those are only a few stories about why the troops consider those at KAF as Hobbits.

WHITE SCHOOL, BLACK MEMORIES

Early in the tour, places like clothing stores and pay offices had specific opening and closing times, like 0800-1200 and 1300-1500 and were closed on Saturdays and Sundays, which was very inconvenient. It took almost an act of Parliament to get them to open outside those hours, especially when the troops had only a little more than a day in camp. If that was our only time at KAF, too bad, the Hobbits needed time off. Eight-hour shifts are hard to do while eating a pizza and salsa dancing.

I don't want to sound bitter or disrespectful to those who worked out of KAF, as they were the folks who made sure we had everything we needed to complete our mission. We were all part of the same team, but these events did not help to expel the 'Hesco Hobbit' concept. Now, I want to make sure that I do not leave you with the wrong idea about those in KAF, as they did tremendous work on behalf of everyone and kept the war machine running.

They deserve our thanks.

BACK TO ROUTE SUMMIT

The thirty-six hours or so in KAF flew by. Before we knew it, we were receiving orders to move back out to Route Summit.

Every road move was considered an operation in itself and required a proper set of orders. Anyone who decided to move about Afghanistan on an administrative road move did so at their peril.

I can recall only one or, maybe, two times out of the many moves that we did anywhere in southern Afghanistan that we were not hit. It was just a fact of life that, if you were going to move by road, you would come across an IED or be ambushed. You needed to be ready. Soldiers always had a loaded weapon; all guns in the LAV were loaded, functional and ready to go. Anytime we had issues with one of our many weapon systems, it needed to be corrected immediately.

On one occasion we were moving from the area of Panjwai to a small village at the edge of the Red Desert. The Forward Observation Officer's LAV had problems with its coaxial machine-gun and had just had the weapons technician fix it. So, while travelling along the road, with about eight other LAVs and about six Toyota pickup trucks filled with ANA soldiers, they asked permission over the radio to fire their coaxial machine-gun into the mountain to the west to confirm it was functioning correctly. The Company Commander told the FOO over the radio to go ahead but to ensure there were no signs of life in the area first.

What we didn't realize was that the Afghan soldiers following along in their trucks did not have Canadian radios and weren't aware of that radio conversation.

The LAV rotated its turret and, after ensuring that there were no signs of life, fired several machine-gun bursts into the mountain about four hundred metres to our west. The Afghan soldiers of those early days may not have been well trained or well paid, but they were brave. And the one thing they did know is war. When they saw the impact of those rounds hitting the desert, they thought that we were under attack from the mountain.

They immediately swung their trucks toward the mountains and drove about fifty metres off the road. Then, they jumped out and started running toward the mountain, firing their weapons. Their mentor just stood there trying to figure out what was going on. I was screaming at them to stop, but the noise of several LAVs and trucks and two dozen AKs firing prevented them from hearing me.

Luckily, the mentor had radio or phone contact with the Afghans, and he had stayed near the trucks. We were able to get word to him that it was just test firing, and he had contact with the Afghan commander. He was finally able to stop the assault about fifty metres from the base of the mountain. The Afghans all returned to their trucks with smiles on their faces and empty weapons, as if they had just defeated a large force of Taliban.

The Afghan National Army was always an element that we had to consider when planning. We would often not have immediate contact with them and would link up with them only a few hours before starting operations. It could be difficult to always know exactly where they were and what they were doing. I still had a lot of respect for Afghan soldiers, especially for the hundreds of them who gave their lives for their country.

During another patrol around the same time, we were travelling with about nine LAVs, including a full platoon of infantry, the Company HQ, a forward observation team, an engineer and an armoured ambulance. The patrol left the area of Sperwan Ghar and headed northeast, eventually ending up travelling west along Highway 1. The plan was to make a show of force and be a presence in the area. We planned to stop in some of the smaller villages and see if there was any interest in speaking with us.

The patrol went well for the first hour as we moved on and off the major routes, occasionally stopping at some villages and bypassing others. However, as we had learned from previous experience, the word spreads once you are out for a while, especially if you are travelling on a specific route or in a particular direction. It was only a matter of time before we got hit.

I was standing in the back of our HQ LAV, wearing a headset to hear what is going on, my rifle on the hatch within reach and a shotgun in my hand. Anytime we were travelling in close confines of a town, village or traffic, I liked to have the shotgun ready to go, hoping that it would allow me to send a message if anyone got too close.

VEHICLE-BORNE IMPROVISED EXPLOSIVE DEVICE (VBIED)

There was only light traffic on the highway this far west, and so it came as a bit of a surprise when the lead LAV came on the radio to say that a white pickup was about three hundred metres to their front and acting strangely.

The pickup had been spotted driving down the highway toward us when the lead vehicle first saw it. Almost immediately, it made a U-turn and pulled off onto the right side of the road. The pressing concern for the lead vehicle was that it could be a vehicle borne improvised explosive device or suicide bomb, which was quite common in our area during this time. It could also just be an innocent Afghan who wanted to get out of the way, though I don't think anyone believed that.

Our convoy slowed down, and orders were passed to move to the left side of the road and be prepared to engage and stop the vehicle. From past experiences, the bombers usually tried to get into the middle of a convoy before blowing themselves up, hoping to cause as much carnage as possible. These were the occasions when your asshole puckered and every fibre of your being screamed to retreat. Approaching that pickup, you'd be as tense and alert as physically possible and prepared for the worst.

The convoy picked up speed, stayed spread out to reduce damage from an explosion and moved as far as safely possible to the left side of the road. From my vantage point, it wasn't easy to see, but I maintained situational awareness using the radio. As soon as the lead LAV was within about fifty metres of the parked truck, it tried to move back onto the road and into the path of the convoy. It had misjudged where it had parked and, like most vehicles in Afghanistan, the tires were shit, the motor was junk, and it was unable to get any traction in the loose sand and rocks. It continued to try to move out but only spun its tires more and more, digging a hole. Over the radio, the lead call sign kept everyone up to date on what was happening.

There was absolutely no doubt in anyone's mind by now as to what was about to happen, and so the lead vehicle fired a burst into the truck's windshield. I believe that once the driver knew the jig was up and he wouldn't be able to ram into the convoy, he decided to set off his explosives. The explosion was deafening, and dust and dirt covered everything.

The convoy stopped with the lead vehicle only ten or fifteen metres from the explosion. Rocks, dirt and pieces of the pickup landed amongst the convoy, but all call signs quickly checked in to say they were okay. We remained vigilant, and everyone was prepared for a second attack, but it didn't come. As the smoke and dust cleared, I heard the commander of the lead vehicle get back on the radio.

"Oh shit," he said, "he's alive and moving toward us."

I couldn't specifically see what was happening, but the story was told to me shortly after. When the smoke cleared, the crew of our lead vehicle saw the pickup driver on the road twenty metres or so to their front. Somehow, he had survived the explosion, but only barely. When the bomb exploded, it appeared that it tore apart the pickup and threw the driver several metres away, missing the lower part of his body. All that remained of him was from the waist up, and even that was a terrible mess. He was dragging himself by his arms toward the lead LAV, yelling something unintelligible. He stopped after a few seconds, adjusted his headscarf, and started dragging himself again. A few seconds later, a burst of 7.62mm rounds ended his life for good.

Even though this guy was bleeding out and was missing the lower part of his body, he remained a threat if. He could have been wearing a suicide vest. So, the right decision was made, and the danger was eliminated.

WHITE SCHOOL, BLACK MEMORIES

After making sure all the pertinent information about the contact was passed to higher, our convoy rolled by the bloody mess on the road and carried on with our task. The Afghan police and Coalition exploitation teams could deal with the aftermath, as we had other battles to fight.

WHITE TOYOTA

We arrived back out on Route Summit around first light, after a couple more minor incidents.

The first occurred while driving through Kandahar City. Traffic was light for the city, but there were always cars and trucks filling the streets no matter what time you went through. The streets were narrow, and there were always vehicles parked on both sides of the road as well as carts and bicycles and many other contraptions. We were forced to squeeze through, aware that there was always the possibility of one of the parked vehicles exploding.

It is essential to understand that in early 2006 in Kandahar, the war was still in full force. Taliban soldiers were trying to kill Coalition soldiers daily with roadside bombs, vehicle borne improvised explosive devices and suicide bombers. People were dying daily.

While travelling through Kandahar City we received a report from our rear LAV that a white Toyota Corolla kept closing up with them and then falling back. They had been waved back several times but were still hanging around. Vehicles filled with explosives were often rammed into the middle of a convoy where they exploded with devastating effects. The air sentry of the rear LAV knew that they could not allow this car to pass them.

After several more attempts by the soldiers to wave the vehicle back, they fired warning shots into the road in front of the car. Usually, this was enough to make the casual, innocent driver pull over and stay away from us. This car started to close faster. The young soldier, following his training and initiative as well as his rules of engagement, fired a burst from his C9 machine-gun into the windshield of the car. The car spun around and slammed into a parked truck on the side of the road. We did not stop. We called it in on the radio and continued.

Stopping in the middle of Kandahar City on a narrow street was suicidal. Our standard operating procedure was to remove ourselves from the situation as quickly as possible and continue with our mission. Afterward, we found out that the car's driver had been killed, and no explosives were found. To me, he was just one more dummy who made a wrong decision and paid for it with his life. We never really found out why someone would act like that, though there was some thought that it could be a dry run to see how the convoy would react, giving the actual bomber the best chance of success. We'll never know!

Many Afghans lost their lives for not following the direction on the sign and the hand signals of the Coalition soldier. Many locals could not read, but everyone knew to stay away from the convoys, and the hand signals and warning shots could not be any clearer. There were times throughout the tour when the escalation of force was perhaps a little too hasty, but I never second-guessed my soldiers in the back of those LAVs.

AIR SENTRY

I had to make the same decision driving through Kandahar City a few weeks later with the same deadly results.

I was standing in the air sentry hatch of Three-Niner and, being the rear vehicle, we were responsible for rear security. I could have had the Company medic standing with the signaller, but I did not believe in putting others at risk while I sat down below in relative safety.

A white pickup truck pulled out of a side street as the convoy passed, and the lone individual in the vehicle closed rapidly on the rear of the convoy. Both the signaller and I began waving our arms frantically for him to stay back. At the same time, I informed the OC over the radio. The truck slowed and pulled to one side of the road. Then, without warning, it pulled out and sped toward us once again. As he closed to within fifty metres, I fired three rounds into the road in front of him, with one of the bullets causing sparks as it ricocheted into the grill.

The vehicle continued.

I immediately raised my aim, fired several rounds into the windshield, and watched as the driver started jerking around. The vehicle spun out and slammed into the side of a bus and then into a building. I reported what had happened, and we continued to our destination.

That evening, we received word that the driver had been killed and that no explosives were found. Although there were several weapons and several cell phones in the trunk, the individual had not yet been identified. Once again, what was this guy doing? We never found out, but the results were almost always the same.

On several occasions, the vehicles exploded early when fired upon. Typically, this means that the convoy was unhurt, but civilians were often killed. On a few occasions when soldiers had to fire warning shots or deadly shots, the bullets ricocheted off the street or the car, hitting civilians who were wounded or killed. It was a terrible result, but we had to put the lives of our soldiers first, and sometimes there was collateral damage. It was tough to live with, but we learned not to think about it while in Afghanistan.

The daily routine of living in the Strong Points became a part of our lives, and we looked forward to the hard work, patrolling and continued operations to secure more extensive areas of Kandahar. As leaders, we understood that keeping extremely busy was a good way of staying focused and not becoming complacent.

Because complacency was an excellent way to end up dead.

STRONG POINT CENTRE

Strong Point Centre was a few metres off Route Summit within sight of Strong Point West, the Arghandab River and FOB Ma'sum Ghar. Strong Point North was about two kilometres straight up Route Summit, and from there they could see Highway 1 and FOB Wilson.

Strong Point Centre used the natural lay of the land to anchor its defence. Two LAVs sat on one flank of the position and covered the western approach and the road. To their front lay a hundred metre swath of sand, and beyond that were marijuana fields, grape vineyards and an array of mud compounds and grape-drying huts. This meant that their fields of view were limited.

Sheltered behind the large mud building that was the centre point of the defensive position and protected by a natural wall to its other side, another LAV aimed its deadly cannon to the north, covering the approach by road. Finally, dug in nearby were two machine-gun pits. One faced south to control the road, while the other faced east to cover the close terrain, mainly grape vineyards, which extended right up to the defensive position. We also augmented this natural fortress with walls made from thousands of sandbags to provide additional protection, fighting positions for the soldiers, and an area to sleep and eat.

Over the next couple of months, we would use tens of thousands of sandbags and build a complex that not only provided a defensive location for seven LAVs to fire from but upward of fifty soldiers to live in and defend. Security was always the main focus, and twenty-four hours a day, seven days a week, we had LAVs crewed and ready to respond with fire. They also used the vehicle's outstanding gunsights to watch for infiltrators during day and night.

In addition to the LAVs, we had dismounted machine-guns and anti-armour weapons manned as well. The area around the position was filled with trip flares, which we armed at night and disarmed during the day. They were always covered by fire, and if one of them went off, a machine-gun would immediately engage the area.

No one wandered around at night without good reason.

We also had Claymore mines set up in front of our positions. These are directional anti-personnel mines that can be either command-detonated or set up to go off by tripwire. Despite the fact that "Front towards the enemy" was written clearly across one side of the mine, people have still been known to mess it up. When these are detonated, they send several hundred steel balls flying at a 60-degree pattern for about a hundred metres. That can cause devastating damage to the human body. Because of the Canadian caveat against using anti-personnel mines, ours were set up as command-detonated only and always under the watchful eyes of our soldiers.

In our defensive position, we had a 360-degree observation and the ability to fire in any direction as well. The main problem we had was that, like much of Afghanistan, the area was full of wadis, walls, compounds, grape fields and drying huts that would allow a small force using discretion and good tactics to get in close enough to fire at us before we could see them. We had to always remain on our guard.

For those not on security watch or operating a weapon system, reveille came at about 0500 hours daily. Depending on the water situation, soldiers might use some in a washbasin to wash and shave. Sometimes, this happened only once or twice a week. Following a quick wash would be an MRE breakfast, heated using a chemical bag that came with the ration. People oftentimes just ate it the way that it was, the air temperature in Southern Afghanistan making it warm enough. If we were lucky, we would have a good selection of both Canadian and American rations from which to choose. As the choices got low, the meals and complaints got worse.

Rations taste good to a civilian who gets an opportunity to eat one at a family day in Petawawa or when the soldier sneaks one home, but after eating them for months on end, they start tasting like crap. The alternative is worse. Many of us lived on noodles and "Cup-a-soup" sent to us from home or issued by the box by the CQ.

FILLING SANDBAGS

Each morning following breakfast, there would be about three to four hours of filling sandbags and building the strong point before it got too hot. By 1100 hours, the heat would already be unbearable.

One of the biggest misunderstandings about Afghanistan is that it is a dry, desolate desert with sand everywhere. There are deserts, dunes, scorpions and all the stuff we imagined in some parts of the country, but Kandahar is not like that. Neither is Panjwai.

The area around Route Summit is a greenbelt. Water was diverted from the mountains and flowed through huge wadis several feet deep and wide from centuries of use. When it was dry the ground was so hard that large digging equipment, like bulldozers and backhoes, had difficulty making a scratch, so those first few days of trying to fill sandbags with a shovel were futile. Eventually, we had to have the engineers and local contractors bring in large truckloads of sand from the Red Desert for us to use, and some of that was more like gravel than sand.

So, hundreds of hours were spent filling sandbags, carrying sandbags and banging them into position with shovels, pick handles and six-foot steel pickets to make sure they were solid and able to withstand attack. We used miles of concertina wire to the front of our position, which had to be continually watched and covered by fire. Other than the guys on duty watch in the LAVs and on the weapons, the rest of us worked. It helped us bond as a team.

There were no exceptions. Major Sprague, myself, the platoon commanders, medics, soldiers and even the interpreters helped build Strong Point Centre. It was a great feeling of accomplishment as the days and weeks went by, and this thing grew larger and more robust. We didn't build it too high, wanting to keep the profile low, and so soldiers had to stoop down in parts of it to walk around. I had to stoop down while walking through parts that would lead from the Company headquarters area to the platoon area and then to each LAV firing position. It was a structure that people wanted to see because they could not believe that soldiers had built this huge and complex structure by hand.

Each morning while the work was taking place, a section from the platoon would do a clearance patrol about a kilometre or so around the position to ensure that no one had penetrated without our knowledge and that all our wire and other defences were intact.

On several occasions, they contacted some Taliban trying to get close, and each time a firefight would be the result, normally followed by us using either artillery or air power to destroy them.

By lunchtime, the heat would prove to be too much to bear, and lunch would be an MRE in any shade that could be found—usually inside—which was always a few degrees cooler. The afternoon was an opportunity for the OC and I to visit the other Strong Points, speak with the troops, and see how the construction of the rest of Route Summit was coming along.

Germany was paying about €1.3 million to complete the final 3.2 kilometres of Route Summit. They refused to provide soldiers for security, as it was outside their government's mandate and was considered too dangerous. They were not the only Coalition allies to decide that Kandahar was too risky to conduct operations. I never blamed the soldiers, as these were government decisions.

The Americans had promised to build a bridge over the Arghandab River after completion of the road. By the time I left, it had not even been started. For three months as it was being constructed, Route Summit became the front line in the battle for Kandahar Province. We heard that the German contractor who was handling the road work met with the Taliban leaders in Kabul sometime in November to try and convince them to leave them alone. I am sure there was money offered as part of the deal, but I don't know that to be a fact.

Around that time a Mr. Dube, the German official in charge of the construction company, made a statement that the road was being built without any interference from the Taliban. This was news to us on the ground and, especially, to the drivers of the gravel trucks or heavy equipment which were targeted almost daily by IEDs, RPGs and small arms.

Perhaps our German businessman should have spoken to the family of Private Frederick Couture of the 2nd Battalion, Royal 22e Régiment. He was seriously wounded when he stepped on an IED while doing a foot patrol along Route Summit. Or perhaps they should have listened in as Brigadier General Howard told a Senate committee in December that the soldiers of the Battle Group were being attacked each day by the Taliban. In January, we fought a three-hour firefight with the Taliban along Route Summit. It was nice to see the Germans, who refused to fight alongside us in Kandahar, had such an easy time of it. Perhaps they needed to see how smooth it was first hand, instead of relying on the view from Berlin.

On Route Summit it was Canadians taking all the risks as we directed earthmovers and local labourers, all the while under the constant threat of rocket attack, small arms fire, IEDs and landmines. For the most part, things went well. We had excellent security along Route Summit and lots of firepower available to deal with anything that occurred. But while we focused on the route, the war continued on around us.

FOB Ma'sum Ghar continued to be attacked, and we could both see and hear it from our locations. Very seldom could we bring fire to bear on the enemy, but the FOB had enough firepower of its own to deal with the occasional insurgent. So as the Taliban continued to cause havoc and destruction, we continued with the work at hand, securing Route Summit while the road was being built.

STRAIGHTENING THE COMBAT ROAD

The combat road that the Coalition had built for Operation MEDUSA was too narrow and followed a twisty route around compounds and fields and wadis. It was not good in terms of security either, as we could not have eyes on the whole road all the time. It allowed the enemy to move a few guys under cover and concealment into the area to either plant IEDs or set up ambushes to hit Coalition soldiers or local workers building the road.

The plan was to make the new road as straight as possible, clear enough space on both sides to prevent interference by the enemy, and then pave it to make it even more difficult to plant mines and IEDs. It was built to improve security in the district and for the benefit of the locals, but it wasn't done with their input. We could have talked this part through a bit better. Anything that blocked our field of view from the Strong Points or anything along the road that the enemy could potentially use to attack us was destroyed.

The terrain was a soldier's worst nightmare. Marijuana fields, as high as nine feet tall, obscured visibility, even when observing from a turret of a LAV. These plants also absorbed energy and heat very readily. As a result, it was difficult to penetrate the forests of "pot" with thermal surveillance equipment. Burning the fields with white phosphorus and diesel fuel also failed because the plants were still too full of water.

All these factors afforded the Taliban a high degree of freedom of movement around us.

While the initial construction phase was taking place, no locals were living in our area. Anyone that we saw moving about was considered an enemy, and we killed them. This response would change when the Coalition decided it was vital that we get locals back into the Panjwai area to earn their support. In return, we would assist them and ensure the Taliban stayed away.

This was easier said than done.

In the meantime, we continued to clear fields of fire. We blew up compounds and homes that had been in the area for hundreds of years. These structures and all others were virtually impregnable strongholds, as their walls were up to a metre and a half thick and could be ten feet high. They were constructed of a mix of mud, thatch and straw. However, once they had dried and baked in the heat of the Afghan sun, they were as solid as concrete and could be penetrated only by powerful munitions.

Compounds could be big or small and house a single family or several, but if they were too close to the road or posed a potential danger, we destroyed them and plowed over the ruins. As the days went by, Route Summit began to take shape. It now went straight from Ma'sum Ghar to Highway 1, and for the most part, it did not have anything close to it for hundreds of metres on either side. Not only did we knock down walls and blow up homes and grape huts, but we also plowed over farmers' fields that were used to grow melons, marijuana, poppies, corn, grapes and whatever else. We filled in ditches, wadis and wells and made the landscape look like it had been destroyed by a tornado that had swept through north to south for five kilometres.

As this construction and destruction was taking place, some locals began to return. This caused us concern because it now allowed the Taliban to infiltrate the area by posing as locals. We had intelligence that though the Taliban had been defeated and destroyed in early September, those who could escape did so by burying their weapons and leaving as civilians. It was believed that dozens of weapons caches were hidden throughout the area. We had found many of them while patrolling and building Route Summit, but many more remained.

Now the Taliban, looking like local farmers, could move back in with shovels and axes and when they had an opportunity, they could dig up a weapons cache and conduct a hasty attack. If they survived, they would hide the weapons and go back to being a farmer. It made our job a lot harder, but the soldiers continued to make me proud.

The arrival of some of the locals caused quite a stir when they realized that they were coming home to nothing. Nobody asked them for permission to destroy their homes and fields, and most of them were very unhappy. I believe that most of the local population in the Province of Kandahar supported the Taliban, whether openly or quietly. I also think many of these local farmers and their sons took up arms during this phase either in support of the Taliban or just because they were pissed that we had destroyed their homes and crops. Now, we wanted them to start growing other crops that would not be as lucrative for them, so they tried to kill us. Many of these young men lost their lives over the next several weeks as we built Route Summit.

As the locals were moving back into the area, we saw more and more of the Canadian Provincial Reconstruction Team (PRT) as well. They tried to work out fair compensation for the farmers whose property and crops had been destroyed. This promised to be a very tricky situation as all kinds of people came out of the woodwork looking for money.

On one occasion, there were about a hundred people claiming title to the same tiny piece of Route Summit, and records were almost nonexistent. I did not envy the PRT as they tried to do the best they could with only a bag of money and word

PART THREE - AFGHANISTAN

of mouth to help them. It was a very time-consuming process, and the local farmers wanted their money immediately. It became a tug of war with them as the PRT tried to sort through the mess.

These things had been furthest from our minds a few weeks earlier as we destroyed anything considered a threat. In Afghanistan, there is a saying: "The only thing that happens swift and sure is death." As far as I can tell, that's true.

To complicate things further, the war was far from over and hard-core Taliban forces also rapidly began infiltrating back into the area. They simply blended among the local population and adopted guerrilla and terrorist tactics. They intimidated locals and coerced them into supporting the Taliban. They planted IEDs and mines, deployed suicide bombers in vehicles, on bicycles and on foot and conducted hit-and-run attacks against Coalition forces throughout the area.

This enemy was skilled and extremely clever. They quickly learned the limitations of the Coalition's capabilities and the constraints embodied in our rules of engagement. Thus armed, the Taliban struck back swiftly with precision. They persistently harassed our thinly stretched troops. During the night, they would stealthily plant IEDs and mines in the sandy furrows that were the unimproved part of the road. In addition, they would deploy small teams who would attempt to surprise and ambush us. Using these tactics, they immobilized two bulldozers and several other vehicles through IED and mine strikes.

SPERWAN GHAR

As we started getting into a daily routine, we received a warning order that we would be the lead for another operation. Charles Company was pushing west to secure an area known as Sperwan Ghar.

This area was chronicled in the book Lions of Kandahar, which tells the story of Task Force 31 and a small contingent of U.S. Army Green Berets whose official role in Operation MEDUSA was to act as a screen to prevent the Taliban from escaping across the border into Pakistan. The 1st Battalion, 3rd Special Forces Group became the first non-Canadian unit to receive the Commander-in-Chief Unit Commendation, awarded for the performance of "an extraordinary deed or activity of rare high standard in extremely hazardous circumstances."

This American unit took and held Sperwan Ghar during the decisive early days of Operation MEDUSA. Against all odds and with extreme bravery, they helped defeat hundreds of Taliban fighters and ensured the Canadian Battle Group was successful. By early October, Operation MEDUSA was formally over, and the U.S. Special Forces had moved on to other priorities. We, however, were trying to hold onto the ground that had cost NATO and Canada so much. The decision was made that Charles Company would roll west and take Sperwan Ghar by force. No large Taliban force was expected to be in the area, but by rolling in a large armoured force, the plan was to surprise and overwhelm any remnants left behind from the initial battle by the U.S.

WHITE SCHOOL, BLACK MEMORIES

Special Forces.

Sperwan Ghar, Pashto for dusty mountain, is an earthen mound approximately six kilometres west of Ma'sum Ghar. It rises sixty metres above a jumbled mix of deeply furrowed grape fields, wadis and compounds around a small village. It was built by the Soviet Union in the 1980s by bringing in thousands of truckloads of sand from the Registan Desert. They then built an elaborate trench system and cement bunkers on it to ensure that they had good lines of sight.

The leadership of Charles Company and our engineer and artillery attachments moved back to KAF to receive orders and plan for the occupation of Sperwan Ghar. Those two days in KAF were busy, ensuring that Charles Company and all our attachments were prepared for this phase. Our team consisted of the usual combat arms folks and air support, including helicopters, fighters and drones, and a platoon of Afghan soldiers and their American mentors. All this also had to be coordinated with all our Coalition partners.

After the OC gave his orders to all the key commanders, we used the cover of darkness to move from KAF to Sperwan Ghar, as we wanted to arrive at first light. We did not include the Afghan Army or police in the initial plan for security reasons and only told them the objective as we were about to leave KAF. The Afghan commander was warned about security and to make sure that none of his soldiers had cell phones. He promised us that he would take care of this and that he trusted all his soldiers. From my perspective , though, those soldiers hadn't yet earned our trust.

We had the engineers move ahead of us to look for IEDs and explosives, followed by the Afghans and a platoon of Canadians and then Company Headquarters. We had a second platoon moving along a different route as a reserve in case something went wrong. After the opening days of Operation MEDUSA, Charles Company soldiers went in with the expectation that this would not be easy. To our relief, we encountered no resistance other than a few small engagements en route and an IED that was quickly disposed of by the Afghan Army.

The most significant moment came when our engineers discovered wires connected to an IED within sight of Sperwan Ghar. We stopped the Combat Team and provided security while waiting for the engineers to either destroy the explosive or make it safe. It seemed that not everyone was willing to wait. To our amusement, the Afghan commander walked by the engineers with an expression of disdain, went up to the explosives and pulled out the wires. He then proceeded to pick up a couple of old Russian artillery shells and a jug that was clearly filled with explosives. The route was clear. While we weren't impressed by this dangerous display, it did allow us to proceed into Sperwan Ghar and quickly secure it.

As we were rolling into Sperwan Ghar, we could see the remnants of the battle during Operation MEDUSA. At the bottom of the mound was a completely burned-out Humvee that had hit an IED during the initial attack. It was a huge relief to take this area without any resistance, and we quickly understood why the Russians had built this hill. The 360 degrees of observation over the local area was magnificent and allowed us to observe any movement for miles around.

We quickly placed our LAVs and our soldiers into positions that would give them the best cover and the best fields of fire if the Taliban decided to take us on.

My initial discussions with the OC were about the best way to defend the position. Sperwan Ghar actually consisted of two hills. The first was several hundred metres in diameter and had a cement building and a second cement structure that the Russians may have once used to hold water. This was where we would have our soldiers eat, sleep, and build their defences to provide all-around security.

In the middle of this area was a second hill that was only about a hundred metres in diameter, but the sides went straight up for about a hundred metres. The top of this was the best location for observation and fire. A small dusty, narrow trail ran in circles around it and allowed us to drive some vehicles up, though it was impossible for most.

When I was going to the top, I usually used this winding trail to walk up, but the Afghan soldiers would just run straight up the side like a mountain goat. A couple of times I attempted that route, but it left me struggling for breath and my footing, so I left that to the ninety-pound Afghans instead.

Once we had initial security in place and the OC and the platoon commander felt comfortable enough to dispel any attack, we were able to relax a bit and look around at our environment. It felt like we had been dropped onto the moon or some other alien planet. The dust here was incredible, and I never saw another location throughout Afghanistan that even came close, including in the Registan Desert, also known as the Red Desert. The sand was so light and dusty it was like walking through talcum powder. Every step brought up a spray of dust.

In some places, the dust was a foot thick, and you had to almost drag your feet through it. It got on everything immediately, and you had trouble breathing as it got into your mouth and nose. As the night moved in and darkness spread over Sperwan Ghar, it became a ghostly looking place. It almost looked like people were moving through a foot of white fluffy snow, and it blew around as they took each step. However, the terrible heat and smell that hovered over everything quickly brought you back to your senses.

Shortly after dark, we took our first incoming rounds from both small arms and mortars. No one was injured, but it quickly told us that this would not be a quiet location. We returned fire into a compound only a few metres from the base of the lower hill, and the enemy fire stopped as quickly as it started. The incoming mortar round had been spotted coming from another compound about hundred metres south of our new home. We engaged with both small arms and cannon fire from the LAVs. An hour later, a second mortar round landed at the base of the hill, and fortunately again no one was injured.

Luckily for us, our Forward Air Controller had an American F/A-18 Hornet fighter in the area, and the OC called in an airstrike on the compound. A few minutes later, it was turned into rubble while Charles Company soldiers shouted out words of praise to the U.S. pilot. We did not send any soldiers out to assess the damage or clear the area, as we had not had the opportunity yet to walk the ground during daylight and clear it of any mines or explosives.

The Taliban must have had enough of Charles Company for that evening, as the remainder of the night was quiet. We spent the rest of the evening either watching the local compounds and fields for movement or trying to catch a bit of sleep. I had become accustomed over the years to being able to sleep on any piece of ground available, and in this case, my bed was my air mattress on the ground with my poncho liner covering me.

SAND FLEAS

I woke up several times throughout the night and eventually gave up and got up around 0500 as daylight started to appear. A few days earlier, while in KAF, I had the opportunity to shower and put on a clean combat uniform, but, for some reason, I felt dirtier than ever. The fact that I was covered in a layer of white dust did not help, but my biggest concern was that I was extremely itchy. I looked at my arms and legs and noticed a bunch of red dots. Then, upon a more detailed inspection, I discovered several more around my neck and my crotch. I knew immediately that these were sand flea bites, and I was not amused.

We knew that we were going to have to endure the relentless heat and put up with the constant churning of dust every time someone or something moved or even if the wind picked up. To add to this misery were the sand fleas and flies, which tortured us relentlessly. I took the opportunity while in KAF to research fleas and learned that Afghanistan is one of the countries where sand fleas and flies are most prevalent. I knew that these fleas could jump only about twenty to thirty centimetres, so most people seemed to have been bitten around the feet and ankles unless they got you when you happened to be lying down. It was also more likely to be bitten during the evening, night or at dawn. It made me wonder if it was possible for us to sleep only during the day, standing up...

My research also told me the same thing my mother had, at least a thousand times: not to scratch. The itch was unbearable, but I resisted scratching and went to see the Company medic, who had some calamine lotion for me to put on. He also told me that he had seen several guys already that day with bites. I never gave it much more thought as we continued to build our defences and sent out the Afghan platoon to do some local patrols to see if there was any pattern of life in the area and check for IEDs and mines. We also wanted them to go to the compound from which the mortar had been fired to see if anyone was occupying it.

Most locals had left the area during Operation MEDUSA, especially around Ma'sum Ghar, but this area had seen some locals remain and others had recently returned. The Afghans were not eager to go out into the village area without Canadians, but they agreed to conduct their patrol after several minutes of arguing with us. Still, they wanted constant coverage by our LAVs and machine-guns on Sperwan Ghar. We agreed, and the patrol departed. Almost immediately after entering the village at the base of the mountain, we heard AK-47 fire and some yelling. A few minutes later, the Afghans were seen returning to Sperwan Ghar. They told us there were too many Taliban in the village, and they did not have the numbers or firepower to take care of it.

To this day, I do not know if they came under fire or just fired a few rounds themselves and came back. Their U.S. Marine mentor said that he had not seen any Taliban, and he did not think they had received any incoming fire but could not be sure. He also relayed that this platoon had shown its bravery on several occasions but was more useful in an assist role, with Americans or Canadians taking the lead. We both knew that the plan was for the Afghans to start taking the lead in these missions, but it wouldn't be easy.

The rest of the day was spent building up our defences, filling sandbags and cleaning and checking weapons to make sure they would fire when needed. It was part of a routine that all Charles Company soldiers followed anytime there was a pause or downtime. The first thing before eating, sleeping or washing was weapons maintenance.

We ate MREs and used some of our limited water supply to drink. We had only the water we carried on us and what was in jerry cans on our LAVs, and you could never be sure that there would be a resupply coming anytime soon. We made sure that Captain Norton back at the Command Post in FOB Wilson started working on a resupply plan for FOB Sperwan Ghar. We wanted to stockpile rations, water and ammunition here for any future operations.

DUSK ATTACK

That evening, just before dark, we received incoming small arms fire again and were attacked with mortars and rockets. No one was injured, and the rockets impacted on the side of Sperwan Ghar. All the soldiers immediately went to their fighting positions, and anyone that could locate where the fire was coming from engaged the enemy with machine-guns and LAVs. At times like this, the chain of command had to be in control to make sure that the troops were not wasting ammunition because, like our water, there was never a guarantee that we would be resupplied any time soon.

We had also set up our Company 60mm mortars, and our artillery brothers set up their 81mm mortar. Both engaged the compound that was identified as the area of concern. I watched as our mortar rounds landed inside the compound, but we continued to receive enemy fire from the same location. As mentioned earlier, these compounds could be set up like bunkers, with each section inside being protected by thick walls.

We spotted three young fighting-age males moving around outside the compound area, but we did not see any weapons on them and did not engage. It can be very frustrating at times to the soldiers, but our rules of engagement are clear. When we know that locals are in the area, we must always consider collateral damage and civilian casualties.

WHITE SCHOOL, BLACK MEMORIES

Like most of my soldiers, I believe that those three males were Taliban, but following the rules is what makes us Canadian and, even if it may cost us our lives, we are better than the bad guys. Over the next hour or so, we continued to receive fire from the compound and the immediate area around it. After another rocket flew over our heads and exploded, Major Brown decided it was time to deal with this before someone was killed or injured.

We did not want to deploy outside the FOB in the dark and possibly walk into an ambush or an IED, so staying in the relative safety of our defensive position made the most sense. Major Brown got on the radio and asked for air support. His timing was perfect as two American aircraft had been dispatched to Ma'sum Ghar for a different Canadian operation but had not dropped their bombs. They were preparing to return to KAF but instead were diverted to our location and arrived overhead a few minutes later. Major Brown made immediate ground-to-air contact with the lead pilot and passed on our enemy contact and location information. A moment later, both aircraft made a pass over Sperwan Ghar, moved toward the objective and then dropped two 500-pound bombs on the target in succession.

The results were devastating. The compound took two direct hits, and the explosions sent mud and rock and debris in a 360-degree arc. The outer walls were completely destroyed. My initial thoughts were that no one inside could have survived. I was surprised that I did not have any emotion other than glee while watching the destruction of the compound and any lives that were inside. I don't know if I had become hardened by war or if I had just put my feelings aside where they would not get in the way of the job that needed to be done, but, either way, it made the task at hand a little easier.

We decided to wait until daylight to send out a Canadian and Afghan patrol to assess the damage and look for any Taliban. For now, we were not receiving any incoming rounds, so it made more sense to stay in the FOB, where we could watch the target area with our night vision capabilities. The night became eerily quiet, and we had the soldiers go about their business, with most manning LAVs and machine-guns and the remainder eating or getting some rest. We had the Afghans manning the two entrances and exits, covered by the LAVs.

We had backed our headquarters LAV up against the cement building and ran wires from our radios through a window to one of the rooms, which became our command post. Within thirty minutes of the airstrike, one of our LAVs reported that a vehicle was approaching the back entrance to the FOB and that it had come from the area of the bombing. We immediately went into high alert, got everyone into their fighting positions, and ordered the LAV to make sure the vehicle did not approach the gate too closely. We had already encountered many vehicle suicide bombers, and this was our concern.

The OC and I moved to a location where we could see the approaching vehicle, and two of the Afghan soldiers at the gate began waving at it to stop. The covering LAV flashed its lights, but the small, white pickup truck continued to approach slowly.

PART THREE - AFGHANISTAN

At about fifty metres, we had the LAV fire some warning shots in front of the truck, and it immediately stopped. Two Afghan soldiers from the gate approached the truck slowly and carefully while the remainder of the company on this side of the FOB was prepared to destroy the truck if it moved any closer.

The two Afghan soldiers could be seen speaking to someone inside the truck, and then one of them came back to the wire surrounding the FOB. The radio came alive, and the Canadian Platoon Commander briefed the OC on the situation. According to the Afghan soldier, two local farmers had just had their home destroyed by an explosion, and they had several injured family members, including children. Local farmers, my ass. But my heart sank. It was one of our worst nightmares that children would be hurt or killed during some of this fighting.

It was a known fact that the Taliban used compounds and homes where women and children were, using them like cowards as personal shields. Plus, local Taliban kept their families in the area to fool Coalition soldiers into not paying attention to them. It was a touchy situation, as we had just been attacked from the village, and after calling in an airstrike that had destroyed the compound, we now had supposed locals asking for help with the injured.

What was our obligation to injured locals? If we encountered them during operations, did we treat them like we did our own wounded? Did this include the enemy? Did it include bringing them into our FOB? My initial response to the OC was to send them away to the local hospital in Kandahar City, but he wanted to help them, especially since we had injured them. He was responsible for that airstrike, and the burden of command was on his shoulders.

Our Company signaller interrupted our discussion by grabbing my arm and pointing toward the road.

All I remember thinking was, "What the fuck is he doing?"

The second Afghan soldier that had remained at the white truck was walking back to the gate with the vehicle slowly following him and, by the time anyone could react, it was already at the gap in the wire that served as a gate. The other Afghan soldiers started to remove injured people from the back. We immediately sent the Platoon Commander and some of his soldiers down to the entrance to ensure these people did not have weapons or suicide vests, a dangerous but necessary job. Major Brown and I waited at a safe distance as the Platoon Commander and his soldiers completed the task.

Almost as quickly as the vehicle had initially appeared, we saw the truck heading back toward the village, and I saw the Platoon Commander become truly angry with the Afghan soldiers. After unloading the injured, they had allowed the two young men who had driven the truck up to the gate to drive away. We knew that those two were either Taliban or had valuable information, but we would never know for sure. It was just one more unexplained occurrence between the Afghan Army and the Taliban. Throughout my tour, there were many times when the Afghan National Army or the Afghan National Police would make decisions that would give you pause. I do not believe there was ever any real trust between them and us.

The wounded were brought up to the top of the hill and placed in one of the cement structures, and we had our first chance to see them. There were three children who appeared to be between the ages of three and ten years old and two adult males. The two men were on stretchers and were both in profoundly serious condition—their wounds were life-threatening. I immediately got our medics working on these two and went to see the state of the children.

All three children were physically uninjured except for a few minor cuts and scratches, but they were obviously in shock. The smallest child, a boy of maybe three or four, just sat against the cement wall and rocked back and forth and stared straight to his front. He was not only in shock—he was terrified. The middle child was a small girl, perhaps four or five years old, and she was covered in debris and sobbing. The third child, a girl of maybe ten, seemed to be almost defiant. She sat there wearing a long dress and headscarf and held the two younger children close and would not respond when the interpreter spoke to her.

We tried to find out if these two injured men were her family and who the two men were who had driven the truck, but she just looked at us with disdain and would not answer. We had soldiers standing close by, covering all five of them with weapons, as none could be trusted at this stage, even the youngest, though all of them had been searched by Canadian soldiers before they were brought up.

It may seem a little bit extreme, but young children had been used as suicide bombers on several occasions already, and I was not taking any risks. Searching females, even little girls, can cause quite a stir in Afghanistan, but, in this situation, we were lucky to have our female medic, and she had been tasked to complete the search of the children.

We got on the radio, notified our higher headquarters of the occurrence and requested medical evacuation for all five. We explained the extent of the two males' injuries and that the only chance these two men had to live was immediate evacuation. The Battle Group authorized helicopters to come to our location to pick up the two men. We got our soldiers to prepare and secure a landing site outside the FOB and then get the two men ready for evacuation.

The one guy, who appeared to be in his early twenties, was extremely thin, almost to the point that his ribs were protruding. His long, black beard was covered in blood and dirt, and his injuries were devastating. He had one eye that was gone, and that side of his head was completely ripped open. His chest and stomach were mangled, and his groin area had been torn apart. The medics did everything they could for him and were able to bring him back to life several times. Forty-five minutes later, when he was placed on the helicopter, he was close to death. I believe that he did not live to see the Coalition hospital at KAF.

The second man appeared even younger. He had a light beard and, once again, looked very thin and in poor health. He had sores and old scabs all over his body. Even though he had only a few outward injuries that the medics quickly looked after, he was unconscious and stopped breathing on two occasions. The Company medic believed that he had severe internal injuries. The medics worked diligently on this individual from when they received him until he was handed off to the American medics on the helicopter. It was their dedication and skill that kept him alive all that time. He was alive when we placed him on the aircraft and alive when he reached the Coalition hospital in KAF, but I do not know if he ultimately survived.

The three children did not react when we took the two men and put them on the helicopter; they just sat there looking straight ahead, the little girl still sobbing and the little boy still rocking. I do not know if that meant that they did not know these two guys or if they were just in shock after having two 500-pound bombs explode in their compound.

After the helicopter left, I was able to get the middle girl to stop sobbing, and she accepted a bottle of water from me. I now saw the little boy looking up at me as well. I offered him water, and, at first, he hesitated, but he reached out his hand and took it and drank long and slow. Even though she was probably very thirsty, the oldest child did not waiver and would not accept anything. One of the soldiers brought over some chocolate from his private stash, and the two smallest children devoured it, but the older girl would not even look at the soldier.

Our higher headquarters arranged for the local police to come to get the children. About an hour later, three Afghan National Police trucks with about twenty police in a variety of dress and weapons came to the front of Sperwan Ghar and took the children away. We never did find out the relationship between the two wounded men, the children, and the two men who drove the truck.

A few days later, I was told by a friend of mine at our Battle Group Command Post that the two wounded men were positively identified by the local police as foreign Taliban fighters, from either Pakistan or Chechnya, an autonomous Muslim republic in southern Russia which has exported many jihadist fighters to battles all over the world. It did not surprise us as we had fought Chechen fighters before. They were some of the most violent and dedicated soldiers in Afghanistan. The children were identified as belonging to a local family from Kandahar City who was loyal to the Taliban. We never knew how they ended up so many miles away in a compound at the base of Sperwan Ghar with several Taliban fighters.

The remainder of that night was quiet, but we remained vigilant and prepared for anything. As soon as I lay down on my air mattress, my mind started thinking about fleas, and the itching returned with a vengeance. I eventually was able to get a couple of hours of sleep and woke up choking on the Sperwan Ghar dust as one of the LAVs moved out of its firing position. It was only about 0600, but I was already sweating because I had slept with my shirt buttoned up tight and tucked inside my pants, and my pant legs bloused and tucked into my boots. My body was then completely wrapped in my poncho liner, all in the battle against the sand fleas.

Over the next several days, I saw the terrible results of sand fleas. We had soldiers who may not have been as dedicated as me to keeping fleas off or not scratching the bites from those that did penetrate the skin.

Two types of sand flea bites occur on humans. The first looks like a mosquito bite and happens when the flea sucks on your blood and then goes on to another victim. They inject saliva to prevent clotting while feeding, and this saliva irritates the skin, which causes it to itch. The second one is a little worse. Breeding female sand fleas cause this second kind of bite by burrowing their way under your skin and staying there until their eggs hatch. It causes swollen areas on the skin with a black spot in the middle, which is the breeding sand flea.

Both these bites will cause itching, pain and irritation, but the burrowing sand flea also causes fever and infection and becomes inflamed, especially if scratched. It can also lead to a serious skin disease, which must be treated to prevent it from spreading. One of the most significant issues we had out there, besides the threat of being killed at any moment, was these little pests. The lack of water, proper sleeping areas and clean clothes made matters worse, and of course like anyone else, soldiers will scratch an itch.

After weeks of this, we had soldiers with terrible infections all over their bodies. These started oozing pus, and the heat and the dirt just helped the infection spread quickly. We had to medevac some of our soldiers because it got to the point where the condition was becoming life-threatening. We passed this information to our higher command in our daily situation reports, but it was not until we started to medevac soldiers that they took it seriously. We initially received calamine lotion, some other creams, and aloe vera. None of it helped much.

The issue was that the living conditions were terrible: we were sleeping in bunkers, on the ground beside our vehicles, and eating and resting in the same location. I made sure we had a fire pit to burn all our garbage. We dug holes to piss and shit in and then filled them in. Because we were on entirely hard rations, they got a lot of use. I continually fought with the American mentor and the Afghan commander about keeping their areas clean and tidy to prevent people from getting sick. We were all living on the top of this fake mountain, and we needed to make the best of it.

It would still be several weeks before we received portable toilets, cots (to get soldiers off the ground and away from the fleas), water containers and other amenities, but until then we lived rough.

A few days later, a vehicle convoy from KAF arrived. It had the last of our replacement soldiers from Canada, a load of ammunition, water, rations, and even some parcels from home. One of the packages I received from the convoy commander had my name on it, and he said it had come from the Task Force Command Post. I tore the parcel open, and inside were about thirty flea collars.

At first, I thought this was just a joke, and it made me laugh. The convoy commander told me that this was something that the medical system in Canada had sent to help us with the flea problem. I was flabbergasted. What the fuck were they thinking? Did they think we were a bunch of dogs? They sent dog flea collars. I got on the radio to the Company CP in FOB Wilson and asked them to get in touch with higher to find out if this was serious. It was. We had a good laugh about it, and I handed them out to the soldiers who had the most difficult time with fleas. I don't know what they did with them, but I sent a report a few days later saying that they didn't work. I told the company that we would have to live with fleas, stay buttoned up as best as possible, and try to get off the ground to sleep—any distance could help.

I remembered an incident just before Operation MEDUSA, Major Sprague had taken the complete Company out into the desert to set up a hasty leaguer for the night. Once everything was secure, and our defence was established, we lay on the ground by our LAV in our poncho liners. There was Major Sprague and I, our driver and gunner and the company medic, as well as our interpreter, all lying on the ground next to Three-Niner. We all slept through the night without incident, and when we woke up in the morning, we were all covered in sand flea bites—that is, all of us except the Afghan interpreter. I do not know if this was some kind of Taliban conspiracy, but I was not impressed with that guy. I would not let him sleep close by for the remainder of his time with us.

There were a few things that pissed me off about the sand fleas. One was the fact that the interpreters did not seem to get bitten. The second was that our higher headquarters did not take it seriously (flea collars?!?). And the third was the fact that we had washed our uniforms back in Canada in a registered pesticide called DEET. It can be absorbed through the skin and into the bloodstream. Several studies have shown that DEET concentrations higher than 30% may have serious health risks, and Canada banned anything over 30%.

I have no idea what percentage was in the liquid that we washed our uniforms in, but we needed special gloves and masks, and we had to do it outside on our base and not at home. Our uniforms were then left hanging in the drill hall to dry, and we were told not to wear them until we got to Afghanistan. After all that and who knows what kind of health risk we had encountered using it, it didn't work. We also received some bug repellent, including some that had DEET in it, but I never used it. I figured I had enough chemicals in my system already.

I remember asking our terps about how they avoided getting bitten, and they said that some local remedies were used, but they did not know what they were. I think that the interpreters were part of a conspiracy designed to have us all laid up in hospital with sand fleas depositing their eggs inside of us.

OUR INTERPRETER, JAMES

We had some good interpreters, and we had some bad ones. One has left me wondering about his plight.

On one of our early trips from KAF, we picked up an interpreter named James. Most of them took western names because we could not pronounce their Pashtun name. Several of them had the same name, and using a typical English name made it easier for everyone, especially under stressful situations.

We had one that we called Michael Jackson because he liked to wear flashy pants and shirts and was always dancing around and singing some local crap. There was another who we called Slick because of the way he combed his greasy hair back over the top.

We were lucky to keep James with us for several weeks before he went to visit his family and then again for several weeks on his return. He was a good interpreter, and we got to know him very well. When you got one that could interpret well, you held on to them.

He was about thirty years old and was born in Afghanistan but had moved to the United States with his mother as a young boy and then lived in Chicago for most of his life. He had been raised a Muslim but did not consider himself to be devout or extreme. His father was a doctor who initially remained in Afghanistan and then moved to Pakistan with James' other siblings. James described his father as a very conservative Muslim. James told us that he had a rough life in Chicago. His mother worked very hard to keep a roof over his head, but he had gotten mixed up with a gang and began doing drugs, drinking alcohol, and engaging in other criminal activity. He had been arrested several times and, after multiple arrests, he decided to turn his life around.

James spoke of how he had met a Christian minister on the streets of Chicago who had been helping youth. He said that he attended one of the minister's sermons, and after that, he found Jesus. He told us very proudly that Jesus Christ was now his saviour and that he believed it was his duty to spread the word of Christ.

He always carried a small bible with him and, when he was just sitting around, he could be seen reading passages aloud. Even though Christianity is forbidden in Afghanistan, the other interpreters did not seem to mind and didn't harass him.

After finding Jesus, he had gone back to school and was planning to be a teacher. He had a place to live, a girlfriend, attended church three or four times a week and was involved in helping the poor. He said he had a perfect life. He had been brought to the United States at age six. He was now in his twenties and, even though he had a criminal record, he felt he was living the American dream. His mother had moved back to join his father while James was still involved with gangs, and now his parents lived in Quetta in Pakistan.

Everything changed for James on September 11, 2001. After the terrorist attacks on the World Trade Center, he was rounded up with thousands of other Muslims who had criminal records and were not American citizens. He was deported to his home country of Afghanistan. He said he was terrified. He understood Pashtun because they had used it at home in Chicago, but his first language was English, and the United States was the only home he knew. His biggest fear was that he would be ostracized in such a conservative Muslim country like Afghanistan since he was a Christian.

Shortly after arriving in Kabul, he crossed over the border and went to his father's house in Quetta. His parents wanted nothing to do with him unless he denounced Christianity and became a Muslim again. He told them the same story that he said to me about Christ being his saviour, and they sent him away and told him never to come back. He said he dressed like a Muslim, grew his beard and tried to fit in.

He remained in Pakistan for a couple of years and then went back to Kabul, where he got a job teaching English to kids. He then applied to work for the Americans as an interpreter, and worked for the Special Forces and the CIA. He said that his favourite people to work for were the CIA as they paid better and treated him well.

He learned from other interpreters that Canadians also treated their interpreters well and that their commanders would write a letter to help interpreters to immigrate to Canada after the war. I told him that I was sure we could get a letter written but that there was no guarantee that he would be allowed to go to Canada. He said that was the only hope he had.

While he was with us, he shaved off his beard, started wearing western clothes, and stopped pretending he was a Muslim. We warned him not to be too open about his Christianity, but he kept saying that Christ was his saviour and would protect him. It started to come to a head during Ramadan in late September or early October.

We were staying at FOB Ma'sum Ghar, and an under-strength company of Afghan soldiers was staying there as well. Their Commander, a Colonel who was also a mullah who had studied Islamic Law in Pakistan and had fought the Russians, forced his soldiers to practice what he called "true" Islam. They all attended prayers together five times a day. He would be seen punishing anyone for even the most minor mistakes—especially if he caught his soldiers doing drugs or drinking alcohol or if they broke their fast during Ramadan.

Our Command Post received a visit from this same Afghan Colonel, who was very agitated. He told us that James had been trying to convert some of his soldiers to Christianity and that he was terribly upset. If he caught James near his soldiers again, he would kill him.

In the Western world, we might say things like that, but not mean it literally. In Afghanistan, when this Colonel said it, he meant it. I had a good sense of how serious he was because of an incident that happened the first day after we arrived in Sperwan Ghar. We were inside the concrete building when a burst of gunfire was sprayed over the heads of some Canadian soldiers. When we ran outside to see what was going on, we saw two Afghan soldiers standing on the roof, laughing.

I was ready to pull them down, place them in handcuffs and hand them off to the police when their Colonel arrived. He started yelling at them and the laughing immediately stopped and was replaced with obvious fear. They came down off the roof and stood in front of their Colonel, who suddenly slapped them both several times across the face and then had them dragged away by other soldiers.

That isn't how we would treat our soldiers, but we had no grounds to interfere. If he had tried to kill them, we would have had an obligation to try and stop that, but not for much that didn't meet that threshold. A few hours later, the Colonel came to the CP and apologized to us, promising that the soldiers would be punished. He was outraged because they had been drinking alcohol and doing heroin, and he further promised that it would never happen again. He added that the soldier who had fired his weapon had not tried to hit the Canadians but was trying to scare them for a laugh.

WHITE SCHOOL, BLACK MEMORIES

We accepted his apology, and he went back to his soldiers.

The following day, at about 1000 hours during the intense heat, I heard a commotion outside. I found the Afghan soldier who had fired his weapon, in full fighting order, belly-crawling across the FOB in dust that was a foot deep, all the while being yelled at by another soldier. That unfortunate soldier crawled the length of the FOB several times in extreme heat. Every time he stopped, the guard would go up to him and yell and kick him until he started moving again. I felt sorry for him and was worried that he would collapse and die. I was just about to see if we could stop it when the Colonel appeared, yelling something to the soldier.

The young soldier, who I judged to be about 18 years old, struggled to his feet and stood shaking in front of his Colonel. He spoke to him in a quiet tone. The young soldier could be seen nodding his head up and down, and tears began to flow. Then the unexpected happened. The Colonel stepped forward, hugged the soldier and kissed him on both cheeks. He then handed him a bottle of water, and they both walked away, hand in hand.

What a strange society.

Knowing what this Colonel could be like, I went and found James and explained to him that he needed to stop approaching the Afghan soldiers about becoming Christians. I also told him that he was not to display public forms of Christianity while he was with us. James was not happy, and he explained that it was his calling to serve Christ and that he was not afraid. I explained to him that it was not only about him, but it was about our relationship with the Afghan Army, which we could not afford to go south. I finished off by telling him that if he could not follow those rules, I would send him back to KAF on the next convoy. He said he would try, which did not comfort me, but I let it go.

There were a few times or so over the next week that I had to pull him aside when I caught him with his bible out and speaking to either Afghan soldiers or police, and even on one occasion, to a merchant at a local market. I warned him again and told him that this was his last chance. I liked James, and he was a good interpreter, but even if I didn't like the way things were in Afghanistan, I needed to follow their rules and customs or, at least, not openly flaunt them, and so did he.

One of the strict customs they followed was fasting during Ramadan, and by the time the month was nearly over, I think all the Afghans were looking forward to it ending. Starving themselves and not drinking water all day did not make it particularly easy to soldier, and their Colonel would not allow any exceptions. On several operations, we either had to stop early or medevac an Afghan soldier who passed out or could not continue.

Eventually things with James came to a head. I was hanging out in the Command Post, listening to the radio, when one of our soldiers ran in.

"They're going to kill James," he said.

The OC and I ran outside towards our LAV, where a crowd had gathered. We found James sitting in the back of the vehicle while the Afghan Colonel and several of his soldiers stood outside with their rifles up and at the ready. Everyone seemed to be yelling simultaneously, and James was giving it back as much as he was receiving it. We were asking what was going on, but no one was listening to us, so I had to grab the Colonel's arm to get his attention. He spun around and had a look that told me that he was ready to kill. I had seen that look on many faces, both friendly and enemy, several times throughout the tour.

After finally getting the Colonel's attention, I used one of the platoon interpreters to speak with him. I first asked him to tell his soldiers to lower their weapons so that he could tell me what was going on. He eventually told his soldiers to relax, and they all lowered their guns, but I noticed they did not place them on safe or sling them over their shoulders. The Colonel used many inflammatory words to describe James and kept saying that he needed to die. We told him that James worked for us, and we could not allow him to be killed like this. Once again, I asked him what had happened. James started to speak to me, and I snapped at him to shut up and say nothing.

I knew that he had probably provoked this.

The Colonel pointed at one of his soldiers and said that he had been walking by the back of the LAV and found James sitting inside reading his bible and eating. Now, after the previous incident at Ma'sum Ghar a couple of weeks earlier, James had started growing out his beard again and wearing local dress to avoid any issues. All the soldier saw was an Afghan eating food and reading a bible during daylight hours during Ramadan.

We had told our soldiers and James that we would show respect to the Afghan soldiers and the other interpreters during Ramadan by keeping a low profile while eating or drinking. We kept our food under wraps, and we would eat in the building or our LAVs with the ramp closed and out of sight. James had broken this rule. I could tell that the Afghan soldiers and their Commander wanted blood, and if they got the chance, they would kill James.

I told the Colonel to leave James to me and that I would send him away. He would not have to deal with him again, and for a while, I did not think this would appease him. After several tense minutes when Canadian and Afghan soldiers had weapons ready to use on each other, he agreed. He sent his soldiers away and then said something to James that was obviously a threat. James just rolled his eyes and continued eating. I yelled at James to stop eating, or I would kill him myself. The Colonel walked away, but I could tell he was not happy.

I sent everyone else away, and I got in to sit beside James. I told him I was terribly angry that he had again put us in a situation where things could have gotten bad fast. I told him that he was to pack up his kit and that he would be going on the next convoy back to KAF, and I would suggest to the Task Force that he needed to be fired. He was not happy with me, and began talking about Jesus Christ and how he would be okay. He did ask if he could get a letter of recommendation for obtaining immigrant status to Canada. I told him that that was probably not going to happen and that he needed to be ready to leave in a few minutes, as we had a meeting at the District Center just outside of Ma'sum Ghar. I told him that he was coming with us but that he would not be the official interpreter. We would use one of the platoon assets.

An hour later we pulled into the District Center, guarded by Afghan soldiers and police as well as armed civilian contractors, for a meeting with the Governor of Kandahar about the area's reconstruction. The Company Commander and his team of engineers and reconstruction folks went inside. I stayed outside in the courtyard with our soldiers and the security folks. There were a lot of Afghans, some in uniform and some not, roaming around with weapons. I did not feel secure, and I had the rest of the Company soldiers stay alert and be ready for anything. I also sent a soldier inside to watch the OC's back.

Before I left the LAV, I warned James to stay inside, keep his bible hidden and not speak with anyone. I also told him that I would restrain him with cuffs and a blindfold if I needed to. He agreed to behave. Just a few minutes later, I saw James in conversation with a few Afghan police and a couple of contractors. As I got closer, I saw his bible.

I called over the rest of the headquarters soldiers and told them that I was putting James in the back of our LAV. We would put the ramp up and bind him with flex-cuffs to keep him out of trouble until we left. I could not take a chance that this could cause a flare-up that would cost lives. I walked up to James, grabbed his arm and viciously pulled him toward the LAV while he complained. I told him to shut up, not cause a commotion and that he would be restrained in the back until we left. He said that he was getting his kit and leaving, and we couldn't stop him.

To be honest, I don't know if we had the authority to stop him or not, but I figured he was a free man and could make whatever choice he wanted. He grabbed his pack out of the back of the LAV and started walking toward the front gate of the District Center. I walked with him, explaining how dangerous this was and that tomorrow, he was leaving anyway. He just looked at me and said that he would be okay with Christ as his saviour. He no longer wanted anything to do with us.

I was expecting him to stop at any moment and come back. He passed the local guards manning the entrance. They just looked at him, then at me, as he pulled open the gate and walked out, shutting it behind him.

James was never heard from or seen again, and I often wonder what happened to him. He would not be welcomed in Afghanistan as a Christian, and his adoptive home of America was not an option. His family had disowned him, and now he was on his own. Perhaps he had made his way back into Pakistan and linked up with one of the many Christian churches spread throughout the country.

I liked James and I just hope he made it and did not end up dead in a ditch on the side of the road.

25

MID-TOUR LEAVE

After another week or so, we left one of the platoons, some armoured assets and a battery of guns at Sperwan Ghar, and the rest of us returned to Route Summit to continue our task of providing security.

When October rolled around, I was personally in a state of agitation. My leave block was coming, and I was supposed to depart Kandahar Airfield on October 15 for Dubai and then back to Canada to spend a couple of weeks with my family. A part of me was extremely excited about getting home. I loved my wife and two children with all my heart. After what had happened to me and what was happening daily to Canadian soldiers, they needed to see that I was all right.

But a part of me also felt guilty that I was leaving these guys again when the Company was just starting to get its mojo back and was finally ready to take on bigger and more prominent roles. That is a terrible feeling and difficult to understand. It is not something you can discuss with your family.

I briefly spoke to Major Brown about delaying my leave and taking it later when things were a little bit more stable, but he gave me the standard answer, "Nope, you are going home. No more discussions."

During the week of October 7-14, there was an increase in the number of attacks on Route Summit, and we had several contacts, sometimes a couple a day. These included mortars and rockets being indiscriminately fired into our areas and IEDs being planted along or near Route Summit. Several times insurgents had gotten close enough to fire their AKs and RPGs at our soldiers and the local workers. It was a stressful time, being constantly under attack. And up until October 13, we repelled all the close-in attacks, and we had no significant injuries from the mortars and IEDs.

But on the evening of October 13, the CP notified me that they had arranged for me to get a helicopter ride the next day from FOB Wilson, a few kilometres north of Strong Point Centre, to take me to KAF to start my leave. It was good news because I was not looking forward to another trip by road through Kandahar City, as there was almost a 100% chance of getting hit. I was still a little apprehensive about leaving the Company during this volatile time but, once again, I had planned for WO Olstad to come out to Route Summit and replace me. I know he had said he didn't want to ever replace me again, but I know he was excited and happy to get the opportunity to again be the Sergeant Major of Charles Company for about three weeks. He was hoping that the second time would be better than the first. Having someone stepping in with his professionalism, knowledge and courage, as well as the respect of the soldiers, was a great relief.

Saturday, October 14 was like most other mornings, hot and dry, and we completed the same routine as on all the other days. I crawled out of the bunker at about 0500 and got an update from the duty watch in the CP on anything that was happening in our area. I sat outside the bunker with Major Brown and had a coffee made by the crew of Three-Niner Tac. They looked after us like no other, and I will be forever thankful to them all.

I did a walk around the defensive area and spoke to the soldiers who were operating the LAVs and machine-guns. I talked to WO Scott Robinson, the 7 Platoon Second-in-Command, as he was preparing to go with one of the sections in their LAV to patrol around the position. I spoke with Sergeant Darcy Tedford, who was only back a few hours after returning from leave in Canada. He could not stop smiling as he told me about his time home with Charmaine and his two girls. I remember telling him that I was heading into KAF today to go home and see my family. He told me to have fun as he went about his business.

The machine-gunner had seen some heat signatures about an hour earlier and had called it into headquarters. The LAVs, which had much better night vision capabilities, looked in the area but found nothing. I told the gunner to remain vigilant and to give that specific area a bit more focus.

As the sun was slowly coming up, I sat outside the bunker area where I had been sleeping for the past couple of weeks and enjoyed what was going to be my last MRE breakfast. I mumbled a few words to Major Brown about staying in theatre, but he just slowly shook his head and remained silent. My spidey senses told me something was up, but everything was quiet. The sun was finally in the sky, and our position was well defended.

What could happen?

I discussed the manning situation with Major Brown, as this was a concern for all of us now that leave had kicked in. We had asked for support from both the Afghan National Army and the Afghan National Police for weeks but were not happy with the response. The Afghan National Government finally sent some Afghan Security Forces into our area of responsibility. Although welcomed, they were of limited value. Those who arrived were relatively professional, adequately trained, but only really ready to fight if Canadians were accompanying them.

The biggest problem with them, though, was that there were too few of them.

Instead of the three hundred soldiers we'd been promised, only forty arrived to assist us. To make matters worse, they were from the Afghan National Police, in many ways the opposite of soldiers. They were young, and in some cases appeared to be no more than fourteen or fifteen years old. They were untrained and answered directly to the governor of Kandahar. They did not have uniforms and resembled and behaved more like common thugs than police. They were notoriously corrupt and untrustworthy, and many of them were suspected of being either Taliban or at least sympathizers.

The 1 RCR Battle Group could not provide us with more soldiers, and our replacements were awfully slow coming in. The Battle Group area of responsibility covered thousands of square kilometres of territory, and we were spread very thin. The Task Force had already suffered fifteen soldiers killed and a further eighty-five wounded, with the majority coming from Charles Company. Adding salt to the wounds, leave had started, and troops were being rotated out of the theatre in three-week periods.

I got up off the sandbag, went around once more to talk to the troops and speak with the Platoon Commander, Lieutenant Ray Corby, to make sure everything was okay and that he had a section gearing up to do a clearance patrol. Lieutenant Corby had taken over only a couple of weeks earlier as part of the re-organization of Charles Company and had been moved from a staff officer job in KAF to Strong Point Centre. He was still trying to get to know his new platoon.

He came into an enormously stressful environment, with troops from 7 Platoon occupying an austere position with Company Headquarters. In Strong Point Centre they baked under the sun, slept rough, and were always labouring under a threat that could materialize very quickly, sometimes under the soldiers' very own noses.

I saw WO Robinson, the only surviving Platoon Second-in-Command from Operation MEDUSA, departing with one of his sections and gave them a quick wave. Everything seemed good to go, and so I went back to the company headquarters. Around me, the troops were getting ready to keep working on the Strong Point, which, at this stage, was coming along well. We had already decided that we would continue improving the defensive position as long as we were here because it was a good routine that did not allow the soldiers to get complacent and relax too much.

IED STRIKE

By now, the heat started to feel like it would suck every bit of moisture out of your body. As I was reaching for a bottle of water, I heard the explosion. There was no doubt in my mind what that was. I had heard many and had been in the immediate area several times when IEDs had exploded. I also knew that this was a big one, and those almost always caused destruction, injuries and death.

As soldiers grabbed weapons and equipment and headed to their fighting positions, I jumped inside the headquarters LAV and grabbed a headset. Immediately, I heard that the section that had just departed our position had hit an IED about six hundred metres from our position on Route Summit. I knew this vehicle had several soldiers inside, but my first thought was of Robinson. Perhaps it was not a politically correct thought, but I didn't want to lose our last remaining original Platoon Warrant.

We got lucky. The vehicle was severely damaged, and from my first look, I didn't think anyone survived. In fact, everyone was okay, including WO Robinson. It was a huge relief that no one had been killed.

We had the vehicle recovered to FOB Wilson, a few kilometres up Route Summit, along with the section who would be checked out by the medics in that location. Everyone seemed fine, but large explosions can cause unseen injuries, to which I can attest.

The significance of this IED was not lost on any of us. It had been placed in the middle of the unfinished road, approximately six hundred metres away from Strong Point Centre. I was mystified as to how this had happened. How had it been planted on a route under constant observation, both day and night, both from our position and by the Afghans located almost directly in front of it?

Over the next hour or so, there was continued activity around Route Summit, which kept everyone on their toes and a little bit antsy. We heard over the radio that 9 Platoon at Strong Point West had spotted three Taliban to the west of their position. It was not a big deal as this was an almost everyday occurrence. Major Brown kept asking 9 Platoon for situation reports. We learned they had asked their local Afghan commander to take his soldiers out, and he had agreed. So, with the platoon's soldiers close at hand and with machine-guns and mortars to support, away they went to find and kill these Taliban.

Moments later, we heard what sounded like an RPG and then some small arms fire from an area about eight hundred metres west of us. Again, Major Brown asked for a situation report. He was told that the Afghans had returned to say that the Taliban were gone. Because 9 Platoon did not have an interpreter, we could never precisely determine if the Afghans had killed the Taliban or just fired some rounds and returned to their Canadian protectors. Nevertheless, the silence seemed to return to Route Summit.

DISTRICT CHIEF VISIT

That morning also found us having some visitors at Strong Point Centre. A local District Chief, with his Afghan National Police bodyguard and our Civil-Military Affairs (CIMIC) folks, were on-site conducting a meeting to discuss the progress of the road, as well as compensation for locals who had their homes destroyed. They also had a combat cameraman and a senior Canadian officer on a technical assistance visit in tow. Even with these visits and the morning's incidents, there did not seem to be any reason to treat this differently than a hundred other contacts. Soon these events were mainly forgotten, and the soldiers got on with the job at hand. We had become used to contacts, and they weren't really a big deal to us anymore.

PART THREE - AFGHANISTAN

While waiting for Lieutenant-Colonel Lavoie and his Tactical Headquarters to arrive, I noticed Lieutenant Corby trying to speak with the District Chief, but the young lieutenant was getting brushed off. We always made fun of how young Lieutenant Corby looked, and Afghan culture put a lot of importance on "being a man." Those without beards and moustaches were boys to them, and most of the senior Afghan locals did not want to speak with boys. Lieutenant Corby then started to talk with the CIMIC Commander, CWO Frank Gratton, a great soldier and warrior. He kept getting interrupted by the District Chief, who was asking when his ride would arrive. During this time, the District Chief also received a couple of phone calls and placed one himself. He seemed to be a bit fidgety and kept looking at his watch and asking about his ride.

As this was happening, small arms fire started to impact around us. It was not something completely unexpected, and so the soldiers reacted as they were trained. Everyone made sure they had their body armour, helmet and fighting gear and quickly went to their fighting positions. Everyone at Strong Point Centre had a site they would immediately occupy if under attack. My post was in the headquarters LAV, and we would provide fire, if required, from our fighting position, or we would be ready with the other headquarters LAVs to move to a location to help.

My position in Three-Niner was in the back of the LAV, usually standing in the air sentry hatch with either the signaller or the medic, providing both rear security and overwatch. I had a headset on and listened on the company net for updates on what was happening while the Company Commander was in the turret to control the battle. We also had our gunner who provided observation and fire. Our gunner was well trained, and he knew that he did not have to wait for orders to shoot. He was able to use his initiative and fire either the cannon or the coaxial machine-gun when he saw enemy targets. Our driver was in his compartment, and the vehicle was kept running, ready to move on command. We were a well-trained team.

The platoon in our strong point reported that their machine-gunner in the southeast section had received about a dozen rounds of small arms fire into his position. There were no injuries, and all incoming rounds had impacted the sandbags. They had provided the protection for which they were designed. The machine-gunner had returned fire into an area of rubble and destroyed compounds about two hundred and fifty metres south of his position. That was the location that he believed from which the enemy fire had originated.

While we were receiving this update, Strong Point West, several hundred metres away, jumped on the radio to say they had seen two armed insurgents in the same rubble and were hesitant to engage across Route Summit. This was understandable now that some civilians were back in the area, and it was not unusual to see a truck or a tractor appearing out of nowhere.

The OC decided that Three-Niner Tac would move out and follow Route Summit south toward the Arghandab River to see if we could either spot the insurgents or allow them to engage us so that we could kill them. It may sound a little crazy, but that is what infantry soldiers do. Our mission is to "Close with and destroy the enemy."

We rolled out and proceeded south with the platoons at Strong Point Centre and West providing overwatch. The Taliban do not like LAVs, and they know every time they have engaged our LAVs with small arms and RPGs, they have lost badly.

The three LAVs of Three-Niner Tac spread out to give us a better chance of survival if we hit an IED or received RPG fire as we moved toward the enemy position. When we rolled up to a location on Route Summit that looked directly east to where the enemy fire had originated from, we saw movement. Two insurgents were suddenly not so keen to be where they were, and they turned their backs on us and ran east as fast as they could, using whatever cover they could find. Both had AK-47s. One had an RPG strapped over his shoulder, with a round protruding out the front.

Normally the LAVs 25mm gun is intended for hard targets, such as vehicles and bunkers, while the machine-guns are for use against personnel.

It doesn't always work out that way.

While standing in the air sentry hatch, I heard our gunner engage the two insurgents and saw the splash of machine-gun rounds impacting around them as they frantically ran between piles of rubble to escape. Both insurgents appeared to have been hit and went down, then popped back up and continued to run, obviously injured. They were able to make it outside of the zone we had cleared and into an area still filled with vegetation and compounds. They both ducked behind a two-foot wall. Almost immediately, Three-Niner Tac started to engage with 25mm, and the wall and everything around or behind it was quickly destroyed.

After using our daytime thermal imaging system to observe and seeing no signs of life, we returned to Strong Point Centre, confident that those two dirtbags would no longer be a threat. Even still, we had the soldiers remain in their tactical positions for another thirty minutes.

It was during this time frame that Niner Tac arrived—the Battle Group Commander's tactical headquarters. It was composed of Lieutenant-Colonel Lavoie's LAV, his forward observation officer's party and his engineer party. They also had WO Olstad with them to replace me while I went on leave. I had forgotten all about that.

The three LAVs rolled into our position to find us all at "stand to", which is when all soldiers in the area are in their firing positions, ready for a fight. Major Brown briefed Lieutenant-Colonel Lavoie on what we were doing and why, and Lieutenant Corby reported on the IED strike.

Lieutenant-Colonel Lavoie looked over at me.

"Why aren't you at FOB Wilson yet? Your helicopter will be here in an hour."

I explained that we had just been in contact, and I did not think it was good to leave now. Maybe I could take my leave later...

I got the party line. "Get your stuff and leave."

I was just starting to brief WO Olstad on some outstanding issues and tasks that needed to be completed when the position again came under attack from the same general vicinity as before. A couple of small arms bursts hit the strong point, but no one was hurt as the soldiers were all in their firing positions. One of the LAVs returned fire, and I thought it was the section that had been fired on earlier, but when I looked, Lieutenant-Colonel Lavoie had repositioned his LAV and was hammering the area from which the firing had come. The firefight lasted only a couple of minutes, and everything went quiet again.

LEAVING THE BATTLE

I heard over the radio that a helicopter was inbound to FOB Wilson, and so I reluctantly grabbed my kit, jumped in the LAV captain's vehicle, and departed. My only thoughts were that I was again leaving in the middle of a fight.

The ride was short, and I got to Wilson just as the helicopter was landing. As I jumped out, I could hear that Strong Point Centre was now under attack again by a much larger force than before. I was torn between jumping in that helicopter and getting back in the LAV. I wondered about the District Chief, the phone calls, and the fact that he was continually checking his watch and was eager to leave the position.

Corruption is everywhere in Afghanistan, and traitors would not be anything new. That beautiful punk rock song "Should I stay, or should I go now," from the appropriately named album, Combat Rock, came to mind. I knew that my wife would understand if I stayed. She was a former military member, the daughter of a career Air Force member, and now the spouse of a soldier for the last seventeen years. But I had two young children who would not understand.

I headed for the helicopter with a sense of dread, knowing my soldiers were again in a scrap, and I was leaving. I said a silent prayer.

"Please, God, protect them."

I jumped in the helicopter and put on one of the headsets for the radio, which allowed me to hear the pilot and co-pilot speaking, as well as the Coalition net. I listened to the pilot being told to leave immediately as the area was under attack and that a large force had been spotted moving into the area of Route Summit. I could not believe my ears. A large force? How many? How well armed? Were there suicide bombers? Did the troops know?

As soon as the radio went silent, I used the intercom to ask the pilot if the Canadians knew about the large force? Immediately he switched to our Battle Group net, which he was already on to land at FOB Wilson. I heard the Company CP telling everyone that a large force consisting of ten to twenty insurgents had been spotted, and they were moving from the east toward Strong Point Centre. Good, they knew. As long as they knew, they would be prepared, and they would be okay.

The helicopter took off and swung south over Route Summit and then over Strong Point Centre before heading back north. I don't know if he did that for my benefit or he had to go that way because of the wind and sand. Either way, I had the opportunity to see my soldiers in action from above and see the LAVs pounding away with 25mm and 7.62mm rounds. I thought to myself, "Those Taliban shit-birds are going to be ripped apart."

We continued to fly toward Kandahar Airfield. Before distance resulted in the loss of communication on the Battle Group net, I heard a request for medical evacuation because Canadian soldiers had been wounded. I was terrified. It reminded me of the morning I woke up in the Role 3 Hospital, knowing that someone had been hit and hoping it was someone other than Charles Company. Once again, I was wondering who had been shot, how badly and whether they would be okay.

The helicopter landed at Kandahar Airfield, and I was met by MWO Rob MacRae once again. He had heard my name come over the radio as inbound to KAF and had gotten a vehicle to meet me at the landing zone. I asked him if he had any more info on what was going on with the attack on Charles Company. He said that the fighting appeared to have ended and that there had been some wounded, but he had no details.

I had Rob take me to the Canadian compound where the main CP and office areas were located. When I got out of the vehicle, I heard people passing the word that we were in a communication lockdown. We did that when Canadian soldiers were seriously wounded or killed to ensure that the word didn't leak out before the CP was able to get accurate information and families back in Canada were notified. The last thing we wanted was for someone to hear that terrible news through social media or from a neighbour who was told by someone else.

This was not good. How bad had it been?

I made my way slowly to the Battle Group CP, and it was a flurry of activity. When the Operations Officer saw me, he came over and shook my hand and said he was glad to see I was safe. He then told me in a very matter-of-fact way that two of my soldiers had been killed and at least three were wounded, one badly. They were still trying to identify the dead through the ZAP numbers, and I could hear WO Olstad on the radio passing on information.

A few minutes later, the Operations Officer pulled me aside and told me that Sergeant Darcy Tedford and Private Blake Williamson were dead. Of course, I knew them both well. I had known Sergeant Tedford for several years, and I had spoken to him a couple of hours earlier about his recent visit back home to his family. I got to know Private Williamson well while we were at Strong Point Centre. What a terrible loss.

The story of what happened that day was told to me by Lieutenant-Colonel Omer Lavoie. As I was flying over the site en route to KAF, a large force attacked Strong Point Centre. Dozens of RPGs were fired at the position, and many were surprisingly accurate. Our soldiers returned fire, and for at least an hour the intense firefight continued, with Lieutenant-Colonel Lavoie firing thousands of rounds from his LAV alone. By the time the battle was over, two soldiers were dead and three were wounded. An unknown number of attackers were also dead.

One of the amazing stories that came out of this attack concerned the heroic actions of Private Jess Larochelle. With the platoon being short-handed after one of the LAVs hit an IED, Larochelle volunteered to man the observation post by himself, normally a two-person task. According to soldiers that were in the area and Larochelle himself, when

PART THREE - AFGHANISTAN

the attack happened a rocket hit his observation post, knocking him unconscious and breaking vertebrae in his neck and back. One of his eyes had damage to its retina and his eardrum on the right side was blown out. When Larochelle gained consciousness, he saw a scene from hell. Two of his brothers lay dead, three more were seriously wounded and his post was under sustained attack. The machine gun he had been using was destroyed and the LAV in his immediate vicinity was malfunctioning. Even though he was severely wounded and exposed to enemy fire, he immediately began to provide covering fire for the remainder of his platoon and company. This would have been very difficult and painful. Private Larochelle's heroic actions allowed the rest of the company to fend off the attack by about twenty insurgents. After it was over, he remained on the battlefield for another twelve hours despite his injuries. Only after being returned to KAF to help carry one of the dead did he finally seek medical attention.

Doctors confirmed that everything Private Larochelle did after the initial attack was completed with a broken back. Private Larochelle was awarded the Military Star of Merit, Canada's second highest honour. He is truly a Canadian Hero

Cpl Bruce Moncur, another soldier from Charles Company who was severely wounded during the opening hours of Operation Medusa has started a non-profit organization called "Valour in the Presence of the Enemy ". With the help of General Rick Hillier and many others they are fighting to have the case of Jess Larochelle and some others reviewed, with the possibility that he will become the first recipient of the Canadian Victoria Cross. They have my full support.

After the attack there was a moment that is an example of the brotherhood forged in war, when WO Keith Olstad, now the acting Sergeant Major in my place, handed two dog tags to CWO Bobby Girouard, the Battle Group Sergeant Major. No words were spoken; the meaning was clear.

Recently Omar Lavoie spoke at the dedication and naming of the Kemptville Armoury as the "Private Blake Williamson Memorial Hall." While talking about the events of that morning and the significance of the passing of the dog tags, I could still hear the raw emotion in his voice, even ten years later.

I spent the remainder of the day walking around KAF in a daze. I had to deal with the administrative guys about money, leave and flights, finding time for a shower, some clean clothes, and getting a haircut. I did not want to do any of it.

By suppertime, I had completed all my tasks and even packed a few things for my trip. It was time to go and try to enjoy a fresh meal. I was sitting in the kitchen picking at an overcooked steak that did not come from Canada when I saw the Operations Officer and MWO MacRae come in. They grabbed their food and joined me at the table. The Operations Officer asked me if I would be open to the idea of escorting Sergeant Tedford's body back to Canada, seeing as I was going back on leave anyway, and the extra days would be added to the end of my holiday. He also stated that he would understand if I did not want to do it. I immediately said yes and that the lost days of my leave did not matter. This was something that would be a privilege to do.

26

ESCORT DUTY

I was listed as the official escort for Sergeant Darcy Tedford. Another young soldier and friend of Private Williamson's from Bravo Company was the second escort. I also learned that these guys were best friends. I tried to comfort the second escort, but he was not ready for that yet.

I received a briefing on the escort duties and learned that I was responsible to always be with the remains while they were being moved. I would have to deal with the folks from Mortuary Affairs looking after the remains from Kandahar to Dubai and back to Trenton. Then, there would be a road move to Toronto for the autopsy, followed by preparations and a final move to their hometowns for the funerals. I would only be responsible as the escort to Trenton, at which point I would hand off my duties to someone from our home unit in Petawawa. They would be responsible for the remainder of the time, and I would head off on my leave. My family had been notified of the changes to my travel and would meet me in Trenton.

I spent the remainder of my time in Kandahar running around, changing paperwork for flights and manifests and getting ready for the Ramp Ceremony. We would be departing Kandahar Airfield immediately afterward for an "undisclosed location" which was Dubai, one of the worst-kept secrets in the world.

During my last few hours at the airfield, there was a flurry of activity as I prepared to leave for three weeks. What I was not aware of and what I was never told is that there was a mandatory briefing that was given to all Canadian soldiers before leaving for holidays. These briefings included a security brief about what you should and should not be talking about as operations were still ongoing. They also included briefings on how to behave, as some soldiers had been in the shit for two or three months. Now they were going to be around ordinary people, around alcohol and around families. They were told that if needed, you should talk to someone about your feelings.

The other part of the briefing was about personal equipment, what was left in

Kandahar and what was left in Dubai, to make sure everything was safe and secure. That last part would come back to haunt me and some other folks.

The Ramp Ceremony was just like the last one I had attended—hundreds of people from every Coalition nation all paying their last respects as the flag-draped coffins were driven by on the ramps of LAVs. Comrades then carried them into the belly of the waiting plane. The aircraft had been set up to accommodate the two caskets at the back. The front half had seats to take about twenty or so passengers who were either heading off on leave or back to their main camp in Dubai. After the caskets were loaded, the escorts remained with the bodies as closer friends and comrades came on board to say a final goodbye. It was tough, and once again, tears came easily.

This time, I did not try to hide them.

There was a process for all the other passengers to board. There were security checks and proper identification like at a regular airport, even though people still had weapons and ammunition. Once all the other passengers were boarded, two Air Force sergeants came and told me and the other escort that it was time for us to now board. They said that we had reserved seats and if there was anything we needed, just to ask. They also said that we were their special guests and would be looked after. I held my tongue as I thought to myself, "The special guests are in the two boxes," but I understood that this young Air Force guy was just trying to do his part in a bad situation.

When I got on the plane, we were taken to two seats just outside the area that the coffins were in and found our gear was already there, waiting for us. I assumed that the sergeants brought it on board.

The flight to Dubai was uneventful, even though we had to do a combat take-off from Kandahar to avoid being shot at or shot down. Both of us escorts were treated like royalty for the rest of the flight, and it felt good.

Once we landed in Dubai, at about 0200 hours in the morning, I was surprised to look out the window and see many soldiers lined up to show respect. Everyone wanted to do their part, and it was much appreciated.

When the plane came to a stop, the same two sergeants briefed everyone on the upcoming process. All the passengers would stay on board until the remains of the two heroes were taken off. As for the escorts, we would depart the aircraft with the caskets.

An Air Force Master Corporal from Dubai came on board. He identified himself and told us that he would look after us while we were here. He also said that he would now take our combat kit, have it stored, and we would pick it up on our return in a few weeks.

All Canadian soldiers going through Dubai on their way out of the theatre left all their fighting gear there, including body armour, tac vests, weapons and ammo. They would then pick it up again on the way back into the theatre of operations.

But I didn't receive the briefing, and this is where it became interesting.

GRENADES IN DUBAI

The young Corporal escort handed over his gear, and, when I reached for mine, I noticed the Master Corporal's face change. He started to back up.

"You have grenades," he said.

"Yes, I do. Here's one, and another," I said, pulling them off my vest.

The other people around us just looked on with curiosity as I held two grenades in the palm of my hand and reached out toward the Master Corporal to give them to him. He started to say something about how I couldn't have them here. They needed to stay in Kandahar. I just spoke over him.

"Stop. I'm here now, and I have these two grenades. As a matter of fact, there are two more in my butt pack, so that makes four. Deal with it. If you don't want to touch them, I'll turn them in myself."

He quickly turned around and headed off the plane, saying something about getting the Warrant.

A few minutes later, an Air Force Warrant Officer came in and looked at me standing there holding two grenades in my left hand and pulling two more out of my pack with my right hand.

"Hey Sergeant Major," he said, "welcome to Camp Mirage. Let me take these from you, and the Master Corporal will take the rest of your kit. If you need anything, just ask."

Now there was someone that knew how to handle a delicate situation.

I expected the senior folks in Dubai to freak out about my grenades, as I found out that only your weapon and one magazine were allowed on the aircraft. I had about five hundred rounds of ammunition on me, as well. Just a day earlier, I had been in a battle with the enemy and, somehow, with everyone being so nice to me and helpful, they missed giving me the briefing that everyone else received.

No harm was done, but I was slightly surprised to hear nothing else about it. I figure this Warrant had been someone who had been in combat himself sometime in the past, or he was just a calm, collected NCO who dealt with what I considered a minor mishap. A few weeks later, I did not get the grenades back on my return, but that was okay. There were lots in Afghanistan.

The caskets were removed from the airplane in Dubai in a very professional and dignified manner and received a salute from the many soldiers, sailors, airmen, and women gathered on the airfield. Then we linked up with the mortuary affairs people from MacKinnon and Bowes, located in Toronto.

At this point it was well past 0200 hours in the morning. I had been living in crappy conditions for the past two or three months. I had been shot at hundreds of times, and here I found myself giggling like a little schoolgirl. The guy who put his hand out and introduced himself as a representative of the Ontario Coroner's Office looked like the guy from the World Wrestling Federation known as the "Pallbearer," the manager for the wrestler called "the Undertaker." I do not know if it was the release of stress or all the pills I had been swallowing, but it was funny, and I couldn't hide it.

The Pallbearer was dressed all in black, with pasty white skin and his ample girth hanging over his pants. He just ignored my laughter and introduced me to his assistant.

I was gob struck.

She was the complete opposite. In her early 20s, she was dressed in a black but very casual, sexy pantsuit that showed that she looked after herself and had all the right curves in all the right places. She was a gorgeous young woman who seemed to be very shy and perhaps intimidated. It made her even sexier.

The only women we had seen in the past three months had been soldiers wearing army green who were as dirty as the rest of us or Afghan women wearing a burka. So, to notice a beautiful young woman did not seem sexist or demeaning to me.

I am sure, as my lovely wife reads this, she will certainly understand.

The assistant was a student in a work placement and wanted to work in Mortuary Affairs as a career. I thought to myself, to each their own, and pictured her in twenty years looking like the Pallbearer.

THE REMAINS

After introductions, we moved the remains of our two Canadian heroes to the American Mortuary Affairs unit, as Canada did not have this capability in theatre. The caskets were then opened, and the pasty white coroner checked the remains and then added dry ice to ensure they were kept as they were for the upcoming autopsy in Canada.

I was not prepared for this part.

There is a nice casket with a beautiful Canadian flag draped on it and a beautiful Ramp Ceremony. The complete trip is made in a sombre, dignified manner. However, the body is placed in the casket, just as it was found on the battlefield, to preserve any evidence of the cause of death. Unless soldiers or medical staff were trying to save the person's life, the remains are still fully clothed with body armour and equipment, minus any ammunition or explosives.

Once confirmation is done, the remains are placed in a cooler within the mortuary and secured for the night. Once I had confirmed that the remains were indeed secure, I was escorted to quarters where an air-conditioned room with a soft bed awaited me. We had about three hours to relax before departing for Canada, and I needed the rest. I had not slept well for months, and a couple of hours in a cool room and a real bed sounded good. I spent way too long in the shower, and when I was done, I crawled into the bed, but sleep would not come.

It was a terrible first hour as every bad thing that had happened over the last three months came flooding back. I was glad that none of my soldiers were around, as they would have seen their hard-ass, grumpy Sergeant Major lose control. That was something that would have been hard for me to recover from.

After tossing and turning for an hour, I got up and got dressed and went for a walk around Camp Mirage to see how the other side lived. I tried to keep my mind on the fact that I would soon be home and able to spend time with Julie, JJ, and Jana, and that was what mattered. I came across some guys standing outside a building, and I roamed over and introduced myself. They immediately invited me in for coffee, probably the best coffee I'd had in months.

The Air Force knows how to make coffee.

I sat there and talked with those guys for probably thirty minutes. I told them how much I appreciated how everyone here at the camp treated the fallen soldiers when they arrived. They told me they all wanted to do their small part; however, it was not just a tiny part. It was instrumental in how we brought our soldiers back home. They wished me luck and told me they were proud of what my soldiers were doing in Afghanistan. I thanked them and said goodbye.

By the time I got back to my room, people were up and getting dressed, as most of them were getting ready to go home either on leave or because they had finished their tour at Camp Mirage. Either way, they would be travelling on the same aircraft as Sergeant Tedford and Private Williamson.

The Warrant Officer that had taken my grenades earlier came and grabbed me and the other escort and took us to the mortuary, where we met up with the Pallbearer and his beautiful assistant. They checked the remains, added some more ice, and then prepared the casket for travel. The whole time both escorts remained at the side of each of the fallen. Soldiers from Camp Mirage then carried the coffins in front of every available soldier from the camp and onto the aircraft. I thought, how many of these ceremonies these young aviators had had to do and what effect was it having on them?

Both escorts were led onto the plane and into assigned seats closest to the caskets. The rest of the passengers, probably around twenty or so, boarded and took their seats. If I remember correctly, this was the Prime Minister's airplane, which he graciously gave up for this journey home for our two fallen soldiers.

Once everyone was aboard, the pilot came on the speaker, briefed everyone on the flight and explained that we had the remains of two Canadian heroes and their escorts. He mentioned both of us by name and said it was an honour to be able to bring our soldiers home. I know everyone on board was touched. We were then approached by members of the airplane crew, told that they were at our beck and call, and if we needed anything, to just ask.

They were first-class the whole flight back, and they deserve my thanks

27
ARRIVAL IN CANADA

I don't remember a lot about the flight because I slept for most of it. I was overtired, on painkillers and once the stress of continually being in combat was removed, I finally started to relax. I was awoken by a voice on a speaker saying that we would be landing in Trenton shortly.

I was immediately awake, and my mind was going a hundred miles an hour. I would be seeing Julie and the kids. How would they be? What would I say to them? I was actually a little bit scared. Then, my thoughts went to the two dead soldiers behind me, and I knew that their families would confront me in the next few minutes, too.

I was terrified.

The speaker came to life again, and the pilot let everyone know that there would be a ceremony at the airfield. He said that several dignitaries and families of the fallen were present, including members of Parliament, the Chief of the Defence Staff and local government officials. All the passengers were to remain on the plane until the fallen soldiers were taken off and placed in the waiting hearses. The pilot then told everyone that they would have to get off and go through customs inside the terminal before seeing their families.

He added that someone from the ground would come on as soon as we stopped, get the two escorts and take us into the terminal to meet the dignitaries and families. We would then join them outside as the caskets were taken off.

The plane stopped, and the doors opened. A Captain came on board, introduced himself and told us to come with him. We walked down the stairs and into the terminal. The first person we met was the Chief of the Defence Staff, General Rick Hillier. I had met General Hillier many times over my career, including in Afghanistan when he joined us in the field for a visit, which was a great morale booster for the troops. He shook both escorts' hands and expressed his great thanks to us for taking on the tremendous duty of escorting our fallen heroes home. He spoke to both of us as if he had known us for years, something for which General Hillier was known. Whether you were a Private or a Colonel, he always made you feel like you were important to him.

Standing with him were the families of Sergeant Tedford and Private Williamson. I quickly reaffirmed that Canadian soldiers have great families and are dignified at the best and worst of times. I looked at Charmaine Tedford and saw the sadness in her eyes. I put my arms around her and told her how deeply sorry I was to bring Darcy home in this manner. She then pulled back a little bit and looked up into my eyes and asked me if I was all right.

I was amazed at how precious she was, with her husband laying in a box a few metres away in an airplane. One of the people responsible for making sure he would come home alive was standing in front of her, and she was worried about me. She held my hand and said how proud she was of all the soldiers of Charles Company and how grateful she was that Darcy had been able to see her and the kids a few days earlier. She then smiled up at me and said, "Julie and the kids are here. Go see them. They've been waiting."

I looked past her, and standing a few feet away were Julie, JJ and Jana. I knew that Julie had not come forward because she knew that I had my duty as an escort to finish first. She has always understood that sometimes she would have to come second, though never in my heart. I probably have not told her often enough that she has always come first. I immediately saw that Julie was sobbing, and Jana was crying uncontrollably too. JJ, at the age of sixteen, was trying to hold it all together. I embraced them all. We hugged for a long time, and there was no one else that mattered.

I never wanted to let go. It was the first time I had felt safe in many weeks.

I remember hugging JJ separately, telling him how happy I was to see him, how much he had grown, and that he was looking more and more like a young man.

He smiled at me and, as he hugged me, asked, "Are you wearing your flak vest?"

"No," I said with a puzzled look on my face.

"I thought you would have lost weight in Afghanistan."

I slapped him across the back of the head in a playful manner. "Thanks, buddy."

He always was and still is a bit of a wise guy.

We were interrupted by a Captain who wanted to brief me on the next phase of the return of our soldiers. I was introduced to the soldier from 1 RCR who would now take over the escort duties and continue until Sergeant Tedford was laid to rest. I spoke with him briefly and thanked him for taking over this tremendous task. He said it was an honour for him to do this for Sergeant Tedford, his family, and the soldiers of Charles Company who have entrusted it to him. We still had a few minutes before they would be ready to remove the remains from the aircraft, and I took that time to assure Julie and the kids that I was okay. Jana and JJ had wandered off, and when I looked over, they were at the window. Sitting with them was General Rick Hillier. He spoke to my children for several minutes, and then he presented each of them with one of his coins, which I hope they will treasure forever.

General Rick Hillier will go down as one of our greatest Chiefs of the Defence Staff. The fact that I got to know him personally and that he was a fellow Newfoundlander makes it even more significant to me.

It was not until many years later that I fully understood what JJ and Jana went through during my deployment to Afghanistan. My children have grown up to be wonderful, successful adults. Most of that I credit directly to how Julie raised them and gave them their values while I was off saving the world. However, I also believe that my children had to experience things that most children could never understand. Living on or near army bases from Germany to Petawawa to Meaford and Kingston, attending schools with mostly military children and knowing that those friends you were making would be leaving for another posting, plus knowing you were moving too and would need to make new friends, teaches you a lot about life.

Living on or near a base and seeing Canadian soldiers wearing our flag with pride every day can be a very gratifying and unique experience for military kids but during times of war and conflict, living around a Canadian base can also be a huge burden. I remember hearing stories from JJ and Jana about how kids were called out of the classrooms to be told that one of their parents had been killed or wounded. How every time the intercom system came on or there was a knock on the classroom door, kids flinched and even began to cry.

I cannot even imagine how that must feel. That terrible feeling of despair while waiting for it to be your turn and perhaps even hoping that it was someone else's parent rather than your own. Having to go to school on a base where the Canadian flag is at half-mast, when you know why and for whom. How did they feel that day when Julie told them to get in the house in a raised voice because a soldier had pulled up to them in uniform? They knew that he was about to tell their mother terrible news about their Dad.

What were they thinking as they peered out the window watching Mark Brander speaking to their mother, knowing that this was their turn and wondering if I was dead? Even after hearing the news that I was wounded but not having enough information to put them at ease, they would have had many questions: Was I going to live? How badly had I been hurt?

Julie didn't want them to hear any bad news from anyone but her. She is my hero.

I have heard stories of spouses and children being diagnosed with Post-Traumatic Stress Disorder and I often thought, how was this possible? Now I know.

I have told the story a hundred times to soldiers, civilians and children about how it was so much easier for me in Afghanistan, even as I was losing soldiers and grieving. All the emotions were short-lived, as I always had to get back to the mission. There was no time to dwell on a tragedy that had just happened, as we needed to be ready for the next fight that was just around the corner. Our daily routine was hectic, and the chance of death was always present, so our thoughts were mostly on day-to-day survival. We never really thought about our feelings or even other people's feelings. We took only a quick moment to grieve for those killed or wounded.

The rest would have to wait until we got back to Canada.

At home, our families had to be living on pins and needles as they waited for the phone call, the knock or the rumours of another battle.

That was much more stressful than anything I have ever done

As I looked at my teenage children sitting by the window of the airport in Trenton with General Rick Hillier, I understood for the first time how difficult it had been on them and how unfair it was to put such a huge burden on them at such a young age. Before I went back to Afghanistan, I knew I needed to sit down and talk with them about what could happen. I had written letters for each of them and one for Julie. I didn't remember if I had left them where they could be easily found in my room in Kandahar or if they had been destroyed with my gear in the attack. I would need to confirm this as soon as I was back on the ground.

My thoughts were interrupted by an announcement. We were to move outside as the remains were unloaded and placed on the waiting hearses. Winter had arrived in Canada, but the cool air felt terrific after three months of extreme heat. As I stood on the airfield waiting for the ceremony to start, I noticed the smell of fresh air—what a concept.

Afghanistan has only one smell: shit. Everywhere you go, there is a smell of human shit—dried shit blowing in the air and getting on your clothes and skin. What a relief it was to be standing in the greatest country in the world and enjoying the cool, fresh air. On top of being back in Canada, being able to hug my wife and children, smelling the fresh air, I also had the opportunity to reconnect with Major Sprague. He, of course, would not have missed this ceremony for the world. These were his soldiers, and he stood beside me as the families were moved into place.

Major Sprague looked good and he said he felt good. He had been hit in several places during the A-10 strike, including the head, but he told me several times he was ready to come back.

"You'll see me in Afghanistan soon," he said.

It reminded me of what I had said to Major Savage in Kandahar when I wanted to go back out with the troops. Major Sprague said that, so far, he had not been cleared to redeploy—but he was not giving up. Once again, it sounded familiar. Later on, I took the opportunity to sit down with Major Sprague and bring him up to speed on what had been happening in Afghanistan since he had left.

CEREMONY IN TRENTON

I was brought back to reality as the ceremony began, and the Honour Guard and Bearer Party unloaded the caskets with the Canadian flag still covering each one in all its glory. In a slow and dignified march, they were placed in the waiting hearses.

Individual family members went up to the caskets one by one. Some placed their hand on top, some quietly said personal words to their loved one. If they only knew what was really inside the coffin. It was not their loved one. It was a destroyed body that was still in the same condition as it was on the battlefield. It reminded me of how delicate the human body actually is and that it was never meant to stand up to hot lead and explosions.

Then it was our turn, and Major Sprague and I went up to the hearse together. I remember placing my hand on each Canadian flag.

"You're now home."

We then stepped back together in a sharp military movement and saluted our soldiers. I looked back at the two families and wished I was anywhere but there at that moment. After we walked back, I said goodbye to the families and told them how sorry I was for their loss.

As I was about to leave and join my family, Charmaine Tedford grabbed my arm.

"John, it's okay," she said. "Spend some time with Julie and the kids. You'll be all right. I'll be all right."

What a woman. When she and her two girls had just received the body of their husband and father, she had a moment for me. I was taken aback, and I just looked at her. I told her that she had our phone number and that Julie and I were there for them. I stood with Julie and the kids as the hearses and the families departed for the Highway of Heroes and Toronto.

What's not often clear to people is what happens to the bodies after they arrive in Trenton. The bodies are preserved as best as possible from the time of death until they arrive in Canada, though sometimes this could take several days. This means placing them in containers with dry ice and not cleaning, preparing, or disturbing them in any way to preserve evidence of how they died. The immediate destination of the bodies from Trenton is the Office of the Chief Coroner, a very plain, two-story building in downtown Toronto. It's just the next step on the long road from the dirt fields of Afghanistan through Camp Mirage in Dubai, then to Trenton, and then on to the small towns and cities across Canada for burial.

In Toronto, the coroner and experts from the Canadian Forces have the difficult job of examining the remains. Typically, the autopsy is meant to try and answer five questions for the Canadian Armed Forces, the public and the family.

Who is the person?

How did they die?

When, where, and by what means?

Typically, coroners are dealing with the unknown when they conduct an autopsy, but not in these cases. The cause of death is not a mystery—more often than not, the person was shot or involved in a catastrophic explosion.

When the coroner hears that a Canadian soldier is on the way, they start getting ready to receive the remains. Once the convoy arrives from Trenton, the Honour Guard and the escort moves the flag-draped coffins inside to the basement morgue. The autopsy room is much like any operating room you would see, with one addition: a Canadian flag hanging on the wall. Once the autopsy is completed, which could take a couple of hours, the Honour Guard again comes and takes the casket away. The remains are then taken to the funeral home, where they are prepared as per the family's wishes. Then, if the family wishes, they receive full military honours at the funeral.

28

HOME LEAVE

The next couple of weeks for me were a blur. It was so good to be home, to be able to choose what I ate, have a beer, watch hockey, or just hang out with Julie and the kids. But what was happening in Afghanistan was never far from my mind. If I was in the house, the television was on a news channel. I was continually calling Mark Brander of the Rear Party for information on what was happening.

I was never able to relax.

I am not sure that we adequately prepare our soldiers to come home on leave and be back in the real world. On the other hand, there is a lot of funding and resources available to ensure that our soldiers can deal with the psychological impacts of Afghanistan before going home at the end of their tour.

Canada had set up a third-party decompression site in Cyprus that soldiers must go through on their way home. In Cyprus, every soldier received briefings on how to readjust. There are psychologists, social workers, chaplains for spiritual support, and many opportunities to relax and enjoy life without stress. It was also an opportunity to speak with people about how you felt and to get anything off your chest before going home.

But there I was, back home after spending more than two months in a war zone and being under constant daily attack, having to kill and see your soldiers being killed. I had gone directly from combat to sitting in Petawawa with Julie and the kids, having a beer. No wonder I was on edge. I was always looking behind me. I only wanted to walk on paved surfaces and crowds made me feel unsafe and caused me great anxiety. Even ten years later, I still feel these things.

When I saw a man wearing typical Pashtun dress in Ottawa, I went into fight-or-flight mode, and I had to use all my internal power to avoid attacking him. I began to sweat. My muscles became tense, and I reached for where my weapon would have been.

WHITE SCHOOL, BLACK MEMORIES

Only a soft touch from Julie kept me from making a terrible mistake. Even today, ten years later, the sight of a man or woman wearing Afghan or Pashtun dress makes me nervous.

What were we thinking? We plucked soldiers off the battlefield, where they might have been killing someone only hours earlier, or picking up Canadian or Afghan bodies, and allowed them to go directly into the rest of the world. No wonder we had issues with Canadian soldiers drinking too much alcohol on flights and causing disturbances and worse. Despite how I was feeling, I tried not to let Julie or the kids see my anxiety or concerns, and I tried to enjoy every moment I had with them.

I don't know if I was successful, and I'm sure that Julie and the kids noticed that I was eager to go back to Afghanistan. That is a tough sell to your family. I had just put them through hell, and now I was finally home, I almost immediately wanted to leave. I couldn't explain it to them at the time, and I believe that made it even worse.

I think that today, as the kids are older and more mature (I would never tell them that), they have a better understanding of why getting back was so important to me. It was not about getting away from them. It was all about getting back to my soldiers in the hope of bringing them all home alive to their families.

While at home, Major Sprague and I attended the funeral service for Sergeant Tedford. It was held in Petawawa at 1 RCR, and I had the opportunity to say goodbye to him surrounded by family, friends, and the soldiers of the Brigade and Base. That was tough, but I kept it together long enough not to make a scene.

It was then time for me to pack up and head back to Afghanistan and my soldiers. Part of me did not want to leave my family again and did not want to leave the comfort and safety of Canada. But I also knew I had a duty to my soldiers. They were expecting me to return, and the job that we had started had not been finished.

I probably could have remained behind if I had wanted to.

My headaches had not gone away, and I walked around with a pocket full of pills that I ate like candy and were not working anymore. I was having dizzy spells and issues with my short-term memory. My hearing loss was worse than I first thought, and I only figured that out when I was trying to have a normal conversation with my family or when the kids would yell for me to turn the TV down, and I could barely hear it. There were also times when I got up too quickly, and I would still lose my balance. It was a genuine concern.

I was able to keep these conditions a secret from my family and friends, or at least they never commented on it, but if I had gone to the military doctor in Petawawa, I am sure I would not have been allowed to return.

So, of course, I did not see a doctor, and I said a painful goodbye to Julie, JJ and Jana. It was much harder this time than three months earlier, as they were now much more aware of the dangers of the mission and knew that there was a good chance that I could be killed or wounded. How do you say goodbye to someone you love with all your heart and soul, knowing that you may never see them again? I've been an incredibly lucky man to have such a loving and supportive family. Julie did a fantastic job at keeping it all together and raising two wonderful children.

My daughter Jana is now Master Corporal Barnes, a member of the Base Military Police in Petawawa. Her husband, Josh, is a supply technician, and they're the new parents of my two beautiful grandsons, Noah and Theo. My son, JJ (John Jarod), graduated from Carleton University and now works for the federal government in Ottawa.

Without question, they are my greatest achievements.

29

BACK TO AFGHANISTAN

My return trip felt like it took an eternity, as sleep would not come. I took a flight from Ottawa to London and then an Emirates flight to Dubai, and finally a bus to Camp Mirage. The trip was uneventful, and the only thing that caught my attention was my Emirates flight.

While checking in at the gate in London, I noticed that all the ladies working the counter and gate wore hijabs, which caused me some apprehension. On the plane, all the female flight attendants were also wearing hijabs. Once the aircraft was in the air, almost on cue, all of them removed their hijabs and stayed like that until we were about to enter Dubai airspace, when they once again put them on. What kind of society forces half its population to follow these types of draconian traditions?

I arrived in Mirage on the night of November 10, exhausted from two days of travelling and thoughts of my family's tears and sadness as I left. What made that especially hard was that I couldn't do anything to help them.

The following morning was November 11, and I had the privilege of attending a Remembrance Day Ceremony at the Camp Mirage Memorial. Every available soldier, sailor, airman and woman attended, and of course, this one had a more special meaning than those of other years. It was a moment to remember all our lost soldiers, but it took on a more personal meaning for me as I thought of the fallen soldiers who I knew.

Shortly after the ceremony and following a nice meal, I was approached by the same Warrant Officer who I had dealt with three weeks earlier on the way through Dubai. He told me that he had my gear ready minus my four grenades and arranged for me to sit up in the front of the CC-130 Hercules aircraft. At first, I told him that I did not want special treatment, as many other soldiers were travelling back to Kandahar as well, but he insisted. I finally agreed.

The flight into KAF was amazing. The view of the ground through the Hercules' windshield is much different than what you get when squeezed into the plane's belly.

PART THREE - AFGHANISTAN

The landing in Kandahar was a combat landing used to avoid being shot out of the sky by missiles or small arms. It was a beautiful thing to see from the cockpit. I have so much appreciation for those pilots, being able to manoeuvre those big planes around the sky like a toy and land softly on a small runway.

Once the plane came to a halt and the doors were open, we were met with the same disgusting smell and heat that I had left three weeks earlier. I told myself that it was time to get my game face on and get back into the battle. There was no room for error and no room for thoughts of home. I was back in the shit, or at least for the time being, in the Hesco Hobbit version of the shit.

I enjoyed a full day of relaxing at Kandahar Airfield as arrangements were made for my transportation to Panjwai. I sat around the boardwalk, had Tim Hortons coffee and doughnuts, and then watched some Canadians playing ball hockey against some Americans in a rink built out front. I don't think I have to say who won that game.

I then strolled back to the quarters, had a nap in my air-conditioned room and was not awakened until I heard two distant explosions followed by sirens going off to let people know of incoming rockets. The only issue was that the missiles landed before the sirens. I heard people running around and yelling to get to the bunkers, doors slamming and more running. Meanwhile, I just stayed in bed. This example would not be a particularly good one for my young soldiers, but I figured if there were more incoming rockets, I had just as good a chance to survive here as I did in the bunker. I reached over, grabbed my weapon, put a round in the chamber, made sure it was on safe and laid it on the bed beside me, just in case. The sirens finally went silent about an hour later, and I heard people returning to their rooms. I rolled over and fell back asleep.

The following day, I was up and ready to go, but the helicopter ride had been cancelled because of other priorities, and I had to wait. I was finally able to get a seat on a convoy leaving that night for FOB Wilson. I was not keen on another road move through Kandahar City, but beggars can't be choosers.

The rest of the day was spent at the CQ, talking with the troops and telling war stories. A couple of the young soldiers had taken advantage of their leave to go to Thailand, and they proceeded to tell us stories about their time over there. I stuck around until the conversation started to swing toward some of their sexual exploits and got into areas I was not interested in or comfortable hearing. When a sexual exploit story begins with 'anything goes for the right price,' it was time for this married man and father of two teenagers to move on.

MOVE TO FOB WILSON

I headed back to my room, where I lay in bed and read a book until I fell asleep. A knock on my door awakened me, and a young corporal stuck his head in to tell me that there would be orders for the night move to FOB Wilson after supper. I skipped supper and made sure my kit was all good to go and that my weapons were functional and clear of any dust or dirt. I emptied all the ammo out of my twelve magazines, let the springs relax for a couple of hours, and then reloaded them.

I was heading back out into disputed territory and the last thing you want to find out when you come in contact with the enemy is that your ammo is not feeding into the weapon because they have sat for too long on a compressed spring. On top of that, I was driving out into the badlands in convoy with many strangers and not my soldiers.

At orders, a young sergeant stood in front of everyone and identified himself as the convoy commander. He told us that, even though there were a mixture of folks from across the military—different trades, senior officers and senior NCOs—that if anything happened, he was in charge. That had made my stomach feel a little weird. Who was this guy? I know he was a reservist and not part of the Battle Group, but what experience did he have? How would he react if we came under fire?

"Ladies and gentlemen, orders."

The young sergeant began giving orders. I have done this many times throughout my career. I have sat in on and received hundreds of orders, and I must say that this young reserve sergeant gave one of the best and most comprehensive set of orders I had ever received. He followed a sequence that made it relatively easy to understand, regardless of which background you came from. His plan was simple but logical, and he covered every possible situation. Once he was finished, there were only a few very low-level questions to confirm some things, and then everyone got up, grabbed their kit and prepared to leave.

As I was about to walk out of the room, the sergeant got my attention and asked me if I had any questions or concerns. I understood that he probably knew that I was the Sergeant Major of Charles Company, knew that I had a lot of combat experience, and he was probably only looking for advice. I told him that he had given a great set of orders and that it was apparent what everyone had to do. His face gave away that he was happy to hear that from me, as an infantry soldier and an MWO.

He went on to tell me that this was his seventh convoy in the past two months and that he had come under fire on every one. Because of the mixture of folks on board, it sometimes became chaotic. He told me that if they came under attack, he would appreciate any assistance I could give. I assured him that I had every faith in him as the commander, and if he wanted my help, he could just ask. He shook my hand, gave me a small smile and rushed off to prepare to lead the convoy.

The convoy was mainly uneventful, with only a minor breakdown that the sergeant handled as precisely as how I would have. We were able to roll into FOB Wilson by about midnight, towing a vehicle behind us. I told the sergeant that perhaps I was his lucky charm, as this had been the first convoy he had led that had not been in contact with the enemy. Then I told him what a great job he had done and wished him luck.

Even though FOB Wilson had about sixty Canadians and another thirty or so Afghan soldiers, as well as about fifteen Afghan National Police, it was very dark and mostly quiet when we arrived, except for the occasional dog bark. We unloaded the vehicles in the dark, and I, once again, thanked the sergeant and headed off to the

Charles Company Command Post in one of the corners under canvas.

CAPTAIN NORTON

I walked in to find the Company Second-in-Command, Captain Trevor Norton, sitting in the back of his LAV with a headset on listening to reports from the platoons while one of his LAV crew, Corporal Gary Mullin, was working over a map.

Corporal Mullin was a career soldier with more than eighteen years of experience and was a perfect fit for the Company Command Post. His role in the success of the Company cannot be overstated. Unfortunately, Corporal Mullin died in November 2007 at forty-four years of age, just eight short months after returning from Afghanistan.

Captain Norton had been the Company LAV Captain and responsible for employing the Company's fifteen LAVs in battle. However, after the tragic losses during September 3-4, he was promoted into the Company Second-in-Command position. I must admit that he went into this new role kicking and screaming. Captain Norton was a combat soldier. He was intelligent, tough and wanted to be in the middle of the fight with the troops—plus, he was good at it. Although a critical position, the Company Second-in-Command is typically kept behind the company and is, at least in theory, out of contact with the enemy. Captain Norton took on this new role with the same vigour as he had to past ones and did a fantastic job until Major Sprague returned to Afghanistan. He was then able to be the LAV Captain again.

Captain Norton went on to have a stellar career, including as the Commanding Officer of 2 RCR. I would not be surprised to see him commanding a brigade or a higher formation in future—he is that kind of officer and gentleman.

He briefed me on what was going on in the area, and I learned that there were no huge changes since I had left. I knew that the ongoing insurgency was not letting up, and soldiers remained in contact with the enemy daily. I decided to stay at FOB Wilson until the following day when I would be taken back to Strong Point Centre and could link up with WO Olstad, who had done a fantastic job during my absence.

My first night back in Panjwai did not let me down. Corporal Mullin had provided a space for me under canvas, but I decided to sleep outside under the beautiful sky. I settled down on my air mattress next to the Command Post LAV, and was remembering the look on the faces of Julie, JJ and Jana as I walked through security at the Ottawa airport for my return flight to Afghanistan. That's when the first mortar round landed just outside the FOB. I immediately gunned up and went inside the LAV to listen to the radio as the remainder of FOB Wilson scurried to their bunkers and fighting positions.

Almost as the dust was settling from the first round, a second and then a third mortar round landed on the opposite side of the FOB. I did not know if they had landed inside or outside the wire, and my thoughts went to the soldiers who were living over there. Luckily, the last two rounds had overshot the FOB and landed about fifty metres outside, and no one had been injured. Next, I heard a machine-gun open fire from the roof of the main building used as the FOB headquarters and medical station. The gunners had located the mortar and were engaging.

As the machine-gun opened fire, the Quick Reaction Force (QRF) had loaded up into their vehicles and was ready to deploy wherever necessary. There was always a QRF on standby at FOB Wilson to come to the assistance of anyone in the area that found themselves in a situation that they could not handle on their own. In this case, it was a platoon from Bravo Company with a couple of sections of Afghans. I heard over the radio that the mortars had been fired from the location of the mosque that was located several hundred metres east of FOB Wilson on Highway 1. That mosque had become a bone of contention since we had been here and had been used on several occasions to fire at the FOB or plan assaults.

We were between a rock and a hard place as Coalition soldiers because the mosques were a place of worship and, unless we were under direct attack from the site and there were no other options than to strike it, our hands were tied. I had become very cynical when it came to mosques. Almost everyone that was searched during my tour had either bad guys or weapons and ammunition. We already knew that most of them preached hatred. We used our Afghan troops to enter mosques whenever time permitted to make sure that the mission had an Afghan face; we tried to avoid upsetting the locals any more than we already had.

I may not be politically correct, but I would have been okay with flattening every mosque in Afghanistan that either harboured or supported the Taliban or terrorists, and if they used them as cover to fire at Coalition forces or to store weapons or ammunition, they needed to be fair game.

In this case, the QRF rolled out to Highway 1 and slowly went toward the mosque, but the enemy had disappeared by the time they got there. They were now probably safely inside the mosque, weapons hidden and, on their knees, praying to Allah as if they were innocent. Permission for the QRF to search the mosque was denied. That mosque and that specific area about a kilometre or so east of FOB Wilson along Highway 1 would continue to be a thorn in our side. Eventually, it would have to be dealt with.

I got out of the LAV and went back to my air mattress with the hopes of a couple of hours of sleep, but it did not come easily. That mosque and the surrounding area continued to creep into my thoughts, and the more it did, the more pissed off I became.

30

SERGEANTS-MAJOR CHANGEOVER

Major Brown was already on his way from Strong Point Centre to pick me up, so I threw my stuff together and eagerly awaited his arrival. I saw two LAVs coming through the gate and identified Major Brown standing in the turret of the first vehicle. He waved and smiled at me. As the LAVs stopped, the ramps came down and WO Keith Olstad came out with his hand reaching toward mine and told me that he was glad I was back. I thanked him for the great job he had done and told him that I'd had coffee with his wife, Becky, just a couple of days ago and that she really missed him.

We headed off to the CP with Major Brown so that they could brief me on what I had missed over the last few weeks. There had not been any huge changes since I'd left, and Route Summit had continued to be attacked almost daily while Canadians tried to provide security to the engineers and local workers. We spoke a little bit about the battle that had occurred as I was leaving a few weeks ago, and I told them about bringing Sergeant Tedford and Private Williamson home and how they had been treated.

We made some more small talk about Petawawa and what was going on there. I told them that Major Sprague had said "hi" and was still trying to get back to Kandahar. It was then time to discuss the daily situation in more detail. Several more families had returned to the surrounding villages and compounds, which made our job even more difficult. We still had a platoon from Bravo Company occupying one of the Strong Points while our platoon secured Sperwan Ghar, which had become a hub of activity and a staging area for operations. There was now a Recce Squadron and an Artillery Battery living there, as well as their supporters, and an Afghan Army platoon had set up shop as well.

Once everyone was happy that we had passed on all the needed information, we jumped into Three-Niner and headed back down to Strong Point Centre. WO Olstad remained at FOB Wilson to set up a small two-person detachment to serve as Charles

Company's CQ, with his other two storemen working out of KAF. We hoped this would give us a better and faster resupply mechanism and allow the CQ to hold some stores and equipment at FOB Wilson. This set-up also enables WO Olstad to remain outside of KAF, and that makes him incredibly happy.

DRESS, DEPORTMENT AND PROFESSIONALISM

Once things started to settle down a little bit, Major Brown told me he wanted to speak to me about a couple of incidents that had occurred while I was away. I expected to hear something about how someone reacted or behaved during combat but instead, he spoke to me about dress, deportment and professionalism. This has been a bit of a sore issue since before we deployed, especially the dress and equipment.

There had been complaints from the troops about the issued boots, tactical vests, body armour, helmet liners, safety glasses, gloves—and the list went on and on. It's often been said that the troops were never happy, and complaining was a soldier's pastime.

The Battle Group had compromised on a few things back in Canada, specifically boots and gloves, and soldiers could purchase and wear what they bought if it was within reason. Still, they were pretty much sticking to the issued kit for the remainder of the items.

The reasons behind this decision are clear. It comes down to safety and professionalism. If soldiers were able to wear whatever equipment they wanted, and it was discovered that after a soldier was shot, wounded or killed that he was wearing gear that was not up to safety standards, someone would hang. The second piece was professionalism. We are part of the Profession of Arms and, as such, we do not want to be some sort of ragtag outfit that one sees on TV or even in other parts of the world. Being a professional army needs to mean something, and this Battle Group was no different.

Shortly after arriving in theatre, the Battle Group allowed some more flexibility and permitted soldiers to wear non-issue tactical vests that allowed soldiers to carry extra ammo and magazines or was more workable for machine-gunners or other specialty positions.

Early in the tour, I allowed soldiers to skip shaving during operations or during periods when water was in short supply. Sometimes, this could be over several days, but the chain of command monitored this to ensure it was not abused. Some individual sections and platoons showed up wearing their own patches on their uniforms, and I quickly put an end to that. I always tried to make sure that Charles Company understood that even though we were in combat, we would not lose our professionalism. If anything, we needed to be at our highest standard.

In this context, Major Brown told me that the Battle Group Commander had spoken to him about a visit that he had made with his RSM and the Task Force Command Team to Sperwan Ghar. They had been embarrassed and disappointed by

PART THREE - AFGHANISTAN

the lack of professionalism they had seen. I understand that soldiers had been walking around in all states of dress without their protective equipment, and most were unshaven and ragged.

Now, I usually am not a person who gets overly excited about these types of things, and on this occasion I believed that it might have been a little blown out of proportion. I would wait to see for myself. Major Brown had already planned on taking Three-Niner Tac out to Sperwan Ghar today, so I decided I would deal with it then. Major Brown was upset because he had been embarrassed by what the Commander had said to him, and he was out for blood. As I had done on many occasions before, I calmed him down and told him we would deal with it after we confirmed the problem.

A couple of hours later, we arrived at the base of Sperwan Ghar and only then did we notify the FOB that we were coming. We rolled up and through the gate manned by two Charles Company soldiers. My first impression of Sperwan Ghar after almost four weeks of being away was that it seemed busy. People were running around, there were many more vehicles and a lot more equipment in the camp, and the defences looked good.

My first impression of the soldiers was not as good.

The two Charles Company soldiers at the gate were both wearing non-issued glasses that were probably not ballistic. They both had full beards and hair hanging over their ears, and one had his rifle leaning against a sandbag. Even though we were clearly Canadians and were quickly identified as the Company Commander and Sergeant Major, we should not have been waved through without being given any directions. I yelled into the intercom for the driver to stop the LAV and drop the ramp, and I told Major Brown that I would meet him at the CP once I was done sorting out some soldiers.

I will not detail my conversation with these two soldiers over the next couple of minutes, but I was not happy.

The ballistic glasses issued to Canadian soldiers have been tested against a standard to ensure that, under normal battlefield conditions, they can save your sight. I am a living example because after September 3, I noticed that two pieces of shrapnel or debris and rocks had hit the left lens of my ballistic glasses but did not penetrate. This probably saved my eye. So, soldiers who decided to wear non-issued glasses, or no glasses at all, earned my ire.

The front gate had a bunker so that one of the soldiers there could always cover the second from a position of safety, but the two soldiers who met us had been outside just standing around, one with his rifle leaning up against the sandbags. I asked the soldiers why they had beards, and they first said that there was little water and that they had to conserve it. Then, one of them told me that the sand fleas were terrible, and shaving caused irritation. They said that they both had medical chits excusing them from shaving. I initially thought that this made sense if their faces were getting infected, so I asked to see their faces a little closer, and they told me that it had mostly cleared up. I reminded the soldiers about the proper posture for manning the entrance to the FOB, made sure they immediately got into appropriate positions for security, and told them that I would be back to speak with them later.

I started to walk toward the Command Post and saw three more Charles Company soldiers coming toward me. They were carrying their weapons like they were on a hunting trip and were not wearing helmets or tactical vests. To my dismay, all three had full beards. I stopped them and asked them where their helmets and tactical vests were. They said they were back in their sleeping areas, and they only had to wear them while on duty. My anger was starting to boil over, but I needed to control myself, as someone had authorized this behaviour and yelling at young soldiers would not prove anything.

We were in the middle of a war zone and could be hit at any time.

I asked them what would happen if someone fired a rocket into the camp at this moment.

They all hesitated until one spoke up. "We would take cover in the closest bunker."

"After the rocket lands," I said, "imagine that we get attacked by a dismounted enemy. Now what?"

"We would stop the attack."

"With what? You have one magazine of ammo, no grenades, and no anti-tank weapons. Are you going to go back to your bed space for your gear?" I could tell that these three guys were finally getting it and knew I was unhappy, but I was not done with them yet.

I asked them why they all had beards, and I got the same story as before, including the fact that they had chits. I asked to see the medical chits, and sure enough, they each pulled out one and showed it to me. Their Platoon Medic, a corporal, had signed the chits. I told them to get the rest of their gear and to never leave their area without it again.

A few minutes later when I walked into the CP, smoke was probably coming out of my ears. We had already lost too many soldiers to start acting like cowboys now.

As I walked through the canvas door, the situation became noticeably clearer. I saw the Platoon Warrant and the Platoon LAV Sergeant speaking to Major Brown while a couple of other soldiers were operating the radios and scurrying around the command post. All of them were in various states of dress, and most of them had beards.

What was going on here?

I tried to always remain professional, and I don't believe in correcting leaders in front of their soldiers or other more senior officers, but in this case, I lost it.

MAKING IT RIGHT

I yelled at the Platoon Warrant for about two minutes, and every time he tried to interrupt, I told him to keep quiet. I then asked him to take me around the FOB so that I could see his defences. He tried to explain to me a few times about the dress and the beards, but I shut him up each time and told him to show me the defences. As we walked around Sperwan Ghar, I noticed that the platoon had done a lot of defensive work over the last few weeks. Fighting positions were looking incredibly good, but the issue with the troops remained. They were just too relaxed and did not seem to be taking things as seriously as they should. I even saw a soldier lying around sun-tanning and, yes, even he had a beard.

During my inspection, I noticed that the FOB now had a water buffalo, which holds about four hundred gallons of water. Stacked beside it was about another hundred jerry cans containing twenty litres each. By lifting a couple at random, I noticed that they were all full. I never said anything to the Platoon Warrant at the time.

After about an hour of inspecting the FOB defences, we returned to the Command Post, and along with the LAV Sergeant and Major Brown, we sat down to discuss my findings. I had already been informed that the Platoon Commander was back in Canada on leave, so the Platoon Warrant was the man in charge. I always like to get the negative out of the way first and end on some positives, so I discussed the soldiers first, including their dress, deportment and professionalism.

After explaining the points I had discussed previously, I told the Warrant that once we were done here, everyone in the FOB would have one hour to be correctly shaved, clean and dressed. If I ever found his platoon looking like this again, he would be relieved of his position. I understood that the Platoon Commander was on leave, but that was no excuse for this mess. I told him that if there were any legitimate medical cases for not shaving, I would be here in the CP, and he was to send the individual and the medic to see me.

I then moved the discussions to the FOB defences. I explained that even though I was not happy with the defensive posture of the soldiers, the positions were looking exceptionally good. Even still, they needed to continue working on them as part of their daily routine and continue improving them. I made it clear that I didn't care how long the soldiers were going to be here or how well this place was defended, the soldiers would always be dressed appropriately, with all their fighting and safety equipment on at all times. If they were on duty, they would be in positions of security and overwatch. I explained that once a soldier was inside his bunker and not on duty, they could then relax a little bit but would always have their equipment within arm's reach.

Once both the Platoon Warrant and Sergeant said they understood, I asked Major Brown if he had anything to add.

"No, Sergeant Major," he said. "You've said it all."

I waited in the CP over the next hour to see if I would have any visitors who needed my attention, but there were none. When I walked around with Major Brown a little while later, the change was incredible.

Any soldiers outside their bunkers were dressed correctly, their weapons were at the ready, and all were clean-shaven. I ran into the Platoon Medic on my second walkabout, and he seemed a little bit withdrawn and probably did not want to speak with me. I knew that this platoon had put a lot of pressure on him, and he wanted to be part of the team, so I didn't blame him. I did not even bring the shaving chits up. Instead, I asked him about his medical supplies and any medical issues, and then I moved on.

Shortly afterwards we gathered the crew of Three-Niner Tac together, said our goodbyes and left. Major Brown told me on the way back that he had never heard such a good jacking in all his years. He added that by the end, he was close to tears. I have been told that I have given some of the best jackings that people have ever heard, but I pride myself by ending them all with what a great disappointment people have been, and that part usually changes things.

I have always made it clear to anyone who wanted to listen that I am not worried about personal friendships or whether the soldiers or the officers like me. All I wanted to do was give every soldier that I had an influence over the best chance possible to go home alive.

The alternative sucks.

On our way back to Strong Point Centre, we stopped in to see the Company CP and the CQ, and I took advantage of this time to check my emails as FOB Wilson now had Internet. I first checked my military account and found an email from the Battle Group's Sergeant Major, CWO Bobby Girouard. He mentioned their previous visit to Sperwan Ghar and told me that the Task Force Commander was not pleased. I was about to reply to him and let him know that the situation was now corrected when I noticed a second email below his. I do not know if CWO Girouard meant to leave it on there, but it was an email from the Task Force Sergeant Major, obviously meant for him only. It talked about their visit to Sperwan Ghar and how he was disappointed in the professionalism of the soldiers he saw there. That would have been okay with me, as it was true, but as I continued to read, the smoke came back.

The email stated that he was disappointed in the Company Sergeant Major (me) and that I could obviously not look after my company in combat. He spoke about my lack of professionalism and that if I could not even have my soldiers be clean-shaven, maybe I didn't know how to survive in this environment. He stated that there was lots of water in the location and that the decision I made to allow soldiers not to shave was poor.

Of course, the first thing that came through my mind was "Hobbit." Who was this guy, who didn't know anything about me, to talk about my professionalism and my ability to be the sergeant major of a combat unit? Did he even know that I was away on leave for three weeks? Probably not.

I put the Task Force Sergeant Major's name in the "To" area of the email and CC'd CWO Girouard. I then commenced writing a reply about not appreciating his comments about me, especially given that he didn't have the facts. I told him that when he could come out and live like my soldiers and I for a few months, then maybe I would listen to him. I also told him that I didn't need his advice on how to run my company. I finished off by telling him that after returning from almost four weeks of leave and escorting two of my soldiers' bodies home, I was not impressed by what I found at Sperwan Ghar and that, after an hour of being in location, it had been corrected. I asked him how long he had been at FOB Sperwan Ghar and why he didn't fix the issues himself?

I held my finger over the "send" button for a few seconds and knew that this could be a career-ender, but I hesitated for only a moment longer and hit send.

I saw the Task Force RSM several times throughout the remainder of the tour. He would always smile at me, call me John, and tell me what a great job we were doing. I spoke to Bobby Girouard on his next visit out to our position, and he only smiled at me and shook his head in the way that meant, "Why did you do that?" I do not know what he said to the Task Force RSM, but he obviously spoke to him, and the situation blew over. CWO Bobby Girouard had a knack for handling these sensitive situations, and I hated putting him in them.

Through this, I learned an unbelievably valuable lesson about allowing small things to erode in combat and how they will continue until you lose control. I stayed on top of the platoons for the remainder of the tour, and I made sure that the Platoon Commanders and their Seconds-in-Command were held accountable for their platoons.

Back in Strong Point Centre, things were much the same as a few weeks earlier, except the position was now built even better, and thousands of more sandbags had been stacked. More of the immediate area around Route Summit had been cleared and plowed over, and the work on the road continued. I didn't know if the word had gotten out about my trip to Sperwan Ghar, but soldiers were in an excellent defensive posture as we stopped at each of the Strong Points on the way to the centre.

Now, it needs to be understood that seven months is a long time to be at a high state of alert, so we did allow the soldiers an opportunity to relax, as long as they were not on duty and were under cover from direct fire. There was always the risk of indirect fire, but that was a risk we mitigated as best we could with our defensive positions. But even when relaxing, soldiers always had to have their equipment within immediate reach in case it was needed.

31

DANGER CLOSE FIRE MISSION

I settled in for my first evening back at Strong Point Centre.

I was just starting to enjoy a beautiful American MRE when the sound of an explosion, followed by a burst of small arms, told me that Strong Point West was under attack. Everyone scrambled to their fighting positions. I jumped inside the LAV and put on the headset. We quickly learned that at least two mortars had been fired at Strong Point West, and one had hit the compound wall. No one was injured, and they had been able to identify the position from which the mortar had fired. I immediately recognized the position on the map from previous attacks as being a cemetery about 800-1000 metres west of the Strong Point.

Major Brown immediately gave authority for the platoon to call in fire support from Ma'sum Ghar, where one of the Canadian artillery batteries was located with the brand new 155mm M777 ultra-lightweight-towed howitzer. It fired a wide variety of munitions, including the precision Excalibur projectile. They also had the lightweight-counter-mortar and HALO Sound Ranging System to bring to the fight.

We had depended on the guns for support since Operation MEDUSA. The guns of the Royal Canadian Artillery had fired thousands of rounds in support of us already. This fire mission was called in by one of the soldiers from the platoon that had eyes on the position of the mortar. After the initial rounds impacted, we moved Three-Niner Tac from Strong Point Centre over to Strong Point West to provide a better location for observation and additional firepower, if needed.

We positioned our LAVs in locations that the platoon considered weakest. Major Brown, the Forward Observation Officer and I dismounted and moved onto a rooftop to get a better view of the cemetery, leaving our gunners in the LAVs with authority to fire at any targets of opportunity. We could still observe movement in the cemetery and called for a second fire mission that impacted almost directly on the spot where we

PART THREE - AFGHANISTAN

had observed activity just a few minutes earlier.

The Strong Point then started to receive small arms fire from a couple of positions much closer to us, and several of the platoon soldiers began to return fire. We could hear the impact of the rounds as they were striking the forward edge of the Strong Point or whizzing overhead. The Platoon Commander tried to call in a fire mission on the two positions about 400 metres to our front but got some pushback from the guns because the target was considered "Danger Close" to friendly troops. Danger Close missions were called in only if soldiers were in imminent danger and had hardcover to be under.

The Company FOO that was part of Three-Niner Tac jumped on the radio and called in the mission himself and passed the word quickly for everyone to be prepared on his word to be under hardcover. Soldiers on the ground looked for hardcover areas while those of us on the rooftop got behind a huge, two-foot-thick wall. We heard the fire mission being called over the radio and then the yelling for everyone to take cover.

"Incoming!"

The rounds landed a little bit closer than called for, and the explosion rocked us. Rocks, dirt and debris flew all around us and impacted the walls. Soldiers could be heard yelling, "too close," as these 155mm rounds exploded. As the smoke and dust cleared, we raised our heads and peaked over the wall; we saw the area where the rounds had impacted. Smoke hung over the ground, and we couldn't see any movement. No one in our position had been injured, but it was a rush of adrenaline.

We remained in our fighting positions for about thirty more minutes and then we sent out a dismounted patrol to assess the damage and make sure the area had been cleared. What a welcome back. I needed to discuss calling in artillery so close to our troops; it didn't make sense. Yes, we were being shot at from a few hundred metres away, but we were not in danger of being overrun. We could handle a few guys with AK-47s without using artillery or air support.

We waited around while the clearance patrol was out in case the LAV firepower was needed. They were gone for about an hour when they called in to report that they were at the cemetery and had located at least two bodies and one weapon, but it was challenging to be sure of the numbers because of the damage. What was more exciting was that they reported that the explosion had uncovered what appeared to be a buried weapons cache. They were requesting engineer support to check it out before touching it or destroying it.

The patrol had to remain in that location for a couple of tense hours while they waited for engineer support to arrive. Engineers were always in demand here, and there were not enough to go around. Once the engineers did arrive, they concluded that the damage done by the fire mission made exploiting the cache unsafe. They asked for authority to destroy it in place.

Authority was given, but first, the two bodies needed to be removed to a safe distance, and the platoon provided cover while the explosives were set. The explosion was massive, and it was a relief to know that one of the Taliban's weapons caches would no longer be available to them. The engineer who set the explosive believed there could have been as many as twenty AK-47s and at least a crate of grenades and several RPGs, as well as a bunch of wire and jugs used for holding homemade explosives. This one was a win for the good guys.

The remains of the dead were put in body bags, and after a few minutes of discussions, the Afghan National Police went forward with two of their trucks and picked them up. On the way back to Strong Point Centre, the patrol walked through the area that the small arms fire had come from and where several rounds of 155mm artillery shells had just exploded. They were able to find an AK-47 and a bunch of burned and charred clothes, but no bodies. They were either completely destroyed, or they were just wounded and somehow crawled away.

We may never know the truth.

LATRINE DUTY

I tried to settle in and over a coffee told a few stories about my return to Canada. Everyone wanted to know about the base, how the families were doing, and if there were any ongoing issues. After an hour of talking, I realized that I was exhausted. As soon as my head hit the cot that was located just inside the bunker, I was asleep. The Taliban could have swept through with a thousand insurgents, and I probably would have only woken up as my head was being removed from my neck.

The next couple of weeks consisted of filling sandbags, building up the bunkers and defensive positions, then clearance patrols around the area while waiting for the daily attack. It was almost like clockwork. At about dusk, one of the strong points would get engaged. Then, usually, they would hit us with a rocket or mortar followed by some small arms. We would fire back if we located their positions, and if we had artillery or air support, we would call that in. Sometimes the clearance patrol would find a body or blood or a weapon, but we would often find nothing.

The following day, I woke up with the worst stomach cramps imaginable. I could hardly get off my cot and make my way the fifty feet to our shitters. I expect the mixture of fresh food for three weeks at home followed by a couple of MREs, and the added stress of being back had caused some lousy diarrhea. I grabbed my gear and, hoping the troops did not see me, half-ran, half-dragged myself the fifty feet while also pulling my gear behind me (no, I wasn't wearing it; the pain was messing with my mind). I immediately gained relief as I emptied my stomach, and almost as fast as the pain had come, it was gone.

When I was feeling better, it was only then that I noticed the work done to our toilet area. The structure I was sitting in was made from massive wooden beams, six-foot steel pickets and hundreds of filled sandbags. It was a two-seater with no privacy in between, but the seat was an actual toilet seat sitting over a cut-down steel drum. You could sit back and relax, and, if you were to come under attack, this place was defendable.

I was admiring the great work as a young corporal came in, took off his gear, dropped his drawers and took a seat next to me.

"How are you doing, Sergeant Major?" he said. "It's a beautiful morning."

"It was," I replied as this young soldier went about his business a few inches away from me. I finished up and bid the young man goodbye. There's no room for embarrassment or shyness on the battlefield. Infantry is not for the weak of heart or body.

Perhaps toilets don't seem to be a significant issue. Still, living in rough conditions for months without proper showers and laundry, it becomes a priority to make sure that your soldiers do not become ill.

After the first few days of having to dig a latrine several feet deep and then burying it daily to avoid smell and disease, we were able to get the engineers to cut a couple of steel barrels in half, which would now become the community toilets. Structures were built out of available wood, six-foot steel pickets and sandbags to allow the drum to be placed under it from the rear and then pulled out from the back each morning. It became part of our daily chores.

A couple of platoon soldiers were tasked with pulling out the drums each morning and burning whatever was inside. They had to pour in diesel, set it on fire and then, over the next hour, or so, they used a steel picket or a stick to stir the contents as the diesel burned hotter until everything was gone. This was not a glamorous job, but it was a necessary one. Soldiers would use masks or scarves wrapped around their faces and gloves on their hands, and, following the task, they would have to go wash.

Many soldiers could be heard gagging or vomiting as they went about this task, and many could be heard swearing and yelling if they found anything inside, such as garbage and urine, that was not supposed to be there. There were piss tubes buried in the ground several feet away for the guys to piss in, and piss in the drums just made it harder to burn the other stuff. I have a picture burned into my brain of soldiers standing above these steel drums full of shit, stirring them with a stick while smoke billows up around them and other soldiers laughing, all the while knowing that their turn would be coming.

This shit detail became a way of punishing minor indiscretions on the part of the soldiers, so they always knew not to be late for their shift or to not have their kit on them.

RETURN OF MAJOR SPRAGUE

Shortly after I returned, we began hearing a rumour that Major Sprague was trying to return to command the Charles Company, but I already knew this from speaking with him a few weeks earlier. The company had not heard much information about him since he had been seriously wounded and medically evacuated to Canada. After seeing him in the hospital in Kandahar, I had not expected him to return.

I guess I underestimated his stubbornness.

However, when I saw him at the airfield in Trenton and the Memorial Service at 1 RCR and then at a coffee break for the spouses while I was back in Canada, I thought he just might make it back. I understand that he almost drove anyone who would listen to him crazy about returning to Afghanistan even before he arrived home. I came to realize that he was a bigger pain in the ass than I was in dealing with Major Savage.

I was sitting with Major Brown at the HQ location at Strong Point Centre, eating an MRE and discussing the next day's plan when the radio buzzed. It was the Company CP located at FOB Wilson up on Highway 1. The commander of Charles Company is known as call sign Three-Niner, and the CP is known as call sign Three.

"Three-Niner, this is Three. Can you send a call sign [vehicle] to this location to pick up Three-Niner?"

Major Brown grabbed the radio. "Three, this is Three-Niner. Say again."

"Three-Niner, this is Three; send a call sign to this location to pick up Three-Niner."

Major Brown was getting a little frustrated.

"Three, this is Three-Niner. I am at Strong Point Centre and do not need a ride."

When the Company Commander is not in his LAV and the LAV crew speaks on the radio, they identify themselves as Zulu Three-Niner.

PART THREE - AFGHANISTAN

The command post sent another message. "Zulu Three-Niner, this is Three. Send the vehicle to my location now."

Major Brown was now getting upset.

"Three, this is Three-Niner. Who needs to be picked up? Over."

The following words made it truly clear as Major Sprague's easily recognizable voice was heard.

"Three-Niner Alpha, this is Three-Niner. Get the fuck up here and pick me up. OUT."

Major Sprague was back in location, and we were shocked but thrilled. Well, everyone except Major Brown who would now have to go back to being Captain Brown, Company Second-in-Command.

Major Brown took over command of Charles Company during some of the worst moments imaginable, and he did a stellar job. When Major Sprague came back, he was able to slip back into the role quickly. There was no noticeable change to the Company as one took over from the other. Major Brown should be commended for his professionalism and tact, as this could not have been easy on him. He would return to the Command Post as the Company Second-in-Command and continue to be a great asset to us all. Today, he continues to serve as a Lieutenant Colonel.

We immediately got Three-Niner Tac together, and all three LAVs moved quickly up to FOB Wilson where Major Sprague was standing outside the CP, with the biggest shit-eating grin I have ever seen.

Major Brown had done a great job, but I must say it was a massive relief to me, personally, to have my Command Team Partner back. He looked good, other than a couple of scars on his head. By now, there were not very many of Charles Company soldiers who did not have scars. A scar was almost like a badge of honour.

We hung around the CP for an hour or so as Major Sprague was briefed on what had been going on and what was coming up. He then made Captain Norton an incredibly happy man when he told him he would be returning to his job as the Company LAV Captain and that Major Brown would be moving back into the CP as the Company Second-in-Command. I know that at least one of them was happy.

An hour or so later, we moved down Route Summit to Strong Point Centre. Major Sprague set foot on the ground for the first time since day one of Operation MEDUSA where he had fought so bravely and where we had lost some great soldiers. I could tell that his mind was racing, and I knew that his feelings would be all over the place. We allowed him some time to himself to figure it out as the rest of us helped Major Brown gather his kit and get ready to head to FOB Wilson. As we were helping Major Brown, we could see call sign Three rolling down Route Summit with Captain Norton in the turret; he was already packed and ready to switch with Major Brown.

After some final words from Major Sprague, Major Brown jumped in his vehicle and headed back to FOB Wilson and the Command Post. The handover was complete.

MENTAL HEALTH PROBLEM

Like most others, the next couple of days started with work on the positions and clearance patrols checking out the local area. Once work stopped, we would get Three-Niner Tac geared up, and Major Sprague would get acquainted with the area and visit all the Charles Company positions. We would typically return to Strong Point Centre at the end of each day except for a few nights spent at Sperwan Ghar.

Most evenings resulted in contact with the enemy, either a random rocket fired in our general direction or perhaps a mortar and a few rifle rounds. Still, it was always more of a pain than a sustained attack. We would respond with LAV fire or artillery or air support, if available. It was believed that the insurgency was probing our positions, trying to find out exactly where our guns were and how we would react.

A few nights after Major Sprague returned, we saw it firsthand while visiting Strong Point North. Shortly after dusk, a lone individual was spotted walking down Route Summit toward the strong point with a sack hung over his shoulder. This was very unusual, and the position quickly stood to, with soldiers in their firing positions. Our immediate concern, of course, was that he was a suicide bomber.

When he was about five hundred metres away, we had the LAVs flash their lights, and we fired a para flare into the sky, which lit him up, as well as the area around him. He just ignored all of this and kept walking. We had the platoon fire two more flares, and we continued to flash the LAV lights, but nothing seemed to affect him; he just kept walking toward the strong point.

Major Sprague was on the radio with our CP, who contacted the local Afghan National Army and Afghan National Police units to see if they were aware of anyone walking around the area or if anyone had left FOB Wilson recently. Even though a few local families had returned, they kept a low profile and would not be out walking around at night.

At two hundred metres, the platoon was given orders to fire warning shots into the road in front of the individual, and one of the riflemen fired a couple of rounds from his weapon. The Canadian C-7 rifle uses a 5.56mm round and when hitting the dirt and dust of an Afghan road it does not leave much of a splash and may even be hard to see. The man kept coming so we had the C-6 machine-gun, which fires a bigger 7.62mm round, fire a burst at the man's feet. The result of the impact of the rounds was even visible from our location, and they hit a lot closer to the man than we wanted, but he reacted for the first time. He stopped, looked around as if startled and then kept coming.

Major Sprague then had the platoon terp yell at the man to stop as he was closing on one hundred and fifty metres, but he continued. Major Sprague had picked a distance that he would not allow the man to pass, and he had already reached that critical point. The order was given to the platoon to stop him.

We are infantry soldiers and not some marksmen from the movies. When we engage a target, we aim for the centre of mass. In this case, that is the chest area. A soldier was identified, and he took aim and fired. The man kept coming. The Platoon Commander yelled out that he had missed and to fire again.

I watched the soldier take aim and fire, and the man continued and was now well inside one hundred metres. Major Sprague yelled out for someone to kill this guy now and a different soldier fired. The man stopped, stumbled back a few feet, and then was walking again. The soldier fired again, and the man went down, but only for a second before he got up again. This time, the machine-gun on one of the LAVs fired, and the man went down and did not move.

I am not a fan of the 5.56 round as I have seen several different occasions when a man was hit several times but was still a threat. The bigger 7.62 round has much greater stopping power and is the round that the Taliban were using in their AK-47s.

We remained on high alert as we waited for the engineers and the Afghan Police to come to make sure the body was safe and take it away. The engineers arrived and were discussing possibilities about approaching the man, including using the bomb suit or their robot, but as has happened on a couple of other occasions, the ANP lost patience and drove up to the body without warning and were seen searching it and then putting it in the back of their truck. These guys were going to get people killed with their tactics, but hopefully only their own. The body was taken to FOB Wilson, where the local Police Chief and his cronies hung out and, in the morning, it was taken away.

The report from the engineers and the ANP was that the man was unarmed and that the sack contained about twenty 25mm empty casings that had been fired somewhere by a Canadian LAV. The police identified the man as being a forty-something single guy from Kandahar with mental health problems. We never knew for sure what this guy was up to, but it was believed that the Taliban probably paid him or coerced or tricked him into walking down Route Summit so that they could watch our reaction.

It may have cost an innocent man his life, but that was never a concern for the Taliban.

SPECIAL FORCES OPS GONE AWRY

Around this time in the tour, Major Sprague received orders to provide a platoon with LAVs to assist our special forces soldiers on an operation.

I am not sure if any of the platoons would have jumped at this opportunity because we never really had a lot of faith or even respect for our special forces guys. They had a bit of a reputation as pretty boys, and they never seemed to assist the Canadian Battle Group. Instead, they always did their own thing. By contrast, we had worked with the American and British Special Forces guys, and they were a joy to be around.

I believe our regular infantry soldiers understand the secrecy and lack of information surrounding special forces operations. Despite that, we are all supposed to be on the same team, but we did not always feel that way. Over the last few years, the level of cooperation changed a lot when a new special forces commander decided to be more like their American counterparts. Secrecy of operations is essential, but it is also vital to allow other folks to know what you are doing.

Major Sprague tasked 8 Platoon, under the command of Captain Jeremy Hiltz, to be attached to our special forces for an upcoming operation. We were not given any details about the operation, only that the platoon would be required for four or five days. Major Sprague and I found out enough about the operation over the next few days to keep us in the loop. The platoon moved into the camp housing our special forces folks and was briefed on the upcoming mission and their role in the plan.

I will not write about specific details of the plan, as it is still how we do operations today, and lives could be put at risk. The platoon would be filling a fundamental infantry role and not intimately involved in the hands-on operation. The training and orders were repetitive, and rehearsals were done until the actions were known in and out and would result in success.

Many criteria need to be met before a special forces operation is given the go-ahead and finally after several days the night operation was given the green light. The target was a location that was believed to have senior Taliban leaders present and both weapons and IED supplies. The makeup of the force conducting the raid was a mix of Afghans, special forces and regular infantry.

While the Charles Company soldiers travelled in LAVs, the remainder travelled in wheeled vehicles. The convoy moved along a highway at night without lights, with the LAVs both leading and in the rear and the wheeled vehicles in the middle. As the target was coming into sight, a couple of incidents occurred that could have been devastating to the soldiers but afterwards were looked at with amusement by many of us.

One lead LAV somehow had its dragon teeth come unhooked and fall off the side onto the road. These are steel teeth attached by a heavy cable and pulled across a highway to blow tires and stop vehicles, and that is exactly what it did, albeit accidentally. The teeth hit the road and in the dark two of the wheeled vehicles rolled over it, ripping their tires to shreds. At the same time, the lead LAV moved too far to the right and the shoulder of the road gave way, causing the LAV to roll over onto its side.

All of this occurred within sight of the objective but not on it. Perhaps the people at the location just thought another coalition convoy had an accident, and they didn't respond. The operation was cancelled, the vehicles were recovered, and the only injury was to their pride.

From that night forward, Captain Jeremy Hiltz, the famous Platoon Commander from this incident, was known as "SF Hiltz." I don't know if it has followed him to this day, but he will always be known as SF Hiltz to me.

33

DEATH OF THE RSM

November 27 started like any other day: an early rise to a crappy coffee and an MRE breakfast, followed by a few hours of work filling sandbags and improving the bunker's defensive positions and living areas.

After an MRE lunch, Major Sprague and I jumped in our LAVs and visited the other strong points to look at the improvements to those positions and see if there were any ongoing issues that needed our attention. It was also an opportunity for us to speak with the soldiers face-to-face and see how they were doing. I always talked to the Platoon Warrants one on one so they could feel free to speak to me about anything. It was usually through these conversations that I learned of any ongoing issues and, more importantly, the troops' morale. On many occasions, the Company Commander would speak with the Platoon Commanders, and when we were alone afterward he would tell me that they had said everything was good, but now he wanted the real story.

Major Sprague knew that I could speak with the Platoon Warrants and the soldiers, and I would more than likely get the truth. In contrast, many young officers told him what they thought he wanted to hear because they believed that anything negative reflected poorly on them.

After a full day of driving around our area of responsibility, always waiting for something to happen, we returned to Strong Point Centre for another delicious MRE supper. Shortly after 1800 hours, while sitting outside the bunker listening to the Battle Group radio, we heard something significant.

We heard Lieutenant-Colonel Lavoie come over the Battle Group radio to say they had been involved in an explosion and to wait for more details. Still, his voice was different from the confident soldier and leader we heard every day. A few minutes later, we listened to the request from his call sign, Niner Tac, asking for immediate medevac with details to follow. One of the other call signs in the location sent a situation report saying that one vehicle had a mobility kill and casualties.

Major Sprague and I moved closer to the radio. Soon several people gathered because we all knew this was different from the dozens of other incidents we had heard and been involved in. The next information was sent as part of the medevac and listed two casualties as VSA (vital signs absent). We always recorded our casualties as VSA and not dead because, officially, the only one that could pronounce someone dead was a medical doctor.

I immediately had a sick feeling in my stomach, even though they hadn't identified the casualties or even which vehicle had been hit. A part of me knew that my friend and mentor, CWO Bobby Girouard, was one of the dead because if he were not he would have been on that radio dealing with the casualties. It was an agonizing wait for confirmation of who was dead. I was already starting to feel depressed and went and found a spot to be alone. I remember seeing Major Sprague coming to find me.

"You were right," he said. "CWO Girouard and his driver, Corporal Albert Storm [Stormy], were both killed in that IED strike." Even though I had kind of known and believed that I knew, the words were like a punch in the gut.

I felt like throwing up. I couldn't speak and I started to cry. Major Sprague just touched my shoulder and left me alone to my thoughts. CWO Bobby Girouard was not only my RSM and my mentor, but he was also my friend. This news was almost unbearable.

CWO Girouard was the first Regimental Chief to die at the enemy's hands in the Regiment's 123-year history, and this was not a first to be celebrated. He was both a soldier and a leader, and he was always at the front, where all great leaders are seen.

I remember speaking with Bobby on the many occasions when he and the Battle Group Commander showed up at our position. During one talk, he said that he was looking forward to getting home and was planning on retiring from the military after more than twenty-nine years of service. He was considering taking the truck driver course and driving large trucks between Canada and the U.S. At first, I thought he was pulling my leg, and then he told me that it had been a dream of his for a long time, and he could see himself and his wife, Jackie, having a blast.

He then told me something that I will never forget.

He said that he was immensely proud of me and how I had handled a terrible situation with Charles Company.

"You are my best Sergeant Major," he said. I was taken aback because I had never expected to hear those words. For them to come from someone like CWO Bobby Girouard, who I highly respected, made me blush. He just tapped me on the shoulder and said, "Look after yourself, John," and he left.

A CBC news article posted December 6, 2006, quoted the Chief of the Defence Staff, General Rick Hillier while he was in Landstuhl Germany. He spoke about Bobby after his death. He said: "Girouard represents the incredible national treasure that we have in uniform". He went on to say "Girouard was an incredible leader, an incredible

PART THREE - AFGHANISTAN

Chief Warrant Officer, an incredible NCO, and an incredible man who inspires us all. His loss is incredible."

Even though our Battle Group was based around 1 RCR, it was a mixture of many other units, and the one thing I kept hearing everywhere I went was: "He was our RSM."

I went back to KAF the next day and was one of the Sergeants Major who carried CWO Bobby Girouard's remains onto the aircraft for his final journey home. Afterward, it felt like a part of me was missing. There was a massive hole in my heart, and my feelings of depression hit a level that scared me.

A couple of hours after the Ramp Ceremony, Lieutenant-Colonel Lavoie came to see me. Even though the sadness and stress were evident on his face, he spoke to me with the same confidence and respect I had become accustomed to. He said that he had lost his Command Team Partner and his friend. Now he needed to pull it together for the troops and get on with the job. He was concerned about how I was doing and whether I was okay to go back into the firefight.

Of course, I said I was good to go.

There was no time to mourn, only time for a coffee with some of the other Sergeants Major on the boardwalk and a chance to talk about Bobby. Then, it was back into our vehicles and back out to the battlefield. There was a discussion about whether I should move into the Battle Group HQ as the RSM, pending a permanent fix. Lieutenant-Colonel Lavoie had spoken to Major Sprague, and he approached me on the subject.

My answer was straightforward. If the CO wanted me to step up and fill in, I would gladly do so. But if he was asking, I had a full-time job with Charles Company which was more important to me. A few hours later, I was told not to worry about it and to stay where I was. That was good news for everyone involved.

34

NEGLIGENT DISCHARGE

A few days later, around the end of November or early December, we received word to go into KAF to get orders for an upcoming operation. Three-Niner Tac moved back into KAF under cover of darkness and spent two days there while Major Sprague and the other commanders received briefs and orders on the upcoming mission. Most of the details for this operation were kept under wraps until the last minute, as this would be a Coalition operation, with not only Canadians.

Back in KAF, we linked up with the engineers, artillery and pilots—and to our great surprise, a squadron of Leopard tanks. The Canadian tanks had only been in the country for a couple of weeks and had been kept quiet, other than doing some training and ranges.

I understood that the new Dutch Task Force commander was not too pleased to have tanks in theatre as he believed it sent the wrong message when we were trying to win hearts and minds. I am all about hearts and minds, but give me a tank any day when that doesn't work.

We gave orders to all the commanders and key folks involved in the upcoming operation and then briefed everyone on our road move out to Ma'sum Ghar the following morning. We would be staging out of there for the forthcoming operation.

OUR FIRST EMBEDDED REPORTER

While in KAF, we enjoyed a fresh supper and then we gave confirmatory orders for our planned move to the FOB the following morning. As orders were finishing up, a civilian with a press card on his shirt walked into the CP. He said he was looking for Major Sprague. He introduced himself as a reporter from a major newspaper in Toronto. He said that he had been granted authority to embed himself with Charles

Company for the next couple of weeks.

From the look on Major Sprague's face, I could tell that he was not aware of this, so he excused himself to speak with the Battle Group Command Post just down the hallway. A few minutes later, Major Sprague came back and I knew immediately that he had not gotten the answer he had hoped for. We had avoided having reporters around any time we could. Other companies liked the publicity and loved to do interviews. Charles Company was here to kill the Taliban, and we did not have time for reporters. We considered ourselves a very professional infantry company that did its job and did not need the recognition that others seemed to crave.

This was the first time that we had been forced to accept the inevitable. Major Sprague gave him the old line of staying out of the way and not doing anything stupid and then told him to meet us here at the compound the following morning at 0600. We had just given orders before the reporter's arrival, and the plan was to depart the compound here at 0400 hours. I was about to correct Major Sprague when I got that look I had received a few times over the years. It meant, "Shut up." So, I stayed quiet. The reporter left to sort out his equipment and told us he would be here to meet up with us around 0545 hrs.

After the reporter left, I looked at Major Sprague, and he just grinned and said, "Let's go grab a burger."

The following day at 0300, the Company and our attachments met at the compound. We got our vehicles and equipment ready to go and gathered everyone at 0345 for a last-minute debriefing. The CQ was there to see us off and check if we needed any last-minute supplies, and he asked us if anyone had seen the reporter. Of course, no one had, and he said he would send someone to try to locate him.

"No, he had the timings like everyone else," said Major Sprague. "If he slept in, that's his problem; we're not babysitters."

I chuckled on the inside as we climbed into our LAVs and prepared to depart.

At 0400 hours as per our orders, we rolled out of KAF and back out into the badlands, while our reporter friend was sleeping soundly in bed. I know there were some heated discussions that morning when the reporter arrived and he was told that he had missed the convoy. He kept saying that he was told 0600, and the CQ said no, the timing was 0400 and it hadn't changed. He must have heard them wrong. I don't know if the reporter knew he was played or if he thought he had messed up the timings, but in either case, Charles Company once again came out on top, and I never saw that reporter again.

DEALING WITH NEGLIGENT DISCHARGES

Before leaving for the Strong Points, I had to deal with an incident that had occurred a couple of days earlier when we arrived in KAF. One of the headquarters soldiers had a negligent discharge (ND) of their weapon, which is as it sounds. It's when someone fires a round without the proper authority. In this case, as we rolled into KAF, there is an area marked by the Coalition for all the vehicles to stop and point their weapons in a designated safe direction, clear them and make sure they are all safe. This was done every time, without exception, and all weapons, including personal ones, had to be cleared. Every soldier dismounted from the vehicle and was responsible for their weapon, as well as the support weapons.

In this case, we had completed the clearance drill and were in the compound where we have parked our LAVs. We were starting to unload our kit when I heard a bang from beside us. One of the Charles Company LAVs has discharged a smoke grenade. The LAV has eight 76mm grenade launchers in two clusters of four launchers positioned on each side of the turret which are used for smoke grenades. The launchers had not been unloaded as was part of the standard operating procedure, and one of the clusters had been fired. The soldier had immediately stepped out of the LAV and admitted that he had accidentally hit the fire button. A few minutes later, I learned that this had caused quite the disturbance when the smoke grenades landed in an American Special Forces compound, who rightly thought they had come under attack. They were not happy, and it took a visit by Major Sprague and I to apologize to finally calm them down. This incident did not do much for the reputation of Canadian soldiers, at least in the minds of this small group of Americans. Afterwards I investigated this incident, charged the soldier, and he was found guilty and sentenced by a summary trial. This ND cost the soldier several hundred dollars.

There would be several NDs happen throughout the tour, most early after our arrival and then again late in the tour when some complacency had set in. In every case except one, the soldiers admitted their guilt, were punished, and got on with the mission.

On one occasion, the soldier tried to cover up his mistake and continued to lie about it even as I investigated the incident and eventually charged the individual. At his summary trial, the soldier continued to make excuses and would not accept responsibility for his negligence. In the end, the Presiding Officer got it right. The soldier was found guilty, given a hefty fine, demoted in rank and sent home early. This soldier had been in a position of authority and leadership. An example had to be set to show the young soldiers that everyone is accountable for their actions, regardless of position or rank.

There was also another ND that was only a few inches from becoming a tragedy for Warrant Officer Olstad or I. We had rolled into FOB Wilson, expecting to spend about an hour while Major Sprague got some final direction from the Battle Group CP. While this was happening, I instructed the soldiers to use the relative safety of the FOB and time while we waited to clean and check their weapons. We had recently received a new Company Medic to replace Master Corporal Somerset while he was away on leave, and she was sitting in the back of Three-Niner. Warrant Officer Olstad and I sat on the ramp discussing the upcoming operation. We had our back to the open LAV and were startled to hear a gunshot and the sound of a bullet zinging by. We immediately grabbed our weapons and got into a firing posture only to observe our Company Medic sitting in the back with her pistol in her hand, her finger on the trigger and her mouth wide open.

I immediately reached inside the LAV toward her and quietly told her to remove her finger from the trigger and slowly lay the pistol on the seat. She did not move, so I squeezed in beside her, gently took the pistol out of her hand, and then took a deep breath and looked at the ramp. A distinctive bullet mark was on the ramp exactly between where Keith Olstad and I had just been sitting, with only inches between us. WO Olstad and I both looked at each other and smiled as we realized we had just cheated either death or a bullet hole in the back.

This young Master Corporal Medic that had just been sent out from KAF for the first time was crying and in shock. WO Olstad explained what had happened to the gathering crowd and sent everyone away to continue whatever they were doing. I knew that we were only a few minutes from heading off on an operation, and I needed my Company Medic, so I forcefully told her to stop crying and pay attention to me. I had WO Olstad check her weapon to make sure it was in good working order and made sure it was safe, as this would be required for any summary trial.

I then turned to the medic and explained to her what was going to happen. I told her that she was not to say anything about what had happened until we had some time to do a proper investigation and that she would then be read her rights. For now, I handed her back the pistol and told her that we were leaving on a mission, and she needed to get her head back in the game. She did not seem eager to get the pistol back, but I knew that now was the time to get her back in the saddle and get her confidence back.

I called over one of the sergeants and directed him to take the Master Corporal aside and spend the next fifteen minutes going over drills on the pistol, including the safety precautions, as she would be carrying it into battle very soon. I also told him that she should come to see me once he was satisfied that she was good to go. As she was leaving the LAV, I told her not to stress over this, that she was not the first and would not be the last to have an ND, and we would deal with this when we were back in a safe location. I had WO Olstad and any other witnesses write down what they had seen or heard and told them I would interview them later.

When Major Sprague arrived back at the LAV, I explained what had happened and what I had done. His only concern was whether she was ready to come with us. I told him that we needed her medical skills for this operation. She had made a mistake and was prepared to go.

This young medic learned a valuable lesson and one that she would not forget very soon. She remained with us only for a few days before being rotated back into KAF. A few weeks later, I was able to do the investigation, and once again, I charged the Master Corporal. She was found guilty.

I do not remember the exact number of NDs that we had during the seven months of our tour. Still, there were too many, and that is unacceptable for a highly trained infantry company. Negligent discharges are something that every soldier understands from the first time they take a weapons class in basic training to the last day they are in uniform. Unfortunately, they are not all dealt with the same way, which has caused some bitterness amongst the troops.

I made a point of constantly dealing with any negligent discharge from the time I was first placed in leadership positions and would investigate every possible incident. The importance of one cannot be overstated. First and foremost is safety. Every soldier who picks up a weapon is responsible for that weapon. A round that is fired without authority and by mistake can kill someone in the vicinity. It has happened several times throughout my career.

From a purely tactical situation, a round fired without authority can give away your position to the enemy, can take away the element of surprise and once again can cost lives. Even though I had never looked the other way when there was a negligent discharge, I also tried not to make too big a deal about it. However, there may have been unintended consequences caused by my hard line on negligent discharges.

We had a few negligent discharges before deploying to Afghanistan and then several more early in the tour. In every case, the soldier was found guilty and punished. This may have caused some soldiers to be more worried about having a negligent discharge than being prepared for the enemy. On a few occasions, the Platoon Warrants informed me that they discovered soldiers without a round in the chamber, despite being in the area of the camp where weapons were loaded and made ready and safe. This was unacceptable and could cost lives during operations. When an attack is sudden, a soldier in this position must take the extra second to grasp the cocking handle, cock the weapon, place a round in the chamber and then fire. This extra time can be the difference between life and death for him and his comrades.

I had a one-sided conversation with the Platoon Warrants to tell them that they needed to make sure that this never happened again. They were to tell their soldiers the seriousness of what they were doing. There were only a handful of soldiers who were doing this, and the Company was told that anyone caught not having their weapon prepared as directed would be dealt with much more harshly than someone who had an ND.

I assume that this sorted out the issue, as it never came up again during the last several months of the tour.

A C9 LEFT BEHIND

A slightly different situation occurred a few months later while Charles Company HQ and a platoon moved into Ma'sum Ghar for a few weeks to replace the PPCLI Company while they were tasked elsewhere. The platoon had been housed in a tented area where cots and electricity had been set up. After they had been tasked out for the day and departed the FOB, I walked through their site to see a soldier who had remained behind because he was ill. I spoke to the soldier lying on his cot for a few minutes and then turned to walk out.

As I passed one of the empty cots, I noticed a rifle barrel sticking out from under a sleeping bag. I grabbed the barrel and pulled out a C-9, which is the section-level machine-gun. Each infantry section has two machine-gunners that provide extra firepower. They are crucial to the platoon and company. I looked at the kitbag and rucksack at the foot of the bed and saw the soldier's name. Turning to the ill soldier, I asked him where this soldier was. I was told that he had deployed with his platoon.

I was confused, and as I walked toward the ill soldier, I could tell he was getting extremely uncomfortable and was squirming. I became a little angry and asked him what was going on and told him that he best not tell me lies. He did not. He explained that the section machine-gunner had come to him just before departing on their operation to ask him if he could take this soldier's rifle and leave his machine-gun behind. He went on to say that the soldier said he wanted to carry the lighter weapon and that no one would know. I told the ill soldier not to say a word about our conversation or the fact that I was taking the C-9 with me.

"I won't, sir."

I briefed Major Sprague on what had occurred and told him that I would handle it and report to him afterwards. As always, Major Sprague just nodded and said, "Sure thing, Sergeant Major."

Several hours later, the platoon came rolling back into the FOB after completing their operation without incident. I approached the Platoon Warrant and asked him how the patrol went and was told that, other than speaking with some nomads, walking through a small village and getting a hateful stare from everyone, there had been no significant incidents.

The Platoon Warrant then said the soldiers would be cleaning their weapons, checking their kit and then eating supper. I walked among the soldiers as they sat on their cots, cleaning the dirt and dust from their weapons and asked several how their day had been. I stopped in front of the cot that I had removed the machine-gun from earlier and saw the machine-gunner cleaning a rifle. When I stopped, he smiled up at me and asked how I was doing, without a worry in the world. If only he knew. I talked to a few more soldiers and went back to the CP to wait and see how long it would be before the soldier discovered his machine-gun was missing and would have to approach his Platoon Warrant and let him know.

I must say a part of me enjoyed the valuable lesson that was about to be learned by this platoon and the company.

I was a little surprised as a couple of hours went by, and no one came to see me to report a missing weapon, but I continued to relax, drink coffee and wait. Finally, about another hour later, I saw the canvas door being pulled open, and in walked the Platoon Warrant looking like he was going to cry.

"Sergeant Major," he said, "can I talk to you alone?"

"No, it's only the OC and Command Post crew. Let's talk here."

He started by telling me a soldier approached him about an hour earlier to say that his C-9 machine-gun had gone missing from his cot.

I acted surprised and said, "How the fuck did that happen?"

The Warrant went on to say that the soldier had left it on his cot when he went to visit the Porta-Potty, and I interrupted and said, "Stop." I got up and went to the back of the CP LAV, removed the weapon in question, and handed it to the Platoon Warrant. He looked surprised, and I asked him if they had given orders and inspected the soldiers before they departed on their patrol. He said yes, the Platoon Commander had given orders, and he had done a quick check of the soldiers and equipment.

I remained calm but said, "You did not do a particularly good job because one of your machine-gunners left his weapon behind." I then told him what had happened. I could tell that he had not known, and he was angry and disappointed with his soldier but, more importantly, at himself for not noticing this before they had departed on their operation. He then said he would speak with the soldier and, more importantly, the Section Commander, as it was evident that no one had been doing their job correctly.

I had the Platoon Warrant do an internal investigation. After bringing me the results, I decided to charge the soldier and place the Section Commander on a recorded warning. This would be a significant negative mark on his career.

I took the time to speak with all the platoon warrants, and the OC did the same with the platoon commanders. We stressed the importance of always maintaining professionalism and ensuring the soldiers were adequately prepared, all the time. Once again, there were no other similar incidents the rest of the tour.

35

OPERATION BAAZ TSUKA

Back at the Strong Point, we passed the word that our platoons would be relieved in place by other Canadian soldiers. Once that was completed, they were to move to Ma'sum Ghar and await orders. All they knew for sure was that this was going to be another major operation, so they started preparing as soon as they arrived in the FOB.

OUR SECOND EMBEDDED REPORTER

As the pieces were coming together, Charles Company's luck ran out again, but this time no lives were lost; we just ended up with an embedded reporter.

I looked on with skepticism at this middle-aged woman who seemed like she would have difficulty carrying her camera, let alone all her gear, and would need an air-conditioned hotel room to survive. She came toward Major Sprague and I with an outstretched hand and a huge smile. She introduced herself as Christie Blatchford from The Globe And Mail and informed us that she would be travelling and living with us for the next week or so. From Major Sprague's face, I could tell that he was not impressed, but we may have been outsmarted this time. He welcomed her aboard, and they sat down to go over some simple rules.

We understood the importance of reporters, and we also understood that getting the right story out from Afghanistan was especially vital to us. We were starting to enjoy some of the best support the military had ever had from the Canadian population, at least in my lifetime. We needed to maintain that. We briefed Christie on how we did things here in Charles Company and her responsibilities.

Major Sprague wanted to make sure that he would have the opportunity to see what she was going to send out beforehand just to make sure that it was accurate and that there were not any security breaches that could cost lives. She was in full agreement. She informed us that she had been embedded several times with Canadians before this and was experienced. Indeed, she proved very quickly to us that she was not only a good reporter but that she had huge respect for what we were doing. She quickly established that her size or gender were not an obstacle, and I would have put her up against any of our soldiers.

A few days later, while rolling through FOB Wilson, I jumped on the internet and looked up her name to find several articles she had written on the Canadian military. I quickly realized that she was more than fair and could be a huge asset to us.

Christie Blatchford would become part of the Company for the next several days, and the soldiers would come to trust her. We warned our soldiers to stay in their lanes, speak only about their specific job and role, and always remember that nothing is off the record.

FALCON'S SUMMIT

We were now getting ready for the Canadian piece of Operation Baaz Tsuka, which was Pashtun for "Falcon's Summit" and conveniently pronounced by us clumsy Westerners as "bazooka."

The plan was to expel Taliban fighters from the Panjwai and Zhari districts of Kandahar, a mission statement that would be used again and again over the next several years. Canadians had been fighting the Taliban here for several months and, although this operation was under British command, most of the moving elements on the ground were Canadian.

As Lieutenant-Colonel Lavoie had so elegantly put it, our method would be: "Soft knock by preference, hard knock as needed." In other words, we were prepared to move into these contested areas and provide reconstruction and additional assistance if we had the support of the locals and the Taliban had moved on. If not, we had the firepower to move in and force our will on the area.

Early in the morning of December 15, Coalition aircraft attacked Taliban command posts in the area, using laser-guided bombs and fuel-air explosives to blast apart fortresses made from concrete, stone and mud that had hardened under the intense Afghan sun for years. That same day, they dropped three sets of leaflets over the area. The first warned the population of the coming battle, the second was a plea for locals to turn their back on the Taliban, and the third consisted of an image of a Taliban fighter with a large X through him to warn fighters to either leave or face NATO. These pictogram-type messages were meant to convince the largely illiterate Taliban foot soldiers to lay down their weapons and improvised explosive devices while they could.

Before these events started, we had Canadian soldiers, as part of the Provincial Reconstruction Teams, visit some local villages to discuss reconstruction and persuade the locals to support NATO. While en route to one of these meetings, a soldier from the Royal 22ᵉ Régiment stepped on a landmine and suffered severe but non-life-threatening injuries. Two Taliban spotted and killed by Canadian soldiers had planted the landmine the night before. Even though the area had been cleared by soldiers at first light, one explosive was missed.

On December 19, offensive operations began with a massive artillery barrage and tank fire that killed around sixty Taliban. The artillery barrage lasted about forty minutes and was supported by tank fire and .50 calibre machine-guns. When the barrage ended, we moved out of Ma'sum Ghar and headed for an area around the village of Howz-e Medad. We went in expecting a fight but hoping that it was not needed. Lucky for us, we did not have to fire a shot.

I expect the Taliban would have been notified immediately of the overwhelming force that rolled out of Ma'sum Ghar. That would have been enough to either have those who had remained behind after the leaflet drop pack up and move elsewhere or hide their weapons and melt into the local population. I expect that both did occur.

We set up a perimeter around the village to speak with the locals and see if they could support us. Howz-e Medad was a typical Afghan village that had popped up around a local bazaar and consisted of mud compounds, farmers' fields and, of course, a big, elaborate mosque. We did our first dismounted patrol along the main dusty road and past the local markets and shabby businesses such as a bicycle repair shop, a slaughterhouse, and a small-engine repair store. All of the shops were located inside small mud structures lined with a mixture of straw and sticks.

The people just stood and stared.

Several men dressed in black with long beards openly glared at us as we walked by, and I suspected they were Taliban. My suspicions were confirmed when I noticed that all three of our terps immediately pulled their scarves over their faces. They told us they did this whenever there was a possibility of Taliban, and, unlike most Westerners, they could see and feel the differences between the people.

Our Company terp leaned over and said, "Those guys are not Afghan." It always amazed me how they could tell the difference. I know it is politically incorrect to say, but these guys all looked similar to me. But the Afghan terps could immediately tell if someone was Pakistani, Chechen, Iranian or even a westerner.

There were no weapons visible, and there were no apparent signs of hostile intent. Because we wanted this to be about hearts and minds, we did not want to overreact. We had our soldiers keep some extra attention on those guys but also kept a close eye on everyone. After patrolling back and forth through the village centre and trying to speak with some of the men who, for the most part, did not want to talk to us, we got nowhere. Trying to set up a shura to discuss any issues with the village elders was also unsuccessful. As we moved about, we continued to receive the stink eye from the suspicious men.

We were concerned about the attitude of the village and the possibility that there could be a small Taliban force hidden there with their weapons and explosives close by. That was one of the negative impacts of informing the village days before rolling in that we were coming.

WHITE SCHOOL, BLACK MEMORIES

We were able to get an American explosive-sniffing dog team to come in and assist us with searching the area to make sure it was secure for any shura that we might plan. At least, that was why we told the locals we were doing it. We provided security and overwatch as the dog team did their work. We kept it as low-key and unobtrusive as possible to avoid alienating the people even more, but it was evident that the locals were not impressed to have dogs sniffing through their market stands and stores. We just had the team walk through the businesses and the street areas and, unless they picked up an explosive scent, we did not search. The team went through the complete main bazaar area of the village and, even though the dogs did react a few times, they did not pick up any specific scent, which came as a big surprise to everyone.

I continued to be concerned, as the village remained very defiant and unfriendly. This was even more obvious as the many children stayed away from us even when our attached Provincial Reconstruction Team members pulled out candy and chocolate bars. The one constant that I have seen from operations worldwide is that children will always gather around foreign soldiers, either because they are curious or because they know we have nice stuff, food or equipment.

The children became an early warning sign to us on many occasions as we travelled through Kandahar City or other smaller towns and villages. For the most part, as we were driving, if kids were waving, begging or even throwing rocks at us, it usually meant that nothing was going to happen. But, when the kids suddenly disappeared, or there were none around at all, it put everyone on edge and, more times than not, we got hit. Even though the Taliban were very violent and killed many more Afghans than foreign soldiers, the children always seemed to know if something was up.

So, in this case, even though we did not get hit, there was no doubt that the village was being watched and reported on. The locals were not going to be seen speaking to us or showing any type of support.

Over the next few days, NATO forces secured several more towns and villages around the area with little to no resistance. Commanders believed that the lack of resistance we had encountered was due to the leaflets dropped during the information campaign. I think it may have had something more to do with the artillery barrage and a pile of tanks and armoured vehicles coming their way.

Maybe we were both right.

Around the village of Howz-e Medad was a ten-square-mile area of mud-walled fortresses containing an expected nine hundred Taliban fighters. Canadian infantry and armour surrounded the area. The complex layout of the site made it almost impossible for the Taliban to escape from it. To the east was Route Summit, and it was under constant observation and fire from Canadians. Ten kilometres to the south was a line of American soldiers, and to the west were the British, making this a genuinely combined effort.

The following day, two rockets flew past us, and we fired into the area from which they had come. There were no casualties on either side. It would still be a few days before Canadian infantry, supported by American helicopter gunships, would sweep through the mud fortresses and rout out any remaining Taliban. Most of the Taliban had decided not to engage us. They left the area or remained behind walled compounds with their weapons hidden and ready for another day.

While the Taliban were hiding, Canadians brought several sea containers filled with hand tools, seeds, blankets, and various household goods to the two districts. A large amount of cash was also handed out to local leaders to entice the half-hearted and local insurgents to commit to the Afghan Government.

I believe all the goods and money ended up in the hands of the Taliban or the corrupt officials.

VISIT BY THE GOVERNOR

As we were settling in, we received word that the Governor of Kandahar would be flying in by helicopter in a couple of hours and would hold an impromptu shura with the elders. We were now responsible for securing a landing site and the outer perimeter of the meeting area. We were not impressed. This area was not safe, and Major Sprague tried to let higher authorities know that this would not be easy.

The word had already gotten out and hundreds of people were already starting to gather. We quickly identified a landing area and had some soldiers begin to secure it. We used our vehicles to form a perimeter and put up some barbed wire to limit access to the area. We were not happy with the site selected for the shura, but that was out of our hands, and the hundreds of people gathering for it were going to be an issue, too.

We briefed our Afghan National Army partners and got them to set up an area that would force people to move through them to join the shura. Everyone would have to be searched, and at the same time, we had our soldiers searching everyone who wanted to get into the area where the helicopter was going to land.

I remember running back and forth between the helicopter landing area and where the shura would be held. The whole time I was thinking, "What an opportunity for a suicide bomber." I was more worried about all the Canadian soldiers they could kill than the Governor or the locals, but that was my inner voice speaking.

As I got back to the village centre and the area set up for searching by the Afghan Army, I found myself getting angry as I saw that there were already hundreds of people gathered. At best, the Afghan soldiers were doing only hasty searches, and I saw several people were sent through without being searched at all. I grabbed the terp, went up to the Afghan soldiers and police who were doing such a shitty job and informed them how dangerous it was. They just smiled at me as if to say, "You're an idiot. We've got this covered." They continued to do a quick tap on some people and let all the women through without a search at all.

I went back and briefed Major Sprague, and he just threw his hands up in the air and swore and went to brief Lieutenant-Colonel Lavoie, who had arrived in the area. We heard the helicopter with the Governor coming in and knew it was too late to do anything more. Once again, we would be doing this the Afghan way: half-assed. Our soldiers did the best they could, but once the helicopter landed, even our half-assed plan went to shit in a handbasket very quickly.

The governor, his aides, bodyguards and many local politicians who had arrived by car just took their own route into the shura and ignored us. To make matters worse, they mingled in with the local people as they went, security be damned. I spoke to our soldiers gathered around the shura site and the search areas and told them to keep a safe distance and watch, as we could not be sure that everyone inside was a good guy.

The following thirty minutes were incredibly stressful as more people arrived, and the searches got even more relaxed. I believe you could have gotten into the shura area with whatever explosives you wanted, and I think the only reason that it did not happen was that this had been an unexpected visit. It had happened so quickly that the Taliban did not have anyone ready. The governor spoke for about fifteen minutes or so and then went around and shook some hands. Then almost as quickly as it began, it was over.

As soon as it ended, the entourage walked back through the crowd and into their waiting helicopter and cars and left without incident. Every soldier in Charles Company breathed a sigh of relief. We had dodged a bullet here, and we all knew it.

No matter how much training you are involved with, no matter your level of experience or authority, sometimes you must work off the seat of your pants and hope for the best. This had been one of those times where it could have been a major tragedy. One bad guy with an explosive could have killed a lot of people, and it would have been on our watch.

All I can say is, "But for the grace of God."

Charles Company Combat Team, which was now about two hundred and fifty people strong, including our mechanized rifle company, a squadron of tanks, a recce squadron, an engineer troop and about a platoon of Afghan soldiers, continued to provide a "ring of steel" about a kilometre outside Howz-e Medad, in the desert but in full view of the village. The Provincial Reconstruction Team and dismounted soldiers continued to hold discussions with local elders. The plan was clear to all, including the villagers. We would keep the heavy armour and weapons in the desert if we were not attacked. If we were attacked, we would roll into the village and impress our will upon everyone.

One of the most significant issues that the villagers had, and continued to bring up in every shura, was that once we left the area there would be no government representatives remaining and therefore no security. How could we expect the locals to support us when the Taliban would return with a vengeance? This concern was a very valid one to which we did not have a good response.

There were not enough Afghan soldiers to spread around, and they were not eager anyway to be left on their own without Coalition firepower, so it came down to a detachment of Afghan National Police. They did not believe it was safe to be out here on their own either, and we knew from past incidents that every time the Taliban came to a village, the police either ran away or were slaughtered.

PART THREE - AFGHANISTAN

The Task Force decided that we would build a police substation that the police could hopefully defend, and that a QRF would be on call from either FOB Sperwan Ghar or Ma'sum Ghar to assist them if required. I knew in my heart that if the Taliban were going to come into this village, the police would be dead and cold before the QRF could arrive, but if it gave them a little comfort, so be it.

The local Police Chief from FOB Wilson arrived and after discussions it was decided that if we built a secure substation, he would order the police to stay and defend this area. We had our doubts, but this was their country, and they needed to start being the face of security, not the Coalition Forces.

ROYAL ENGINEERS

We enlisted the help of the British Royal Engineers from neighbouring Helmand Province to come and build this police substation. Late that evening, after enduring several hours of harrowing driving, they rolled into Howz-e Medad. It was a sight for sore eyes. The convoy consisted of several British Land Rovers and an array of heavy equipment, about twenty vehicles in total.

The fragility of the British Land Rover was an issue that had already hit the British media, where it had been dubbed 'the Deathtrap.' Much like our Canadian G-Wagon, it was never meant for heavy combat operations, as it provided only minimal protection from small arms and nearly none from IEDs and explosions.

As the weary Brits arrived, they could be seen standing in the open-top Land Rovers handling .50 calibre machine-guns and looking like they might have looked sixty years earlier as they rolled through the desert against Rommel. They were a courageous bunch and as soon as we got together on the ground it was like we had known each other for years. There is something about soldiers that cause us to immediately bond with others like us, and other than the Americans the Brits are our closest allies.

We kept the tanks and most of the armoured vehicles out in the desert where they were set up in all-around defence but ready to rumble to our location if we came under attack. After driving several hours in their death traps, I could tell that the Brits were excited about having a Canadian armoured combat team for security while they worked.

Major Sprague wanted to know if they wanted to eat and rest for the night and start in the morning. They declined and said they would eat as they worked and wanted to be completed and gone by first light because as bad as it was here in Kandahar province, Helmand was worse and they were needed there. That was quite the task they had given themselves and a timeline that did not seem within reach to me.

Boy, was I wrong!

These Brits immediately got to work, and they had everything they needed. The best location for both security and defence was selected. It had to be plowed over, levelled out, and then packed with gravel. Part of the location included a small mud structure that had a sign hanging over the steel door which identified it as a bicycle tire repair shop. This shop was about fifteen feet square, part of one wall was falling over and holes could be seen in the straw roof—but it did have some tires and tools hanging on the wall. The owner came toward us as the British bulldozer started heading toward the hut, and he was waving his hands and yelling while he dragged a small boy of about five years old along with him. We explained to him, through the terp, that this structure had to go to build a police substation to protect his village. He wanted no part of it and told us that this was how he made his living. It was his family's business, and we couldn't touch it. We came into this operation thinking of using either the soft knock or hard knock approach, and even though the idea was explicitly meant for the Taliban, we were not going to allow one local with a $100 mud hut get in the way.

We had been here in this tiny village for about three days, and I had seen only one bicycle. However, these guys weren't stupid, and he wanted money. We called CWO Frank Gratton over, who was with us from the PRT. Frank was a fellow Royal Canadian and had a storied career in our Regiment and the Special Forces. He looked the part. He was a grizzled guy with a huge moustache and easily fit into any shura with the locals because he had that elder look about him. I was a little concerned about Frank in the early days of our tour when he roamed around the local villages without any real security. At least now, he had us to provide protection.

Frank told the owner that his bicycle shop would be flattened and that the discussion was over, but they could now discuss what it was worth and he would pay him cash. The guy's eyes lit up and he started to barter with Frank. Christie Blatchford and some of our soldiers stood around, watching in amusement as Frank pulled out a wad of cash. The owner then brought Frank over to a hole in the ground that we had not even seen. He told us that this had been his family's well for hundreds of years and that his shop was the only one in the village and was a necessity, so he would need money to buy land, rebuild and dig a well. He continued for several minutes to barter until I could tell that Frank was getting a little fed up, and the Brits were getting impatient. Finally, a deal was made. I do not know how much money exchanged hands, but the guy walked away with a smile on his face and at least several hundred dollars in his pocket.

He didn't even take anything out of his shop or stick around to watch as a minute later it disappeared into the dust and dirt of Afghanistan, tires and tools included. I am not even sure today as I write this that we confirmed the guy was the owner. Perhaps he was just in the right place at the right time, and maybe he was even Taliban. Either way, some Afghan got some money and the Brits rolled over a hundred-dollar shop.

All in a day's work.

The Brits worked throughout the night, filling Hesco containers with dirt. The Hesco Bastion is a collapsible wire mesh container with a heavy-duty fabric liner initially designed by the British to prevent erosion on beaches and marshes. It now had military use as a blast wall. They are filled with dirt and lined and stacked to build a structure that can be very defendable. They were lined up along the main road so that traffic would have to slow down to go through it and then could be forced into an area where the vehicle could be searched or the driver questioned by police. The Hesco was positioned so that if there was an explosion, it would be contained within the search area. The Brits also used large sea containers that were cut and had access points from one to another to build an office area, a sleeping area and an area to eat. These containers were then enclosed with more Hesco Bastions, made several feet high.

I do not believe these fine soldiers stopped throughout the night other than to grab a drink. By first light, the British Engineers and their security were already mounted up and ready to depart for Helmand Province and the British Sector. Before they left, the local Police Chief and the provincial government official arrived for pictures and accolades on the new police substation. They were rightfully amazed at the amount of work that had been done in only a few hours. I was impressed with the skills and the professionalism of the Royal Engineers and their incredible work habits. They were second to none.

With lots of handshakes and even a few hugs, we watched as these desert rats departed our location and made the dangerous journey back to Helmand Province. I wished them well and hoped that they would all make it home safe.

We spent the rest of the day getting the local police in location, making sure their numbers were sufficient for the task, explaining how the QRF worked and speaking with the locals about how vital their police were to them. The problem with the police was that almost all were poorly trained, poorly equipped and corrupt, so the locals did not trust them.

Shortly after this operation, we would begin to embed Canadian Military Police with the Afghan National Police, which immediately had a positive impact. But for the moment, most locals told us that the police were even worse than the Taliban and charged them a tax to go through the checkpoints. We detained several police officers during our tour for suspicion of collaborating with the Taliban or because they fired on us. We also had police that would leave their weapons at their checkpoints and just walk away because they had not been paid for months.

All the money provided by the Coalition to build, train and pay the police went through the provincial governors to the district Police Chiefs, who would then pay their police or not. I saw Afghan police as young as fourteen years old, who got the jobs through family or tribal connections. Once they were enrolled, they had enormous power despite having no training. A lot of these guys were illiterate, and some had no formal education at all. Many of them did drugs regularly and on more than one occasion we found alcohol bottles and heroin in their checkpoints.

During my tour, hundreds of these young men were found dead at their checkpoints because they were either asleep, too drugged up to defend themselves, or they surrendered to the Taliban insurgents hoping for mercy. They would not receive any. By early 2007, there were some positive changes slowly occurring within the police force, but in 2006 they were more of a hindrance than an asset.

We remained in a location outside of Howz-e Medad until the following morning when another Canadian unit would replace us and remain in place for a few more days.

WHITE SCHOOL, BLACK MEMORIES

The local police and elders did not want us to leave, as the Taliban were still around and retribution would be swift for what would appear like cooperation with NATO.

December 21 came and while we were waiting for the Canadian unit that would replace us, I took the time to acknowledge that it was our Regimental Birthday. That day is a good memory from Afghanistan that I kept with me for a long time.

Operation Baaz Tsuka was in full swing. The majority of Charles Company Combat Team was still in an all-around defensive position overlooking the village of Howz-e Medad. The police substation was built and manned and the locals seem to be coming around to our way of thinking. Until the sun started to rise and remove the chill from the frosty night, our Regimental Birthday was the furthest thing from our minds. But that day was the 123rd birthday of The Royal Canadian Regiment, and it needed to be recognized.

ORTONA TOAST

Weeks earlier, Lieutenant-Colonel Lavoie realized that the vast majority of his Battle Group would be deployed forward for the birthday and so he ordered his team to get all the ingredients together, namely dark rum and brown sugar, so that his soldiers could celebrate with the "Ortona Toast."

This tradition originated during the Regimental Birthday celebrated at the Ortona Crossroads in Italy on December 21, 1943. On that day, the Regiment's 60th birthday, Lieutenant-Colonel Spry (Acting Commander of 1 Canadian Infantry Brigade) was invited to visit the Battalion Command Post and drink to the health of the Regiment, despite the fact that it was being shelled at the time.

They prepared a punch made of issued rum, sugar and water. Then, Lieutenant-Colonel Dan Spry, Major Strome Galloway, Captain Sandy Mitchell, Captain Marty Upper, Lieutenant Walter Roy, Captain [Padre] Rusty Wilkes, MC, and RSM Archie McDonnell all participated in the toast. Just as the ceremony was about to begin, Captain Dick Dillon, MC and Lieutenant Buck Bowman, MC reported in from two fighting patrols they had been leading with considerable success. The toast was drunk from white china mugs salvaged from a nearby farmhouse.

And so, it is with some surprise and delight that I saw Lieutenant-Colonel Lavoie and his tactical headquarters pull into our headquarters position, with the CQ in tow. We gathered all the soldiers that we could without compromising security around our Headquarters LAV. WO Olstad had enough white mugs to hand out to all the senior leaders and paper or Melmac cups to the rest. The drivers had all started boiling water, knowing what was coming, and soon everyone had a drink in hand.

Lieutenant-Colonel Lavoie spoke for a moment about how proud he was of Charles Company, that we had bounced back from our losses and continued to be the best Company in the Canadian Army. He then explained the significance of the Ortona Toast to all those gathered.

"To my knowledge," he began, "this is the first time, since the original Ortona

Toast in 1943, that it has been done in combat." He then invited Colonel Jonathan Vance, Commander of 1 Canadian Brigade Group and the senior Royal Canadian present, to lead the toast.

Colonel Vance jumped up on the ramp of the LAV. "To all my dear friends, to all those present and to all those who have departed, and in honour of our 123 years of service. To the Regiment, Pro Patria."

Everyone drank up and slapped each other on the backs and wished Happy Birthdays all around, and then it was time to get back to reality and back to the war. The significance of that moment has not been lost on me. Every year since on our Regimental Birthday, I tell this extraordinary story no matter where I am, and I hope it becomes part of our great history.

THE OPERATION ENDS

The purpose of Operation Baaz Tsuka was clear to everyone. Through a campaign of dropping leaflets and other soft tactics, NATO was hoping that a secure enough environment could be built for reconstruction, without heavy fighting to expel the Taliban that would destroy the area.

One of the main objectives of Baaz Tsuka was to persuade the tier two Taliban, mostly uneducated local farmers, to put down their weapons and support the Afghan government. This was a failure. Few dared to abandon the Taliban, and none wanted to join National Auxiliary Police, a paramilitary outfit described at the time as kind of an armed neighbourhood watch. That program was abandoned early in the New Year, and this hard-won territory would again fall to the insurgents.

We had learned early on, while travelling around the villages and towns, to stick to paved routes or make our own routes. Once they were cleared and were known to be safe, they were kept under observation.

The path from Howz-e Medad to our desert defensive site was noticeably clear and easily recognizable, but for some reason the incoming Canadian unit rolled off the road in front of the police station, taking an old local route to our location in the desert. Seconds later there was a massive explosion, followed by a plume of smoke and dust. The lead LAV had hit an IED that had probably been planted there days before we arrived, expecting us to use routes that were already available. Luckily, only the LAV was damaged and everyone inside, other than being shaken up, was okay.

This incident reminded us all that becoming complacent was not an option.

36

AFGHAN NOMADS

After departing the area around Howz-e Medad, we drove south and then east through the desert to an area about five hundred metres from a Kochi village. Nomadic herders, like Arabian Bedouins, they had set up there temporarily for a few months and would eventually pack up and move on.

During the Taliban era, Kochis were supporters of the Taliban and their leader Mohammed Omar. There had also been centuries of conflict between the Kochi as they migrated northwards and the people settled around their summer pastures. As a result, many non-Pashtun ethnic groups—Hazaras, Tajiks, Uzbeks, Turkmen and others—generally distrusted the Kochi. In turn, the Kochis (and many other Pashtuns) saw the other ethnicities as non-Afghans. The Kochis always seemed to play the victim game whenever we came across them, but they could not be trusted.

We left the vehicles outside and walked into the village with about twenty soldiers, including our medics. After linking up with the elders, we asked them if they needed anything, and they complained about the government starting to make it harder for them to move around freely. If they left their pastures completely, others would try to take over the land. It was also getting harder to access the public lands that had been used for grazing for centuries. We told them we would pass on their concerns to our officials and offered some low-level medical care, which they quickly accepted.

We set up a checkpoint in a private area, as well as an area where everyone had to pass through where our soldiers could search them before they were allowed to see the medics. At first, it was only men and boys with cuts and infections and a couple of more serious things we could not handle. Eventually, our female medic was able to see some of the women and girls. However, we always kept armed soldiers at the ready, even if not in visual sight of the women. After a couple of hours we departed, telling them that we would have our people speak with the government about the restrictions

PART THREE - AFGHANISTAN

that the tribe was feeling about their lack of freedom of movement. We also told them that we would return in a few days, and if the Taliban came to see them, they should let us know. Deep down, we knew that this was not going to happen as the Taliban paid many nomads to smuggle weapons, drugs, people and money across the country and in and out of Afghanistan and Pakistan.

We tasked the lead platoon to find an area in the desert with about a kilometre clearance and set up a Company Leaguer for the night. The platoon headed off, followed shortly by the remainder of the Company. As we had done many times, we did not follow existing routes but made our own and set up about fifteen hundred metres from the closest occupied compound and village. It took a couple of hours to prepare defensive positions and sort out a plan for the night. Then everyone settled down for what we hoped would be a quiet night.

For once, we were able to rest the whole night without any incidents. Soldiers were up, packed and ready to move out at first light.

We had just raised Three-Niner's ramp when the LAV beside us rolled over an IED, and the explosion sent dust and debris over everything. The radio remained silent as the dust started to clear, and I could see the LAV beside us was damaged quite extensively. We had all the vehicles stop and stay where they were while we gathered any information possible.

We knew that there were minefields scattered all over Afghanistan. Many were left over from the Soviet invasion. Most were marked on the ground or, at the very least, we had accurate locations of them on our maps. Our first concern was that we had wandered into one of those minefields. We got the word over the radio that no one inside the damaged LAV had been injured, only shaken up, but the vehicle could not move. We checked and rechecked our maps and GPS, and we were at least a kilometre from the nearest minefield, which we could see off in the distance. We were not on any existing route or trail. So how would the Taliban know to plant an IED here, when even we didn't know this would be our spot for the night?

We passed the information over the radio to higher and told them that likely this was a mine because of where we were. Engineers were not immediately available to come to our location, so our soldiers dismounted from the vehicles and cleared the area around their LAVs. The soldiers were trained to look for any signs of mines or IEDs. After an hour of looking, we didn't find anything, and so we hooked up the damaged LAV and rolled out to the main road. We stayed as best we could in the same tracks we made coming in, keeping our fingers crossed that there would not be any more mines.

Once again, we had been lucky.

After briefing the engineers on where we were and what had happened, as well as the damage to the vehicle, they assessed that the moving desert sands, over the many years since the Soviet invasion, had probably shifted the mine, and we had just been unlucky. The Platoon Warrant in the damaged LAV said that it had moved only a few feet when it hit the mine, so there was no doubt that soldiers had been walking back and forth over the mine all night, and someone had probably slept on it. It is sometimes better to be lucky than be good.

We moved back to the area of Route Summit, where one of the platoons was securing FOB Zettelmeyer, built on the very spot where I had been injured and our soldiers had lost their lives. The FOB was located between Strong Point Centre and Ma'sum Ghar and was only a few hundred metres square, but it had a great view up and down the Arghandab River. We had a squadron of tanks and a platoon for security, and they were able to engage targets with great success, but, as Major Sprague had said to anyone who would listen, "Where are the Afghans?"

There was a marked absence of Afghan soldiers and police. We had been promised Afghan soldiers on many occasions, but very seldomly did it work out that way.

Major Sprague was a thinking man. "That's the difference between guilt-based societies like ours and a shame-based society like theirs," he said, "where honour and respect are what matters and motivates people, not remorse or conscience." Even though Afghan troops had been promised on many occasions and none had arrived, no one in the Afghan government was embarrassed or concerned about it.

We did get twenty or so Afghan soldiers a few times, and they would be around for a couple of days. Then something more important would pull them away and, without warning, they would be gone. We had learned to plan everything without them and, if by some miracle, we got some Afghan troops, then we inserted them into our plan at the last minute. It was tough trying to carry out all the tasks assigned to us in one of the nastiest places in Afghanistan when we did not have the support we required.

There is no doubt that the leave policy was putting us in a bad situation. We just did not have the numbers to put soldiers in all the areas that we needed to. Every time we packed up and moved, the Taliban came in behind us. It was very frustrating for the soldiers to be fighting for the same piece of dirt over and over or to have people killed or injured by IEDs planted on the same portion of the road because we did not have the numbers to keep an eye on it, and the locals were not helping.

Soldiers voiced their concerns that both Canada and NATO were not providing the resources required.

The number of "Hobbits" that were hanging around KAF also became a point of contention. The uneven ratio of "boots on the ground" to "supporters behind the wire" at KAF and in bases around Afghanistan was very frustrating to us doing the daily fighting. The numbers just did not make sense; they almost seemed backwards. As I overheard one of Charles Company's young soldiers say to a reporter, "What we need are more combat troops and less support."

I don't know what the final numbers would be. Still, there is no doubt in my mind, after spending a few days in KAF and Dubai, and speaking with folks that had been to Bagram, Blackhorse, Julien and Bastion (which are only a tiny portion of the Coalition bases involved), that the number of soldiers in support roles was phenomenal. To the eye of an infantry soldier living in the dirt and the filth (admittedly by choice) and fighting or prepared to fight daily, the numbers did not add up.

How do you persuade a combat soldier, who is under the constant threat of death or worse and is continually shorthanded for all their missions, that they are receiving all the support needed and that there is no more to give? Then, these same soldiers go into KAF for forty-eight hours and find thousands upon thousands of people playing ball hockey, drinking Tim Hortons, eating Burger King, and even salsa and line dancing. And if they pulled a muscle attempting these new dances, there was always the Lai Thai Spa, where they could receive a massage!

We lost many good people over the first few months, and that experience hardened us to the reality that more death and terrible injuries would come. So, yes, perhaps our attitude had changed, and maybe there was frustration with the politicians and the Hobbits and anyone else we found in our path. But, we continued to do the best we could with what we had. You just couldn't ask us to be happy about it.

CHRISTMAS

The rain began late on Christmas Eve, and it was hard and steady. The dirt and dust we had to deal with for months immediately turned to mud as dawn broke on Christmas Day. As I sat inside my bunker at Strong Point Centre on Christmas Eve, I thought about Julie and the kids and how they would be excited about the coming holidays but worried about me. As midnight approached, I lay awake listening to the sound of occasional machine-guns and rifle fire coming from the east, but, for once, none of the Company positions were under fire. There was only the rare glow of soldiers firing flares into the night sky to light up areas of concern and then darkness again.

It was almost surreal. The rain was pounding on the corrugated steel that lined our positions, and soldiers could be heard moving around the position in the dark, as any light was forbidden. The occasional burp or fart reminded me that many soldiers occupied this bunker. Major Sprague had put away his Grinch hat and allowed anyone not on duty to sleep in until 0800 hours, instead of the usual 0530 reveille. I guess that was his Christmas gift to us all. Sleeping in these tight confines for months on end teaches you to appreciate your own company and time alone.

We were a very tight-knit Company, but we did have some personal issues that we had to correct. Soldiers living and sleeping inches from each other during stressful times must respect each other and each other's space. If not, we got on each other's nerves and that team spirit can be lost. We sat around the headquarters LAV and celebrated Christmas morning with a hot coffee and some stories.

A few soldiers were seen around the position fully kitted up for battle with a Santa hat or some other Christmas article. I let it go, as there are times when a little fun is warranted. I had a long, red Santa hat that I had received in a package from home, and I forced our Company terp to wear it. After several attempts to explain what it was and who Santa was, I gave up, and he just wore the hat around all day. When you grow up in a society where things like Santa, the Easter Bunny, Halloween and the Tooth Fairy are known by everyone from the time they are toddlers, it is hard to believe at first that there are people so different that they have never heard of these things. I am sure that if the Taliban had captured him when he was wearing that Santa hat, he would have been executed on the spot for supporting some pagan Christian tradition. For now, he was in ignorant bliss as he strolled around the position.

An hour or so later, we rolled into FOB Zettelmeyer, and I sent a couple of our vehicles the two kilometres up to Ma'sum Ghar to fetch our Christmas meals. The Battle Group had prepared hot meals for all the unit locations to have an authentic Christmas dinner. I did not initially support this idea, as I could not see how we would live with someone killed to deliver a meal. However, it became one of my favourite moments of the tour.

With the help of the CQ, we set up some tables under hastily hung tarps to protect us from the cold rain, dug out paper plates, and prepared to serve a traditional Christmas dinner. Those on duty in the tanks and the LAVs, as well as those handling the machine-guns, remained in place, but I called everyone else into the centre of this tiny FOB and allowed them to remove their kit as long as they stayed close to it while they ate. I then turned the floor or more appropriately the sand over to Major Sprague.

CHRISTIE BLATCHFORD'S ARTICLE

The next few moments were captured in an article written by Christie Blatchford, who for the moment may have been forgotten. Major Matt Sprague is a man of few words, but it is from the heart when he speaks. He says what he thinks, and the consequences be damned.

"I hate fucking Christmas," he started, "but I can think of no other place for Charles Company to have Christmas than here, right on the ground where this thing all started about four months ago. This place, I think, will always have a special meaning, for a lot of reasons, not necessarily all good ones. No group of people in the entire Canadian Forces more deserves this than you do. When you guys look in the mirror, be proud of what you have done, of what you have become. You are the fucking best, and that is the way it is. Padre, Grace."

That was how Major Sprague was. That was how we were. We could go from profane to sacred in an instant as is the soldier's way, and no one was offended. That was Charles Company's world: death, loss, pain and black humour, a way to get through it.

Padre Guy Chapdelaine said a few words of thanks, and then it was time to eat. What a meal we had: turkey, mashed potatoes, veggies and all the sweets a person could ever ask for, and seconds was called. For the time being, everyone ate their fill, but most would pay for overindulging the following day, as our bodies had been used to MREs for months. All this fresh food would not cooperate with many, and our homemade bunker toilets would get constant use. But, that was far from anyone's thoughts as they ate their fill.

Major Sprague had been right. We could not find a better, more inspirational location to have a Christmas dinner. This was ground zero for Charles Company and

PART THREE - AFGHANISTAN

this was a special spot, as Major Sprague had said for all of us, perhaps for different reasons. This was where Charles Company had its first real baptism of fire. Yes, we had been in firefights before, but not like what we faced here in early September. Everywhere that I looked, I could see the hallowed ground, areas where blood had been spilled. The white school, which became a rallying cry for the Company, the objective where so many lives from both sides were lost was now just some rubble...the dirty brown fields that were so lush and green with marijuana plants that towered above us a few months ago and the ditch where one of the LAVs got stuck and was surrounded by Taliban. And, of course, buried beneath my feet was the armoured Zettelmeyer that gave us some much-needed comfort when things were at their worst.

Dinner was cleared away, and soldiers picked up their kit and separated into small groups, a practice that they no longer needed to be told to do. It was second nature and meant that an explosion might only kill a few and not everyone. I kept a close eye on the interpreters as we celebrated because not only did I not fully trust them, Christianity is not allowed in Afghanistan and open celebrations can be deemed disrespectful. However, all our terps seemed to enjoy the day and especially all the food and sweets. We allowed them to take as much as they wanted.

After dinner, Padre Chapdelaine had a small service for those interested, including offering Holy Communion to those who desired it. I was raised a Catholic in a close-knit family in a small fishing community on the Avalon Peninsula in Newfoundland, but I had not been practicing for several years. I still considered myself a Catholic and believed in the church's teachings but had not routinely attended mass.

As I sat there considering my options, I realized that I had spoken to God on several occasions over the last few months, when things were going bad and I needed his help and there was nowhere else to turn. Now, when I had an opportunity to attend a mass in relative peace here on this hallowed ground, I wanted to be part of it. We pulled up water cans and ration boxes for seats, and a small group of us gathered in a corner away from the centre of the FOB and, with the icy rain hitting us, Padre Chapdelaine did a short but significant mass. He then offered Holy Communion and, at first, I hesitated, remembering the words of many priests and my parents as I was growing up, "You can only receive communion after you have gone to confession and confessed your sins." That was not going to happen here at FOB Zettelmeyer, at least not to this Padre, so I closed my eyes and asked God for forgiveness for all my sins and stood up and received Holy Communion. I was lost in the moment, and I do not remember anyone taking photos, and I especially do not remember Christie Blatchford taking any. However, a few days later, I learned that she did.

On December 27 or 28 I had access to a satellite phone and could speak with Julie and the kids to tell them how much I loved and missed them. As I was about to say goodbye, Julie said that she was glad that the soldiers had a chance to have mass and communion. I paused because I had not told her about that. She said that her Dad, a Baptist and a deeply religious man, had read an article in The Globe And Mail about Charles Company and I. She told me it had an entire page, close-up photo of me receiving Holy Communion, as well as an article about Charles Company. She said that her Dad had pointed out that the picture did not necessarily go with the words of the article as it talked about me reading stories from a porn magazine to the soldiers over the radio as they were fighting. I was shocked at first and then a little angry, but as always Julie did not make a big deal out of it. However, I needed to know.

An hour or so later at FOB Wilson, I looked up the article online, and sure enough, I confirmed what Julie had said. On the way back to FOB Zettelmeyer, I was complaining to Major Sprague. I told him that I would let Christie Blatchford know that I was not happy and that she was not very professional, as the story was factually untrue, and I had not told her any of it. Yes, there were a few times when we were sitting around in the LAV, either during or after a firefight, that I would grab a magazine and read it aloud over the intercom for laughs. They were always articles from MacLean's, Canadian Geographic and others, but never from porn. Major Sprague started to laugh and told me that during his interview with Blatchford, he might have mentioned that I sometimes read to the troops for laughs or to lower the stress of the ongoing situation.

"Did you tell her that I read from porn magazines?"

With a half-smile, he said, "I don't remember saying that, but I might have."

Case solved. Of course, he had, and he probably didn't think it would make it to a full-page article of The Globe And Mail, but it did. By itself, there was no harm but added to a large picture of me receiving Holy Communion, it was not so good. When I got home a few months later, I found out that Julie had the article professionally placed into a beautiful wooden frame to hang on the wall.

Now that ten years have passed, I look at the whole thing with amusement and enjoy the enormous contrast between the photo and the article.

VISIT BY THE CDS

With our Christmas activities now behind us, we needed to take care of only one more event. We had to get as many soldiers as possible to FOB Wilson the following day to greet General Rick Hillier and his special guests. He had talked some politicians and a few celebrities into giving up their Christmas to join soldiers on the battlefield. We were expecting Rick Mercer and Mary Walsh from This Hour Has 22 Minutes and a Montreal rock band called Jonas.

When we pulled into FOB Wilson the following day, some Hobbits were running around organizing things, but, for the most part, it was just Charles Company and the FOB Wilson folks. I organized Charles Company into a hollow square. While waiting for the arrivals, I was told to make sure that Master Corporal Leblanc was upfront and to identify himself to the CDS because he had a gift for him. I had no idea what was going on. Leblanc had just recently been promoted to Master Corporal, so what else was there? I would find out with everyone else.

As I was getting everyone organized, I yelled at Leblanc in a nasty tone to get upfront so that I could keep an eye on him. He said, "Yes, sir," probably thinking he was in trouble for something. Our guests arrived, and the OC and I met them first. General Hillier and I had met several times, and we knew each other well. We chatted for a moment, and then he asked me if Master Corporal Leblanc was here. I told him yes and discreetly told him where Leblanc was. He thanked me and started walking around shaking hands, with a Dutch combat camera guy following him.

General Hillier spoke to every soldier and told them how proud he was of them. When he got to Leblanc, he did the same. He then looked at his nametag and said, "Master Corporal Leblanc, I've been looking for you. I have something to deliver. Just look into the camera." I watched as Leblanc looked at the Dutch cameraman, and the General, still grasping his hand, leaned in and kissed Leblanc on the cheek.

We were all stunned and started laughing and clapping as the CDS asked Leblanc if he was embarrassed.

"Maybe a little, sir."

Hillier then gave him one of his coins and said, "That kiss was from your fiancée, Melissa, but the coin is from me. Keep up the good work and get home safely to that lovely young lady."

A little later, I learned the whole story.

A few days earlier, General Hillier had visited the 1 RCR Wives' Club in Petawawa, located in the Battalion Lines. He had spoken at length about the great work that the soldiers were doing and, when he had finished, he went around shaking hands and taking photos.

Melissa was asked what unit her husband was in, and she told General Hillier that he was with Charles Company. She was then told that Hillier would be spending Christmas with them. He asked Melissa if she had a message for him to deliver.

"Tell Master Corporal Leblanc 'hello' and that I miss him," she said.

The General had a better idea. He told her to give him a little peck on the cheek, which she did. He then said, "I'll deliver that to him myself."

That incident said everything that needed to be said about General Rick Hillier. He had the knowledge and skills required to lead the Canadian Military and make sound operational decisions. He could also inspire soldiers and had their loyalty, devotion and even love. General Hillier was an authentic Newfoundlander who never tried to be anything but himself. He could be professional one minute and silly the next and the troops loved it. It was the first time in my career that every soldier starting with the newest recruit knew the CDS name and didn't run the other way when he approached.

I believe he was the best CDS that I have known during my thirty-six years of service. I understand that this is not the overall consensus. Most of those with a negative view of General Hillier were folks that had to find a way through or around Canadian government and military policies to fulfill one of the CDS's many promises to the families of dead and injured soldiers. General Hillier would make decisions that would be beneficial to these soldiers' families and I would suggest that he was right and the naysayers had their priorities wrong.

37

COLD AND DAMP

Christmas Day and the hot, or at least, warm turkey dinner as well as a surprise visit by the CDS and his team was a great respite from what now had become months of intense fighting and less-than-ideal living conditions. Our soldiers all returned to their Strong Points and FOBs, and the routine for the next few weeks would be much the same as the last few, including the daily firefights with the enemy.

The weather, for the remainder of December and January, was unforgiving. It still got hot throughout most days, but the temperature would drop dramatically at night. We would wake up to a layer of ice covering the ground. We had days of rain, and we discovered that the wadis and ditches that crisscrossed the battlefield and had caused us so much heartache during Operation MEDUSA were once again going to wreak havoc on us, but this time through our ignorance.

We had previously cleared fields of fire several hundred metres wide on both sides of Route Summit by flattening compounds and homes and plowing over fields and walls. It was all done in the name of security and for the most part it had worked. During the early days of trying to secure the district, we found out that the Taliban used the wadis to move in and out of the area under cover from our view to attack us and plant IEDs. So, we had the engineers block these routes with dirt and obstacles, and we placed trip flares to make them harder to move through undetected.

While sitting around in unbelievable heat in August and September, who would have imagined that in December and January this same area would have, as one of the locals told us, more flooding than they had ever seen in their lifetime? The rain came down in amounts not seen in more than a decade. We spent day after day, clogged down in the mud. There were several days when we could not move our LAVs or get resupply, but the water amazed me. A large amount of rainfall caused the natural mountain cisterns to fill. The water ran from the mountains down into the valley, following the same path it had done for thousands of years, and hit the destruction Canadians had levied upon the landscape. It spilled over onto the fields of Panjwai.

Strong Point Centre was flooded, Route Summit was under several feet of water, and the unpaved remainder was under twelve inches of mud. Any movement was next to impossible, and everyone was wet, miserable and looking for ways to dry out drenched kit. We had to ration our drinking water because resupply could not get to us, and the troops were once again allowed to skip shaving.

Even the Taliban seemed to be affected by the rain, as this was one of the few times that we had a break from the constant attacks. The only folks who were probably happy were the locals in Kandahar, who were finally able to celebrate the end of the drought. They now had renewed hope.

Soldiers would wake up shaking from the cold and the dampness. Those who decided that their sleeping bag's weight was more than they wanted to carry in the Afghanistan desert and only brought a poncho liner suffered even more. I had both pieces of my sleeping bag and loaned one of them out to a young officer who had not brought his. I could no longer deal with having him shivering and shaking, and I felt a little bad for him. After several days of this, I could not believe I caught myself wishing for the hot days of August. Luckily for us, this lousy weather lasted only for a few weeks, and then we got back to cool nights and warm days again. The attacks returned, as well.

SHARK ATTACK

During this time, I was involved in an incident that had become synonymous with my tour in Afghanistan. Whenever I find myself in a group of friends or military acquaintances, the story gets retold, usually by my wife or kids, who got it from Major Sprague.

While living at Strong Point Centre, Major Sprague and I had an area just inside the entrance to the bunker where we slept and had our extra kit. It was a square, sandbagged area that had just enough room for our two cots and a foot or so on either side to stand. There were just six inches in the middle of the two cots that separated them. It almost looked like one bed.

I do not typically remember my dreams or nightmares in detail, but one night was different. I took Mefloquine, a medication used to prevent or treat malaria that was given to all Canadian soldiers while in Afghanistan. It was taken weekly and did have some side effects, which differed from person to person. Some of the side effects could be mental health problems, hallucinations, anxiety, or things like poor balance, seizures and ringing in the ears, most of which I already had from my previous attack.

On that night, I was sleeping on my cot under my poncho liner, fully dressed except for my boots. Sleeping peacefully, about six inches from me on his cot, was Major Sprague. I woke up several times throughout the night because I was having a nightmare, but I couldn't remember it once I was awake. Finally, I fell into a deep sleep, and I found myself having another nightmare. In it I was underwater, wearing a diver's suit with a large knife in one hand and being chased by several sharks.

I have never dived in my life, and even worse, I'm a non-swimmer. In my dream I swam as fast as possible, but the sharks were catching up, and one was almost at my feet. I stopped suddenly, and there was a quick and vicious hand-to-flipper battle that took place, with the shark slowly sinking into the water with vast amounts of blood coming from a large wound in its chest. The other sharks were almost right next to me, so I started swimming again. I was going as fast as possible, but the sharks were catching up, and I panicked. There were too many of them, and I was by myself. I needed to swim faster. I needed to get to shore. Which way was the shore?

I was panicking more, and I was swimming as fast as humanly possible. My arms and legs were going a mile a minute, and the sharks were still catching up. I believed I was going to die. As the sharks surrounded me and the end was near, I heard, "Sergeant Major, Sergeant Major," and my world was shaking. My eyes popped open, and I was breathing hard, sweating, scared, and laying on my stomach. Major Sprague was using his foot to kick my cot.

It took me a few seconds to realize where I was and what had happened. Major Sprague had a look of concern on his face, and he asked me if I was okay. I was still panting as I told him about my nightmare. When I was about to put my legs over the side of the cot, I realized that I was in real pain. While escaping from the sharks, I had been thrashing on my bed and had been driving my legs and shins as well as my arms onto the metal bar at either end of the cot. As I looked down, I saw blood and huge bruises. Both my feet and shins were swollen to about twice their normal size. My arms were aching, and I had huge bruises on both my forearms. It hurt just to raise them.

What had just happened?

Major Sprague told me that he'd been woken up by some loud banging and his cot being shaken. When he looked over, I was on my stomach, my legs and hands were swinging wildly and I looked like I was holding my breath. At first, he said he was scared to wake me because he didn't know how I would react. He moved my weapons out of reach and then used his foot to shake me. It took him several attempts to get me to wake up and by then I was gasping for breath and terrified.

"If you had stopped breathing," he said with a smile, "I was not doing mouth to mouth on you. You'd be dead."

Daylight came shortly afterward, and it was only then that I saw the full damage I had done to my legs and arms. The bruises were extensive, and the swelling would take days to go down. I could not get my boots on and spent most of the day lying around on my cot with my feet up on something to help with the swelling. The Company medic wanted to send me to FOB Wilson to get looked at, but I wanted no part in that. It was embarrassing enough without being medevacked.

I was not naive enough to think this would remain a secret. Others in the bunker had heard the commotion, and as is the Army way, this story would need to be told. As Major Sprague had already shown with the story about reading over the radio, he would be sharing this with anyone who would listen, all for a good laugh. I understood that, as I would have done the same thing in his place.

I don't know if Mefloquine had anything to do with this episode, but it was one of several occasions in theatre that I had terrible nightmares that left me scared and confused. I continued to have bad dreams and nightmares, especially in the months following my tour, but nothing to that extreme. Even so, I kicked and injured Julie during some of my dreams and nightmares, but none were as realistic as the one with the sharks.

For the record, I do believe that Major Sprague, as my Command Team Partner and friend, was ready to perform mouth to mouth if I needed it, but he'll never admit to that.

BITS AND PIECES

Around that same time, the Company went into KAF for a day or so to get a hot shower, clean clothes, a fresh meal, and a comfortable bed in an air-conditioned room. I do not think any of us were looking forward to the road move back through Kandahar, but the thoughts of a Tim Horton's coffee were enough for me to take the risk.

Once again, Three-Niner Tac and three LAVs from one of the platoons would travel together. It was one of the few times that we travelled anywhere in this province that we did not get hit. We did, however, once again have an escalation of force.

A white pickup truck continually closed on the rear LAV and then fell back. After several attempts by the soldiers in the air sentry hatch to wave him back, they fired a warning shot into the road in front of the vehicle. The pickup truck did stop after the warning shot, but I heard later that a woman on the street had been hit with a ricochet and had a severe wound, although not a life-threatening one. This was another one of those situations where we were told by our higher headquarters that we needed to be more professional and make better decisions when it came to an escalation of force.

We typically just ignored them because they were not on the ground.

Both Major Sprague and I were hesitant to second-guess our soldiers when they made decisions because we did not want them to hesitate. It could cost lives. They understood their rules of engagement, and we believed that our soldiers would make the right decisions when called upon. We told them many times that if they made the decision based on the rules of engagement and their experience, we would support them fully. And we did. We also told all our soldiers that if they did not follow the rules of engagement or made unethical decisions, we would prosecute them fully.

We made it safely into KAF at around 1900 hours, and, after a shower and a pizza on the boardwalk, I got a message to call my brother-in-law working in KAF. Tim was not a soldier, but he served his country for many years and now found himself in the same dangers as everyone else in KAF. Tim worked behind the wire in a compound that had very controlled access, and only those with specific requirements could enter. A few months earlier, Tim had been with Julie and the kids when MWO Mark Brander had linked up with them on the road in front of our house to tell them that I had been wounded. Now, he was here in Afghanistan with me.

I couldn't wait to see him, and I almost ran over to the compound. At the compound gate I had to use a speaker to ask for Tim. A few minutes later he came out, and it was like a weight had been lifted off my shoulders. At times like these, the familiarity of family means so much. Tim is Julie's younger brother, and he had accepted me into their family right from the beginning. He had also done a lot for Julie, JJ, and Jana when I was not around. Tim always stepped up. Tim and his wife, Julie Cullen, have served Canada and the people of this great country for many years, but unlike those of us in uniform, they would not receive the public recognition they deserved. To both Tim and Julie, thank you for your service to this country.

I met up with Tim again after his shift. We had supper together in one of the mess halls, where I introduced him to the Battle Group Commander, Lieutenant-Colonel Lavoie, and the Battle Group Sergeant Major. We hung out for about an hour or so, and then we once again had to go our separate ways—Tim back to get ready for another shift and me back to my room to get some rest and depart for enemy territory again. Having the opportunity to see and speak with Tim rejuvenated me and boosted my morale.

As January slowly slipped by, my thoughts started going to our redeployment back to Canada. Even though we did not have any dates, we knew that beginning in February, the 2 RCR Battle Group from Gagetown, New Brunswick, would begin arriving. January had been a quiet month compared to the previous six, but we still had daily engagements with the enemy. Usually, it was only one or two insurgents sneaking in and taking a few shots at us or firing an RPG. Then they disappeared into the countryside as we pursued them with air assets or our high-tech LAV sights.

We started hearing bits and pieces of the redeployment plan. We had already seen the leadership of the new Battle Group, who had done their tactical recce a few weeks earlier. The tactical recce consisted of all the senior leaders of the 2 RCR Battle Group.

There was only one noteworthy incident that occurred while the recce was in our area of operations. A senior officer from 2 RCR and several others from across the Battle Group were in FOB Zettelmeyer when Omer Lavoie put them in their place. The officer spoke to his fellow visiting officers, talking about how he would do things differently once he was in command. He did not like how we were in bunkers and defensive positions. He said he would take his soldiers out, find the Taliban, wipe them out and not hide behind sandbags. I heard the conversation, and so did Lavoie. He immediately approached the officers and told them to shut the fuck up, as they had no idea what they were talking about. He went on to say we had lost a lot of soldiers on this tour and that they would lose many as well with that kind of attitude.

The officers walked away with their heads hung low and silent.

We learned a short time later that Charles Company would be replaced by a company of soldiers from the PPCLI attached as part of the 2 RCR Battle Group. This news also informed us that we would be the last Company to be replaced because the PPCLI Company would not deploy in LAVs but would use RG-31s. The RG-31 was a 4x4 multi-purpose, mine-resistant, ambush-protected infantry vehicle manufactured in South Africa, and was selected because it is highly resistant to mine and IED strikes. The major drawback was that it was not as heavily armed as our LAVs.

Because this decision had been made late, the Patricias were now scrambling to get their soldiers qualified as drivers and gunners on this new vehicle and needed to take the extra time in Canada to make sure they were ready. This fact would also change the plan for our handover, as we would not be able to integrate together as fully as we had done in August. We would be travelling in two completely different vehicles, and they would all have to be manned separately rather than mixing crews and sections. The worst part for most of our soldiers was that while portions of our Battle Group would be heading home as early as the first week of February, it would be close to mid-March before Charles Company departed. We would be engaging the enemy up to that last day.

We had always been the Company to step up, and this was no different.

DEPARTURE FROM AFGHANISTAN

Around the third week of February, we received word that one of the Companies from 2 RCR that had arrived already would take over our positions on Route Summit. We would move into KAF and prepare to redeploy back to Canada. Everyone was excited, and, over the next few days, we were able to hand the Strong Points over and move safely to KAF. We would not get the treatment we thought we would get or even deserved as we rolled onto the airfield. I think everyone was looking forward to relaxing in comfortable quarters with air conditioning, some privacy and relative safety while waiting for our flights to Canada.

Within hours of rolling in, we got the word that all our soldiers would have to move out of their comfortable air-conditioned rooms and into the BAT (the "Big Ass Tent"). Instead, all the incoming Hobbits would have our rooms while they were there handing over with our outgoing Hobbits.

The BAT was a large canvas structure that had hundreds of bunk beds minus mattresses stacked and lined up so that you had everyone living on top of each other. The roof was torn and leaking. The floor was mud and dirt, and there was zero privacy. Now, this is not complaining for the sake of complaining, as even this was better than what we had for most of the tour. I was frustrated once again with the system. How is it possible to bring in a company of soldiers who had spent the last six months fighting and dying in the dirt of Panjwai and put them in a shithole for two or three weeks while they are waiting to go home? And all so that the Hobbits, who have just come to Afghanistan from their comfortable beds in Canada, have a nice, air-conditioned room on their arrival?

Once again, Charles Company made the best of a bad situation. We took advantage of the relative safety of KAF and the fresh food and hot water to get our equipment and ourselves ready for the handover.

PART THREE - AFGHANISTAN

The first members of the Patricia Company arrived somewhere around March 1. So, Major Sprague, I, and the last of the Company prepared to depart Afghanistan on March 10. It is surprising how quickly you become acclimatized to the good life in KAF. After a couple of days of this fine living, it was a bit of a downer when we received orders that we would be doing some low-level operations a few kilometres outside of KAF. Some of the soldiers were only a few days from leaving, and the most anyone had left was perhaps a week, so we were now short timers. I could see the apprehension and concern on the faces of some when we told them we were going out again. These were not essential missions, and most included three or four LAVs and maybe a couple of RG-31s with about two dozen RCR and PPCLI soldiers.

The first one was a hasty roadblock on Highway 1 about three kilometres from KAF with a handful of the Afghan police. We used the LAVs, barbed wire and dragons' teeth to set it up. The police searched each car under our watchful eye and heavy firepower and questioned the drivers and passengers. After about an hour, which was long enough for the word to get out, we packed up, moved to a new location, and set up all over again. We did this for about four hours, and then we packed up and moved back to KAF.

Mission accomplished for day one. No one had been hurt or killed.

We did this same sort of task on several more occasions over the next few days. Each time, we held our breath that no one would get hurt.

CLUSTER BOMBS

We came awfully close on one of those occasions to having disaster strike. We had moved to a location astride one of the roads believed to move fighters and weapons into Panjwai. After setting up the roadblock and placing our vehicles to provide overwatch and firepower, we moved our headquarters LAV off the road where we could keep an eye on the whole operation. We lowered the ramp and stepped outside when one of our soldiers noticed that the ground was littered with what looked like some tiny metal objects. We automatically froze; we were in the middle of either a minefield or a bunch of unexploded anti-personnel cluster bombs. We slowly had all the soldiers follow their steps back into the LAV and look over the side to make sure we hadn't run over anything. We then had the driver track his route back out to the road.

This took a few terrifying moments, but, finally out on the paved route we stopped to look back at where we had come from. There were hundreds of these cluster bombs everywhere. Somehow, we had pulled in among them but not on them. We maintained security in the area and had to wait a few extra hours for the engineers to send out some explosive folks to get rid of these things. We learned from the engineers that these were probably dropped from an American B-1 Bomber and were extremely dangerous. These are intended to be used against enemy vehicles or personnel. However, many do not explode on contact and so have killed and maimed many civilians because they are shiny, look harmless and people will pick them up. The engineers collected about sixty of the bomblets and destroyed them in place with explosives.

We said goodbye to another group of our soldiers from Kandahar, and now we were only three days away from leaving ourselves. We were short timers. The Battle Group change of command had taken place and 2 RCR were in control. Only a handful of soldiers from 1 RCR were still present. 2 RCR received orders that they would be moving by force into the same areas we had previously gone into during Operation Falcon's Summit, and initially we were to be part of it. We explained that we were leaving in three days and had no intention of leaving KAF again. We were dropped from the plan.

As my final day in Kandahar came, I was of two minds and a little bit sad. This country had taken so much from us as a Company and from me personally. Now it was over, and I don't know if we ever accomplished what we wanted. However, I was going home alive, which was more than many others did.

As I was sitting in the BAT on my last night in Kandahar, the emotions flooded over me. I was frightened and overwhelmed. I had some emotional days over the past seven months—losing soldiers, seeing them perform heroically, seeing my family or having to say goodbye to them—but this was different. These emotions were confusing. There was a sense of relief and joy, but there was also an almost-paralyzing feeling of guilt which shook me to the core.

I had to get off my bed and walk away as I was overcome with emotion and started shaking. I spent the next hour walking around KAF, trying to pull myself together. Eventually I did, but not until I had torn myself up over having survived. Losing soldiers is a terrible burden that many have faced before me, and more will face in the future, but it is an empty gut-wrenching feeling when it is you. I have heard it called "survivor's guilt," but it was much more than that for me. It was very personal. I had a feeling of pride and love for these guys that most could never understand, and to make matters worse, some of those who died were personal friends.

To top it all off, I placed extra blame on myself for Warrant Officer Frank Mellish's death.

As I walked around the dark, dusty roads of KAF, I wondered how I was ever going to be able to be happy and enjoy life after my decisions had cost Frank his life. I was going home to my family, I had all my parts intact, or, at least, most of them, and I would be able to watch my children grow up, graduate, go off to college or university, fall in love and get married. What about Frank's boys?

Ten years have passed since that lonely walk around KAF, and there is hardly a day that passes that I do not feel the guilt return. It is the first thought that comes to my mind when I see my wife or kids smile, see them accomplish something or even when I accomplish something myself. At those moments when I should be happy, there is always a bitter taste in my mouth. Why me, why do I get to be here?

Over those seven months, many soldiers of the Battle Group had been killed and wounded. Charles Company Combat Team took the brunt of that, with several killed and dozens injured, with many of those still suffering today. As the Officer

PART THREE - AFGHANISTAN

Commanding Charles Company, Major Matthew Sprague, and, to a lesser degree, Captain Steve Brown have had to live with the burden of command and the decisions they had to make on the battlefield that cost lives and left soldiers terribly wounded.

I don't envy them for a moment, but I've taken it personally as well. As the Sergeant Major of Charles Company, I was part of the Command Team that sent our soldiers into situations where they were killed or injured and that is something I have to live with. The part that hurts the most is always wondering if I could have changed any of those outcomes.

DECOMPRESSION IN CYPRUS

I did not really get a sense of safety or security until I was on the ground in Cyprus and en route to our hotel in Larnaca. We arrived at a beautiful resort with water and sand, it was clean and smelled fresh and I was excited to be here. I tried to push the feelings of guilt to the back of my mind.

We were some of the last soldiers from our Battle Group to go through decompression, so the hotel staff and the Canadian military staff who were there to assist were prepared for us. Over the past few weeks, there were several incidents as soldiers came through, including a sergeant being attacked and beaten badly in his room by some young soldiers who believed they had a bone to pick. Alcohol gave them the courage to act. A hotel TV dropped from the 10th floor down into the lobby area caused quite a stir as well, and several soldiers got so drunk that the local police were called to either arrest them or remove them from a local establishment.

Although some of the staff has been to Afghanistan, they had not been part of our Task Force. They had decided that soldiers were becoming too excessive in their drinking, resulting in some disciplinary issues, and they had placed some restrictions on us as we arrived. This decision included being back in the resort at a specific time and allowing no alcohol in the rooms. Lots of the young guys wanted to head downtown, get drunk and maybe get lucky. We older married guys just wanted to lie in our room and have a few beers. Now, even this was forbidden.

My soldiers and I had just come from a war zone and had put our lives on the line daily, and now we had some Hobbit treating us like children. I am a firm believer in holding individuals responsible for their actions and not punishing everyone for the actions of a few. I was a little pissed that those who had come before us had acted so unprofessionally that they had forced the staff to make drastic decisions. There was a genuine concern that someone would be injured or arrested for something terrible. Near the top of the problems was the probability of something making it to the papers and embarrassing Canada and the Cypriot government. I understood all of this, and that was not what I wanted, but, at the same time we were grown men and women who had just been fighting on behalf of our country. They needed to show us the respect we deserved.

I spoke to the Charles Company soldiers and warned them about being idiots, to watch their drinking and behaviour, and to enjoy themselves. Afterward I wondered how many of them heard a word I said? I recalled those same types of talks from my Sergeant Major many times over the years, and usually as he walked away, we would forget every word.

As I was thinking this, Warrant Officer Dave Marsh, a fellow soldier from 1 RCR and now part of the Canadian staff, came up to me with a female Canadian MP who I also knew. He said that I should come with them as they had gotten my room key already and I didn't need to wait at the front with everyone else. As the rest of the soldiers were getting their room keys, Dave and the MP sergeant escorted me outside the hotel and into a separate area where suites were. I asked them what was up, and they said they had been able to acquire a few upscale suites from the resort and provide them to some special folks as they arrived.

This was, by far, the nicest suite I have ever had. It was two bedrooms and two stories, all marble, including the two bathrooms and the living room. It had an outdoor patio with a barbecue and an outdoor fridge with a stereo and surround sound. I was shocked and could only say thanks.

Dave just smiled. "You deserve it. And by the way, there's a surprise in the fridge for you."

I rushed over and opened the fridge. It was full of local beers and wine, and on the counter were two bottles of whiskey. So much for no booze in the room!

I really appreciated what they had done for me, but I kept it quiet. I didn't want to send the wrong message to the troops. Dave told me that the staff and the MPs would be very lenient with the soldiers if they did not cross the line.

"And that line is very wide," said the MP sergeant with a smile. That made me feel better, knowing that these guys were here to ensure the troops were safe and looked after.

That night was free time for everyone, but at 0800 the following day, there would be some mandatory briefings and time for individual sessions with psychologists, social workers, or religious leaders. The troops had been warned that if they failed to make it at 0800, they would not be allowed to drink for the remainder of the stay.

We also had the opportunity to sign up for some relaxing stuff, like golfing, fishing and local tours. I signed up with a small group of guys for the fishing trip and a dinner evening with belly dancing. There were lots of more aggressive and fun things for the younger guys, but my generation just wanted a fine meal and to relax. My first night was spent at the hotel bar having a few drinks and telling stories, but by 2200, I was already starting to feel the effects of alcohol and a lack of sleep. That feeling of anxiety and guilt also started to return. Alcohol has a strange way of affecting emotions, so I headed off to bed in my luxury suite.

I had a couple of sleepless hours as I tossed and turned as my mind raced back and forth between Afghanistan and home. After I did fall asleep, I woke up twice in a cold sweat and screaming but had no memory of what had occurred. Eventually, I fell into a sound sleep and got some well-needed rest.

PART THREE - AFGHANISTAN

THINKING OUTSIDE THE BOX

The next morning, I was awake at about 0500. I got dressed, headed for the pool for a quick dip in the shallow end and then returned to the suite for a shower and breakfast. I grabbed a notebook, headed to the main lobby area and then to the conference room for the first briefing. As I approached the conference area, I saw several people standing around and heard a commotion. As I pushed my way past some senior officers and NCMs, I found one of my young soldiers from Charles Company curled up on the floor in front of the door, obviously still in his jeans and t-shirt from the previous night. One of the civilian briefers who had arrived early to set up was a little concerned.

The officers in the area were talking about getting the MPs to come and get this drunk soldier and that he was in big trouble, but I just brushed by all of them.

"You guys don't have to worry," I said, "I've got this." I reached down and woke up the soldier, and as soon as he saw me, he jumped up.

"Sir, I'm not late, am I?"

He said he had gotten back to the resort at about 0300 or so (long past curfew) and wanted to make sure he wasn't late for the brief. He figured the best place to sleep was in front of the briefing room door as someone would have to wake him up to get in.

I told him he had twenty minutes to get to his room, shower, brush his teeth, and return. He hardly allowed me to finish, and he was already running toward the elevator. I started laughing as some of the senior officers looked on.

"Gentlemen, that is the kind of soldier I want in my company, always thinking and not afraid to think outside the box."

A few of the officers were senior staff officers from the Task Force who had been in KAF (Hobbits), and I could tell from their looks that they disagreed, but I didn't give a shit. They didn't question my decision. As we sat down for the first brief, I saw the young soldier sitting in the back with wet hair and a smile on his face.

I never spoke of the issue again other than to tell the story over a few beers for a good laugh.

I attended all the mandatory briefings with my soldiers, and after people got comfortable there were some excellent discussions. I believe that at least some of my soldiers found it helpful, even if most just wanted to get to the relaxing stuff.

I spent most of my time relaxing by the pool and reading, except for the fishing trip and the dinner. I had signed up for the Lebanese Mezze dinner and belly dancing. About ten of us sat together. The meal was terrific, the wine flowed, and halfway through the dinner, the lights dimmed, and the music started. A sultry figure appeared out of the back, wearing lace and flowing gowns and gyrating to the music. There was only one other table occupied, so we had the full attention of the dancer. We were all watching with amusement, and then as our belly dancer got closer and removed her face veil, we all gasped. She must have been sixty years old, and her face, as well as her belly, showed the strains of age.

I will admit that she was a good belly dancer, but she was not what we nine male and one female Canadian soldier expected. However, like most Canadians, we got on board and cheered her on and clapped as she performed. The more we hollered and cheered, the more she gyrated. I had a great meal, good entertainment, and great company, so it was a huge success.

The following morning, all those who had signed up for the half-day fishing trip met at the pier at 0500. It was a small boat with no luxury, but the captain made the day. Once we were all aboard, he opened a beer and whiskey compartment, and we headed out. The fishing was unsuccessful, as we caught only an eel and some sculpin, but the comradeship amongst the seven or eight Canadians and the Greek captain was great. We had to stop along the shore to pick up some more beer to finish the trip.

The remainder of my time in Cyprus was spent relaxing and preparing myself to reintegrate into my family. The briefers told us not to be surprised if we had difficulty fitting in immediately because our wives and children have had to move on without us. Their lives didn't stop for seven months.

I had to deal with one situation when one of my soldiers had gotten really drunk and ended up in a bar that was probably owned or at least controlled, by the mafia. When he eagerly decided to buy drinks for the lovely lady who wanted to spend time with him, he failed to realize that each glass was $100 and meant that she would spend a certain amount of time with him. When his bill arrived, and was expected to pay about $800, he got agitated and the local police were called. We were able to have our Military Police intervene, and they negotiated the price down to $200. The soldier was told not to return.

A second incident happened with one of my soldiers who arrived in Cyprus as I was leaving and was part of the last group of soldiers from our Battle Group to redeploy. I received word while in Canada that one of my soldiers had been arrested. He was in a local jail—the Cypriots were not happy with him, and it had made the local paper. As the story goes, he was highly intoxicated and somehow ended up at a bar by himself. This was against the direction that had been given to remain together in groups. However, you couldn't force someone to go back to the hotel if he didn't want to go.

He was drunk enough that he kept falling off his chair, smashing glasses, and just being a pain to all the locals in the bar. Because no other Canadians were around, the local police responded. They were sick and tired of dealing with drunken Canadians. According to the soldier, when he didn't cooperate he was grabbed by several Cypriot police, handcuffed, and treated very roughly.

As they are walking him outside toward the police car, the Canadian soldier lowered his head and then brought it back up viciously, driving it into the face of the cop holding him. The police officer's nose was shattered, with parts of it pushed up into his skull. The media had found out, and it had been published in the local paper. It would be several days of waiting to see what condition the police officer was in and, if he had died, this would be a completely different tale. The cop was lucky, and the Canadian soldier was luckier.

The Military Police and the Canadian consulate negotiated the charges down so that the soldier was sentenced to days served, awarded a huge fine, and kicked out of the country. That soldier also had to face me on return, as well as military justice. This soldier was fortunate that the police officer had not been more seriously injured or died, as he would have been facing years in a Greek Cypriot prison.

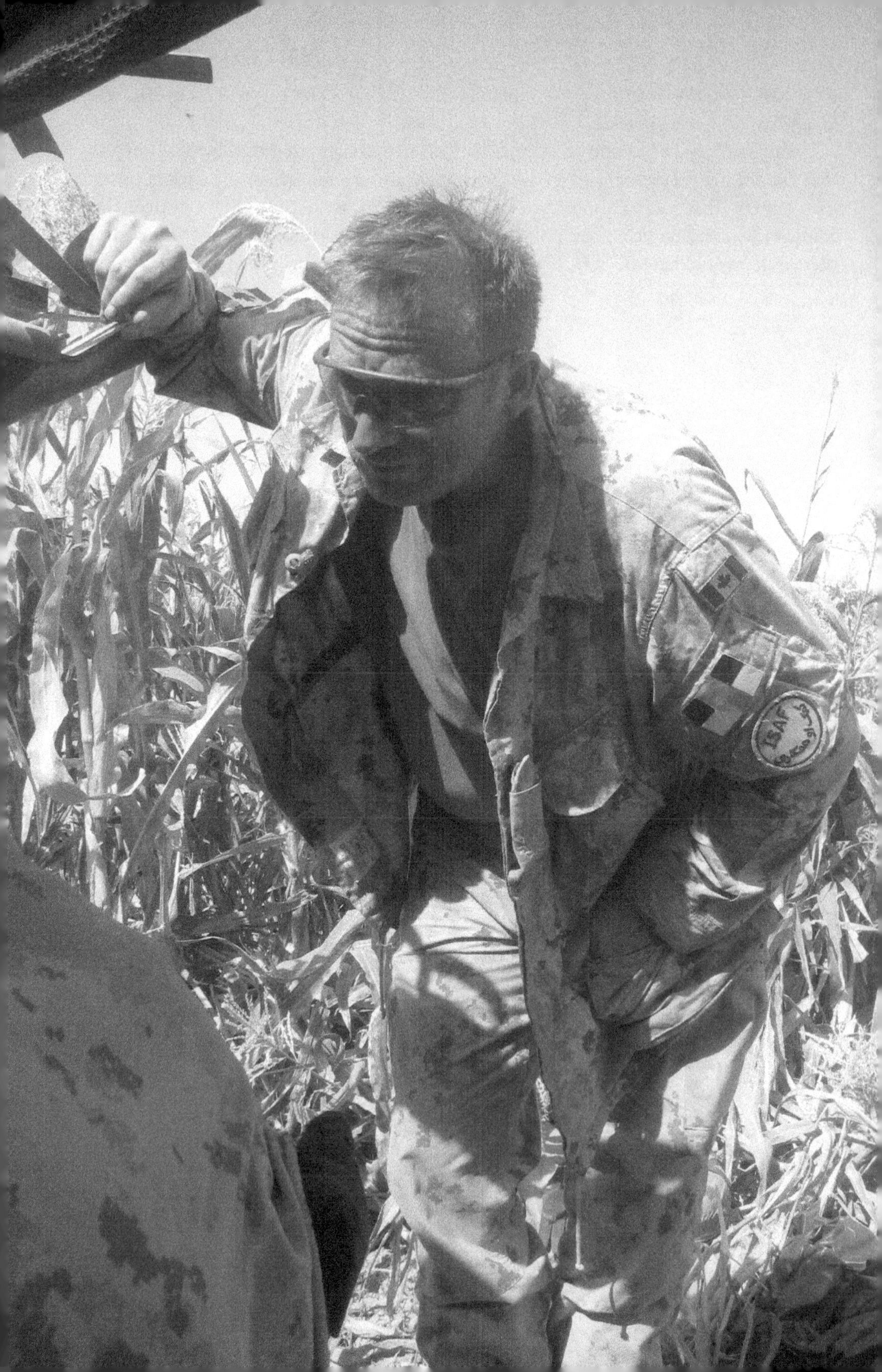
ISAF

OPPOSITE: Too much sun, Objective Rugby, 2006. (Charles Company photo)
ABOVE: Strong Point Centre, overlooking what would become Route Summit. (Author's photo)
BELOW: Some of 39er Tac at Strong Point Center, MWO Barnes 3rd from the right. (Charles Company photo)

ABOVE: FOB Zettlemeyer. (Charles Company photo)
BELOW: Carrying my friend and mentor, CWO Booby Girouard, to his last flight home. (DND)

ABOVE: Two avid Habs fans, Lieutenant-Colonel Lavoie and I, during Operation Baaz Tsuka. (Charles Company photo)

BELOW: Colonel Vance and Lieutenant-Colonel Lavoie conducting the Ortona Toast (Charles Company photo)

ABOVE: Lunch with Maj Sprague at Strong Point Center. (Author's photo)
BELOW: Award of medals by the Governor General. Left to right, Barnes (Meritorious Service Medal), Funnell (Medal of Military Valour), Teal (Star of Military Valour), O'Rourke (Medal of Military Valour), Somerset (MSM), Niefer (Medal of Military Valour), Fawcett (Medal of Military Valour), Sprague (MSM). (DND)

ABOVE: *Myself and Rick Mercer in FOB Wilson, December 2006. (Author's photo)*
BELOW: *Major Sprague and Christie Blatchford during Operation Baaz Tsuka. (Charles Company photo)*
FOLLOWING PAGE: *Receiving communion on Christmas Day, 2006. (Author's photo)*

...iers celebrate an Afghan Christmas amid shadows of the...

...receives communion from Padre Guy Chapdelaine as troops from Charles Company attend a Christmas Day service in Afghanistan's Panjwai...

Dark humour on a grim holiday

CHRISTIE BLATCHFORD

FORWARD OPERATIONS BASE
WILMEYER, AFGHANISTAN

The rain began late on Christmas Eve.

It was not midnight mass — that and the sound of fates and the occasional burp of machine-gun fire and the claps of thunder and the roar of light ar-

moured vehicles and the crunch of machine and boats on gravel, all of it melding into the low ominous rumble that forms the elevator music of this spooky place.

The soldiers of Charles Company Combat Team, 1st Battalion the Royal Canadian Regiment, got some extra shut-eye, with reveille at 8 on Christmas morning not the usual 5:45 or 6. And then they went up for the normal standing-around period, or one of them, which

make up the grunt's life when all is quiet. Next thing, a couple of vehicles went the few kilometres up to Masum Ghar, the next little Canadian base south of here and just down the Panjwai Valley, to fetch the Christmas meals.

Sergeant-Major John Barnes gathered the boys around them, in the centre of the gravel that, with a row of HESCO bunkers and a few Sea Can trailers and some tents, is this little base, nothing more.

"Make sure you know your kit [flak jacket and...] he said, "in case we start coming rounds."

The 40-year-old Officer manding of Charles Com[pany] Major Matthew Sprague, words. He's not one for [many] but managed to be pos[itive] revealing despite himself [that] he is.

See BLATCHFORD on pa[ge]

...nmerry season for Bédard

PART FOUR
POST-AFGHANISTAN
(2009-2017)

39

AFTERMATH

The flight home, going through customs and the bus ride to Petawawa were all a blur, and I only really remember the moment when we were rolling onto the base in Petawawa. I was excited but cautious, and I didn't know why. I was thinking about the families that would not be at the drill hall to meet their soldiers and the families whose lives have been changed forever because of their loss. Guilt is a terrible thing, and it came back in a flurry as the bus stopped.

I stayed seated on the bus as others rushed off to meet their loved ones. I thought back to each soldier we left behind, and I wondered if the families would ever forgive us and whether I would ever forgive myself. I remember it was cold, and I shivered as I got off the bus and saw all the families, primarily women and children, as they rush toward their heroes. Then I saw Julie, JJ and Jana, and I knew that everything would be all right. I was home, safe, and that needed to be enough, at least for now. As I stood there holding my family, I told myself that I would not allow the guilt and the negative emotions to control my life. I had suffered headaches and neck pain since September 3, and I promised myself not to let that define me.

As I sit here today, I believe that I failed on both counts, and it is only now, ten years later, that I am trying to fix myself.

Julie would say to me over the years, "You always look after your soldiers. When are you going to look after yourself?"

I admit that I did not pay that much heed. I initially used prescription painkillers and then pockets full of Tylenol with codeine to take away the pain or at least get it to an acceptable level. Julie would make jokes about us being drug dealers because Tylenol with codeine is controlled. It's kept behind the counter at the pharmacy, and even though you do not need a prescription, you need to ask for it.

We started driving around the local area because we were embarrassed to keep asking at the same place in Petawawa or Pembroke, as these bottles would contain up to two hundred pills and would last me for only about three weeks. Anytime we went anywhere to visit, or for work, we would buy more pills. There were times we would have several bottles at home. I never left the house without having a pocket full and, if I was leaving the area for an extended time, I carried a bottle. If I saw that I was getting low or, by some strange occurrence, I found myself without pills, I panicked. There were days I took only seven or eight, but most days, I took between fifteen and twenty, depending on my daily activities. I hid the extent of the headaches and my neck injury from the military for years, as I did not want my career to suffer, but I could not hide them from my family.

After returning from Afghanistan, I was lucky to be placed in positions of authority that allowed me to have flexibility in how I performed my job. I could close my office door and turn off the lights when the headaches were terrible, and if needed, I could sneak away and go home early. No one ever questioned my actions. I was truly fortunate to have some great bosses whom I did tell about my issues, but I also told them it would not affect my ability to do my job. They were incredibly supportive when things were bad. For years, my life was about taking pills to numb the physical pain and allow me to function. I believe I was successful—I continued to have a great career, get promoted and moved into senior jobs. But it was all at the expense of my health and quality of life, and my family as well.

The first few days and weeks after my return from Kandahar were not easy for me, but I could always find my way through the most challenging times. During those first few days, I never felt comfortable, even in my own house, and I had to force myself to remain calm. Everyone wanted to see me and welcome me back and thank me for my service, but deep down, I did not want to be part of any of it.

I had a plan to visit the families of all my soldiers who had been killed and injured. I quickly realized that I could not do that because of my immense feelings of guilt, anger, and what would be later diagnosed as anxiety and depression. I had difficulty going out in public, and I was always afraid that someone was watching, ready to do me harm. I panicked if I was forced to leave a paved surface and walk across the grass in case of mines or IEDs. If a car backfired or a horn honked, I would jump and start sweating and shaking, sometimes unable to control myself.

All those things were happening while I was trying to adjust to these new surroundings. I was also trying to redefine my role with Julie, JJ and Jana and get help for my massive headaches, troubling neck and loss of hearing. The nightmares had remained from Afghanistan, and on a few occasions, my thrashing and uncontrollable fear caused injuries to Julie while we both slept. I felt terrible and was grateful that my wife laughed off the few bruises and sores, and she never made a big deal out of the nightmares.

After a couple of weeks, I began feeling a little bit more comfortable, and things were starting to get into a new normal. The kids were in school, Julie was back at work, and I found myself happy to be alone and not have to deal with people.

PART FOUR - POST-AFGHANISTAN (2009-2017)

NEWFOUNDLAND VISIT

It was around this time that I decided to take a trip to Newfoundland to visit my family.

Even though my Mom and Dad had passed, I still had brothers and sisters who had been very worried about me and needed to see that I was all right. I spoke with my sister, Karen, and told her of my upcoming trip. She immediately asked me if I could bring my dress uniform with me for some pictures. I said yes and thought no more about it.

I knew something was up when Karen asked me to make sure I had my uniform readily available because they wanted me to change into it at the airport in St. John's for the one-hour trip to my hometown of Riverhead. I initially fought the idea and told her to make sure that there was no big deal made of my coming home. She said that just the family wanted to gather and welcome me home. I had a nagging feeling, but the headaches and stress I was under just allowed me to ignore it.

I landed in St. John's around mid-morning and was met in the baggage area by my oldest brother, Randy. While we waited for my bags, he asked me to go into the washroom and change into my uniform and, once again, I felt a little uncomfortable but followed directions. As we are driving on the highway, I asked Randy what was going on, and he told me that there was going to be a small gathering at the Legion in Riverhead, mostly family, to welcome me home. I still remember the look on his face, and I knew there was more to the story, but I let it go.

When we were a few miles from my hometown, Randy told me that a few cars were going to be meeting us at a place known as the "two-mile stretch," because of it being long and straight. As we came over the last hill before the stretch, I was forced to sit up and stare in awe as I looked at the vehicles waiting for us.

Riverhead is a small fishing village in a vast bay called Saint Mary's, and the population of the whole area is only in the few thousands, spread out over hundreds of miles. To say I was shocked is an understatement. There, waiting for us, must have been well over a hundred vehicles. They had banners and flags flying, and horns blared as we went by. Our car led a procession through Riverhead, then on to Coots Pond and down through Saint Mary's. Anyone who was not following us in a vehicle was standing in their front yard, waving, and clapping.

It went on for miles and miles.

I was a little bit in awe and a whole lot embarrassed. I had to hold back the tears as I read the dozens of signs thanking me for my service and welcoming me home. After driving through Saint Mary's, we turned around and took the same route back to Riverhead. When we pulled in at the Legion, the crowd of people, young and old, was overwhelming.

I put my beret on and stepped out of Randy's car to loud applause. A young female cadet walked over to me, saluted and asked me if I wanted to inspect the guard. At first, I was not prepared for this because, in all my shock, I hadn't noticed the local cadets formed up. I stammered, "Yes," and the young cadet took me to the formation. I walked up and down the files, speaking to each person. The weather was wet and miserable, but I figured if these young kids took the time and effort to do this for me, I was going to thank each one of them. I didn't know any of them personally, but I recognized almost all their last names, as they were the kids and grandkids of people with whom I had grown up. That was, by far, the highlight of the event, and I was so appreciative of those young boys and girls.

Following my inspection and a few words of praise for the cadets, everyone went inside the Legion. It was then that I noticed the sea of people. There were kids and the elderly and everyone in between. There were many people I knew and many more I did not. The Legion put on a grand affair as they welcomed me home and made me feel special. People were genuinely appreciative of what I had done, and everyone there took the time to come up and shake my hand. There was food and drink and lots of speeches, and I had an opportunity to respond with an address. I know that this was an effort between my brothers, sisters, the Legion, and the people of my hometown. They will be forever in my heart.

The one regret I had from this trip was that I had been asked to go to my old high school and speak to the kids, and I declined. I am sure that this was probably taken as a snub, but I was terrified to embarrass myself. I am considered a great speaker, and I can speak with or without notes for hours, but I think everything came to a head after the celebration at the Legion. I felt that I was not deserving of all the accolades, and I was afraid that I could not stand in front of those kids and talk about Afghanistan without saying something that I would regret, so I avoided it. In hindsight, I wish I had taken the time to speak with the kids at my old school. Perhaps there will be a second opportunity in the future.

The week in Newfoundland flew by and, before I knew it, I was back in Petawawa, my leave had ended, and I had to return to work.

ESCORTING FAMILIES TO AFGHANISTAN

I had settled into the job of Drill Sergeant Major (DSM) for 3 RCR, and the battalion was in full training mode for their upcoming deployment to Afghanistan.

CWO Ernie Hall came to see me with a request from higher to ask if I would be an escort as part of a plan to allow family members of the fallen to go to Afghanistan. I believe this was the brainchild of General Hillier, but my initial response was no and that I thought it was a terrible idea.

The war was still raging in southern Afghanistan, and soldiers were dying. KAF continued to receive incoming rockets and even direct attacks against the airfield. What was Canada thinking, sending grieving civilian families into an active war zone?

I was told that this might come down as a task and to be prepared to go. I remember thinking that I didn't want to return, especially as an escort for grieving families with hundreds of questions. A day or so later, I was pulled aside and told that Ottawa explicitly asked for me as some of those attending would be families of the fallen from Charles Company. I was taken aback as it had only been a year since I had returned. These families would still be in a state of grief, and I wasn't sure that I'd be able to handle the task.

I'd been able to suppress the feeling of guilt and anxiety for the past year. But now, those feelings and terrible memories came flooding back.

TASKING

A few days later, I received an email from some staff officer in Ottawa with the task's details, including dates and a list of family members. It was as if I was being told the decision had been made, and I was going.

I read the list very carefully and saw family members from Trooper Darryl

WHITE SCHOOL, BLACK MEMORIES

Caswell, Corporal Paul Davis, Corporal Brent Boland, Private Richard Green, and, to my dismay, Warrant Officer Frank Mellish. The names all jumped out at me, but one gave me a moment of pause: Officer Cadet Kendra Mellish, Frank's spouse, who had recently joined the military. I hadn't seen or spoken to Kendra since before we had deployed to Afghanistan in 2006, but her message about Frank had never been far from my thoughts. I immediately thought that there was no way that I would be able to face her, and I did not want to return to Afghanistan with her.

I remember telling CWO Hall that I was not interested in doing this task and that they would have to find someone else. He seemed good with that at the time, but obviously, someone put pressure on the 3 RCR Command Team, who then put pressure on me to do it. I was not ordered to do it or was threatened or coerced. In the end, I decided to accept this task as I was probably the best person and, as I've always done, I follow directions well.

The days leading up to my return to Afghanistan were a whirlwind as I had to quickly go through Departure Assistance Group, get all my shots, go through medical and dental, and see a social worker to make sure I was fit to go. I even had to do a piss test. I guess they do not test for excessive amounts of codeine, or I would have failed miserably.

I found this a little amusing, as I had been back from Afghanistan for only a year. I would be in the country for only two days, but I had to go through a whole barrage of stuff to ensure I was fit to return. I convinced my family to give me their blessing, as this was only a short task and was safe because if it were not, then we would not be taking families with us. I never really received any specifics about the role of the escort and what my duties were, except to say that we would be looking after the family members from start to finish. I would be responsible for Kendra and Frank's father, Barry Mellish, who would also be attending. I had never met Barry, but a quick check told me that he was a retired RCMP officer and a dedicated father.

BARRY AND KENDRA

I was very apprehensive as I walked into the airport and had my first contact with Barry and Kendra.

Barry was a large and confident man who shook my hand with a strength that said a lot about his character and attitude. His eyes, however, betrayed his grief and sadness and was something that I would focus on over the next several days. I introduced myself as MWO John Barnes and then identified myself as Frank's Sergeant Major in Afghanistan, as I did not want any secrets. I was unsure if he knew this fact, however, I would have been surprised if Kendra had not told him. I told him that I was deeply sorry for his loss and that Frank was a great Canadian hero and a good friend. All the time I am speaking with Barry, Kendra was standing a few feet behind him and I was avoiding all eye contact with her.

"I believe you know Kendra," he said. As my stomach turned and tightened, I

PART FOUR - POST-AFGHANISTAN (2009-2017)

looked her in the eyes and moved toward her.

I was almost sick, and the feeling of guilt and horror was overwhelming, but I forced myself to reach out. The tension was obvious as we hugged each other and, like a robot, I told her all the things I knew I needed to say. I told her about the honour of being asked to be their escort and how this was an opportunity to recognize Frank again for his heroics and sacrifice. I added that I would be at their beck and call.

As we sat and waited to board our aircraft for our flight to Dubai, we spoke quietly about day-to-day stuff and avoided the challenging topics, each of us knowing that we would be forced to confront all those demons before this trip was over. Barry remained very calm and collected. We spoke about Afghanistan and what it was like, what the people were like, and Charles Company. He never asked about specifics regarding Frank or his death, and I did not offer that information. Kendra and Barry seemed remarkably close, and they could continually be seen comforting each other. I looked around and saw the other escorts and families interacting, many sitting and speaking quietly while others laughed or just huddled together, and I thought, "How do they do it?"

I felt the tension between Kendra and myself and, to a lesser extent, Barry throughout the trip, but I tried my best to be a good escort and friend. I knew that when the time came, I would be prepared to speak honestly and tell them both all the details, including the last few moments of Frank's life. If requested, no details would be spared.

While sitting in Dubai, Kendra and Barry came to me with a request from another family on this journey to visit a small chapel in Spin Boldak. With the war ongoing, I knew it wasn't going to happen. The chapel was special to Barry and Kendra as well, as Frank had spoken about it in a phone call and a letter. Spin Boldak is a small town on the border with Pakistan where we had initially deployed in early August 2006. I tried to explain that it was unsafe to go to Spin Boldak and that we would not be allowed to leave Kandahar Airfield for security reasons, but the family of the fallen soldier was very persistent. I told her that I would check but that the chance was extremely low. I did mention the request to those leading this endeavour and was told that it would not happen.

I later told Barry and Kendra about our few days in Spin Boldak, described the camp and the surrounding area, as well as the small chapel that Frank had really fallen for. The French Special Forces that had occupied the camp before us had built the chapel. I had taken pictures of the chapel but told Kendra and Barry that my camera had been destroyed in the explosion or had been burned with my contaminated kit.

But, I found out that Kendra had pictures from Frank's camera of the chapel that she later shared with me. It was a special place in her eyes, as Frank was not overly religious but he did hold onto his faith. In his last letter to her, which she received after his death, he seemed to be making his peace with things. He told her he was not afraid to die, and besides, it didn't matter, he said. His exact words were powerful: "I loved you, always have and always will." That must of been so hard for Kendra to digest, knowing what had happened just before that letter arrived.

I was pleased to discover that we would be taking one of Canada's new CC-177 Globemaster strategic aircraft from Dubai to Kandahar. This large, beautiful aircraft is leaps and bounds ahead of the CC-130 Hercules I had taken each time I flew in or out of Afghanistan. I was amazed by the size and comfort. After ensuring everyone had on their helmets and protective gear, we boarded for our short flight to Kandahar.

I could tell from the faces of the family members that they were excited, scared and sad about this trip. When we touched down in Kandahar, many began to cry. I took a moment to reflect on where I was and the fact that I had believed that I would never be back here again. Yet here I was. I briefed Barry and Kendra on what to expect once the doors opened and to be prepared for the heat and the smell, which was already filling the plane.

The doors opened and as my feet touched down on the ground, I was almost floored by memories and events that had occurred here. There was a quick moment when I thought, "I'm not going to be able to do this." My thoughts were interrupted by someone who told us to move inside the hangar, which was still partially bombed out from earlier battles and where we would receive our safety briefing.

The briefing was typical and had not changed much from the previous year when I had arrived the first time but was particularly important for the families that would be here for the next twenty-four hours. It told them what to expect and how to react if the airfield came under attack from rockets or direct fire. It told them where they would be sleeping and where the closest bunkers were. There would be a camp tour, a good meal and then tomorrow, a ceremony at the cenotaph in honour of their fallen heroes. Then, they would be leaving to return to Dubai.

PROVIDING THE DETAILS

After supper that evening, Barry approached me and wanted to speak with me in private. My worst fears were about to be realized. He was not angry, but he was a little agitated and wanted to know what was happening. Why was I so distant from him and Kendra? Even though I had decided to be very honest and speak the truth, I did not. I told him some story about how I was still grieving, how I probably should not have come back because I was not ready, and that I was sorry that my emotions were getting in the way of assisting them to find some sort of closure. Barry just smiled and said he understood that this was hard on me as well, and I felt terrible about not being honest about my true feelings. We chatted about things for a few minutes, and Barry headed back to his room, and I walked around KAF, lost in my thoughts.

An hour or so later, I found myself outside Barry's door and asked him if I could have a few minutes of his time. He invited me in, and I started by telling him that I was sorry that I had not been honest with him and Kendra from the start and that I would tell him exactly what was going on. I told him the story of Kendra's concerns before deployment and that she had said to me that if Frank went, he would not come

PART FOUR - POST-AFGHANISTAN (2009-2017)

back alive. Barry just put out his hand, touched my shoulder and said that it was not my fault and that Kendra didn't blame me either. He suggested that I speak with her.

Barry then asked me with tears in his eyes if his son had suffered in his last moments and asked if I could go through those final moments with him. I explained to Barry that I was a little confused over events immediately after the explosion but would tell him everything I knew. I told him that Frank had not suffered and had died very quickly. I spoke candidly about the battle from the orders to move across the river early to the actual fight. I think he appreciated the honesty.

I told him that I believed that Frank died doing exactly what he always did, taking care of the troops and that he would not have had it any other way. I explained to him that Frank had been with the reserver platoon at the Casualty Collection Point, which is kept slightly behind the battle so that the commander has options if things go wrong, as they did.

I told him that when Frank had heard that Warrant Officer Rick Nolan was dead, his friend and fellow Platoon Second-in-Command, he had come running forward with Private William Cushley to help retrieve Rick's body. Seconds after speaking with me, the 82mm recoilless rifle round had hit him and taken his life, as well as killing Cushley. I explained that both soldiers received grievous wounds and died very quickly.

We cried together for a few moments, and then he asked me several other questions about the event. I answered as honestly as possible. I explained that Frank was a true Canadian hero and that he had died doing something that he firmly believed in, and that his loss was not in vain. I explained that Frank was a great soldier and a great father and committed fully to both. I told him that Frank was always looking out for his soldiers and put their interests ahead of his own.

Even though Barry was very emotional, I believe there was a sense of relief and comfort in hearing this from me. At least, I hoped that this might help with closure in the future.

That night while sleeping, the alarms went off, and a rocket landed somewhere in the camp with no casualties. It was a stark reminder to everyone of the dangers that were still present as we rushed to our bunkers.

The next morning after breakfast, I had the opportunity to sit down with Kendra and speak with her one on one. For some reason, the details of our chat have slipped away. I am at a loss as to the actual event. I know I told her how sorry I was about Frank and that I have carried the guilt of his death with me every day. I also said I would continue to feel guilty for the rest of my life. I don't remember her exact response at the time, but she's since reminded me that she told me that she could feel my grief and pain as if it was her own, that she didn't blame me, and that it was all in God's hands anyways.

At the time, though, I continued to feel uncomfortable, but I also have fond memories of Barry and Kendra following our chats. I also remember Kendra insisting on trying to get her a helicopter ride out to Ma'sum Ghar so she could see the exact area where Frank had died. This was still a very volatile region, and there was no way for the military to get that kind of authority for a civilian, though I understand that on some later visits, families may have gotten that wish.

COMMEMORATION CEREMONY

Later that second morning, we gathered at the beautiful marble cenotaph built to honour Canada's war dead. Surrounded by hundreds of soldiers from Canada and other Coalition nations, as well as a contingent of Afghan soldiers, the families were able to place a wreath at the foot of the marble monument.

It was a very sobering and unscripted moment when, following the Canadian and Afghan National Anthems, Jim Davis stood up to speak. His son Corporal Paul Davis had died on March 2, 2006, and he stood up in front of hundreds of Canadian and Afghan troops.

"Your bravery makes me extremely proud to be able to call myself Canadian," he said, "and I thank you for that." He then turned to the Afghan contingent and told the touching story of how a local Afghan family in Canada had attended his son's funeral to honour Paul's commitment and sacrifice. "When I looked into their eyes," he said, "I saw their hurt, and that is when I realized the true meaning of why my son died in your country. Now, I stand for the Afghan National Anthem as proudly as I do for the Canadian one."

Brigadier General Laroche, the Canadian Commander, thanked the relatives for their long and arduous journey and pledged that the sacrifice of the fallen soldiers would not be in vain. Colonel Abdul Bashir, Commander of the 1st Brigade, 205 Corps of the Afghan National Army, also paid tribute to those Canadians who had lost their lives.

"In the fight against al-Qaida and terrorism," he said, "the great country of Canada sacrificed a lot of its children, and today we are here to remember these heroes. Their names will be written in honour in the history of Afghanistan and Canada."

Next was a moment of silence, followed by a bagpipe rendition of Amazing Grace, which left no one with dry eyes. Then, one after the other, the families were escorted to the Cenotaph to place wreaths and flowers and to look at the gold-framed plaques commemorating their loved ones.

I heard Barry speaking to a reporter and telling them that he was glad that more children were now in school, farmers are getting more help, and Canadians had rebuilt many schools and hospitals. He said that he had come to Afghanistan because he wanted to know that Frank's death was not without meaning or was not careless or useless.

Those words struck me hard as they were remarkably like the words I had been saying to myself since that tragic day.

Barry then went on to say that he knew that his son had died in battle, trying to gain some freedom for the Afghan people, and we, as Canadians, sometimes take these freedoms for granted. Frank had given his life to try and get those freedoms over here and that he was satisfied that his son had not died in vain.

I felt tears flowing down my cheeks as I stood there and thought to myself, "There is a fine Canadian man."

As Barry finished up, a soldier walked by, turned to face the cenotaph, and offered a brisk salute. Barry was moved to tears and said, between sobs, "That is just respect for his fellow man."

Many families, including the Mellishes, remained around the cenotaph long after everyone else had left. It was almost as if leaving would be like saying a final goodbye to their loved ones. We just hung back and allowed them as much time as they needed. An hour or so later, when Barry and Kendra were ready to leave, it was almost like a weight had been lifted off their shoulders. There seemed to me to be a sense of peace about them.

I cannot put myself in their shoes, and I don't know what it is like to lose a son or a husband in the war, but I hope that the trip brought some sort of peace or closure to a terrible event. A part of me had hoped that this trip would also give some kind of closure for me, but it did not.

I continue to wonder if any of it was worth the huge cost we paid.

Upon return to Canada I made a promise to myself that I would keep in touch with Barry and Kendra, but especially Kendra.

The truth is: I did not.

I was a coward and I took the easy road, or at least an easier road.

Once again, I had failed.

I continued to ask for updates on Kendra and the two boys whenever I would meet someone that knew them or knew about them. This also became less frequent. I will never know if things would have turned out differently if I had stayed in touch, but what I do know is that I have lived with that feeling of guilt and failure for almost seventeen years.

My hope is that Kendra and the boys have found a way to move on with their new lives, all the while having to live with the grief of losing a husband, friend and father to a war that many are unsure was worth the sacrifice.

41

THE REAR PARTY

Several months after returning to Petawawa from Afghanistan, I received a phone call from the Regimental CWO asking me if I was interested in being posted from 1 RCR to 3 RCR as the Drill Sergeant Major. It is a great honour and a great opportunity, as the role is the senior MWO in the Battalion and is a stepping-stone to becoming a CWO.

I admit that I was hesitant because I was still suffering from severe headaches and some other medical issues from my head trauma. I had recently moved into Administration Company in 1 RCR as the Sergeant Major, and I enjoyed it immensely. It also allowed me to hide my medical issues. The other reason was that 3 RCR was training for its deployment to Afghanistan, which meant I would be looking after the rear party, which would be an incredibly stressful time.

After some more prodding, I accepted the posting and was looking forward to the challenge. On the bright side, this meant that I would be remaining in Petawawa for at least a couple more years, and JJ would be able to graduate from school with his friends.

DSM, 3 RCR

For the first few months, I was very much a part of 3 RCR. I fulfilled the role of DSM and talked about my expertise and experiences to a Battalion soon to be on its first deployment to Afghanistan, even though some individual soldiers had deployed previously. With training completed, the 3 RCR Battle Group, commanded by Lieutenant-Colonel Roger Barrett and CWO Ernest (Ernie) Hall, were deployed to Afghanistan in September 2008. While Ernie survived Afghanistan, just months after retiring several years later he was killed by a speeding car while walking across the street in Pembroke, following a night of watching a hockey game. Rest in Peace, brother.

While the troops were enjoying a few well-earned weeks of leave before their flights, we reorganized the Rear Party for what we knew would be a busy time. The situation in Afghanistan had not changed much from March 2007, when I had returned from deployment with 1 RCR. Canadians were still fighting the Taliban in Zhari and Panjwai districts, and the bad guys continued to inflict as many casualties as possible. Their use of IEDs had increased, and they continued trying to gain the support of the locals by discrediting the Afghan Government and the Coalition through intimidation and terror. We knew that the possibility of Canadian casualties was high. Rear Party was not going to be fun or relaxing.

I was fortunate to work with some great people, which made a bad situation at least tolerable. The Officer Commanding of the Rear Party was Major Mike Percy and the Adjutant was Captain Sebastien Niles. They were two great young officers who took their tasks very seriously.

My responsibilities as the Rear Party Sergeant Major were immense and more significant than I had anticipated. For starters, the Rear Party was over two hundred soldiers strong, but had only a handful of experienced NCOs and officers that could be depended upon during serious situations. A large majority of the soldiers in the rear party had been left behind for medical or disciplinary issues, including drug and alcohol abuse. A mandatory urine test administered to all members of 3 RCR resulted in many failures because of marijuana, cocaine, and to my surprise, even harder drugs. We had to look after those soldiers and administer drug testing as part of their rehabilitation. We also had to get soldiers trained as possible replacements. And on top of that, we received about sixty new soldiers just out of basic training and a handful of young, inexperienced officers also right off their training.

All of this took up a lot of our time. Still, it was looking after the families of our deployed soldiers that was our fundamental mission, keeping them informed, having social gatherings, coffee mornings and Christmas parties. And when our soldiers were killed or wounded, we had to fulfill the one part of our job that none of us wanted.

NOTIFYING THE FAMILIES

In December, the 3 RCR Battle Group received its first significant casualties, with nine soldiers killed in two separate incidents on Highway 1. It would not be their last.

The Rear Party had trained several senior non-commissioned members and a few young officers to be Assisting Officers. Their role would be to help the families of those wounded or killed, as long as was required. In one case, the Assisting Officer remained in contact with the family for more than a year.

Major Percy and I went and notified the families of those killed who lived in Ontario, while others notified families from other provinces. I have done many difficult and dangerous things in my life, but none of them compared to this task.

As soon as we had confirmed information on casualties, we geared up the notification team consisting of Major Percy, me, and the unit Padre, Captain Francesca Scorsone. We would have to get to the location as quickly as possible because the word could get out even though there was a communication lockdown in theatre. We did not want that to happen.

We quickly learned that a staff car and driver, with three people in full dress uniform, rolling through military housing or a small subdivision in Petawawa or neighbouring Pembroke caused an uproar. All military families on that street or area started to panic, and rightfully so. Knocking on that door and standing there knowing that we had to give this terrible news was devastating to me. But it could not even be compared to what that wife or parent was about to hear.

I remember it like it was yesterday, knocking on a door at about 0600 hours and hearing a baby that was only a few months old crying and seeing the light come on upstairs as the young mother and wife looked out the window. That look will be forever ingrained in my memory. She knew as soon as she saw us that bad news was about to be given to her.

There is no easy way to pass on that news, and Major Percy was the one with this terrible task. He did it with dignity and compassion. We understood that we could not play with feelings, and the initial words had to be direct and truthful. You can't leave an opening for misinterpretation. If a soldier has been killed, you couldn't start by saying that there had been an incident in Afghanistan and an explosion has injured several soldiers. That your husband was hurt very badly. That he was medevacked to Kandahar Airfield and pronounced dead.

That takes too long and leaves hope where there is none.

You are better off saying, "Ma'am, I am sorry to inform you that your husband has been killed." After that, there may be time to explain how, or maybe not, depending on what the person needed to hear.

Every reaction is different, and I was not prepared for that. I saw a young wife and new mother who could not be consoled. I saw a parent whose anger was beyond explanation. I saw a spouse who threw herself on the floor and was uncontrollable and a mom who screamed and yelled at us for killing her son. It was all a very humbling experience.

We were lucky to have a young female reservist as our Padre, Francesca Scorsone, who was one of the most compassionate and understanding people I had ever met. She would become the rock for many of those families, though there's no doubt that it took a toll on her.

I remember sitting and speaking with her on several occasions, and she was always able to leave me feeling better about things. It helped that she could also be just another soldier in 3 RCR when that was required, too.

42

EXTRA-REGIMENTALLY EMPLOYED

In January 2009, CWO Ernie Hall, the RSM of 3 RCR, interviewed me about my career and the Regiment's future for me. I was told that I was in the top tier of MWOs and that I could expect to be promoted within the next year or so. That was exciting news for me, and I wanted to know the plan for me until then. I was told there was already a plan for the next DSM to replace me at 3 RCR to get the experience and points he required on the promotion boards.

Once again, the Regimental Mafia decided that I would need to move on because I was already in the promotion zone. CWO Hall told me that I would be moving as soon as logistically possible to Kingston to take over as the Land Force Doctrine and Training Systems Headquarters Sergeant Major. Kingston sounded reasonably good even though LFDTS was as foreign to me as something in outer space. What the heck, I was up for it.

Before leaving CWO Hall's office, I asked him about my promotion to Chief Warrant Officer and where I could end up once it arrived. The news was a little bit uncertain, as there was no guarantee that my promotion would get me a posting back to one of The RCR battalions as the RSM. A lot would depend on the timing and availability of positions. The Army and the Regiment were trying to extend the length of our RSM positions from two years to at least three. It meant that there was no guarantee that I would be posted back to Petawawa to 1 or 3 RCR the following year as the RSM. It could be to 2 RCR in Gagetown, or even elsewhere outside the Regiment. This wasn't the news I was hoping for, but as I had learned over my career, I kept my head up and moved forward.

I briefed Julie about being in the promotion zone and my immediate posting to Kingston on arriving home that afternoon. I also told her that it did not necessarily mean a posting back to Petawawa when my promotion came. It helped us decide whether we would move to Kingston as a family, knowing that we could quickly move somewhere else the following year. As always, Julie took it in stride and started planning. We decided almost immediately that we would not be selling our home in Petawawa and moving as a family because the housing market is not great in February-March in Petawawa. Jana was still in her last year of school and JJ was already living in Ottawa and attending Carleton University. Once again, I would head to Kingston on Imposed Restriction. Julie and Jana would remain in Petawawa, put the house on the market in the summer and move once a sale was arranged.

I learned from the administration staff that military members posted to Kingston on Imposed Restriction would not be given rations and quarters on base but could rent suitable accommodations in the city. Once I was told the amount that the military would cover, Julie and I went to Kingston to find a place to live. We were lucky that we had good friends in Kingston who knew someone willing to rent their condo to me for the allocated amount the government would provide. I was able to get a fully furnished apartment with cable and phone as part of the rent for exactly what I was allocated, and I was within walking distance from the main base and only fifteen minutes from downtown Kingston.

LFDTS HQ SERGEANT MAJOR

A week or so later, I packed up my military kit and a few other comforts and moved to Kingston. The following Monday, I cleared into the Base. I was surprised to learn that I would be working out of Fort Frontenac, located downtown, separate from the base and the Royal Military College.

My first impression of the Fort was that it was going to be great working there.

The Governor of New France, Louis de Buade, Comte de Frontenac, built the original Fort in 1673. It was rebuilt in 1675 and again in 1695. The Governor of New France used it to control access to the fur trade. It was considered the "key to the west," and was the base of LaSalle's explorations and a French outpost against the Iroquois and the English. The British took control of the Fort in 1758, and it remained in their possession until the end of the war of 1812. It was then deemed obsolete and was gradually demolished. In 1982, archaeologists discovered several sections of the original limestone walls, which have been left uncovered for viewing today, as the Fort is a National Historic Site of Canada.

My office would be in one of the newer buildings on this beautiful site. My childhood dream had come true. I had my own fort, or at least I was the Sergeant Major of a fortress.

I started work in early spring, and immediately I immersed myself in the duties of the LFDTS HQ Sergeant Major. I worked for the CO of LFDTS HQ, Major Kent Stewart, an armoured officer who loved his Scottish heritage and never let an opportunity go by to display it. My job was by no means overly intensive or exciting. I found myself looking after the day-to-day running of the fort as well as the HQ staff.

PART FOUR - POST-AFGHANISTAN (2009-2017)

The Fort was occupied by LFDTS HQ as well as the Canadian Army Command and Staff College. The other occupant was the Fort Frontenac Officers' Mess. It is a beautiful mess, advertised as a home away from home to the students and staff of the College, as well as any lodger units in Kingston. The Mess also had many associate members, retired officers and civilian professionals who worked and lived in the Kingston area.

For the first time in my career, I looked after a civilian workforce, including a large cleaning and kitchen staff. I learned very quickly that civilians do not listen to an army guy because he is a Sergeant Major. One of the first things I received in my handover was the civilian workforce union handbook. This book detailed everything from work hours to pay to holidays and the process for any disciplinary or performance issues. The book was thick and confusing, and after reading it several times over a few days, I still had no idea how to deal with civilian employees.

It was definitely a feeling-out process, and I didn't always get it right.

During my year and a bit in this position, I lived alone in my rented condo and looked forward to the weekends when I usually drove the three hours to Petawawa to be with Julie. I would typically arrive home around suppertime on Friday and would leave around noon on Sunday. Any weekends that I couldn't go to Petawawa, Julie would drive to Kingston.

My time at Fort Frontenac was good, but I knew that it was just a holding position while waiting for my promotion to Chief Warrant Officer to come in. In late December 2009 and early January 2010, I received several phone calls from my career manager and the Regimental Chief to discuss my upcoming promotion and my future. I had assumed that I would be posted to one of the three Regular Force battalions as the Regimental Sergeant Major, and I must admit that I was a little concerned and apprehensive. Even though I was doing a great job as the LFDTS HQ Sergeant Major, as both my boss and the Commander told me, I was struggling both physically and emotionally. I had spent almost my entire career in an infantry battalion or at least with the army, and I understood the rigours of leadership. I lived by our unofficial regimental motto, "Never pass a fault," as well as leading by example, and I was concerned that I would no longer be able to live up to that expectation.

I always believed that the time to leave is before you can no longer do the job.

I continued to have daily headaches, and there were mornings when my neck was so sore and stiff that I could not hold my head up. I was now having issues with my knees, and even a gentle run or march would mean being crippled for days. I was dealing with doctors for my physical issues, but I was still several years away from seeking help for my emotional baggage. How could I be the RSM for an infantry battalion and not lead from the front?

I could not do that to the troops, and I did not want to embarrass myself at this stage of my career.

Over my long career, I had seen and worked with many RSMs, and I learned from every one of them. The problem was that while some of them were great, the lessons learned from a few were not so positive, and I had no intention of being in that second category. I spent several days considering my options, including releasing from the Canadian Armed Forces or turning down my promotion to Chief.

Luckily for me, the Regimental Mafia stepped in again, and this time it was to my benefit.

The Regimental Chief called sometime around February 2010 to say that my promotion message had been sent. It was backdated to January 1, and he wanted to congratulate me. He then said we needed to discuss where I would be going. Because RSMs now held their positions for three years versus two, there was no immediate position available for me. The plan would be to leave me where I was, over ranked as a Chief until a Battalion opened up or I could be considered for a position outside the Battalion. Inside, I was grinning, as this could be the answer to my concerns. I remember telling the Regimental Chief that I had always wanted to be an RSM in a Battalion, but I was not keen on remaining in LFDTS as a Chief doing an MWO's job. I was told to wait a few days while he looked at some other options, and he would get back to me. A few days later, I received a call from the Regimental Chief asking me if I would be interested in becoming the Unit Chief at the MSU, also in Kingston.

I had been in Kingston almost a year, but I had never heard of MSU and admitted as much. I was surprised to learn that my Regimental Chief didn't have much info on what the unit did either, or even where they were on base.

All I knew was that this could be the answer to my prayers, and so I made my decision.

"I would love to be posted to MSU Kingston."

PROMOTION TO CWO – MSU CHIEF

Sometime around March 1, there was a small gathering of LFDTS HQ folks, and I was promoted to the rank of CWO.

A couple of days later, I received a posting message to CDI Ottawa, and I was a little freaked out. I didn't remember hearing anything about Ottawa, and what the heck was CDI? I was told that, for both security and manning reasons, all postings to MSU were sent out by the Chief of Defence Intelligence (CDI) Ottawa.

I was to learn more over the next few weeks.

I started asking around about MSU. I learned it stood for Mission Support Unit, which didn't help me understand anything more about this unit. But as I asked around, I learned more and more. The MSU was in an old building up on the main Base in Kingston. They were not an official unit, but a project under Chief of Defence Intelligence in Ottawa. They had been put together to support the ongoing mission in Afghanistan, hence the name MSU.

The unit consisted primarily of Human Intelligence Operators (HUMINT), plus supporters. The HUMINT folks were either "Source Handlers" or "Interrogators." Most were intelligence personnel, but source handling had been opened to other trades, and there were folks in the unit from across the military. The unit CWO that I was replacing was a PPCLI soldier who had spent a lot of his career with the Special Forces. I called and told him I had received a posting message to replace him. He invited me over for coffee. I learned that he had put in his thirty-day release and was happy that I was coming in early. He had only a couple of weeks left, and we would begin the handover immediately.

Gib Parrell, the outgoing Chief, spent an hour or so explaining what the unit was and what they did and the fact that its members were involved in the ongoing war in Afghanistan. Gib was someone with an expansive level of knowledge from his years of experience with the PPCLI, Special Forces and the HUMINT community, and I was going to soak up as much information as possible. We spent that afternoon talking and completing a tour of the building. The building was in worse shape than it even looked from outside. It was rough, with paint falling off the walls and water-stained ceilings and floors. When we got to the stairs leading to the top floor, the staircase was blocked by tape. Gib ducked under, and I followed. He told me that it was out of bounds and not safe as it was musty, wet and had dead pigeons on the floor. I learned that this would not be a permanent home for the unit.

Even though we were still the MSU on paper, everyone referred to us as Joint Task Force X (JTFX). Over the next week or so, Gib was able to do an excellent handover with me and when he was getting ready to depart, I thought I had at least a rudimentary understanding of JTFX. Many unit members were deployed to Afghanistan. Those roaming around were either just returning or training to replace those in the theatre of operations. Almost everyone was in civilian attire, and most of the male soldiers had long hair and beards, a little strange to this RCR guy.

On Monday morning, I arrived at JTFX as the Unit Chief. I had on my best combats, clean boots and a fresh haircut, all ready to meet the day. I had been introduced to the CO, a Lieutenant-Colonel from the intelligence branch and a source handler. He was not around, so I found myself coming to attention at the DCO's door. He was dressed in casual civilian attire and had a beard. Looking up from his desk, he just smiled and said, "We don't do that here." I ignored his comment and introduced myself as CWO Barnes, the new RSM. He stood up, put his hand out and introduced himself as Terry, the DCO.

"I'll call you sir or Major," I said, "and please call me RSM. I'll even accept Chief."

He sat back down, and we started some small talk when a sharp-dressed young man in civilian clothes pushed by me.

"Hello, Terry," he said. They spoke for a few seconds about meeting downtown at a local pub for a beer after work and some other chit-chat. Then, the individual turned around, brushed by me and walked out.

My initial thought was that maybe he was the Adjutant. I made a note to speak to him next about who I was and how I expected him to show respect and never interrupt me again.

"Who was that?" I asked the DCO.

His answer surprised me. "That's Corporal so and so."

I just stared. "He's a Corporal?" When I got the nod to the affirmative, I turned around and, in a voice that was close to a bellow said: "Corporal, stop!"

The next few minutes were my way of setting the tone for the next few years. In infantry terms, I ripped that Corporal a new asshole.

I remember seeing a few heads sticking out of doors to see what the yelling was about, and that just made it better. I reminded the Corporal, and everyone else in earshot, that they were still in the military and the next person who disrespected me would be looking for a new job. I had no idea how much authority I would have here

PART FOUR - POST-AFGHANISTAN (2009-2017)

or even if I could have someone moved, but I didn't care.

Through some blubbering and whining, the Corporal tried to apologize, saying he didn't know who I was. I told him it didn't matter who I was: he saw the rank and how dare he interrupt my conversation with the DCO. I also added, "If I hear you calling him Terry again, you'll get to know me real fast." I saw the DCO standing at his door, and I smiled.

That was a rather good welcome to JTFX, at least for my first hour.

Over the next few weeks, I took the time to study my surroundings and to see how things were running. I had no intention of coming in and upending the unit until I knew what needed to be changed, if anything. I had excellent conversations with some very senior folks within CDI over the next couple of months, and they were all excited to have me in the unit. They were all incredibly positive about the unit's work in Afghanistan, but there was a genuine concern about the cavalier behaviour of some of its members. I was an outsider, I was not from the intelligence world, and was not a source handler. That would be something I would hear being whispered throughout my tour, but in some circles those were seen as positives.

I learned very quickly that the unit was split into camps. There were the source handlers, the interrogators and the supporters. The source handlers were selected and trained from across the military to gain intelligence from human sources. The interrogators (intelligence personnel) used their interrogation techniques to get information mainly from combatants captured in conflict. The supporters were required to enable the unit to succeed, including a headquarters, clerks, mechanics, supply folks, and others.

Even though I have been calling this a unit, officially, it was still a project, controlled and funded by Ottawa to ensure we had a HUMINT capability to bring to the fight in Afghanistan. It was well under strength, and there were dozens of positions unfilled, causing the unit to continually send the same folks into the theatre of operations.

One of the first tasks I took on was to fix the manning shortfall. I sent an email to all the career managers in Ottawa, who represented the hundreds of different trades in the Canadian Armed Forces. I introduced myself and explained that as a high-priority unit, JTFX would immediately emphasize recruitment for source handlers, interrogators and supporters. I explained that this was a Canadian Armed Forces-wide priority, and I was looking for their full support. Over the next few years, through some newfound friendships and some arguing and coercing, I was able to fill all the unit positions to an unprecedented 100%.

Another task that I took on was the process of the MSU becoming an official military unit. It was both frustrating and rewarding. By the time I departed the unit, this was also completed, and JTFX was a stand-alone unit. I dealt with the Canadian Heraldic Society to get the new unit badge recognized. It was time-consuming, but it was a proud day when the badge was unveiled. I continually sent the ideas and drawings to unit members for comments and suggestions to ensure we had their input. Not everyone was pleased with the result, but it was still a day of pride when it became official.

The badge is officially described in heraldic terms as: "Per saltire. Argent and Purpure, in Chief and Base." There is purple to represent the joint nature of the unit, and white to represent the integrity of its members. It is divided into four quarters that resemble an "X," which represents both the name of the unit and Camp X, the Second World War special operations training establishment, which has historical links to JTFX. In two quarters is a raven, a symbol that represents the idea of being a guardian, a bringer of knowledge, a trickster, shapeshifter and a cunning creature. As such, it represents the source handlers and interrogators. Its black colour represents the clandestine nature of the unit's covert role. In the other two quarters there is a shield with a rose on it and a Fairbairn-Sykes fighting knife. The shield represents force protection and the red rose is a Roman symbol of secrecy. The Fairbairn-Sykes fighting knife was initially issued to Canadian Source Handlers trained at Camp X. It symbolizes targeting and striking, the two primary roles of the unit. The unit motto in Latin is "Quaerite et invenietis," or "Seek, and you shall find."

Shortly after I arrived in JTFX, there was a Change of Command, and Lieutenant-Colonel Bill Maclean became the Commanding Officer. Lieutenant-Colonel Maclean was from Sydney Mines, Cape Breton, and we had an immediate connection. He was an intelligence officer and a qualified source handler, which gave him immediate credit in the unit, unlike me. However, Bill Maclean saw the big picture, and he understood that the unit needed professional leadership, discipline, and a team goal.

We immediately started to work toward that end. Even though there were several bumps along the road, I believe we succeeded. We made it clear from the beginning that, from this day forward, people would be held accountable for their actions and leaders would lead or get out of the way. We changed the policy on beards, which now meant that only those who were about to deploy could begin growing it a few months out. This direction received much more pushback than I expected, but in the end, it was a success. Today, the military has authorized all soldiers to have beards kept to a specific trimmed standard, but those early JTFX beards I am talking about were neither short nor trimmed.

We started to enforce military dress policies and the use of rank during work, which once again was more challenging than expected. It was essential to maintain the line between friendship and leadership. I saw several occasions when friendship got in the way of leaders making the right decisions, causing discipline to lapse. It got corrected quickly as the Commanding Officer and I cracked down on disciplinary issues. There was some whispering, as members of the unit at all rank levels found themselves being charged and attending both summary trials and courts-martial.

The change came slowly, but there was a change, and within a few months, the unit started to resemble a disciplined Canadian military one.

PART FOUR - POST-AFGHANISTAN (2009-2017)

DUMB MOTORCYCLE TRIP

It was late in 2010 that I made a decision that could have cost me my life. I had my truck and motorcycle in Kingston, and the condo I was renting gave me one outdoor parking spot. I used my bike most days for work and used my truck to drive home to Petawawa for the weekends. The weather that fall and early winter was unusually warm, and I kept delaying my decision to bring the motorcycle to Petawawa to put into storage. I remember driving my bike around Kingston in December and finally decided that it was time to take the bike on the three-hour trip to Petawawa.

I woke up early on a Saturday morning, and it was a little brisk outside but not cold enough for ice, so at about 0900 hours, I started on my motorcycle. I took Highway 401 West for a few minutes and then hopped on Highway 41 North. Everything seemed okay.

About an hour into the trip, it began to rain lightly and got a little colder. I zipped up my jacket tighter and carried on. About thirty minutes from Eganville, the temperature suddenly dropped significantly, and the light rain turned to freezing rain. The cliff faces along Highway 41 were covered in ice and snow.

I began to worry. I was in the middle of nowhere on a motorcycle, with no cell phone.

The freezing rain began to stick to my windscreen, and I had to stretch my neck to look over it to see the road. Ice started to form on the road, and I felt the tires slip on several occasions. I travelled along at a snail's pace, and the thirty-minute drive to Eganville took well over ninety minutes, including several stops to scrape the windscreen and my face shield, and to get the feeling back in my fingers and toes. I was cold to the bone and began shivering uncontrollably.

When I finally rolled into the gas station and restaurant in Eganville, I must have been a sorry sight. The bike was covered in ice. A layer of it was on me from my feet to my head. An older gentleman sitting on a bench outside the store smoking a cigarette came over and asked me if I was okay. I couldn't even answer. It took me several minutes to get off my bike, as my body wouldn't respond. Finally, I got off and, with the older man watching, I struggled to walk inside. After a cup of hot coffee and about thirty minutes of drying off, I felt like a new person.

I called Julie and told her where I was. After she stopped yelling at me about how stupid I was, we discussed a plan. Julie wanted me to leave the bike where it was, and she would come to pick me up. I looked outside. It had stopped raining, and the sky was bright, so I told her I could make the last forty minutes home. When I finally pulled into our driveway, I was exhausted. I often wonder about some of the decisions I made throughout my life and if I had learned anything along the way.

It was a decision that could have ended a lot worse than it did.

SPECIAL REQUIREMENTS COMMISSIONING PLAN

My three years at JTFX were thoroughly enjoyable. I learned a fantastic amount about HUMINT and what a force multiplier they are. I hope I had a small part in getting a disjointed project formed into a professional, knowledgeable and capable unit. The folks in this unit do fantastic work, putting themselves in positions that most would not. They have saved many Canadian and coalition lives, and their contributions cannot be overemphasized.

As 2013 rolled in, I started hearing that my time in JTFX was ending and that I would be posted. I had completed about thirty-two years of service, and I was a little apprehensive about my final few years in uniform. I had several conversations with my CO, as well as the CDI Chief. I also spoke with senior Regimental and Army folks about the way ahead.

One of the issues was that my posting possibilities were limited due to several factors as a Senior Chief. One was that I had a max of four years before retirement, and the second was that I did not speak French. I could not control the first, and the second was something that I had tried to resolve several times over my career but it never seemed to work out.

Lieutenant-Colonel Maclean and I spoke about a program called Special Requirements Commissioning Plan (SRCP). The purpose of this program was to provide a means of commissioning officers for the Regular Force to meet the unique and limited needs of the military. I was not excited about this path, as I have been a very proud member of the Non-Commissioned Members Club for my whole career. I never wanted or thought about becoming an officer. There were positives about spending my last years in uniform as an officer, including a pay raise and a better pension, but I wasn't persuaded.

As the days turned into weeks, I learned that there were no open positions for Chiefs in Kingston, so I would be posted to a new location, probably Ottawa. In discussions with the CO, we believed that we could try to keep me here in JTFX as a Captain if I took the SRCP. I reluctantly accepted.

Lieutenant-Colonel Maclean put my name in for the Special Commissioning Program, hoping to stay in JTFX and Kingston for my final years. Before March Break in 2013, I received a letter from an Army Colonel in Ottawa responsible for the SRCP congratulating me on being accepted to become a Captain. Once I signed the attached contract, which stated I had seven calendar days to do so, I would receive my promotion message to Captain and my posting message to Winnipeg.

I almost choked on the words as I read them. It had to be a mistake. I had never even heard anything about having to go to Winnipeg.

This was all happening on the Friday before March Break. As was the usual procedure before holidays, everyone from Kingston to Ottawa had gone home early. I emailed the Colonel about the message stating that seven days would not be enough to make my decision. I had dozens of questions and no one to ask due to March Break. This guy must have been the only person in uniform in Ontario still working because he replied immediately, telling me that the timeline was firm. It would be considered a refusal if I didn't send the signed document within seven calendar days.

I was not happy!

I looked up this Colonel's phone number on the military site and called him. His first words were that this program had specific requirements and was used to fill empty Captain slots identified as essential, and I should have known that. My first thought was "Hobbit." It became almost a shouting match as I tried to tell him about the vacant Captain position here at JTFX. It was a Canadian military priority and it would cost the Army nothing to keep me there, as opposed to moving me to Winnipeg. He wouldn't listen and even interrupted me several times. I finally told him that I did not have time to listen to his garbage, and I hung up.

I spent my March Break trying to reach people at home, and I even reached out to senior folks across the Canadian Armed Forces, Army and the Regiment for help. Everyone proclaimed to be in my corner, and several sent emails directly to this hobbit Colonel asking that I be placed in the empty Captain position in JTFX or, at the very least, a Captain position in Kingston. There were almost twenty vacant Captain positions in Kingston at that time.

Lieutenant-General Peter Devlin, Commander of the Canadian Army and a fellow Royal Canadian, sent the best message. He asked this Hobbit Colonel to reconsider the decision and that I would be a greater asset by remaining in Kingston for the last few years of my career. All the folks who reached out on my behalf had their comments fall on deaf ears. I have seen what can be done within the system if there is a desire, but for some reason I found myself on the losing side this time.

A week after I had received my message, I sent an email to the Colonel in Ottawa. I stated that the system was flawed and that two other Chiefs who were in senior positions to me had competed for SRCP and had been successful. One had remained in his unit in an under-ranked position, and the other had a new role invented for him in Trenton, where he intended to retire. I actually used the word 'Hobbit.' I said that I was not signing anything and that he could make another lousy decision like the one he had already made.

The following Monday, the CDI Chief called to say that my name would be forwarded for three senior positions in Ottawa as a Chief, and he would keep me informed. I accepted that I was moving to Ottawa, where I said I would only go kicking and screaming.

Obviously, I had already done the kicking and screaming.

44

MILITARY POLICE GROUP CHIEF

A couple of weeks later, I was informed that my name was on a shortlist to become the Military Police Group Chief, and that I was the first non-MP to ever be considered. As I had done several times in my career already, I asked myself: "What the heck is that?"

I spoke with the Army Chief, and he did what he could to explain the role to me, but this was new because the Military Police had just recently become a Canadian Armed Forces Group. The Military Police would now fall under a centralized command, unlike how it had been for most of my career. MPs typically came under the control of their units and bases, but now the Provost Marshal would command this centralized group.

I received an email from the Military Police Branch Chief and temporary Group Chief, CWO Rick Day, a career military policeman. He told me that MP Group Commander and Provost Marshal, Colonel Grubb, wanted me to come down to Ottawa for an interview. It was part of the process required before I was confirmed to this new position. It would be my first in-person interview for a job in the military, but how bad could it be?

The first issue arose when Rick Day said the interview would be two days later in Ottawa, and the dress would be 3B or 3C. Now, I will admit that, as a Senior Chief and someone who has served for more than thirty years in the military, the different states of dress should have been known to me, but unfortunately, they were not. I had spent my whole career on Army bases where the dress of the day was combats. The only other uniform we wore was our full dress, and even then, only on Remembrance Day and other special occasions.

A quick search of the dress regulations told me I needed my short-sleeved dress shirt, dress pants and undress ribbons or a sweater. I hadn't seen my sweater since I'd worn it many years earlier while shovelling snow in Petawawa. After some scrambling to get a new shirt and a pair of dress pants that would fit, followed by some ironing, and I was almost ready to go. Where the heck were my undress ribbons? They were nowhere to be found. After a quick trip to clothing stores, I was ready.

Two days later, I drove one of the unit cars from JTFX to Ottawa and arrived at the Military Police Group Headquarters on Walkley Road in Ottawa. I couldn't remember the last time I was that scared. I was trembling as I sat in the car, my head was pounding, and I felt a sense of panic. Several painkillers later, I walked into this strange new environment and was met by a commissionaire who was expecting me. He made a phone call, and a few minutes later, I met CWO Rick Day.

We went upstairs to Rick's office, soon to become mine, and we had several minutes to chat before my appointment with the Provost Marshal. Rick tried to brief me on the organization of the MP Group, but he was using terms and descriptions that I had no idea about, and I just smiled. Now and then, I would ask a question. Luckily, I was handed paper copies of all the briefings, and later I would be able to do some research and better understand what I was looking at. I learned that Colonel Grubb wore two hats: he was the Military Police Group Commander and the Provost Marshal, who had command over all the police functions.

Even today, it doesn't sound very clear.

INTERVIEW

As I got up to go to Colonel Grubbs' office, Rick Day informed me that Grubb was a hard army guy and expected folks to act accordingly. He also said he expected folks to come to attention at his door and to salute and call him "Sir." I didn't know why he said that, as I thought it was the norm and so wasn't anything new to me. I walked up to the door, snapped to attention in my best RCR drill and saluted. I presented myself with an introduction, and we shook hands.

Rick remained for the first ten minutes or so as we discussed mundane stuff. Once Colonel Grubb was ready for the interview, Rick departed and closed the door. Colonel Grubb asked me if there was anything that I wanted to say or ask before we started? I replied in the affirmative. I looked him straight in the eyes, and I told him that I had gone to the Chief of Military Personnel website to look at the prerequisites for this position and that there was one concern. It had stated that this was a bilingual position and that French was a necessity. I told him that I did not speak French and that it was too late in my career to try and learn it now, but I would try my best. I figured that this would be the end of the interview because French was necessary for this position, especially with more than 30% of the MPs being in Quebec. Colonel Grubb just smiled and said that he had already been briefed on this and considered it. He said several files had been given to him and the VCDS Board to review, and mine was first in all the board members' choices.

That surprised me.

He was extremely impressed with my file and said that there was only one issue that he needed to discuss with me. As part of the process, he said there had been a very extensive background check done on me, including by the Military and Canadian Civilian Police and International Police. The concern was that they had not found anything, not even a speeding ticket. He kind of smiled and asked, "How does a Newfoundlander spend thirty plus years in the infantry, especially The RCR, and never have gotten in shit?"

I remember laughing and telling him that I lived by three rules. One, never waste the opportunity to shut up. Two, always know when to leave. And three, always keep some money hidden in your wallet to make sure you have an escape plan after one and two.

It worked for me then, and it still works for me today.

The interview went on for about thirty minutes, and I answered a variety of questions on leadership, the Canadian Armed Forces, and on some more personal stuff, and then it was over. Colonel Grubb said he was impressed by what he saw in my file and in person. He said he had spoken with several senior folks within the Canadian Armed Forces, the Army, and the Regiment about me as well. He thanked me and said, "Someone will get back to you shortly."

The next day, the Army CWO career manager called me to discuss a posting date to become the first non-MP Military Police Group Chief.

I was going to Ottawa.

Within a few days, a message was sent out across the military congratulating me on being selected as the Military Police Group Chief. Personal emails and messages started to come in from everywhere. Many senior folks sent private messages, and many of my soldiers and comrades had to get in on the fun. Their messages were light-hearted.

Chief, you spent thirty years hiding from the police, and now they work for you?

Are you really becoming a "Meathead"?

Should I tell them about the time we got away with that thing?"

There were many funny messages, they were all in jest, and I laughed along.

To be honest, I was a bit surprised to be going to work with the Military Police myself.

During my four years in Kingston, we had sold our home in Petawawa and purchased a new home. Now, Julie and I had to discuss the move from Kingston to Ottawa. We had reason to delay the action. Jana was living with us in Kingston and attending the Police Foundations Course at St. Lawrence College, so, once again, I would go alone on Imposed Restriction. Julie and I spent a week in Ottawa, where we looked at the different options for renting an apartment. After looking at many other locations, I settled on a monthly room at Extended Stay on Cooper Street, only a few minute's walk from Parliament Hill in downtown Ottawa. It had a small kitchen, a living room with a pull-out couch and a separate bedroom. It also had indoor parking—everything I needed.

A couple of weeks later, I cleared out of JTFX, packed up my pickup truck and moved myself and my military kit to Ottawa.

It took me a couple of weeks to just get acquainted with the organizational chart for the Military Police. It took me much longer to figure out Ottawa and the bureaucracy that existed there. The Military Police Group fell directly under the Vice Chief of The Defence Staff (VCDS), and I dealt directly with VCDS Chief, CPO1 Geoff McTigue. Geoff would become my mentor as I tried to find my way through the upper echelons of DND.

Shortly after arriving, Colonel Grubb let me know that he would be leaving that summer and that his Deputy Commander, Colonel Rob Delaney, would replace him. Colonel Delaney was from Cole Harbour, Nova Scotia, and at the time he loved to tell everyone that he was the second most famous person from his hometown, after Sidney Crosby. I learned that Changes of Command and Appointments in Ottawa were quite different from the elaborate affairs on Army bases. In Ottawa, most took place in a room with a table and a few spectators and were essentially a signing ceremony. It made sense, in most cases, as most higher commands did not have a whole lot of subordinates working for them to put on parade or be spectators.

CHANGE OF COMMAND/CHANGE OF APPOINTMENT PARADE

CWO Day, who was now the Branch Chief, spoke to me about planning the upcoming Change of Command between Grubb and Delaney and himself and me. He envisioned a small signing ceremony, followed by a small social gathering. My thought was a little different, and as soon as I had the first opportunity to sit down alone with Colonel Grubb and Colonel Delaney, I presented my idea. It was a Change of Command for the whole Military Police Group, and it was a big deal. I suggested that we have a Change of Command Parade and a Change of Appointment. I also recommended a marching guard with weapons, officers with swords and either the VCDS or the CDS as the Reviewing Officer. At first, I believe they were both a little skeptical, but they both agreed as I explained how we would accomplish it.

A few weeks later, the Change of Command and the Change of Appointment took place on the Parade Square at Connaught Ranges in Ottawa. Two guards of soldiers, sailors and airmen and women from bases and garrisons across Ontario marched onto parade behind a band, all under the command of CWO Rick Day. The officers promenaded with their swords at the side of the square and then marched on to take their positions. Colonel Grubb took over the parade and welcomed the VCDS as the Reviewing Officer. The Change of Command between Grubb and Delaney took place, and then the Change of Appointment between Rick Day and me. Colonel Delaney and I, as the new Command Team, conducted the march past. Once the officers were dismissed, I marched the guards off and officially started my new tenure as the MP Group Chief.

The Change of Command received many positive accolades throughout the Military Police and the senior staff in Ottawa. It would be the first of many marks I would leave upon the Military Police.

The first few months of my time with the Military Police were a huge learning curve. I found myself attending many meetings at the MP Group and VCDS levels, where I only understood half of what I was hearing. The acronyms and the subjects being discussed were as foreign to me as the French used some of the time. I would take notes, and then when the meeting ended, I would ask Rick Day or one of the other Chiefs who had attended to explain some of the stuff to me. As I got more comfortable with my surroundings and began to understand my role better, I would ask questions during the meetings.

Almost immediately upon my arrival, I started feeling that everyone within the MP Group was not happy about my appointment. Some of the Chiefs and senior officers were especially defiant. In some cases, there were pronounced cold shoulders. I understood what was going on. I was an outsider, and the Chiefs, especially, took it as a personal insult that one of them had not been appointed as the Group Chief.

Following the Change of Command Parade, I saw positive changes in how the senior folks treated me and having Colonel Delaney as my Command Team Partner ensured my success. I took the time over the first few weeks to have all the MP Chiefs come to my office for a coffee and a chat. I told them that I understood why some would feel betrayed, but this was not personal. I was here to help this Group become better and ensure that the MPs were respected for their outstanding work. I started using the words "us" and "we" to describe the MPs. Every time I had an opportunity in front of others, especially senior members of DND in Ottawa, I would sing the praises of the MPs.

HONOURS AND AWARDS

One of my secondary tasks was to sit on the VCDS Honours and Awards Board. I believe there were nine of us from across the VCDS Group, mostly Colonels and Chiefs. The VCDS Chief of Staff, an RCR general, chaired the board. We were a diverse group—Navy, Army and Air Force, male and female. In the beginning, I was the only combat-arms type and the only infantry guy on the board.

Before each board, we would receive a bunch of confidential files, both electronically and on paper. Sometimes, there would be as many as thirty or forty files, each several pages long. Then, we had to read and study each one and vote for the files that we thought were deserving of a specific award. There might be thirty candidates for the Order of Military Merit and only seven medals available, so it was competitive. After each of us voted individually, our scores were sent to the VCDS staff to compile them. We would then meet as a board, and all the names would be put up on the screen in order of our combined rankings. The ranking would often be remarkably close to what we all expected, but sometimes there would be a vast discrepancy where I would rank someone number one, and someone else would rank them number thirty. We would then have to present why we scored them as we did and vote on that file again.

Sometimes it was because something got overlooked in the file, and that was easy to solve. Other times, it came down to the experience and knowledge of the board member. For myself, as an infantry CWO that had been to war and saw combat firsthand, I looked at a soldier's performance under fire differently than a Colonel would who was a career lawyer and had never seen combat. I believe I had a significant impact on getting combat soldiers the recognition they deserved.

After attending a couple of boards for a variety of medals and awards, something became very clear. Out of the hundreds of files I had reviewed in the first four or five months, there were none from the military police. I had heard stories in my new position about MPs who were doing amazing things, and I wondered why they were not being recognized. For example, there was an MP who threw himself on a suicidal person who had poured gasoline all over his body and had a lighter in his hand, saving his life. There were dozens of other stories like that. I held a meeting with Colonel Delaney and told him that I would be taking over the Military Police Group Honours and Awards. I spoke with each MP Command and made it clear that I expected to see our folks recommended for honours and awards.

If I did not receive a couple of files each month from each MP group, I was on the phone, jacking someone up. The results were immediate. MP files started reaching the VCDS board, and not all were successful, but within the year, several folks from the Military Police Group received honours and awards. It continued for my whole time as the Group Chief. When I left, at least a hundred folks from the Group had been recognized, from the lowest level commendations to medals of bravery.

I had some pushback about forcing the groups to send me nominations for our MPs. The Chiefs, MWOs and officers would say, "The MPs are only doing their job." It was the same thing I heard from some of the members of the VCDS Board as well. I would always say that we should not be looking at whether it was their job or not, but how they performed it. I would always give the example of my soldiers from Charles Company during Operation MEDUSA. It is an infantryman's job to close with and destroy the enemy, and he expects to get shot at while doing it. If wounded, he needed to keep fighting and help others that are wounded too—this was all part of the job. But that's not to say he doesn't deserve recognition for those actions. When he is wounded and runs into enemy fire to rescue his buddy and drag him to safety, that is his job, but what bravery. By the end of the first year, I was receiving files from our MPs across the country. There were almost always one or two on every VCDS board.

It was a huge success, and I hope our fine Military Police continue to receive the recognition they deserve.

WHITE SCHOOL, BLACK MEMORIES

It was my great honour to serve as the Group Chief for the Military Police. I immediately began working the system to get my position changed to a senior appointment. It met all the prerequisites, and this detail was perhaps overlooked when the new Group was formed. There was also an effort both from within the MP Group and senior elements of the Canadian Forces to have the Commander's position upgraded to a Brigadier-General. The Chief Warrant Officer position was eventually upgraded to a senior appointment. Shortly after I was replaced, the incoming Chief got the rewards of my three years of hard work.

I was very happy for him.

Colonel Delaney was promoted to Brigadier-General, and the MP Group began to get even more of the recognition it deserved. Even though Delaney had been part of what I call the "Big Boys Club" since taking command and attending all the Chief of the Defence Staff senior meetings and planning sessions, things changed the day Rob Delaney became a general. I remember General Delaney saying the atmosphere was completely different when he walked into the room, and the respect and networking were very different. It was an opportunity for us to ensure that the Military Police were considered and consulted in planning for all operations and not an afterthought, as was the usual procedure.

RECRUIT COURSE GRADUATION

One of the highlights of my time with the MPs and of my career was when I received a call from the School Chief in St. Jean, Quebec, to see if General Delaney wanted to be the Reviewing Officer for one of its graduating recruit courses. It was obviously intentional as my daughter, Jana, was on a course in St. Jean during this time. I was given a few different graduation dates, but we accepted that date as soon as I told General Delaney that my daughter was graduating. I got to inspect the graduating course with General Delaney and spoke to my daughter as I went by. General Delaney did the same, knowing that she was going to Base Borden to commence Military Police training.

After the recruit course was dismissed, the staff had them form up again off-site, where General Delaney and I promoted Jana and two others to the rank of corporal. MPs who have completed the Police Foundations Course in college are promoted to corporal following their basic recruit course. One of the three promoted was a cook; he had received his civilian papers before joining the military.

General Delaney and a few other senior MPs knew that Jana was attending the Military Police Course in Borden, but no one else was aware. A week or so into the course, Jana called to tell me the cat was out of the bag. The candidates had to write their autobiography and had to stand in the class and present themselves. One of the staff asked Jana if she had any other family in the military, and she said yes, CWO Barnes in Ottawa. Jana had to put up with a few comments, but they were always in fun. There were a few times throughout the course when someone would say, "What would your Dad think?" or "What would your Dad do here?" But, for the most part, she was treated just like every other candidate. She did say it was a little eerie having to walk by my photo every day on the way to class, and sometimes other classmates or staff would say something, but, as time went by, I was soon forgotten, and Jana was successful on her own merits.

At about the course's halfway point, each candidate was asked to give their top three posting preferences. Jana called me the night before to ask for advice. I explained that she was in a great position, and she could choose a posting anywhere in Canada and that there were some lovely Air Force and Navy bases. I mentioned to Jana that I was in a great position to influence any decision on her first posting, and I thought she would ask for Esquimalt or Halifax, but she said she wanted to go to Petawawa.

A couple of months later, Jana was posted to Petawawa, and her Mom was happy.

INTERACTION WITH THE CF MEDICAL SYSTEM

During my last year with the Military Police, my headaches and neck issues began to take a greater toll. I had been to several pain specialists, muscle and tissue specialists, Traumatic Brain Injury (TBI) specialists, and it was always the same result. Nothing seemed to work.

I found myself not wanting to be around people and definitely not wanting to socialize after work. I found myself alone more and more. Julie and the kids were worried about the amount of time I spent in the basement or bed. They were also concerned about the number of pills I was taking each day just to remain active. I found myself sitting in my office during work hours and closing the door, turning the lights out and closing my eyes.

Many days, I would come in late and leave early.

I always seemed to stay on top of any work that needed to be done, as for the most part I was in a position that allowed me some significant flexibility and leeway. I spoke with General Delaney and let him know about the issues I was having and that I was trying to get the medical system to finally help me out.

I believe it was in early 2015 that I was placed on my first "temporary category," meaning that the medical authorities placed official restrictions on my physical activity. I suffered from massive headaches, followed by dizzy spells and excessive sweating while conducting even minimal physical activity. It was a huge setback for someone who loved walking, playing ball hockey, and working around outdoors. The headaches had been going on for almost ten years, but these new symptoms scared me. I had exhausted the medical system over the last decade, and the only thing that seemed to help was taking more pills.

Around this time, I set up an appointment at the military hospital at Montfort to discuss my ongoing issues again. I showed up early for my appointment and while sitting in the waiting room I endured the worst headache I'd had for a long time.

When called, I went in expecting to see the same military doctor I had seen for the last couple of years, but instead it was someone new. I asked where my original doctor was and was told that it was almost impossible to see the same doctor each time, and this civilian doctor told me he had read my file.

His first question was, "What can I do for you?"

I explained my headaches, dizziness, fatigue and excessive sweating, and he asked how long I had these symptoms. I explained in a few words that the headaches and fatigue were about ten years, and the rest were more recent. He asked me if any specific incidents had caused the initial symptoms. When I told him about having a traumatic brain injury in 2006, he reacted as he had never heard of this.

My head started spinning, and I could feel the anger begin boiling. I had told my story to dozens of medical professionals over the years and had gone into details about how I had been injured. I decided I was not doing it again.

DR. GUPTA

Let me say that Dr. Gupta had been very professional and very polite to me, but for some reason, ten years of pain, anxiety and frustrations all came to a head, and I lost it. I stood up, and I don't remember the exact words, but what I remember are embarrassing and hurtful. I towered over Dr. Gupta, and I screamed about not telling him anything. I said, "You have the fucking file! Read it! Do your fucking job! Once you've read the file and you have a plan, give me a call, and maybe I'll come back in."

I know he tried to say something. I cut him off, turned around, opened his office door and slammed it shut with all the strength I could muster. I stormed out of Montfort Hospital and jumped into my car.

It took me about ten minutes of just sitting there in the parking lot to calm down and compose myself enough to drive back to the Military Police headquarters. By the time I arrived, I was sweating, lightheaded, and my head was pounding like someone was beating me with a baseball bat. It took me several minutes to make it upstairs to my office and close the door. I sat at my desk, put my feet up and stayed that way for about an hour. Once I had regained my composure, I went in to see General Delaney and explained what happened.

I assumed that by now someone from the hospital would have called because of my erratic behaviour or because they were concerned about me, but this hadn't happened. I told General Delaney to expect a call, and I told him exactly what I had done. I was still angry and said to him that my reasoning was just even though my behaviour was inexcusable.

I'm not sure I actually believed that.

I don't know if General Delaney called Dr. Gupta or someone else at the hospital, and we never really spoke of it again. I was only back in the office a few minutes when the phone rang. It was a secretary from Montfort. She explained that

PART FOUR - POST-AFGHANISTAN (2009-2017)

Dr. Gupta had finished reviewing my file and asked if I could come in later that afternoon. I reluctantly made an appointment for 1500 hours.

That afternoon, I sheepishly walked into Dr. Gupta's office and sat down. I apologized for my earlier behaviour and explained that I was extremely frustrated with the medical system. Dr. Gupta told me that he could not do anything about the past ten years but said he would do everything possible to help me. We talked about things that may have had some positive effects in the past, and he set out a path for me to which I was agreeable. He said that he would discuss every step with me and that he would like me to be open to some non-conventional ideas.

Over the next two years, under Dr. Gupta's watch, I tried many different measures. Some had short-term positive effects, others did not. I visited Dr. Gupta's private practice in Montreal, where he wanted to temporarily block some nerve endings in my neck to see if it would help with my headaches. If successful, we would then make it permanent with surgery.

Jana was visiting, and she volunteered to drive with me to Montreal because I would not be allowed to drive after the procedure. A Corporal and his wife were sitting in the waiting room, and I understood that he was going in for the same procedure. His appointment was first, and he went into the inner area and was gone for about thirty minutes. When he returned, I asked him how it went.

"Not too bad," he said, "a little painful."

I was used to pain, so I dismissed it as a minor concern. I noticed he was a little pale and sweaty, but once again, not a big deal.

I began the procedure by laying on my stomach looking at a large screen. Dr. Gupta told me that he would be able to see exactly where the nerve endings are on the screen, and he would apply a substance about the strength of what a dentist uses to numb a tooth. There would be some pain, and it would be uncomfortable, but I mustn't move. I watched the screen as the large needle entered the base of my skull and headed for some nerve endings. At first there was a pinch and a little discomfort, and then pain shot through me like a knife. I held the edge of the table and screamed. This went on for about ten minutes as several nerve endings were deadened, and then it was over.

I was told to remain in the waiting area for about thirty minutes before I could leave. As I went back into the waiting room, I saw that Jana was a little worried, and she asked me how I was and how painful the procedure was.

"Where's that Corporal?" I said. "He lied."

Jana laughed. "He didn't want to frighten you."

After I had left the room, the Corporal had told his wife and Jana that the procedure was the most painful thing he had ever endured. Over the next couple of days, I prayed that the procedure would be successful. But, like so many other attempts, there was no difference in my headaches. Thankfully, I didn't go through with permanent surgery.

After a few weeks, Dr. Gupta had me see a specialist about Botox. At first, I thought it was a bit weird, but I agreed after doing some research. Botox studies had shown positive outcomes for people who have terrible migraines, and Dr. Gupta and I thought it was worth a try. I found myself getting about two hundred needles in my head, face and neck every three months for a year, but other than some very minor effects the first time, it also failed.

At the end of my second visit with Dr. Gupta, he said he wanted to talk about how pain can be physical and psychological. I sat there and listened, but my inner voice was saying, "Bullshit, this is all physical." But I was willing to play along. I had listened to similar advice over the years and was not really open to the idea that pain could have a mental aspect. All I heard was, "You are exaggerating or making it up."

Dr. Gupta asked me if I would be open to speaking with someone about how the pain had affected my life and impacted my family, social and work environment. I tentatively agreed, but a part of me believed that this had more to do with my outburst and unprofessional behaviour a few days earlier.

I set up an appointment and went to see a military psychiatrist a few days later. She asked me many questions about how I was doing, how I felt, and I gave the same answers I had been giving to others for ten years. I'm good. I told her that I was frustrated with the medical system, and it had boiled over a week ago, but I was okay. She said something about pain and how it can be affected by emotional and psychological stresses. All I heard was, "Blah, blah, blah." She wrote a report saying she believed I was good to go.

My ability to lie and manipulate had improved.

Dr. Gupta started to change up some of my medications, and I began to feel a little better. This lasted only a few months. Then, the headaches, neck pain, and other symptoms would return with a vengeance, and we would repeat the process. Dr. Gupta remained professional and explained everything he was thinking in detail and discussed what we could try next. Dr. Gupta was one of the first doctors who I allowed myself to trust since those fine doctors at the multinational hospital in Kandahar.

I had mentioned to Dr. Gupta that I was having difficulty concentrating and that my memory had started to deteriorate. He said that my brain trauma, medications, age and stress could all affect this, and so he set me up to see a specialist in Ottawa that conducted cognitive testing. It was a two-day process that included several interviews with psychologists and hours of testing.

Most of the tests were like puzzles, word games and drawing from memory. Someone would read me a short story, and then we would move on to something else. Then they would ask me questions about the story. I was shown a picture and then asked to draw it from memory and, after doing several other things, asked to draw it again. I found these to be very frustrating, and some things that I should have been able to ace were difficult

A few times I became angry, and I got up, walked out and went for a stroll so that I would not lose it on the fine people doing their jobs. Each time my frustrations boiled over, the person doing the test would just smile and tell me that it was okay, just to relax and that many people found this difficult. At the end of the second day, I was ready to get away from this nightmare and get back in my basement.

A few weeks later, Dr. Gupta called me to go over the report from the cognitive testing centre. I expected the worst but was slightly surprised to find that, overall, I tested in the low normal category. There were some areas that I had more difficulty with than others, and there were areas that I excelled in, but there were no major concerns. Dr. Gupta told me this was good news. Even though there was memory decline and some cognitive areas of concern, there did not seem to be any major issues. I thought we were finished when he said there was one other area of concern that the lead psychologist mentioned.

POST-TRAUMATIC STRESS DISORDER

In the report, a section said that it was in the belief of several psychologists who interviewed me and watched my testing that I was suffering from some mental impairment. It said that, without a proper assessment, they could not be sure, but they believed I was also suffering from PTSD and perhaps some depression. I just rolled my eyes and said something like, "That's crap." Dr. Gupta spoke to me for several minutes again about pain and how psychological issues can affect it, and this time I listened.

I remember getting emotional and not understanding why. It was nothing new other than the letters PTSD. As I have mentioned several times, I have seen PTSD up close. I had to deal with several of my soldiers after returning from Afghanistan. I have attended funerals of those who committed suicide and watched as my friend spiralled downward, out of control.

And all those issues were because of Post-Traumatic Stress Disorder.

I received a call a few hours later about attending a session with a military psychiatrist, which I had supposedly agreed to. I didn't remember agreeing to it at the last meeting with Dr. Gupta, but truthfully, I didn't remember much after hearing the letters PTSD.

This was the slow beginning of my acceptance of the idea that I needed help. It was a huge step for me to go back to see a psychiatrist, and there was still part of me that did not believe I had PTSD.

My initial meeting with the psychiatrist was disappointing. After letting my wall come down and speaking to this guy about stuff that no one else had ever heard, he put me on some medication. He became concerned when I told him about the nightmares and that I had hurt Julie in my sleep a couple of times. I spoke to him about how I had reacted a short time earlier when driving in Ottawa, and a woman in a hijab pulled in front of me. I remembered how my son asked me if I was all right, even though I had not done anything outwardly. I had stopped driving, was staring, sweating and breathing hard.

WHITE SCHOOL, BLACK MEMORIES

I was so tired of medications. I reluctantly took the pills for a couple of weeks, but they made me feel very strange like I was someone else. I had no energy, no appetite and just overall felt lousy. I stopped taking them, and life went back to my normal. I saw the same military psychiatrist a few more times, but I could tell that he was not impressed with me for stopping the pills. It caused me to not open up to him again. Each time we talked, I told him that I was frustrated about the daily pain, and the psychological stuff came second.

Around this time, I was booked an appointment with Dr. Lorraine Overduin, a civilian psychologist in Ottawa. She had worked with several other military soldiers and veterans with emotional baggage. She would become a positive influence in my life during a time most medical professionals were not. I found her very easy to speak with, and she never looked or acted like she was judging me. I would continue to see her for several years, and she would never know what she meant to me or how she allowed me to get my life back. After several months, when she told me that she believed I had PTSD, depression, and anxiety, I actually believed her.

My medical awakening was taking place as my military career was coming to a head. In early 2016, I received word that my three-year tenure as the Military Police Group Chief was coming to an end. There would be a board set up to look for an appropriate replacement for that summer.

I discussed my career choices with Julie, and as we have always done, we made the decision together. The new CWO charter stated Chiefs could serve for thirty-five years or until age fifty-five, whichever came last. July 2016 would be thirty-five years of service for me, but I would be only fifty-four years old, meaning I could serve one more year. I had hoped to get an additional year with the military police to retire with dignity in a unit that I adored and that had shown me great respect.

It was not to be, so my initial plan was to retire in July 2016.

Around this same time, I started getting my medical situation sorted and documented so that my release could be completed and Veterans Affairs would look after me. I met up with Warrant Officer John Hobbs, a physician's assistant. He would be instrumental in ensuring my needs were accommodated and that my medical history was reviewed and appropriately written. The first thing that WO Hobbs did was review my file, and he asked me why I had been placed on three consecutive temporary categories and not put on a permanent one. I had not completed the Army Fitness Test in three years because of restrictions, and I should have been placed on a permanent category. My file should then have been reviewed to see if I still met the "universality of service" requirement. All Canadian military members had to meet this minimum standard.

Around this same time, I got a call from the Army Chief and future Canadian Forces Chief, Alain Guimond. He offered me a new Chief position in Canadian Army Headquarters as the Army Joint Personnel Support Unit (JPSU) Chief. General Vance was looking at how we could best support our ill and injured members as they either recovered to go back to work or transitioned into civilian life. There had been many complaints about this process from our sick and injured over the past several years, especially since Afghanistan.

The plan was to take the JPSU, a centralized unit that looked after members from across the military and give it back to the Army, Navy and Air Force to look after their own people. I explained to Alain that I was being placed on a permanent category and that I only had a year left to serve.

"No problem," he said, "and if you need more time to sort out your medical issues, we can extend you for a second year." After speaking with WO Hobbs, I knew it could take some time to sort out my medical issues in hopes that a permanent category would get me a 3B medical release, along with all the benefits it provided.

With that in mind, I told Alain I would do it and reported to Army Headquarters in July.

THE ARMY ILL AND INJURED CELL AND MY DEPARTURE WITH DIGNITY EVENT

When I walked in that first day, there were many blank stares and confusion because no one knew I was coming. After a couple of hours of running around, I got a desk and computer that someone on parental leave had given up. A captain and I were the only staff, and we started the Army JPSU, or, as some paperwork called it, "The Army Ill and Injured Cell." No one knew for sure what it was or how it worked. We had to start from scratch and figure out what we needed to do, including what personnel we would need to be posted in to fulfill this task. The captain and I did a lot of work independently with little or no direction, except a message from the Chief of the Defence Staff that outlined what he wanted.

I continued to see WO Hobbs and Dr. Overduin at least weekly. I started calling WO Hobbs and others at the base hospital to ask for updates on my category. WO Hobbs had briefed the base surgeon. They had both agreed that because I no longer met the universality of service requirement and my injuries were attributed to military service, I should be medically released on a 3B.

The next several months would be some of the most frustrating of my career as I tried to manoeuvre my way through a complicated medical system and a job with no satisfaction. It took months of interviews and appointments to eventually get placed on a permanent category and then several more months to get a 3B release.

I told my career manager that I was to be released on July 14, 2017, after completing thirty-six years of service. I had explained that the Base Surgeon was recommending a 3B medical release, but it was slow in coming.

Sometime in early 2017, I received my release message, but with a different category. It was called a "5A," or "Service Completed – Retirement Age." This did not please me, and I started to be a pain in the ass for anyone who was involved in the release system.

WHITE SCHOOL, BLACK MEMORIES

I walked into the Base Surgeon's office without an appointment and thought I might get thrown out, but he agreed to speak with me. I was told that if my 3B release did not come through before my release date, I shouldn't be concerned because it could be changed after the fact.

"Not a chance," I said. "I don't have that much faith or trust in the system."

Meanwhile, the Army JPSU position never really got off the ground. Over the first few months, there were many meetings and discussions on the way ahead, but no one wanted to commit funds or people to the task. Eventually, around December 2016, we heard that the Chief of the Defence Staff was cancelling the plan, and the positions would not be maintained. The Canadian Armed Forces would go back to the old model, a similar but refocused JPSU.

I spent the next few weeks driving into Ottawa to work, having a coffee or two, writing some of my story and then going home. I did this for several weeks, and then, in discussions with Alain Guimond, we decided that I would concentrate on getting my medical situation sorted out, and my release changed to a 3B. I wasn't working for anyone, so I made my own hours. I came and went as I saw fit. When I was at work, I would be sitting at my desk writing my story, sometimes for hours. There were days I never went to work at all, and there were even times that I never went for a whole week.

It sounds pretty good, but I was not happy to be ending my career like this. I went from a CWO who was admired and excelled in both JTFX and the MP Group to a CWO without a job. It was a bit of a letdown and just added to the stresses already in my life.

A couple of months before my release was to take effect, I received a letter stating that I no longer met the universality of service, and there was no chance that this would change. I was going to be released on a 3B medical. That was great news, and I started preparing for my last day in uniform.

In hindsight, not having a real job for the last six months of my career was a big positive. I concentrated on my release, planned all the required meetings and appointments well in advance, and spaced them out to avoid being overwhelmed. I know folks who were being released medically and had thirty days to complete everything while still working, which became a huge stressor. Thankfully this was changing around the time I was releasing, and folks were beginning to be posted to the JPSU for their last few months or were given time in their unit to process their release.

My good friend George Myatte had volunteered to be the OPI for my Depart With Dignity ceremony and, even though I really didn't want a big affair, I am glad that we did it. It was held in the WOs and Sergeants Mess in downtown Ottawa on a sunny June day.

There were more than a hundred folks in attendance, and I will be forever grateful for them taking the time to wish me luck in my retirement. There were soldiers who joined with me thirty-six years ago, mentors from my early career and soldiers I had served with in Afghanistan and other areas of operations. There were soldiers and friends from JTFX and the MP Group, and, of course, family and friends. I had a great career, and George gave everyone there that day an opportunity to hear about it.

There were several highlights from that day, but I will remember most when Corporal Jana Barnes, wearing her uniform and my son, JJ, both got up and spoke together. Their words were warm, funny, and from the heart—I will be forever thankful. It was both a happy and sad day, but like all days, it ended.

I spent the next month or so practicing how to be a civilian while still in uniform.

Before I had a chance to blink, it was July 14, and I was walking around Army Headquarters, getting my final clearance paperwork all signed off and turning in my ID card. As I placed my ID card on the Commissionaire's desk, I had just a brief moment of sadness, and my thoughts went to my soldiers and friends who would never retire, and then I turned around and walked out into the light.

During my drive back home alone, it felt like a weight had been lifted off my shoulders. I had been living a lie for more than a decade. I had been afraid that the truth would negatively affect others' perceptions of me as a soldier. I had lived this life of fraud and deception and put my career and ego ahead of my health and even my family. Now, I found myself a civilian and I no longer had the uniform to wrap around myself like a security blanket. I was both scared and relieved.

I threw myself into my writing and continued my bi-weekly meetings with Dr. Overduin, and I began to feel okay. I continued to attend pain clinics, mindfulness clinics, and so many others I no longer remember all of them. Some helped, some didn't, but I always felt like I was okay. I had lots of bad days, but also a lot more good days than I'd had in a long time.

I started volunteering to deliver Meals on Wheels in my small town of Winchester and driving seniors to appointments, and it felt good. I volunteered as the Service Officer at our local Legion in Winchester, where I tried to give back and support veterans whenever I could. I spearheaded a community initiative to have our small Winchester monument updated to include our modern-day veterans. We had two additional pieces added to the existing memorial through donations and fundraising to recognize those veterans from Afghanistan and Peacekeeping.

ABOVE: *A couple of Newfies, General Hillier and MWO Barnes. (DND)*
BELOW: *MWO Barnes receiving the Sacrifice Medal. (DND)*
OPPOSITE: *The JTFX crest. (DND)*

QUAERITE ET INVENIETIS

ABOVE: Promoted to Chief Warrant Officer by Major Stewart. (Author's photo)
BELOW: Corporal Barnes with the Military Police Group Chief (Dad) on graduation from the MP Academy. (DND)

45

WRITING AS THERAPY

Through it all, the one constant that continued to help me was my writing. What had started as a therapeutic means to speak about Operation MEDUSA became the story of my whole tour in Afghanistan. I would spend hours writing and then hours reading it back in the privacy of my home office. There were nights I hardly slept, but I would write, cry, laugh and then eventually fall asleep.

I found writing to be my friend. I could speak to it as honestly as I wanted, and it never judged me. I always knew that no one else would ever read it. It was for my eyes only, and I felt safe. When I finished the story about Afghanistan, I just kept writing, and I told the story of growing up in Newfoundland and continued until I had written about my life.

When my grandkids, Noah and Theo, came into my life, it was like a new beginning. I wanted to be part of their life, and they needed to know their grandfather. I was still in pain daily, and there were still days that were not good, but seeing Noah or Theo on FaceTime just brought a smile to my face.

My good friend, Gilles Sanstere, the Deputy Provost Marshal at the MP group, once said to me, "I would love to read your story." For some reason that I still am not sure about, I agreed. I gave it to him, as rough and uncut as it was, and waited in horror for his response.

He was someone who I respected and admired. A lot of thoughts ran through my head as I waited for his comments.

What have I done?

Why would I let him read this?

He'll never look at me in the same way again.

There were hundreds of pages, and I figured it would be a week or so before Gilles would be able to get through it, but, to my surprise, the next day, he sent me a message.

WHITE SCHOOL, BLACK MEMORIES

He said that he was up all night and couldn't put my story down and that it made him sad, angry, smile, laugh, and that, overall, it was an amazing story that others needed to read. I was a little surprised but relieved that he had similar reactions to what I had each time I read it. After Gilles, I had several other people read my story, and most made remarkably similar comments. I started to feel a little more at ease about releasing it.

Around this time, I came across a message from Colonel (ret'd) A.D. (Sandy) McQuarrie of The RCR Association saying he was interested in sharing short stories by Royal Canadians. I sent him an email saying that I had written a story about Operation MEDUSA but that it was a bit long and disjointed. Sandy was eager to see it, and so I sent it off.

Since then, I learned that Sandy was my first Battalion CO when I was posted to 1 RCR in London in 1981. I sent Sandy some photos of my career, and he sent one of them back with a message. It was a black and white photo of my QL3 graduation platoon and sitting in front of the platoon was none other than him and his RSM Wayne Northrup.

It is a small world.

Sandy did a lot of work to make my story of Operation MEDUSA presentable and then made it available to some members of The RCR Association. It resulted in me receiving dozens of positive comments from throughout the military and the veteran community.

Lieutenant-Colonel Trevor Norton, the CO of 2 RCR, had his officers and senior NCOs read the story, and then we had a live Zoom meeting where they could ask questions and give comments. It led to another Zoom meeting with the Brigade Commander and officers and NCOs from 2 Brigade. Overall, it was very positive, and I thoroughly enjoyed the interaction.

I mentioned to Sandy that I had continued to write after the portion on Operation MEDUSA. I ended up telling my story, from growing up in Newfoundland to joining the Army and retiring. He helped me make sense of my writing and put it into a form that is both legible and more easily read. Even more importantly, Sandy has made sharing my story okay. He has been able to show me that my story is important and should be shared. He helped me better understand the fact that I'm my own worst critic and that writing my tale with ghosts, demons and friends on my shoulders is okay as well. Something that was never meant for public viewing is now out there for the world to see. If the people who read this judge me, disbelieve me, or bully me on social media, that's okay; I'm in a good place.

The years 2020 and 2021 were a bit strange and bizarre, but like all the curveballs life has thrown at Julie and I, we survived and are looking forward to a new normal. Spending an entire winter in Winchester instead of enjoying a visit to Arizona or Florida, as we did a few years ago, was a disappointment. Still, it allowed me to concentrate on my writing.

I find it hard and sad that due to COVID I don't get to hug and squeeze my beautiful grandsons, but seeing them almost daily on FaceTime has been a blessing.

PART FOUR - POST-AFGHANISTAN (2009-2017)

Being forced to spend all my time with Julie has reminded me of how lucky I am to have such a beautiful, wonderful and caring lady in my life. Even though she will never admit it, I know that she has been forced to deal with my issues for way too long. She has never judged me and will always be my biggest supporter. She is a veteran who gets lost in my shadow, but I thank her for her service to Canada and for what she has done for our kids and me.

46

REFLECTIONS

When I look back at my career, I often ask myself, "Why me?" I have now started asking, "Why not me?"

I had never envisioned a long military career thirty-six years ago when I walked into that recruiting centre in St. John's. I don't think I had any goals or ambitions other than finding a way out of the boring and dead-end life that I was living in Riverhead, and if that could be considered a goal, then I certainly achieved that and much more.

As I sit here today in my home, fully retired and surrounded by a room full of plaques, statues, medals, coins and awards, all those things that would tell an outsider how successful and accomplished I have been, all I think about is the guilt of being a survivor and of those soldiers who will never be able to enjoy their retirement.

I try to explain why I feel the way I do, but it never seems enough to satisfy my needs. Am I guilty because I came home alive while many of my friends and soldiers did not? Is the guilt because I honestly believe that if I had done something differently or made a different decision, the results would have been better? Maybe the guilt comes from how I behaved on the battlefield, which resulted in me being safe while others were in much more danger? I am not sure. Maybe it is a combination of things, but the feeling is real, the resulting pain and confusion are real, and I continually find myself alone and sad.

From the early days of my military profession, I was taught that responsibility is key to being a good person and especially a good leader. To avoid responsibility or not to be held to the highest standard is a failure. As part of the Senior Command Team for a Rifle Company, the Officer Commanding and the Sergeant Major are responsible for all the soldiers under our command. Any failures or lapses are taken personally.

My belief in taking responsibility during the good times and the bad and my unconditional loyalty to The Royal Canadian Regiment and its unofficial motto,

PART FOUR - POST-AFGHANISTAN (2009-2017)

'Never pass a fault,' has probably made it a little bit more difficult for me to move on and accept what has happened.

As I have mentioned several times throughout my story, I believe I had the power to change the outcome in at least one situation and could have affected a few others. I have been told by many friends, comrades and professionals that I did everything right. What happened in Afghanistan was not my fault, and I could not have changed it. However, even while nodding my head in agreement, a part of me did not buy that argument.

Even though I have finally accepted a diagnosis of PTSD or, at least, stopped fighting it, I am still looking for other answers. I know that I have changed from who I was before my first rotation in Bosnia, and again with each follow-on tour, including Afghanistan. Even though it was something that has been told to me several times over the years by friends, comrades in arms and professionals—I was never ready to accept that these changes were due to a combat stress injury. It didn't help that I always believed that PTSD only happened to someone else.

I guess, as my career was coming to an end, I no longer felt that I had to keep my true feelings locked inside. Perhaps now, the stigma of PTSD would not be so threatening, and I could finally speak to someone honestly about what I had been living with in silence for many years.

I am still very hesitant to speak of this out loud, and even when a conversation about PTSD or mental health comes up about someone else, I find an excuse to move along. A part of me is perhaps a little scared that fully accepting a PTSD diagnosis would be an excuse for how I feel about the loss of my soldiers and would somehow make their deaths okay. I don't ever want that to be true.

It has been many years since the deaths of Shane Stachnik, Rick Nolan, Frank Mellish, William Cushley, Mark Graham, Darcy Tedford and Blake Williamson. I remember them all like it happened yesterday. I'm not sure I ever want that to change, even if it would be better for me. I want to keep them in my heart. But by allowing ghosts from my past to influence my life, I know that I have not allowed myself to be the best husband and father that I could have been.

In some ways, that is as hard to live with as the deaths of my soldiers.

I hope I have many years left and can find a way to make up for the past eleven. I am lucky and blessed to still have Julie in my life after thirty-plus years and to be able to see my children, JJ and Jana, who are my pride and joy.

In February 2018, Jana and her wonderful husband, Josh, gave Julie and I our first grandchild. My world changed when Noah entered our lives. In March of 2020, it changed again when our second grandson, Theo, arrived.

I will continue to struggle daily with chronic headaches, neck pain, and a body and spirit broken many times by thirty-six years of being an infantry soldier and defending this country. I hope that maybe now I will not be alone as I fight this last battle. Perhaps the next time that I am sitting alone and lost in the deafening silence, the pitter-patter of tiny feet and the smile of a grandson will bring me back to reality and remind me about how much I have to live for.

This is my story. This is my truth, and it has been written with the help of thousands of soldiers who have crossed paths with me over the years. It is written to pay homage to those who made the ultimate sacrifice for Canada and those who suffer daily because of their service. This story is written for the thousands of families that have had to sacrifice in secret and without support for way too long. It is for the next generation of soldiers, sailors and airmen and women who will continue to serve with honour and courage in a world that needs them now, more than ever. This story is to say to them that it's okay to ask for help, it's okay to fail, and it's okay to be human.

Now, my only hope and desire are that tonight, and every night after, I get to fall asleep to Noah and Theo saying, "Poppy Poppy," and wake up to Julie.

To all Canadian soldiers serving and retired, thank you for your service. Remember that you are not alone.

For those who have made the ultimate sacrifice, especially Shane, Rick, Frank, William, Mark, Darcy and Blake, you will never be forgotten.

To my good friend and mentor, Bobby Girouard, rest in peace. I hope you are still as proud of me today as you were in the killing fields of Panjwai so many years ago.

To my good friend, George, you are a special person, and I hope you know what you have meant to me.

Today, when I think about the guilt that I have carried around for ten years and the sadness and anger at losing those fine young soldiers, I try to remember those courageous family members who went to Afghanistan in 2008. I try to remember the words of Jim Davis or Colonel Abdul Bashir, and they bring me a slight sense of peace. I think about the incredible courage and bravery that the soldiers of Charles Company displayed...how some of Canada's greatest sons and daughters made the ultimate sacrifice for the soldier on their right and left and not for the bigger picture.

I wonder if that is how we should all feel.

There are times when I am alone, the headaches are bad, and my neck is so sore that it feels like my head's too heavy for my body, and I think about Frank, Rick and those other fine soldiers, and I remove my hearing aids.

All I hear is a deafening silence!

LEXICON

Like many other professions, the military has a unique language that can be very confusing to a person with little or no military experience. The military also uses many abbreviations in both conversation and documents, which only adds to the confusion.

Perhaps one of the more confusing items concerns ranks and appointments.

For example, in this book, the terms 'Master Warrant Officer,' 'Company Sergeant Major,' and 'Sergeant Major' seem to be employed in a confusing array of usage. The differences are that one is a rank (MWO), one is an appointment (CSM), and one (Sergeant Major) is a shortened form for both. Another inconsistency concerns the rank of 'Chief Warrant Officer' (CWO). Sometimes shortened to 'Chief,' a CWO can be appointed as a 'Regimental Sergeant Major' (RSM), a Battle Group Sergeant Major, a Task Force Sergeant Major or a Group Sergeant Major. Other than the RSM, all of the other appointments are often referred to as the Sergeant Major. Every soldier worth their salt strives to reach the rank of CWO and to be appointed as RSM of a unit.

In this book, my unit in Afghanistan was the First Battalion, The Royal Canadian Regiment (1RCR). I often refer to this unit as a 'Battle Group.' This title is used to describe a unit (such as 1RCR) with attached supporting troops placed under command—an artillery battery, an armoured squadron, a squadron of engineers, military police, etc.

The term 'Task Force' also occurs regularly. In the Canadian Armed Forces, a Task Force is defined as 'a temporary grouping of military forces under one commander for a specific mission. Technically, the 1RCR Battle Group was known as 'Task Force 3-06.' This Task Force included:

Headquarters Company, 1 RCR
Alpha Company, 1 RCR

WHITE SCHOOL, BLACK MEMORIES

Bravo Company, 1 RCR
Charles Company, 1 RCR
Support Company, 1 RCR
Echo Battery, Second Regiment, Royal Canadian Horse Artillery
ISTAR Squadron, Royal Canadian Dragoons
23 Field Squadron, Second Combat Engineer Regiment

Radio call signs are a simple means of identifying an element in the Battle Group. A rifle company consists of a headquarters and three infantry platoons. In Charles Company, the headquarters is known as call sign "Three," the platoons as call signs "Three-One," "Three-Two" and "Three-Three." The three sections of the platoon were identified as Alpha, Bravo, and Charlie. For example, Three Platoon's sections were assigned call signs "Three-Three Alpha," "Three-Three Bravo," and "Three-Three Charlie." Some call signs are also assigned to key members of the company. For example, the officer commanding Charles Company has call sign "Three-Niner," the second-in-command is "Three-Niner Bravo," and the Company Sergeant Major is "Three-Niner Charlie."

The next point involves the designation of unit and sub-unit commanders. In the 1RCR Battle Group, a lieutenant colonel was appointed as the commanding officer. A rifle company is commanded by a major, and that appointment is known as the 'officer commanding.' A rifle platoon is commanded by a captain or lieutenant, and their title is 'platoon commander.' Every commander has a second-in-command—for the unit a major, for the company, a captain, and for the platoon, a Warrant Officer.

Finally, an astute reader may wonder why the 'T' in The Royal Canadian Regiment is always written in upper case. 'The' is part of the official title.

DOUBLE✢DAGGER

Double Dagger Books is Canada's newest military-focused publisher. Conflict and warfare have shaped human history since before we began to record it. The earliest stories that we know of, passed on as oral tradition, speak of war, and more importantly, the essential elements of the human condition that are revealed under its pressure. We are dedicated to publishing material that, while rooted in conflict, transcends the idea of "war" as merely a genre. Fiction, non-fiction, and stuff that defies categorization, we want to read it all.

Because if you want peace, study war.

www.doubledagger.ca

ABOUT THE AUTHOR

Chief Warrant Officer John Barnes served in the Canadian Armed Forces as an infantryman for thirty-six years, primarily in the Royal Canadian Regiment. He served in Germany, Cyprus, the Former Yugoslavia, Qatar and Afghanistan. While serving with 1 RCR in Afghanistan in 2006, he was the Company Sergeant Major of Charles Company. He has been awarded the Sacrifice Medal, the Meritorious Service Medal and was appointed as a Member of the Order of Military Merit.

Now retired, he lives in the National Capital Region with his wife of 33 years, Julie.